THE YEAR THAT MADE AMERICA

From Rebellion to Independence, 1775–1776

TOM MCMILLAN

Essex, Connecticut

An imprint of The Globe Pequot Publishing Group, Inc.
64 South Main Street
Essex, CT 06426
www.globepequot.com

Distributed by NATIONAL BOOK NETWORK

British Library Cataloguing in Publication Information available

Library of Congress Cataloging-in-Publication Data
Library of Congress Cataloging-in-Publication Data

Names: McMillan, Tom, 1956– author.
Title: The year that made America : from rebellion to independence, 1775-1776 / Tom McMillan.
Description: Essex, Connecticut : Lyons Press, 2025. | Includes bibliographical references and index.
Identifiers: LCCN 2024037300 (print) | LCCN 2024037301 (ebook) | ISBN 9781493090587 (cloth) | ISBN 9781493090594 (epub)
Subjects: LCSH: United States—History—Revolution, 1775-1783. | United States. Declaration of Independence. | United States. Continental Congress—History. | Seventeen seventy-six, A.D.
Classification: LCC E208 .M3975 2025 (print) | LCC E208 (ebook) | DDC 973.3/13—dc23/eng/20241228
LC record available at https://lccn.loc.gov/2024037300
LC ebook record available at https://lccn.loc.gov/2024037301

Contents

Introduction 1

CHAPTER 1: "The Greatest Debate of All" 7

CHAPTER 2: A Brave New World 23

CHAPTER 3: Creating a Congress 41

CHAPTER 4: Spirit of '75 57

CHAPTER 5: "Open and Avowed Rebellion" 75

CHAPTER 6: The Ninth of January 87

CHAPTER 7: The Fifteenth of May 103

CHAPTER 8: The Seventh of June 119

CHAPTER 9: The Twenty-Eighth of June 137

CHAPTER 10: The Second of July 153

CHAPTER 11: The Ninth of July 169

CHAPTER 12: The Second of August 187

CHAPTER 13: The Twenty-Fifth of December 205

CHAPTER 14: Forgotten Document? 221

CHAPTER 15: Adams vs. Jefferson 237

CHAPTER 16: "Four Score and Seven Years" 253

CHAPTER 17: More Modern Perspectives 271

Acknowledgments 285

Appendix A 287

Contents

Appendix B 293

Abbreviations for Notes 299

Notes 301

Selected Bibliography 357

Index 369

INTRODUCTION

POSTERITY

Less than a year after American colonists declared their independence from England, John Adams, the brilliant but cantankerous congressional sage, sent a message for future generations that was equal parts heartfelt and skeptical.

In a letter to his wife, Abigail, on April 26, 1777, Adams wrote, "Posterity! You will never know how much it cost the present Generation to preserve your Freedom! I hope you will make good Use of it. If you do not, I shall repent in Heaven, that I ever took half the Pains to preserve it."[1]

Let that sink in for a moment. Adams's words resound more than ever today, when our centuries-old system of government faces repeated attacks from extremists on both sides of the political spectrum. On January 6, 2021, when presidential election deniers stormed their way into the U.S. Capitol, a sitting member of Congress tweeted, "Today is 1776!," and a swarming throng of protestors chanted "1776! 1776!" At a rally near the White House on the eve of the event, an internet provocateur shouted, "We declare 1776 on the new world order!" Months later, after taking time to reassess his actions, one man facing federal charges still claimed, "we are finding ourselves in a situation similar to what the Founders found themselves in 1776."[2]

Some of those folks thought they were starting a new American revolution, channeling, at least in their minds, the "Spirit of '76"—which brings us to a stark and altogether necessary question as the 250th anniversary of the founding approaches: Do most people know what *really* happened in that transcendent year? Emphasis on U.S. history in public education has been declining for decades, from middle schools to universities, including a dearth of detailed study on the revolutionary era and the long, raucous fight for independence. Many celebrate the Fourth of July with red-white-and-blue clothing, flags, banners, parades, picnics, and fireworks without any real grasp of why and how—or even exactly when—it all came to pass.[3]

Rejecting the more prevalent system of hereditary monarchy, Adams and his eighteenth-century cohorts sought to establish a newfangled republic that derived its "just powers from the consent of the governed."[4] The American version of democracy evolved over the years from that foundation, but there were no guarantees that it would work at the start, much less endure for parts of four centuries. In fact, it came close to *not* happening as early as it did. In mid-May 1776, less than two months before the Continental Congress took its historic vote, only six of the thirteen colonies were firmly committed to breaking from England.[5] In early June, after a resolution on independence was tabled for three weeks, one South Carolina delegate wrote that "the sensible part of the House opposed the Motion . . . they saw no wisdom in a Declaration of Independence."[6] A preliminary vote on July 1 showed that there was still no united front—nine for, two against, one deadlocked, and one abstaining—and it likely took some secretive, backroom arm-twisting in those final twenty-four hours to move reluctant colonies along. The formal tally to declare independence on July 2 was 12–0, with one abstention, although New York came around a week later to make it unanimous.[7]

Thus did the great American experiment in self-government begin, tentatively at first, fueled by disagreement and jammed through with some last-second maneuvering by the quarreling Founding Fathers. Our politics have been divisive from the start.

A maddening cloak of mystery still exists around those world-changing days in early July 1776. Part of the reason is that colonial congressmen signed pledges of silence to prevent leaks of information (and, no doubt, to protect their personal safety) while deliberations were underway. One such "Agreement of Secrecy," passed in November 1775, forbade them from revealing "directly or indirectly any matter or thing agitated or debated in Congress before the same shall have been determined."[8] It is not surprising, then, that the official records, published in the *Journals of the Continental Congress*, are purposely lean on details of what took place behind the scenes on July 1–4. A few members violated the code in private correspondence (thankfully), and many wrote about their activities after the fact; however, real-time reports from that period are limited, and only two of their letters dated July 4, 1776, and discussing independence have ever been found.[9]

Much of what we know today has been influenced by accounts that Adams and Thomas Jefferson wrote more than forty years later in the 1820s, when the memories of both men had faded—and when the vain Adams, in particular, saw that Jefferson was getting more credit for independence. That they disagreed or misremembered on several key points only adds to the confusion.[10] There is, of course, another perfectly valid reason for the lack of real-time accounts from the summer of 1776: In the weeks following the vote, participants were more intent on winning the war and ensuring independence than rehashing in great detail how it all occurred in Congress. Lives were on the line, and they turned to more urgent matters. Historian Pauline Maier also cites a lack of curiosity from newspaper reporters, authors, and regular citizens during this period. "Questions hadn't been asked of the Founders [in the 1770s and 1780s]," she said. "Nobody bothered to ask the questions, really, until after the War of 1812, when the younger generation of Americans became very interested in the Revolutionary past."[11]

Even the tradition of celebrating our independence on July 4 can be called into question. Evidence is indisputable that separation from England was made official by a congressional vote two days earlier on July 2. A document written to justify the move, what we now know as the Declaration of Independence, was debated strenuously and edited substantially on July 2, 3, and 4; was approved late on the morning of July 4; and was delivered to the printer that night (hence the date at the top of the hallowed document).[12] Impactful as it has become today, however, with its preamble seen as the melodious treatise of American freedom, the Declaration was not legally binding, did not in itself make the colonies independent, and would have been nullified had the Continental army lost the war.[13] At the time of its release in 1776, the Declaration served mostly as a brilliant marketing piece to reinforce what Congress already had accomplished. July 2 is our *real* Independence Day.

And yet the revolutionary process cannot be distilled to a single date or moment in time. It took years of angst and fierce conflict that splintered families, destroyed livelihoods, and spilled copious amounts of colonial blood. Independence fever may have existed in very small pockets of Massachusetts as early as 1774, but the First Continental Congress that gathered in September of that year was focused on restoring American rights *within* the British Empire. It was not until shots were fired at Lexington and Concord on April 19, 1775, that the movement found a broader purpose. The Second Continental Congress did not convene until a month after the shooting started, and, even then, most members still sought reconciliation while waging war against the greatest military power in the world. Some continued in that vein even after King George III refused to read their conciliatory Olive Branch Petition and declared the colonies in "rebellion" in fall 1775—vowing to enforce their subjugation from his tiny island across the ocean.[14]

The purpose of *The Year That Made America* is to reexamine all of this for a modern audience weaned on prepackaged snippets of American history. Special focus will center on the first eight months of 1776, when the "United Colonies" reached and passed the point of no return, with delegates committing treason in the eyes of England's monarch and ministry. The final push began uncommonly enough on January 9, with the publication of Thomas Paine's *Common Sense*, which explained to the public in clear, uncompromising terms why separation was the goal. Paine, a most unlikely revolutionary, was not even a member of Congress and had arrived from England barely a year earlier, but he stoked the flames of liberty that had been flickering on and off for months.[15]

A group of radical congressional patriots took it from there, overcoming nagging resistance from colleagues who thought they were moving too quickly (perhaps fearing they would all be hanged as traitors, which may have happened if the process had played out differently). Opponents such as John Dickinson worried that a premature declaration would not only send the Continental army to humiliating defeat but provoke even more oppression from the king and Parliament. It is instructive to note, however, that while Dickinson neither voted for independence nor signed the Declaration, he bravely took up arms to serve in the Revolutionary War.[16] His example of setting ego aside to put country first in the earliest days of American history should resonate with some of our ivory-tower politicians today.

The book also will examine the process that Jefferson, Adams, Benjamin Franklin, and their peers in Congress took to write, edit, alter, and produce their declarative document, and how the American public came to learn of its existence (spoiler alert: while newspapers began to publish the text as early as July 6, the Declaration was not signed by members until August, and Congress did not release the list of signers until January 1777).[17]

Some names will be familiar to modern-day Americans, but many among the key participants will not—Edward Rutledge, George Wythe, Caesar Rodney, Roger Sherman, Robert Treat Paine, and Charles Thomson. A case will be made that Richard Henry Lee, whose role in the founding is much overshadowed, deserves a place alongside Adams and Jefferson in the great pantheon of U.S. independence. We also will explore how and why some men who were not even serving in Congress in early July 1776—and were therefore not part of the process—still signed the Declaration of Independence and had their names committed to history.

The overarching goal will be to recount the work of ordinary lawyers and planters who found themselves living in extraordinary times, risking their lives by making a violent break from the most powerful empire in the world. They fomented political unrest based on radical ideas, argued furiously among themselves, changed their minds from time to time, and looked past hypocritical stances—refusing, for instance, to address slavery while advocating freedom—to form a new nation under the most extreme conditions imaginable. Americans observe our "Independence Day" every year with pomp and circumstance, but the astonishingly complex story of how we reached that point is often blurred by a singular focus on the "Fourth of July."

For the record, we even celebrate two days too late.

CHAPTER I

"The Greatest Debate of All"

ANXIOUS BUT RESOLUTE AFTER A NIGHT OF FITFUL SLEEP, CONGRESSIO-nal delegate John Adams of Braintree, Massachusetts, felt the daunting weight of history as he slid out of bed in his rented room on Second Street in Philadelphia.[1] The date on the calendar was July 1, 1776. Independence was in the air.

Lighting a candle to guide him through the predawn darkness and girding for the drama of the day ahead, he sat down to write a letter to his friend and former delegate, Archibald Bulloch, the newly elected president of the colony of Georgia.

> This morning is assigned for the greatest debate of all. A Declaration that these Colonies are free and independent States has been reported by a committee appointed Some Weeks ago for that Purpose, and this date or Tomorrow is to determine its fate.[2]

Adams thought back briefly to the time it all began, a mild dispute in 1761 over British search warrants.[3] That affront of imperial overreach was followed over the next fifteen years by the Sugar Act, the Stamp Act, the Boston Massacre, the Boston Tea Party, various Intolerable Acts, the Continental Congress, Lexington and Concord, Bunker Hill, the Olive Branch Petition, Lord Dunmore's Proclamation, and a dozen other flash points, leading to the release in January 1776 of the best public case yet for colonial independence, *Common Sense*.[4] No single date or incident captures the beating heart of revolution—history is never that tidy—but in the early morning hours of July 1, as Adams walked three blocks to the Pennsylvania State House on Chestnut Street, alone in his thoughts, he knew a decisive moment had arrived.

The day dawned sunny and warm in the provincial capital of Pennsylvania, with temperatures creeping toward 80 degrees, according to records kept by Adams's fellow delegate at the Second Continental Congress, Thomas Jefferson.[5] These two men, a forty-year-old New Englander and a thirty-three-year-old Virginian, so different in style and appearance, had pushed the rebellious assembly to the cusp of a world-changing verdict. They were, by now, the inseparable odd couple of independence: the squat, vain, stridently boisterous Adams and the tall, demure, soft-spoken Jefferson. Jefferson had been tasked with composing a rough draft of principles, asserting the right of thirteen disparate colonies to separate from Great Britain against that empire's wishes, but now it was left to Adams to make the closing argument on the State House floor.

There had never been a day like this in any country, anywhere. England staked its claim to the land here as far back as 1584, when Queen Elizabeth I granted Sir Walter Raleigh a charter to "discover, search, finde out, and view such remote, heathen and barbarous lands, countries and territories, not actually possessed of any Christian Prince, nor inhabited by Christian People."[6] Raleigh failed to gain a foothold in three trips to the Outer Banks of what is now North Carolina, but his exploratory zeal caught the notice of adventurers elsewhere. From that time forward, starting with the first permanent settlement in Jamestown in 1607 and continuing through the French and Indian War in the 1760s, New World colonists built their societies with English laws and customs, felt a kinship with their English brethren across the ocean, and pledged fealty to the English king or queen. Presently, however, in direct defiance of the royal status quo, a new breed was choosing to rise up and declare itself free.

To do so took remarkable foresight and chutzpah, and more than a little luck. As historian Joseph Ellis tells us, "no shared sense of American nationhood existed in 1776," and all domestic alliances formed that year "were assumed to be provisional and temporary arrangements."[7] The resolution that brought Adams to the floor, in fact, placed its primary emphasis on the common link of independent statehood. Introduced on June 7 by delegate Richard Henry Lee of Virginia, it declared at the start that "these United Colonies are, and of right ought to be, free and independent States," followed in order by other key initiatives.[8]

Congress tabled Lee's resolution after several days of debates, postponing a decision because it knew that half the delegations still would not (or could not) vote for independence. Representatives in the extralegal body had to follow orders from provincial assemblies back home, and some of the local leaders had yet to move past their long-held goal of reconciliation. Not even a war that had raged now for more than a year—since the first shots were fired at Lexington and Concord in April 1775—was able to sway them. By Jefferson's estimate, a ballot in mid-June would have found seven colonies for immediate independence and six against or undecided—hardly an emphatic message for England or the rest of the world. "Desirous of unanimity," he said, "and seeing that the public mind was rapidly advancing to it, [Congress] referred the further discussion to the 1st of July."[9]

Oratorical battle lines had been drawn for almost a year, but they hardened during the combative congressional debates of June 8–10. Speaking against the proposal, or at least advocating for more delay, were John Dickinson and James Wilson of Pennsylvania, Robert R. Livingston of New York, and Edward Rutledge of South Carolina, a persuasive quartet of moderate colony leaders. "They were friends to the measure themselves," Jefferson wrote, "and saw the impossibility that we should ever again be united with Gr. Britain, yet were against adopting them at this time." Several colonies still were forbidden by formal decrees to consent "to such a declaration," and others had received no clear instructions either way. On the opposite side, arguing vociferously for independence, were Adams, Lee, and George Wythe of Virginia, urging their colleagues to "declare a fact which already exists."[10]

The roster changed in significant ways by the time Congress reopened the matter three weeks later. Radical stalwarts Lee and Wythe had been called back to Virginia on June 13 to work on a new state constitution, which—though it is hard to imagine today—was considered of greater importance back home in Williamsburg.[11] That left Adams alone to spearhead the debate on July 1. No other delegate could match his passion or grasp of the issues, but he worried there was nothing new to say after so many fiery speeches in the same setting. He groused later that the main points on behalf of independence had been "repeated and hackneyed . . . [a] hundred Times for Six Months."[12]

Many delegates on both sides spoke that day in an exhausting session that lasted nine hours, with Dickinson providing the most ardent voice for delay.[13] A wealthy Philadelphia attorney who once studied law at the Middle Temple in London, Dickinson was among the earliest defenders of colonial liberties and published a series of powerful essays that galvanized opposition to British tax policies in the 1760s.[14] As the independence movement grew, however, he moderated his public stance, fretting that they were moving too quickly, and at times offered strangely conflicting opinions. In summer 1775, he helped author both the "Declaration of the Causes and Necessity of Taking Up Arms," a justification of American military action against the British, and the "Olive Branch Petition," a desperate attempt to mend relations with King George III. His closing argument on July 1 called for Congress to withhold a decision until the colonies were better prepared for such an overtly disruptive act. "When our Enemies are pressing us so vigorously, When We are in so wretched State of preparation, When the Sentiments & Designs of our expected Friends are so unknown to us," Dickinson said, "I am alarm'd at this Declaration being so vehemently presented."[15]

Rain was starting to pelt the windows of the State House when the venerable Adams rose in response. It is one of the great misfortunes of history that he did not write his July 1 remarks in advance or keep contemporary notes, because his biographer, David McCullough, called it "the most powerful and important speech heard in the Congress since it first convened, and the greatest speech of Adams's life." We can attempt to reconstruct part of what he said by referencing private correspondence during this era, when Adams was experimenting with phrases and refining his radical message. In one unfeigned passage to a colleague in Massachusetts, he wrote, "Objects of the most Stupendous Magnitude, Measures in which the Lives and Liberties of Millions, born & unborn

Figure 1.1. John Adams. *(Wikimedia Commons)*

are most essentially interested, are now before Us. We are in the very midst of a Revolution, the most compleat, unexpected and remarkable of any in the History of Nations." In another, he added bluntly, "We never can again be happy, under a single Particle of British Power."[16]

Whether the speeches changed any minds that day is uncertain. When a preliminary vote was taken in the evening, nine of the thirteen colonies were on the side of independence, with two opposed, one deadlocked, and one abstaining. Recent instructions from provincial assemblies had allowed Maryland and New Jersey to join Connecticut, Georgia, Massachusetts, New Hampshire, North Carolina, Rhode Island, and Virginia in the affirmative, making for a strong majority. Delegates from Pennsylvania and South Carolina were still stubbornly, and perhaps intractably, opposed. Delaware's delegation was tied at one vote apiece, but a third member, the pro-independence Caesar Rodney, was said to be returning from Dover overnight, riding a series of panting horses to Philadelphia. New York could not support independence without new instructions from its provincial leaders, which would not be coming for at least a week.

A final tabulation of 9–2–1–1, had it been official, would have achieved independence by a comfortable margin. But any hint of dissension, no matter how small, would shatter the facade of "union" and expose a weakness for England to exploit. It was fortuitous for Adams and his allies that Edward Rutledge sensed the gravity of the situation and called for a delay of one more day. As Jefferson remembered it, "Mr. Rutledge of S. Carolina requested the determination might be put off to the next day, as he believed his colleagues, tho' they disapproved of the resolution, would then join in it for the sake of unanimity."[17]

It still took an otherworldly set of circumstances for Congress to reach that oft-stated objective. South Carolina, prodded and cajoled by Rutledge, reversed its stance at the last minute and voted yes. Rodney, who had ridden through "thunder and rain" and arrived at the State House door in splattered "boots and spurs," broke the tie for Delaware. Pennsylvania came around after Dickinson and one of his cohorts, Robert Morris, voluntarily absented themselves at the crucial moment. New

York still was prohibited from voting by the provincial assembly, but its abstention, under such circumstances, was not a major deterrent.[18]

The resolution for American independence passed the Second Continental Congress by a 12–0–1 vote on July 2, 1776—an astonishing feat, given the chaos of the previous few weeks.[19]

No public announcement was made that day, but word of such vast, earth-shaking nature could not be kept quiet for long, and, despite the vow of secrecy, a small group of delegates impulsively spread the news. Elbridge Gerry of Massachusetts wrote to a friend that "the great question of Independency" had been debated on the floor and "the Facts are as well known at the Coffee-House of the city as in Congress." Working on a tip, the *Pennsylvania Evening Post* even managed to squeeze in the 1776 equivalent of breaking news on the final page of its July 2 evening edition: "This day, the CONTINENTAL CONGRESS declared the UNITED COLONIES FREE and INDEPENDENT STATES."[20] The secret did not last for more than a few hours.

Unable to contain himself, John Adams was among those who broke the rules. In another of his massive contributions to history, he wrote two letters on July 3 to his wife, Abigail, addressing the decision of the previous day, the euphoria over the achievement, and the realization of the rugged road ahead. "Yesterday the greatest Question was decided which ever was debated in America, and a greater perhaps never was or will be decided among men," Adams wrote.[21] But even as he contemplated the fearful toll of blood and treasure required to ensure independence, he was confident that the congressional vote would be memorialized by American patriots far off into the future.

> The Second Day of July 1776 will be the most memorable Epocha in the history of America. I am apt to believe it will be celebrated by succeeding Generations as the great anniversary Festival. It ought to be commemorated as the Day of Deliverance by Acts of Devotion to God Almighty. It ought to be solemnized with Pomp and Parade, with Shews, Games, Sports, Guns, Bells, Bonfires and Illuminations from one End of this Continent to the other from this Time forward forever more.[22]

Barely twenty-four hours after the historic vote, Adams was convinced that Americans already had their Independence Day, the "Second of July." He was correct, but popular culture remembers it differently.

* * *

That Adams's vision did not come to pass was due to a series of related but tangled events that overshadowed the legacy of the vote on July 2. Congress believed a printed document was required to explain its decision to the world, and Jefferson had been working on a draft since mid-June, in the hope that it might soon be necessary.

Contrary to a myth that developed over the years, however, Jefferson was not the singular author of the Declaration of Independence. Instead, he was the draftsman for a five-man committee, including Adams and Benjamin Franklin, that had oversight over the historic text. Jefferson's original draft was edited by Adams and Franklin, mulled over by the committee, submitted to Congress for review on June 28, tabled briefly while the vote took place, and edited again by the full body group session (as Jefferson sat squirming). Scholars have determined that eighty-six changes were made to Jefferson's language, and Congress removed roughly 20 percent of the content.[23] The wording was approved, finally, on July 4 and sent that night to the printer, which explains the date at the top of a document titled "A DECLARATION by the REPRESEN-TATIVES of the UNITED STATES OF AMERICA, in GENERAL CONGRESS assembled."[24]

But their work was far from finished. The document was sent out by courier on July 5, published in a newspaper for the first time on July 6, and read in public at a jubilant ceremony in the State House Yard on July 8. More than a week later, after news arrived that the New York provincial assembly had at least grudgingly approved independence, the heading was changed to "The *unanimous* Declaration of the thirteen United States of America."[25] (Fun fact: it was never formally titled the "Declaration of Independence.")

No one had even signed it by the end of July. The names of John Hancock, as president of Congress, and Charles Thomson, as secretary, appeared in type at the bottom of the original printed version, but the earliest handwritten signatures were not added until August 2. A number of key figures had left Philadelphia by then and did not sign until they returned to the city. Because of the fear of reprisals, and especially because the war wasn't going well in fall 1776, the list of signers was not made public until January 1777.[26]

None of it fits the happy narrative that all of this happened on the Fourth of July, but "facts are stubborn things," as Adams once famously said.[27]

The evolution of Jefferson's text provides another startling peek behind the scenes of independence. His preamble, with its soaring rhetoric about self-evident liberty and equality, became the most famous passage in American history, but it was changed in meaningful ways from the version he first crafted in June. Jefferson no doubt made some edits himself, then turned it over to Adams, to Franklin, to the committee, and to Congress as a whole.[28] Their potentially awkward group effort turned a sound but choppy statement into an eloquent disquisition on freedom and individual rights.

The second paragraph of Jefferson's earliest surviving draft began this way:

> We hold these truths to be sacred & undeniable; that all men are created equal & independent, that from that equal creation they derive rights inherent & inalienable, among which are the preservation of life, & liberty, & the pursuit of happiness.[29]

By the time it was finalized a few weeks later, with edits and suggestions from Adams and Franklin, the updated language came to represent the young country's aspirational vision of itself:

> We hold these truths to be self-evident, that all men are created equal, that they are endowed by their Creator with certain unalienable Rights, that among these are Life, Liberty and the pursuit of Happiness.[30]

It is important to note, however, that despite its prominence in our lives today, as the very essence of the American creed, the preamble was far from the focal point of Jefferson's literary effort in 1776. Its breathtaking language made stunningly little impact at the time.[31] Jefferson's primary task was to justify the case for independence, and he achieved it by presenting a lengthy series of indictments against King George III, charging that the monarch had established "an absolute Tyranny over these States" and "plundered our seas, ravaged our Coasts, burnt our towns, and destroyed the lives of our people."[32] That section, largely ignored by readers in the twenty-first century, represents almost two-thirds of the word count of the Declaration of Independence.[33]

Jefferson laid out twenty-five charges in the draft presented to Congress. As the text was assessed over the next few days, allegations were edited and reformatted, with a few added, for a final count of twenty-seven. The most provocative change Congress made between July 2 and July 4 was the deletion of Jefferson's claim that the king was personally responsible for the Atlantic slave trade—the only place in the document where he referenced Black slavery. "(H)e has waged cruel war against human nature itself," Jefferson wrote, "violating [its] most sacred rights of life & liberty in the persons of a distant people who never offended him, captivating & carrying them into slavery in another hemisphere, or to incur miserable death in their transportation tither. This piratical warfare . . . is the warfare of the CHRISTIAN king of Great Britain, determined to open a market where MEN should be bought & sold."[34]

The greatest conundrum facing Congress was the presence of slavery in a country where all men were now said to be "created equal." Jefferson himself enslaved hundreds of Blacks in his lifetime, forcing them into perpetual servitude at his vast planation in Virginia, and many of his congressional colleagues either held slaves or benefited from the slave trade in meaningful ways.[35] To attempt to place all the blame on King George for a wretched colonial practice that far predated his reign was bizarre, foolhardy, and astoundingly hypocritical. Congress solved the problem by cutting any mention from the Declaration, kicking the can down the road (for eighty-five years, until the American Civil War).[36] Its ultimate goal was to attain independence in 1776, and any formal attacks on slavery or the slave trade would infuriate Southerners and threaten

Figure 1.2. Thomas Jefferson. *(Wikimedia Commons)*

already-fragile colonial unity. True equality for anyone other than white males would have to wait.

The contradiction was not lost on the rest of the world, particularly in England, and among those Americans still loyal to the Crown. English essayist Samuel Johnson raised the topic as early as 1775, asking, with some indignation, "how is it that we hear the loudest yelps for liberty among the drivers of negroes?"[37] After the Declaration was published, one of the most damning retorts came from the former royal governor of Massachusetts, Thomas Hutchinson, who wrote in October 1776, "I could wish to ask the Delegates of Maryland, Virginia, and the Carolinas, how their Constituents justify the depriving (of) more than a hundred thousand Africans of their rights to liberty, and the pursuit of happiness, and in some degree to their lives, if these rights are so absolutely unalienable."[38] No answers were forthcoming, and the lack of any plan to address slavery or the slave trade was the most indefensible weakness of the Declaration—a permanent stain on the legacy of the Founding Fathers.

In a final edit, Congress also chose to alter the language of the document's last paragraph, replacing some of Jefferson's text with the exact words from Richard Henry Lee's independence resolution of June 7. Members thought it was a stronger and more consistent summation of their radical action of July 2. As a result, Lee's assertion—"That these United Colonies are, and of right ought to be, free and independent States, that they are absolved from all allegiance to the British Crown, and that all political connection between them and the State of Great Britain, is and ought to be totally dissolved"—became part of the penultimate sentence, leading to a rousing crescendo that proclaimed independence to the world. (A small segment of that passage is engraved on one of the walls at the Jefferson Memorial in Washington, DC, although Jefferson did not write it.)[39]

The writing and editing of the Declaration over the three-week period from June 11 to July 4 will be examined in greater detail in chapters 8, 9, and 10. Once it was approved, however, events moved so quickly that the doddering pace of eighteenth-century news coverage could not keep up. Only one newspaper reported on July 2 that the resolution had passed, limiting exposure to readers of the *Pennsylvania Evening*

Post—albeit achieving for the *Post* one of the great media exclusives of all time. Following up on its scoop, the *Post* was the first to publish the Declaration in full on July 6, taking up the entire front page, but it took several more days for formal public readings to take place in Philadelphia and nearby colonies, where printed copies had just arrived.

On July 8 in Easton, Pennsylvania, it was reported that "the Declaration was read aloud to a great number of spectators, who gave their hearty assent with three huzzas, and cried out MAY GOD LONG PRESERVE and UNITE the FREE and INDEPENDENT STATES OF AMERICA." Similar festive events were held in two New Jersey cities, Trenton and Princeton. July 9 saw public readings to the various brigades of the Continental army in and around New York City, followed by public ceremonies at Boston, Massachusetts (July 18); Portsmouth, New Hampshire (July 18); Newport, Rhode Island (July 20); Huntington, New York (July 22); and Baltimore, Maryland (July 29). By the first week of August, as copies traveled south, there were additional "grand" readings at Richmond, Virginia, and Charleston, South Carolina, "amidst the acclamations of a vast concourse of people."[40]

The meandering progress of news from Philadelphia to the most remote spots in the country took more than a month, blurring details for many as to when independence had actually occurred. What everyone seemed to remember, however, was a line at the top of the document: "In Congress, July 4, 1776." By the end of August it had been reprinted in at least twenty-nine newspapers and fourteen broadsides, the sheer repetition of a single date planting it firmly in the public's mind.[41] The *Journals of the Continental Congress* make it clear that Lee's resolution was passed on July 2, but complete printed volumes of those records would not be widely available for years, long after the war had ended and the new nation had taken its place on the world stage.[42] Most Americans who experienced the revolutionary period never had the chance to assess or even read them and, as a result, never knew the full story. July 4 became "Independence Day" almost by default.

Even John Adams fell into the trap. On July 5, 1777, while he was still in Philadelphia, Adams wrote to his daughter, Nabby, that "yesterday, being the anniversary of American Independence, was celebrated here with a festivity and ceremony becoming the occasion." Adams and other delegates were so busy managing the war that they had *not even thought* of holding a commemoration until July 2, and made no formal plans for doing so until July 3. The first-ever celebration on the "Fourth" was magnificent, nonetheless. A wide-eyed Adams felt the impact as he took his daily stroll after dinner:

> In the evening, I was walking about the streets for a little fresh air and exercise, and was surprised to find the whole city lighting up their candles at the windows. I walked most of the evening, and I think it was the most splendid illumination I ever saw; a few surly houses were dark, but the lights were very universal. Considering the lateness of the design and the suddenness of the execution, I was amazed at the universal joy and alacrity that was discovered, and at the brilliancy and splendour of every part of this joyful exhibition. I had forgot the ringing of bells all day and evening, and the bonfires in the streets, and the fireworks played off.[43]

Independence celebrations were held sporadically from city to city in those early years, depending on the state of war and other matters affecting day-to-day life, but the "Fourth of July" became ingrained in the American psyche when both Adams and Jefferson died exactly fifty years to the day that the Declaration was approved—a few hours apart, one man in Massachusetts, the other in Virginia, on July 4, 1826. It remains the most astonishing quirk of fate in U.S. history. Many in the mid-nineteenth century also thought it was a sign from God that the date had a religious meaning, made even more so after a third former president, James Monroe, who served in the Continental army and fought at the Battle of Trenton, died on July 4, 1831.

President Abraham Lincoln added to the growing deification during the Civil War by alluding to the Declaration in the opening sentence of the Gettysburg Address in 1863. "Four score and seven years ago," he said, referencing 1776, the country had been "conceived in liberty, and dedicated to the proposition that all men are created equal."[44] Congress passed a law establishing July 4 as a federal holiday on July 28, 1870, and the Library of Congress noted that "even far-flung communities on the western frontier managed to congregate on Independence Day." Additional legislation addressing its importance and making it a formal "public holiday" passed in 1939 and 1941.[45]

"The Fourth" is now ensconced as the most patriotic of all U.S. traditions, celebrated with picnics, fireworks, backyard barbecues, and omnipresent red-white-and-blue memorabilia. But as historians in the twentieth century probed details of the independence movement, tapping sources that were overlooked by previous generations, they discovered an intricate, fascinating, labyrinthine narrative—one far more complicated and controversial than the antiseptic version often foisted on students and the public. There were hot-headed debates, messy compromises, name-calling outbursts, and petty feuds among clashing egos, but also a cool determination through it all to set the new nation on a course for prosperity. The most important date in the process was July 2, 1776, when Congress cast the historic vote, but no day in the riveting eight-month period from January to August was inconsequential in the revolution that changed the world.

The story, warts and all, is at the very core of our national existence. After almost 250 years, with another milestone anniversary approaching, and the country once again in turmoil, it deserves a modern retelling.

CHAPTER 2

A Brave New World

ENGLAND'S FLIRTATION WITH LIFE ON THE EASTERN SEABOARD BEGAN with the charter granted by Queen Elizabeth I to Sir Walter Raleigh in 1584. That was almost a full century after Columbus "discovered" the New World, and several decades after Spain, France, and Portugal created strongholds on its northern and southern continents.[1]

Raleigh was keenly aware that odds were stacked against him. His half brother, Sir Humphrey Gilbert, lost his life in a calamitous attempt to claim the island of Newfoundland in modern-day Canada in 1583, but Raleigh was inspired by the challenge and dreamed of a better fate farther south. Accordingly, he organized three daring missions to the Outer Banks from 1584 to 1587 and made two attempts to establish English colonies in what is now the United States.[2]

Two centuries later, Thomas Jefferson found evidence that those early trips had been funded by private sources, proceeding without financial help from English royalty—and that, in his opinion, made them *independent* from the start. Jefferson made the point repeatedly, including in his original draft of the Declaration of Independence, which read, "We have remined them of the circumstances of our emigration & settlement here . . . that these were effected at the expence of our own blood & treasure, unassisted by the wealth or the strength of Great Britain." His fellow delegates could not bring themselves to include it in the final version, however, deleting much of the language and settling only for a vague reference to "the circumstances of our emigration and settlement," which offered no details or context.[3]

All three Raleigh missions *did* receive private funding, but it is ludicrous to suggest that the substantial "strength of Great Britain" was not inherent in the queen's decree. The word *England* was mentioned fourteen times in the charter's eight paragraphs, and the intent to colonize was evident from its first sentence, which granted Raleigh rights to territories "not actually possessed of any Christian Prince." Day-to-day life would be conducted "according to the lawes of England," and new possessions would be considered to be part of "our Realmes of England." Moreover, Raleigh's colonists and their heirs would have "all the priviledges of free Denizens, and persons native of England . . . as if they were borne and personally (reside) within our saide Realme of England."[4] The Jeffersonian thinking was flawed.

And yet it should come as no surprise that Jefferson studied, and at times obsessed over, Raleigh's efforts in the 1580s. Though the history of those trips seems ancient by modern standards, they took place less than two hundred years before the American Revolution and, despite their failure, planted seeds for the ideas Jefferson himself championed in the 1770s. The narrative of coastal colonization in its earliest form was a compelling way to make his point, even if he ignored some contradictory facts.

Much of what Jefferson wrote was adapted from *The Principal Navigations, Voyages, Traffiques and Discoveries of the English Nation*, authored by Richard Hakluyt, one of Raleigh's chief advisors. Neither Raleigh nor Hakluyt made any of the three journeys—the queen, who adored Raleigh, would not allow him to risk his life that way—but Hakluyt's book, published in 1589 and gleaned from first-person accounts of the survivors, offered a fascinating glimpse of initial contacts between English citizens and this strange new hemisphere. Part of his work was an influential chapter titled "Discourse of the necessitie and commoditie of planting English colonies upon the North partes of America."[5]

Raleigh's first group of explorers came ashore in summer 1584. Beyond the fact that these were the first Englishmen to set foot on land that would become the United States, the trip was memorable because of a list of dates compiled by one of its commanders. "The second of July we found shole water, wher we smelt so sweet, and so strong a smell, as if we had bene in the midst of some delicate garden," he wrote. "The fourth of the same moneth we arrived up on the coast, which we supposed to be a continent and firm lande." July 2. July 4. In 1584. *How eerie.* They eventually found an inlet in the Outer Banks and scouted several nearby islands, including one called "Roanoak" by the natives—modern-day Roanoke Island, North Carolina.[6]

Flushed with excitement over this brief achievement, Raleigh organized another trip to create an actual foothold in spring 1585. As Jefferson described it almost two hundred years later, "they visited the mainland for the first time . . . chose for their habitation the island of Roanoke . . . (and) put into the ground seeds sufficient to produce them a plentiful subsistence for two years."[7] Alas, the colonial roster was hastily chosen and poorly constructed. It consisted of 107 men, mostly soldiers and sailors, but no women or children, making it a military outpost with little chance for long-term success. These well-armed marauders managed to explore as far north as the Chesapeake Bay but clashed violently with native tribes and, despite their modest planting efforts, soon became "distressed for provisions." In summer 1586, when famed English explorer and privateer Sir Francis Drake sailed by to check on "Raleigh's colonists," they eagerly agreed to his offer for a transatlantic trip home.[8]

Raleigh's strongest attempt to establish a permanent settlement in the New World came in April 1587, when three vessels loaded with 118 adventurers, including seventeen women and nine children, left England for Roanoke Island. After what they hoped would be a brief stop in the Outer Banks to pick up items from previous colonists and check for any stranded survivors, the plan was to settle at a new site along the Chesapeake.

This is what came to be known in history as the "Lost Colony," still celebrated today with a heavily fictionalized outdoor drama near the Fort Raleigh National Historic Site. Dropped off at Roanoke in the summer, but fretting over their odds for long-term survival, the colonists convinced their leader, John White, to return to England to obtain much-needed supplies. White set off immediately, but he was prevented from making a return trip to Roanoke for three years because of the Crown's ongoing war with Spain. When he finally traveled back to the Outer Banks in 1590, the colonists he left behind had vanished, offering only small hints—the carving of the word *CROATOAN* on one of the gateposts, and the letters *CRO* on a tree—as to their possible whereabouts.[9]

They were never seen again by European eyes. The assumption is that they split up to improve their chances for survival, some heading inland, others to an island inhabited by the friendly Croatoan tribe (modern-day Hatteras Island). Those who arrived safely probably were absorbed into the native populations; however, numerous theories of their fate abound, and definitive proof still eludes us. The perplexing mystery of the "Lost Colony" continues into the twenty-first century.

Few scholars in the eighteenth century were more interested in the story than Jefferson, who continued to probe the legacy of Raleigh's colonists, using the most positive aspects of their efforts—guile, courage, relentless resolve—to underscore his thesis of British settlement. He stated it most emphatically in a piece titled "Refutation of the Argument that the Colonies Were Established at the Expense of the British Nation," composed early in 1776, just a few months before the Declaration. "This short narration of facts, extracted principally from Hakluyt's [writing], may enable us to judge the effect with the charter to Sir Walter Raleigh may have on our own constitution," Jefferson wrote. "It serves also to expose the distress of those ministerial writers, who, in order to prove that the British parliament may of right legislate for the colonies, are driven to the necessity of advancing this unpalpable untruth that 'the colonies were planted and nursed at the expense of the British nation.'"[10]

He never wavered in that belief, still claiming as late as 1781 that Raleigh had been forced to proceed "without a shilling of aid" while being "obstructed occasionally" by the Crown.[11]

* * *

Raleigh's failure nonetheless begat an empire.

Aroused by his raw ambition but aware of his many mistakes, Englishmen working under a new charter for the "Virginia Company" established the first permanent colony in Jamestown in 1607. A persistent flow of settlers from all walks of life crossed the ocean over the next 125 years, buoyed by boasts of unprecedented opportunity in a seemingly exotic setting—so strikingly different from the cramped, dank streets of London. There were twelve predominantly English colonies by the end of the 1600s, ranging along the coast from New Hampshire to South Carolina, and a thirteenth was added when Georgia received its charter in 1732. The early population also was bolstered by small pockets of non-English arrivals, including French, Dutch, German, Swedish, and Scots-Irish, as well as hundreds of thousands of enslaved Africans.[12]

Colonial charters varied from place to place, depending on how they were granted, and to whom. Some were "royal" colonies, under the auspices of the king and his ministers; some were "proprietary," granted by the king to favored individuals; others were purely "corporate," or joint-stock companies.[13] The freedom of limited self-government within the empire was much of the attraction. Given the thirty-five-hundred-mile distance between, say, Philadelphia and London, and the long weeks it took for transatlantic travel in the eighteenth century, "Americans" enjoyed a reasonable amount of autonomy as a loose amalgamation of British outposts, free from the direct, daily control of Parliament. But most were proud to call themselves "English," and none ever questioned the king's sovereignty.

"The colonies had been founded under the authorization of the Crown," wrote historian Robert Middlekauff, in his book *The Glorious Cause*, "and governmental authority in them had always been exercised in the king's name, though rather ambiguously in the three proprietary colonies, Maryland, Pennsylvania and Delaware, and tenuously in Rhode Island and Connecticut, the two corporate colonies. What had lasted long apparently seemed left unchanged."[14]

The first major fissure in colonial relations came in the mid-1700s, during a clash over North American dominance called the French and Indian War. Some of the opening shots were fired in 1754, when a young British colonel from Virginia named George Washington brashly attacked French troops in western Pennsylvania before war had even been declared. That act of youthful hubris helped touch off an international conflict between England and France that lasted nine costly and controversial years, draining national treasuries, changing imperial boundaries, and ending, finally, with a worldwide British victory and the first Treaty of Paris in 1763.[15]

England claimed French lands in North America and expanded its territorial possessions on other continents almost overnight, creating an enormous domain that it suddenly had to govern. Historians often trace the start of the American Revolution to a heavy-handed shift in policy toward the colonies in this immediate post-treaty period. It is intriguing to note, however, that John Adams thought the struggle for independence began in February 1761, two years *before* the end of the war, when British authorities sought the liberal use of warrants to search private homes for evidence of smuggling. Colonists considered these "writs of assistance" to be outrageous breaches of liberty.[16]

James Otis Jr., a Massachusetts lawyer and one of the earliest proponents of colonial rights, led the opposition at two hearings in Boston, charging that the writs violated fundamental principles of law. At the second hearing in November 1761, he went as far as charging that "[this] appears to me to be the worst instrument of arbitrary power, the most destructive of English liberty . . . that was ever found in an English law-book."[17] A British-appointed judge ruled against Otis and upheld the writs, as expected, but Adams never forgot the mesmerizing impact of his performance in fiery debates with royal leaders:

> Otis was a flame of fire! . . . With a promptitude of Classical Allusions, a depth of research, a rapid summary of historical events & dates, a profusion of Legal Authorities, a prophetic glance of his eyes into futurity, and a rapid torrent of impetuous Eloquence, he hurried away all before him. . . . Then and there was the first scene of the first Act of opposition to the Arbitrary claims of Great Britain. Then and there the Child Independence was born.[18]

The more traditional and widely accepted view is that the breakdown began with the Treaty of Paris in 1763, as British officials clamped down on the colonies following the French and Indian War. Their first step was a royal proclamation in October 1763, prohibiting settlers from moving west of the Appalachian Mountains, in a vain but odious attempt to keep the colonies contained.[19] Next in line were two legislative acts to raise revenue, intended to offset massive British debt incurred during a decade of military action around the globe. There was a growing sense in London and throughout the empire that colonists who benefited from the Crown's protection should pay their fair share.

The Sugar Act of 1764 was intrusive enough from the colonial perspective, calling for stricter enforcement of duties on foreign imports, but it was the Stamp Act of 1765 that caused great public outrage. Approved by Parliament in March, it placed a tax on paper products ranging from official documents to newspapers, pamphlets, academic degrees, and playing cards (each embossed with a legal "stamp"). This was the first direct tax imposed by England in the New World, and it infuriated colonists who believed that only locally elected assemblies should levy taxes. They deemed it a brazen infringement on their natural rights as British subjects—the first manifestation of "taxation without representation."[20]

Opposition began immediately, although the Stamp Act would not go into effect for eight months. An angry Patrick Henry proposed five resolutions in Virginia's House of Burgesses, claiming that taxation by elected representatives "is the distinguishing Characteristick of British Freedom." Farther to the north, mindful of festering street protests by the Sons of Liberty and other activist groups, the Massachusetts assembly sent a letter inviting other colonies to a meeting in New York "to consider of a general and united, dutiful, loyal and humble representation of their condition to His Majesty and the Parliament; and to implore relief." The result was the Stamp Act Congress, the first joint assembly in colonial history.[21]

Twenty-seven representatives from nine colonies met at the Federal Hall building in New York from October 7 to October 25 (Virginia, North Carolina, Georgia, and New Hampshire royal governors prevented their respective delegations from taking part). Attendees included a list of soon-to-be prominent patriots, among them Samuel Adams of Massachusetts, John Dickinson of Pennsylvania, Caesar Rodney of Delaware, and John Rutledge of South Carolina. They formalized a declaration of rights, the first of its kind in America claiming that Parliament had "a tendency to subvert the rights and liberties of the colonists"—and demanding that the act be repealed. But in the first of a lengthy list of fourteen resolutions, they respectfully acknowledged that "his Majesty's subjects in these colonies owe the same allegiance to the crown of Great-Britain . . . and all due subordination" as all others living in the empire. Independence was not yet on their minds.[22]

The colonists were startled that the sheer force of their opposition led to the repeal of the Stamp Act in March 1766. At least part of this was due to the coercive power of British merchants, who feared the destructive impact of an American boycott of their goods. But any chance to celebrate was offset by another decree—the Declaratory Act—issued on the same day that the Stamp Act was abolished. Composed in the cumbersome language of eighteenth-century politics, it declared that the American colonies "are, and of right ought to be, subordinate unto, and dependent upon the imperial crown and parliament of Great Britain," and that Parliament was authorized to make binding laws "in all cases whatsoever."[23]

(The severe wording was so impactful in the colonies that one memorable phrase—"are, and of right ought to be"—was co-opted by Richard Henry Lee in his independence resolution to the Second Continental Congress on June 7, 1776. But that act of one-upmanship was far off in the future.)

The Declaratory Act set off a verbal and legislative tug-of-war between England and the colonies that endured for the next decade, threatening imperial policies and activating the most radical revolutionaries, including Samuel Adams, John's older second cousin. British officials in London heard alarming reports of clandestine meetings leading to "mob rule" in the streets and governmental leaders being hung in effigy. In an effort to gain more of control over the king's subjects, Parliament passed the even more controversial Townshend Revenue Acts in November 1767.[24] These called for specific taxes on seventy-two types of imported paper products, in addition to lead, paint, and tea, while establishing a five-man board of customs commissioners to supervise trade and prevent smuggling.[25]

The new board was to be housed in Boston—another purposeful finger in the eye to Sam Adams and his "Sons of Liberty." Adams responded by writing a letter for the Massachusetts House of Representatives in February 1768, protesting the Townshend Acts as "an infringement on [our] natural and constitutional rights." His hope was to provoke a reaction from other colonies and facilitate a unified opposition. Adams *did*, however, try to soften the blow by expressing "firm confidence in the king, our common head and father, that the united and dutiful supplications of his distressed American subjects will meet with this royal and favourable acceptance."[26]

It turned out to be a waste of time and ink, because those "dutiful supplications" were promptly rejected. King George III and Parliament were in no mood to back off in the face of increasing colonial resistance. They also were aware of another set of published complaints, John Dickinson's "Letters from a Farmer in Pennsylvania to the Inhabitants of the British Colonies," composed over a two-year period from 1867 to 1868, that took further aim at the Townshend Acts. The erudite Dickinson wrote under a veil of anonymity—among other things, he was a lawyer, not a man of the soil—but his no-nonsense prose found a receptive audience among the mostly rural colonial citizenry. The fifth letter noted that it was the "indisputable [and] acknowledged exclusive right of the colonies to tax themselves," which became a popular talking point as more Americans were exposed to his work.[27]

British royalty could not do much about a series of unsanctioned letters from an anonymous author, but it sought to crack down on the defiant action of the Massachusetts legislature. Allowing a locally elected government body to criticize the Crown in such an unfettered manner would be seen around the world as a sign of weakness. Accordingly, Lord Hillsborough, secretary of state for the colonies, demanded that the Massachusetts men rescind the letter. When they refused to do so—by a lopsided vote of 92–17—the colony's royal governor, Francis Bernard, stepped in to disband the house of representatives.[28]

The impact rumbled through the colonies, touching off a spike in protests and even more support for a boycott of British goods. Bernard became so desperate that he asked for troops to "rescue the government," because Boston was now "under the uninterrupted dominion of a faction supported by a trained mob." British authorities had endured the Stamp

Act crisis without the need for military intervention, but he knew they would not be able to do so this time, in the wake of such public discord. It was another inflection point in a burgeoning transatlantic dispute that showed no signs of abating.[29]

* * *

A British fleet and two infantry regiments entered Boston on September 28, 1868, adding the daunting presence of royal musketry to an already-strained civic atmosphere.[30]

Furious citizens coalesced behind Samuel Adams, who, in addition to his usual verbal rabble-rousing, used the pseudonym "Vindex" to publish their thoughts in the *Boston-Gazette and Country Journal*:

> Is there anyone who dares to say that Americans have not the rights of subjects? Is Boston disfranchised? . . . Will the spirits of the people yet unsubdued by tyranny, unaw'd by the menace of arbitrary power, submit to be govern'd by military force? No. Let us rouze our attention to the common law, which is our birthright—our great security against all kinds of insult and oppression.[31]

Adams chose to write anonymously during this period, adopting as many as thirty pseudonyms and sometimes appearing in different newspapers under different names on the same day. He was, alternatively, "Vindex," "A Layman," "A Tory," "A Bostonian," "A Puritan," "Shippen," "E. A.," "T. Z.," "Populous," "Candidus," and "Determinatus" (and, on very rare occasions, "Samuel Adams"). The astounding literary facade was a window into his brilliance as a master manipulator and propagandist. "The impersonations allowed him to stretch the truth in various directions," wrote his most recent biographer, Stacy Schiff. "Without fear of reprisal, he could audition and venture out on limbs. He could provoke, contradict and disavow."[32]

The first year and a half following the arrival of British troops in Boston offered fertile territory for America's new provocateur. On December 12, 1768, "Vindex" wrote that "it is a very improbable supposition that any people can long remain free with a strong military power in the very heart of their country." On January 9, 1769, "T. Z." asserted that "it seems to be generally agreed that every man who is taxed has a right to be present in person, or by *his own* representative, in the body that taxes him." On December 16, 1769, writing under his own name, Adams opined that "it is with astonishment and indignation that the Americans contemplate the folly of the British Ministry in employing troops to parade the streets of Boston. . . . Britain may fall sooner than she is aware; while her colonies who are struggling for liberty may survive her fate and tell the story to their children's children."[33]

Detached as he was from realities on the ground in America, King George III seemed to sense danger more acutely than other members of his hierarchy. In a speech to Parliament on January 9, 1770, he said he wanted to "recommend to the serious attention of my Parliament the state of my government in America," declaring that "in some colonies, many persons have embarked on measures . . . calculated to destroy the commercial connection between them and the mother country." Unfortunately for the king, his warning failed to spark any substantial reaction from Parliament. The assembled Lords and Commons were far more focused on domestic issues than the angry musings of Samuel Adams and a few American rabble-rousers.[34]

Adams was not the only patriot raising his voice in the colonies, but he was the most effective at creating compelling narratives. And he had no problem turning tragedy into opportunity, as happened on February 22, 1770, when, amid rising tensions over the importation of British goods, a customs informer fired randomly into a crowd of protesters at his home and killed eleven-year-old Christopher Seider. The *Boston-Gazette* summed up public opinion by identifying Seider in its obituary as "the unfortunate Boy who was barbarously Murdered."[35]

Adams sprang into action, organizing a theatrical funeral procession on February 26 that attracted two thousand local residents. Led by five hundred school boys marching in pairs and six young pallbearers chosen by Seider's parents, the mourners passed Faneuil Hall, the Old State House, and the Liberty Tree before arriving at the Granary Burial Ground. Adams and his cohorts were delighted at multiple printed tributes, considering "this little hero" to be "the first martyr to the noble cause." The brisk outpouring of emotion convinced the *Gazette* that a positive change in British attitudes might even result: "It is hoped the unexpected and melancholy death of young [Seider] will be a means for the future of preventing any, but more especially the soldierly, from being too free in the use of their instruments of death."[36]

Tensions boiled over into a much more famous event on the night of March 5, 1770, when British "instruments of death" were involved again. A mob of several hundred irate residents gathered on Boston's King Street, near the customs house, and began to harass the single sentry posted there, heaving snow balls and oyster shells, feeding off their colleagues' rage. Some Bostonians were armed with clubs. Fearing for his safety and worried that the crowd would soon plunder the "King's money," the sentry sent word to Captain Thomas Preston for help and reinforcements. Preston gathered eight well-armed soldiers and raced to the scene.

It was a recipe for disaster. Details of exactly what happened in the next few minutes are hazy—so many conflicting accounts exist—but there can be little doubt that Preston and his red-clad troops were pinned against the customs house, pelted with taunts and physical threats from the rabid, jeering throng. "The Mob still increased and were more outrageous," Preston said later, "calling out, 'come on, you Rascals; you bloody Backs, you Lobster scoundrels; fire if you dare . . . we know you dare not." After several long, taut moments, one British soldier was struck with a club and fired his musket. His compatriots reacted by popping away in terror, spraying bullets randomly and felling eleven colonists—five of them killed or mortally wounded.

Many in the crowd ran away, others cowered, and a few scrambled to their homes to retrieve firearms. Additional carnage was avoided only when someone had the presence of mind to summon the acting governor, Thomas Hutchinson, who lived nearby. Hutchinson brushed off threats to his own well-being and defused the turmoil, speaking with participants on both sides, interviewing witnesses, and pledging himself to a full legal inquiry. Captain Preston and the eight soldiers who came to their sentry's aid were arrested and imprisoned in the wee hours of March 6, calming the city's nerves.[37]

The history of the country had changed in an instant, but no one knew it yet.

There is no evidence that Samuel Adams was present that night in the King Street cauldron (Schiff, his biographer, said he "may have been"), but he clearly and defiantly was involved the next day, determined to capitalize on what he considered outrageous British behavior. At 11:00 a.m. on March 6, with "the Blood of our Fellow Citizens running like Water thro' King Street," a committee of fifteen men, led by Adams and wealthy merchant John Hancock, met with Hutchinson to demand the removal of British troops from the city. Hutchinson was reluctant to give up control of his own military, but, seeing no other way out of the crisis, grudgingly agreed to relocate the soldiers to Castle Island in the harbor. The *Gazette* reported that he "gave his word of Honor that he would begin his Preparations in the Morning, and that there should be no necessary delay until the whole of two Regiments were removed to the Castle."[38]

Just as important, Boston won the propaganda battle—led again by Adams, who was the first to describe it as a "massacre," despite its relatively few casualties. Two artists created engravings of a much-exaggerated one-sided attack by British troops firing in unison at innocent, unarmed civilians (Paul Revere's version, which became more famous, was titled "The Bloody Massacre perpetrated in King Street, Boston").[39] Adams saw the value in drawing black-and-white distinctions between attackers and victims. Writing to America's agent in London, Benjamin Franklin, he said he was pleased that the Boston narrative had the desired PR effect, "in some measure preventing the [blame] being cast on the Inhabitants as the aggressors in it . . . it has been thought necessary that our friends on your side of the Water should have a true state of the Circumstances of the Town."[40]

The trials of Captain Preston and his eight imprisoned soldiers promised to be spectacular affairs. It was important for Adams and other leaders, however, that the accused men receive fair treatment in the case of the "Boston Massacre," if only to show Parliament that the colonists still followed the laws of England. Many were surprised when Adams's younger second cousin, John, agreed to be part of the British defense team, but it is unlikely that he would have done so without Samuel's knowledge or approval. John Adams was, at the time, a thirty-four-year-old Boston lawyer of ascending reputation, and he could be counted on to do a good job for Preston and the others as they faced sensationalized murder charges and potentially biased juries.[41]

Perhaps he did *too* good of a job. John Adams weaved a clever tale in the courtroom, making the distinction that, while the soldiers did, indeed, kill five local residents, they were being openly harassed by "a motley rabble" that included "saucy boys, negroes and molattoes, Irish teagues and outlandish jack tars." He was careful not to characterize the group as a riotous mob of regular Boston citizens. This is also when Adams made his famous statement that "facts are stubborn things; and whatever may be our wishes, our inclinations, or the dictates of our passions, they cannot alter the state of facts and evidence." Against all odds, Preston and six of his eight soldiers were acquitted in fall 1770. The other two men were found guilty of manslaughter, a lesser charge, and had their right hands branded with the letter *M* (for *manslaughter*) as punishment.[42]

Samuel Adams would have preferred more convictions, including one or two on murder charges, but he saw the benefit in Massachusetts appearing to be a bastion of judicial fairness. Behind the scenes, he continued to hammer away with his anti-British narrative in other ways, writing about the verdict under the pseudonym "Vindex" in ten published pieces between December 10, 1770, and January 28, 1771. The challenge for Adams was sustaining the same sense of rage among the public. Back on March 5, on the very day that violence broke out on King Street, politicians in London began the process of repealing most of the Townshend Act taxes, maintaining only a tax on tea. Those decisions calmed tempers in much of America, at least temporarily, and, combined with the relocation of troops and other factors, helped usher in a two-year period of relative calm.[43]

* * *

Samuel Adams did not remain idle, however. He wanted each colony to create a "committee of correspondence" to share news and opinions with provincial leaders up and down the seaboard.

This was not a new concept. Richard Henry Lee of Virginia had written to John Dickinson of Pennsylvania as early as 1768, suggesting that the colonies communicate in a coordinated way. "To understand each other," Lee wrote, and "to be informed of what passes, both here and in Great Britain, it would seem that not only select committees should be appointed by all the colonies, but that a private correspondence should be conducted between the lovers of liberty in each province."[44] Nothing much came of it, however, until Adams revisited the issue in 1772.

Parliament had been slowly encroaching on American rights in the early 1770s, using subtle and often-unnoticed legislative maneuvers. The breaking point came in fall 1772, when England ruled that judges in the colonial courts would be paid directly by the Crown, instead of by local legislatures, as had always been the case. This placed the judiciary beyond the control of the colonists for the first time and struck an unsuspecting Adams "like thunder in the ears."[45] At a public meeting at Faneuil Hall on November 2, he proposed forming committees in towns throughout Massachusetts "in order to ascertain the Sense of the People of the province."[46] The idea spread across the colonies, especially after Lee opened correspondence with Adams on February 4, 1773, to discuss "the most easy communication of sentiment." Adams replied, "I had often thought it a misfortune, rather than a fault in the friends of American independence and freedom, not taking care to open every channel of communication."[47] Those two letters helped forge a close relationship between the Lee and Adams families that had a massive impact on the success of the revolutionary movement.

Virginia's House of Burgesses took the formal step of establishing a standing committee of correspondence on March 12, 1773, appointing eleven members, including Lee, Patrick Henry, and a relatively unknown twenty-nine-year-old lawyer named Thomas Jefferson. The stated goal was "to bring our sister colonies into the strictest union with us." Massachusetts followed in early April with its own provincial committee, and it was not long before the colonial agent in London, Benjamin Franklin, heard from Boston delegate Thomas Cushing that "if the colonies are not soon relieved, a Congress will grow out of this Measure and perhaps render a settlement of this unhappy dispute still more difficult." Franklin agreed, saying, "I do not see how it can be prevented."[48]

Franklin and Cushing were premature in their assertion, but only by a year. It would take a sensationally disruptive event in 1773 to convince moderate colonies that such an assembly was necessary. The impetus came when Parliament passed the Tea Act on May 10, giving the financially troubled East India Company a virtual monopoly on selling imported tea. It was not long before ships with hundreds of crates of East India tea set sail to major colonial ports in Boston, Philadelphia, New York, and Charleston. Merchants and consumers were outraged, calling it yet another British affront to their freedom, and a widely distributed handbill warned newly appointed tea agents that "you are marked out as political Bombadiers to demolish the fair structure of American liberty."[49]

Time passed. Some agents wavered and resigned under pressure, but those in Boston refused to be intimidated, calling themselves the "TRUE SONS OF LIBERTY." Backed by Governor Hutchinson, they remained at their posts as the tea ship *Dartmouth* sailed into the harbor with 114 chests of East India product on November 28. Colonists were aware that the ship had twenty days by law to unload the tea; accordingly, they organized protests to prevent it from being "landed, stored, sold or consumed" and demanded that it be sent back to England. The stalemate simmered until the night of December 16, when a group of Sons of Liberty, some "dressed as Indians," clambered aboard the *Dartmouth* and two other ships and gleefully tossed the contents of 342 crates of tea overboard.[50]

The *Gazette* reported that "a number of brave & resolute men, determined to do all in their power to save their country ruin that which their enemies had plotted, in less than four hours, emptied every chest of tea on board the three ships . . . into the sea!!"[51]

The "Boston Tea Party," as it came to be known, had an indelible impact on the country and the world. John Adams felt it immediately, writing to a colleague on December 17: "The Dye is cast: The People have passed the River and cutt away the Bridge: last Night, Three Cargoes of Tea were emptied into the Harbour. This is the Grandest Event which has ever yet happened Since the Controversy with Britain opened!"[52] An even more momentous reaction took place during the third week of January 1774, when word of the American tea insurgency reached London. Blindsided by the news, King George III dashed off a scathing letter to Lord Dartmouth, admitting that "I am much hurt that the instigation of bad men hath drawn the people of Boston to take such unjustifiable steps."[53] Retaliation against the colonists was bound to follow.

CHAPTER 3

Creating a Congress

HUNCHED OVER HIS DIARY ON THE DAY AFTER THE TEA PARTY, JOHN Adams wondered with some trepidation how England would respond to the audacious act of anti-Crown defiance. His thoughts came together in a rapid-fire stream of consciousness:

> What Measures will the Ministry take, in Consequence of this?—Will they resent it? will they dare to resent it? will they punish Us? How? By quartering Troops upon Us?—by annulling our Charter?—by laying on more duties? By restraining our Trade?[1]

Frenzied as those words may have seemed in December 1773, we know now that Adams peered out over the tea-stained harbor and saw the future with remarkable foresight.

British officials met in February 1774 to ponder options for sanctioning the rebellious New Englanders. The king's men knew that George III wanted to "stop the present discourse," which was leading to a "dangerous spirit of resistance" among his "deluded subjects."[2] Accordingly, over the next few months, Parliament proposed a series of regulations called the Coercive Acts, designed to reassert authority, punish the Boston insurgents, and isolate radical Massachusetts from more compliant colonies. They were seen as so draconian that Americans eventually came to call them the "Intolerable Acts."

The first of these, passed in March and scheduled to take effect on June 1, was the Boston Port Act, which shut down commerce in the harbor and imposed severe fines on violators until the East India Company was repaid in full for the destroyed tea.[3] The Port Act was followed by

- the Massachusetts Government Act, seeking to preserve "the peace and good order" by ending most free elections, restricting town meetings, and trampling the colony's charter (just as Adams had feared);
- the Act for the Impartial Administration of Justice, allowing the trial of any royal official to be moved to England; and
- the Quartering Act, calling for British troops to be housed wherever needed, including public buildings and uninhabited houses—essentially an amendment to the previous Quartering Act of 1765.[4]

As if that weren't enough, General Thomas Gage, commander of British troops in North America, was installed as the new royal governor of Massachusetts. He arrived in mid-May, just as news of the Port Act reached Boston from London.[5]

But the king and his ministers had overplayed their hand. The first hints came when colonial leaders in Massachusetts and Virginia began to agitate for a "congress" to share information and discuss organized resistance. Instead of driving a wedge between New England and other regions, the Coercive Acts brought the colonies together in a spirited defense of Boston. David Ramsay, a South Carolina surgeon who penned one of the first histories of the American Revolution in 1789, wrote that "these acts of Parliament, contrary to the expectation of those who planned them, became a cement of a firm union among the colonies from New Hampshire to Georgia." In the minds of many Americans, the new acts imposed a complete system of tyranny.[6]

When the Boston Port Act became law on June 1, Samuel Adams was so outraged that he dared mention *independence* in a letter to a friend. This was at a time—two years before 1776—when no one in the colonies was bold enough to discuss the topic publicly.

"An Empire is Rising in America, and will not this first of June be remembered at a time . . . when it will be in the power of this Country amply to revenge its Wrongs?" Adams wrote. "If Britain by her multiplied oppressions is now accelerating the Independency of the Colonies, which she so much dreads, and which in time must take place, who will she have to blame but herself?"[7]

Less than three weeks later, Massachusetts legislators proposed an American congress to address grievances and refute the Coercive Acts. Governor Gage sent an aide to disrupt them, but Samuel Adams, always one step ahead, barred the door to prevent intrusion. It did not even matter that Gage intended to ban the upstart legislators from ever meeting again; while the governor and his staff fumed, the men inside elected five delegates to the upcoming congress, led by the two Adams cousins.[8]

The next day, an assembly in Pennsylvania agreed that "a congress of deputies from the several colonies in North America is the most probable and proper mode of procuring relief for our suffering brethren" and "securing our rights and liberties." That language was shocking to many—Pennsylvania had always been a bastion of moderation—but it inserted clauses to assure Parliament that its overriding goal was "re-establishing peace and harmony between Greater Britain and these colonies on a constitutional foundation."[9]

Similar meetings were held up and down the coast, most notably in Virginia, where the idea of a congress had been under discussion since May. Richard Henry Lee wrote to Samuel Adams on June 23 that the goal of the continental assembly would be to "adopt such measures as may be most decisive for securing the rights of America against the systemic plan formed for their destruction." Lee and several like-minded Virginia zealots arranged their own provincial convention on August 1 in Williamsburg, seeking to share ideas and determine an appropriate platform.[10]

Despite all the rancor, however, no less a patriot than Adams told Lee that "[s]hould America hold up her own importance to the body of the nation, and at the same time agree to one general bill of rights, the dispute might be settled on principles of freedom, and harmony be restored between Great Britain and the colonies."[11] Even Massachusetts rebels still wanted their rights and liberties to exist within the context of the world's greatest empire.

A new and decidedly radical voice rose in Virginia that summer, well in advance of the colony's August convention. Thomas Jefferson did not yet hold a position of leadership, but he took it upon himself to "prepare a draught of instructions to be given to the delegates whom we should send to the Congress." It was an intrepid move by a still relatively unknown, thirty-one-year-old county representative, and it helps to explain why he soon became a key revolutionary figure. Jefferson said the Crown's punitive acts against Boston jolted him and other Virginians "like a shock of electricity," arousing "anxiety and alarm" across the region.[12]

His sixty-six-hundred-word tract was originally titled "Draft of Instructions to the Virginia Delegates in the Continental Congress," but it came to be known as "A Summary View of the Rights of British America." Much to the surprise of the delegates, and probably to young Jefferson himself, it became one of the most influential documents of early American history. Jefferson's dazzling literary skill was on display to the public for the first time, but the most compelling aspect of "Summary View" was his focus on King George III as a target for criticism. Until that point, colonial anger had been directed solely at Parliament and various other ministers; the king himself was off-limits. In Jefferson's earth-shaking view, however, George III was complicit in illegal acts and negligence toward his subjects.[13]

Jefferson began by asserting that the king was not a divine being but, instead, was "no more than the chief officer of the people, appointed by the laws, and circumscribed with definite powers, to assist in working the great machine of government erected for their use, and consequently subject to their superintendence." That was followed by a damning and voluminous list of illicit activities: restricting free commerce, abolishing local assemblies, quashing public demonstrations, and sending armed troops to threaten law-abiding citizens. Through "inattention to the necessities of his people here," Jefferson wrote, "his majesty permitted our laws to lie neglected in England for years." For good measure, he added, "the British parliament has no right to exercise authority over us." Historians would note that the "Summary View" was actually a warm-up act for the

Declaration of Independence two years later, featuring much of the same language and same tone from the same author.[14]

And yet Jefferson was just as careful as Samuel Adams to stop short of a call for independence in summer 1774. His conclusion of the "grievances which we have thus laid before his majesty" made it clear that "it is neither our wish nor our interest to separate from her." It would take much more time, and even more royal transgressions, for independence to become a practical option. Affronted as he was, Jefferson expressed hope that the king would "procure redress of our great grievances," restoring harmony throughout the empire. "That [it] may continue to the latest ages of time," he wrote in his rousing final sentence, "is the fervent prayer of British America."[15]

Jefferson sent a copy to Peyton Randolph, speaker of Virginia's House of Burgesses. Notwithstanding the softened and upbeat final passage, the convention thought his charges against the king were far too controversial to be shared with the larger congress. (Jefferson later explained that it was "thought too bold for the present state of things.") The Virginians instead adopted a list of eleven resolutions calling for the non-importation of goods from England and a pause to the transatlantic slave trade, while demanding the restoration of America's natural-born liberties. Knowing that news of Jefferson's "Summary View" would find its way across the ocean, they led their published resolutions by pledging "our inviolable and unshaken Fidelity and Attachment to our most gracious Sovereign."[16]

In its final act, the convention appointed a delegation of Randolph, George Washington, Patrick Henry, Richard Henry Lee, and three others as Virginia's representatives to the colonial congress, scheduled to meet in September at Philadelphia. Jefferson would not become involved for another year.[17]

* * *

The Massachusetts delegation left Boston to much fanfare on August 10, 1774. Joining the Adams cousins were Thomas Cushing and Robert Treat Paine (the attorney who, ironically, had opposed John Adams in the Boston Massacre trial). Their first stop was Watertown, nine miles away, where they were feted with food and drinks by "a large number of gentlemen" who gathered to rub elbows at Coolidge's Inn. "About four in the afternoon we took our leave of them," John Adams wrote, "amidst the kind wishes and fervent prayers of every man in the company for our health and success." Short-term hoopla aside, no one could have known they were embarking on an adventure that would establish the foundation of American government for centuries to come.[18]

Reports of a First Continental Congress in defiance of Great Britain electrified the public, and similar scenes played out as the Massachusetts men made their way through Connecticut, New York, and New Jersey on their way to Pennsylvania. This was at a time when, given limited modes of transportation, even the most learned, successful men rarely traveled long distances from their hometowns and almost never into other colonies. Everyone was transfixed by the spectacle. At Harford they connected with Silas Deane, one of Connecticut's delegates, who predicted the Congress would be "the grandest and most important assembly ever held in America." Deane offered helpful background information on several New York delegates, among them James Duane and John Jay. At New Haven they met another Connecticut man, Roger Sherman, a staunch patriot, who believed that Parliament "had authority to make laws for America in no case whatsoever."[19] It was the first time Adams took the measure of Sherman, who would join him two years later on a committee to draft the Declaration of Independence.

The Massachusetts men enjoyed a week of sightseeing in New York City, at one point "walking up the Broad Way, a fine street," Adams said, before meandering south through Trenton toward Pennsylvania. Nearing Philadelphia, they stopped at the village of Frankford and were intercepted by several local patriots who warned them that they were "all suspected of having independence in view." The advance word was unexpected but crucial; timing was not yet right for aggrieved Bostonians to overreach in this first-ever national assembly. Recalling the meeting years later, Adams wrote, "they said you must not utter the word Independence, nor give the least hint or insinuation of the idea, neither in Congress or any private conversation; if you do you are undone; for the idea of Independence is as unpopular in Pennsylvania and in all the middle and Southern States as the Stamp Act itself." Properly chastened, they kept a low profile as representatives from other colonies dropped by to introduce themselves—Thomas McKean of Delaware, Nathan Folsom of New Hampshire, and brothers John and Edward Rutledge of South Carolina, to name a few.[20]

There were fifty-six delegates from twelve colonies elected for the historic body; Georgia declined to attend because it needed British military support in a war against native tribes. Nine of these men had worked together briefly at the Stamp Act Congress in 1765, but most had never met anyone outside their own colonial delegation. Some were naturally curious; others seemed wary of those from different regions. It led to an awkward feeling-out period. John Adams, who took copious notes for his diary, provided some of the most fascinating and detailed assessments from those early days in Philadelphia. Thomas Lynch of South Carolina was "a solid, firm, judicious man." Peyton Randolph of Virginia was "large, well-looking" while Richard Henry Lee was "tall, spare." Charles Thomson of Pennsylvania was "the Sam Adams of Philadelphia, the life of the cause of liberty." James Duane of New York had a "plodding body" and a "very effeminate, feeble voice." Caesar Rodney of Delaware was "the oddest-looking man in the world . . . tall, thin and slender . . . his face is not bigger than a large apple, yet there is sense and fire, spirit and wit, and humor in his countenance." John Dickinson of Pennsylvania was "a shadow; tall but slender as a reed; pale as ashes; one would think at first sight that he could not live a month; yet, upon more attentive inspection, he looks as if the springs of life were strong enough to last many years."[21]

Despite a vow of secrecy to keep information from British spies, John Adams and several others dropped hints in their diaries and spilled intriguing details in letters to loved ones. It was during these early days in Philadelphia that John began to supersede his cousin, Samuel, in revolutionary influence and fame. John proved himself to be a robust orator and master strategist as well as a brilliant, relentless writer and historian; Samuel, by contrast, preferred to work behind the scenes. "[Samuel's] task was to make himself invisible," wrote his biographer, Stacy Schiff. "The idea was to fade into the background, to feel the pulses, sound the depths, and act through others."[22]

Warming to his new and expanded role, John Adams was astounded by their surroundings—not just the city of Philadelphia, with its spacious grid of tree-lined streets, but the intriguing roster of delegates in this quasi-governmental body. "The Congress is Such an Assembly as never before came together on a Sudden [impulse] in any part of the World," Adams wrote to a friend. "Here are Fortunes, Abilities, Learning, Eloquence, Acuteness equal to any I ever met with [in] my Life." But the enormous range of views and backgrounds, blended suddenly in an unfamiliar setting, made him wonder what they could accomplish. "Here is a Diversity of Religions, Educations, Manners, Interests, such as it would Seem to be almost impossible to unite in any one Plan of Conduct," he wrote.[23]

The concern was not unique to Adams. Joseph Galloway of Pennsylvania, an ardent pro-British voice, was wary of the Massachusetts men and saw little hope for unity. After meeting two delegates from New Hampshire for the first time, Galloway wrote to a fellow loyalist: "I think neither of them intends to attach himself more to the particular cause of Boston than will be for the general good." There was more pessimism in a second letter, after he crossed paths with colleagues from other colonies. "The Virginians and Carolinians, [John] Rutledge excepted, seem much among the Bostonians," Galloway wrote. "The Gentlemen from New York have as little Expectations of much Satisfaction from the Event of Things myself."[24]

The First Continental Congress got down to work on September 5 at Carpenters' Hall on Chestnut Street, less than two blocks from the Pennsylvania State House. Forty-four of the fifty-six delegates were present that day and conducted their first business by electing Randolph of Virginia as president and Thomson of Pennsylvania as secretary. They went on to consider some key procedural issues, including whether each colony would get one vote, regardless of size, or whether voting power would be determined by population (it ended up being one colony / one vote).[25] A statement made during their second day of debate had a profound effect on James Duane of New York. "Mr. Henry from Virginia insisted that by the oppression of Parliament all Government was dissolved & that we were reduced to a State of Nature," Duane wrote. "That there were no longer any such distinctions as Colonies. That he conceiv'd himself *not a Virginian but an American.*"[26]

Congress had been in existence for barely twenty-four hours when its proceedings were roiled by a report that the British had attacked and bombed Boston. "It was a confusing account," Adams wrote on the night of September 6, "but an alarming one indeed." The news turned out to be greatly exaggerated. British troops under General Gage had indeed acted aggressively, seizing stores of colonial munitions in Charlestown, but there was no massive military assault or bloodshed. Nonetheless, Philadelphia was on edge, the mood nervous and pensive. "The City is in the utmost Confusion," Silas Deane wrote to his wife. "All The Bells toll muffled, & the most unfeigned marks of sorrow appear in every Countenance."[27] They wondered, understandably, if the mere news of a colonial congress had impelled Gage to action.

Back in session on September 7, the men organized themselves into several committees, including one to "State the rights of the Colonies in general, the several instances in which these rights are violated or infringed, and the means most proper to be pursued for obtaining a restoration of them." The Adams cousins, Lee, Sherman, Duane, Galloway, and Rodney were among those appointed. The committee had a "most ingenious, entertaining debate" on September 8 before breaking into two subcommittees to establish and quantify rights and infringements. One of the most hotly contested issues was considering whether they should deny the authority of Parliament in all cases.[28]

Discussions continued in this manner for the next week as congressmen settled into their roles, aligned with similar thinkers, and welcomed the arrival of the North Carolina delegation on September 14.[29] It was three days later that a second bolt of news from Massachusetts brought an unexpected topic to the agenda.

Courier Paul Revere galloped into town with a series of resolutions adopted by the leaders of Suffolk County and written primarily by Dr. Joseph Warren, a close friend of John Adams from Boston. These nineteen "Suffolk Resolves" declared provincial grievances and outlined methods for resistance. They called on residents to reject recent acts of Parliament as "the attempts of a wicked administration to enslave

Figure 3.1. Carpenters' Hall in Philadelphia, meeting place of the First Continental Congress. *(Author photo)*

America"; accused the British of gross infractions of rights "to which we are justly entitled by the laws of nature"; demanded the immediate with-holding of "all commercial intercourse" with Great Britain, Ireland, and the West Indies; and encouraged residents to "acquaint themselves with the art of war as soon as possible." Congress likely would have acted even without rumors of a British attack on Boston, but there was no waver-ing under the present circumstances, with a sister colony under siege. Delegates pledged support to Massachusetts and unanimously approved Warren's resolves in what amounted to the first formal declaration by an "American" body of government.[30]

There was spirited talk about multiple issues over the next ten days, including another potential boycott of British goods. Moderate members from Pennsylvania and New York worried about the growing strength of radicals during this period and sought to stem their momentum by diverting focus to reconciliatory measures. Galloway introduced a plan on September 28 that called for a joint British/American legislature to regu-late "the administration of the general affairs of America." The intention of Galloway and his allies was to convince King George III that, even while raising complaints, the colonies "hold in abhorrence the idea of being considered independent communities of the British government" and wanted "the establishment of a Political Union with . . . the Mother State." Reconciliation was the preferred remedy for most delegates at the point, but Galloway's statement that he would acknowledge the supreme authority of Parliament over the colonies was a nonstarter for many. The plan was tabled and then dismissed.[31]

Delighted as John Adams was with these developments, especially the adoption of the Suffolk Resolves, it was clear that, after a few short weeks in Congress, he no longer held his colleagues in the same high esteem as he did in early September. Frustration mounted daily, as argu-ments broiled and factions clashed. "I am wearied to Death with the Life I lead," he complained to his wife, Abigail, on October 9. "The Business of the Congress is tedious, beyond Expression." Debates over decisions were "drawn and spun out to an immeasurable Length," and every man thought he was "a great Man," seeking to show off his abilities. "I believe if it was moved and second that We should come to a Resolution that

Three and two make five, We should be entertained with Logick and Rhetorick, Law, History, Politicks, and Mathematicks concerning the Subject for two while Days, and then we Should pass the Resolution unanimously in the Affirmative."[32]

But many years later, aided by the clarity of hindsight, Adams acknowledged the gargantuan challenge they faced in those early weeks of organized revolution at Philadelphia. To develop a cogent strategy in such a limited period of time seemed almost too much to ask of a hastily assembled group of strong-willed strangers with varying backgrounds and views. Short-term inertia was a price they had to pay as part of the embryonic feeling-out process.

As Adams saw it:

> The Colonies had grown up under Constitutions of Government so different, there was so great a Variety of Religions, they were composed of So many different Nations, their Customs, Manners and Habits had So little resemblance, and their Intercourse had been so rare and their Knowledge of each other So imperfect, that to unite them in the Same Principles in Theory and the Same System of Action was certainly a very difficult Enterprize.[33]

Against this backdrop of apparent dysfunction, the First Continental Congress still managed to produce and approve six documents in its final two weeks of operation in October 1774. It was a remarkable feat under unprecedented circumstances, made even more risky by the presence of British informants nearby.

First among them was a bill of rights and grievances, asserting that colonists were "entitled to life, liberty & property, and they have never ceded to any sovereign power whatever, a right to dispose of either without their consent."[34] That was followed by a formalized boycott of British goods and three letters aimed at separate audiences: to the people of Great Britain, the British colonies and the province of Quebec. Their messages were summed up best in the address to the British people, composed by John Jay, a noted moderate and the future chief justice of the U.S. Supreme Court. "The cause of America is now the object of universal attention," Jay wrote. "This unhappy country has not only been oppressed, but abused and misrepresented."[35]

The sixth and final document was of vital importance to the delegates because it took their case directly to King George III. Congress still could not be certain that the "most gracious Sovereign" had been fully apprised of America's indignation, so it chose to bypass Parliament and various royal ministers by submitting a petition to "lay our grievances before the throne." It was a bold and potentially calamitous move for dissatisfied subjects to complain so formally to the king. The list of objections was familiar by now—ranging from unfair taxation to one-sided justice to oppressive restrictions on commerce—but delegates naively clung to the hope that George III, once properly informed, would intervene on their behalf:

> We ask but for peace, liberty, and safety. . . . Your royal authority over us and our connexion with Great-Britain, we shall always carefully and zealously endeavor to support and maintain. . . . We therefore most earnestly beseech your majesty, that your royal authority and interposition may be used for our relief; and that a gracious answer may be given to this petition.

The formal title was "The Petition of the Grand American Continental Congress to the King's Most Excellent Majesty," approved on October 25, their next-to-last day in session. The fifty-one signatories included the Adams cousins, Washington, Lee, Dickinson, Duane, Jay, Sherman, Rodney, the Rutledge brothers, and Galloway—the biggest, most influential names of this grand legislative experiment. Multiple copies were sent to Benjamin Franklin and other American agents in London to increase the odds that the king would receive it. Then Congress brought its unprecedented two-month assembly to a close.[36]

Facing an uncertain future, but strengthened by the bonds of this unlikely union, the delegates decided to meet again in Philadelphia on May 10, 1775, "unless the redress of grievances, which we have desired, be obtained before that time."[37]

* * *

The men who gathered at Carpenters' Hall on the morning of September 5, 1774, had almost no sense of the history they were making. Coming together from different regions with different backgrounds, and often conflicting agendas, the First Continental congressmen pounded out a template for future American governments in less than two months, achieving a rough consensus—against all odds—on several crucial matters.

They passed the Suffolk Resolves and declared that the once all-powerful Parliament held no power over the colonies other than to regulate trade. They formalized the harshest acts of economic resistance in the history of the British Empire, far more serious than dumping tea in Boston's harbor. They affirmed the necessity of locally elected colonial legislatures to tax and govern on their own terms, albeit within the framework of the empire, at least for now. They stopped short of sanctioning military support for freedom fighters in Massachusetts, where the colony was threatened by British troops, but left open the possibility of armed conflict in the future.

Finally, and most unexpectedly under the circumstances, they made it clear that Parliament, and maybe even the king himself, would have to make the first series of concessions if a new, more harmonious partnership was to be reached.[38]

Some delegates felt that a day of reckoning was inevitable. There was such a "determined and unanimous" resolution among the colonies that further British missteps might set off to a clash of arms. Dickinson wrote to an agent in England on October 27: "The Colonists have now taken such grounds that Great Britain must relax, or inevitably involve herself in a civil war, likely in all human probability to overwhelm her with a weight of calamities." Five days later, Galloway addressed the "unfortunate Dispute between The Mother Country & her Colonies" by fretting that "it is now arrived at such a Heighth that it will be with great Difficulty accommodated." Although he had affixed his signature to key documents issued by Congress, Galloway judged them, in a private letter, to be "too warm & indiscreet in my Opinion."[39]

British officials in North America were rattled by the steady drumbeat of news in late October and early November. They no longer chortled at the idea of inexperienced, self-styled legislators leading the colonies in opposition to Parliament. "The proceedings of the Continental Congress astonish and terrify all considerate men," General Gage wrote from Boston to Lord Dartmouth in London on November 15. "Though I am confident that many of their Resolves neither can or will be observed, I fear they will be generally received, as there does not appear to be resolution and strength enough among the most sensible and moderate people in any of the Provinces to openly reject them."[40]

Little did anyone know at the time, but King George III had already hardened his stance. Weeks before the congressional petition arrived in England, he sent a furious note to Lord North on November 18, decrying the state of the colonies—no doubt after receiving word from Gage that Massachusetts and Connecticut were preparing to take up arms. "The New England Governments are in a State of Rebellion," the king wrote, fairly seething. "Blows must decide where they are to be subject to this Country or independent."[41] It was a crucial turning point in this thinking, and the first indication that George III foresaw war as a solution. Less than two weeks later, in a speech to both houses of Parliament on November 30, the king noted that "a most daring spirit of resistance and disobedience to the law still unhappily prevails" in Massachusetts and other colonies. He assured them that the ferocity of his commitment to crushing rebellion was growing daily. "You may depend upon my firm and steadfast resolution to withstand every attempt to weaken . . . the supreme authority of this Legislature over all the dominions of my Crown."[42]

The petition from Congress did not reach Franklin's residence in London until December 20. The king's speech was clear that no accommodations would be made, but Franklin sent it along to Lord Dartmouth anyway, in the hope of gaining an audience. Finding "nothing improper to present," Dartmouth took the unexpected step of showing it to George III, who received it "very graciously" (Franklin's words) before passing it onto Parliament. Alas, the petition was placed at the bottom of a stack of 149 documents that went to the governmental body and never was formally addressed. A separate attempt by Franklin to be heard by the House of Commons was rejected by an overwhelming vote of 218–65.[43]

The time required for news to cross the Atlantic kept the colonies in suspense, but reports of the king's explosive November 30 speech finally arrived by ship in Boston on February 1, 1775. The full text appeared the next day in the *Massachusetts Spy*. John Adams was out of town at the time, serving in the provincial congress at Cambridge, but his wife was well versed on the politics of the day and made a stark assessment of the royal assertions. "The die is cast," Abigail Adams wrote to a friend on February 3. "Yesterday brought us such a Speech from the Throne as will stain with everlasting infamy the reign of George the 3. . . . Infatuated Britain! Poor distressed America! Heaven only know what is next to take place, but it seems to me the Sword is now our only, yet dreadful alternative."[44]

Her husband once wondered if he would ever return to Philadelphia. Now it was almost certain that he would be back again for a second congress in May 1775.

CHAPTER 4

Spirit of '75

THE PROSPECT OF A SECOND CONTINENTAL CONGRESS WAS NOT THE most urgent issue facing British officials as the calendar turned to 1775. Far more concerning was the colonial effort to collect and store military supplies that one day might be used against His Majesty's troops in New England.

"Nothing can be more provoking than the conduct of the inhabitants of Massachusetts Bay," King George III wrote in mid-December 1774, his famous temper flaring again. "Some measures must undoubtedly be adopted after Christmas to . . . bring them to a due obedience to the mother country."[1] The king did not want to sit back and become victimized by ungrateful subjects from thousands of miles away.

It was against that backdrop that Lord Dartmouth issued orders on January 27, 1775, for General Thomas Gage to smash the rebellion in its earliest stage. "The king's dignity, and the honor and safety of the empire require that . . . force should be repelled by force," he wrote. Dartmouth and others believed the colonists were a rude rabble, operating haphazardly, and that even a small force of well-trained British regulars could promptly quash the insurgency. To ensure future compliance, Gage was told to arrest and imprison leaders of the provincial congress, "whose proceedings appear in every light to be the acts of treason and rebellion."[2]

A series of legislative and weather-related delays meant the formal copy of orders did not reach Gage for almost three months. Arriving, finally, on April 16, they promised reinforcements and reeked of overconfidence, predicting a quick, almost pristine victory. Gage selected as his target the town of Concord, eighteen miles inland from Boston, where the provincial congress sometimes met, and where, far more important, British spies told him the colonists were stashing supplies, including cannons.[3] He sent clear, blunt instructions to Lieutenant Colonel Francis Smith, commander of the Tenth Regiment of Foot:

> Having received intelligence, that a quantity of Ammunition, Provision, Artillery, Tents and small arms, have been collected at Concord, for the Avowed Purpose of raising and supporting a Rebellion against His Majesty, you will March with the Corps of Grenadiers and Light Infantry, put under your command, with the utmost expedition and Secrecy to Concord, where you will seize and destroy all artillery, Ammunition, Provisions, Tents, Small Arms, and all Military Stores whatever. But you will take care that the Soldiers do not plunder the inhabitants, or hurt private property.[4]

It was April 18, 1775.

Gage could not imagine the world-changing fury he was about to unleash.

* * *

The march of seven hundred red-clad British soldiers from Boston to Concord was not conducted in the secrecy Gage had hoped. American informants had been monitoring their actions for days, and patriot Joseph Warren had organized a series of swift-riding couriers to deliver real-time updates through the countryside. Warren knew that Samuel Adams and John Hancock were holed up in the small town of Lexington, about six miles east of Concord, and feared they were prime targets for capture. Couriers Paul Revere and William Dawes were assigned to alert them to the danger and warn local militias and other residents that the British, indeed, were coming.[5]

Traveling different routes on lathered horses to avoid detection, Revere and Dawes arrived in Lexington shortly after midnight, in the wee hours of April 19. They soon found the residence of Reverend Jonas Clarke, where Adams and Hancock had taken up temporary quarters.

The ambitious Hancock was feverishly cleaning his gun to take part in the militia fight, but Adams intervened and talked him out of it. "That is not our business," he said. "We belong to the cabinet." Gage's main goal was seizing supplies in Concord, but the two radical legislators knew they were vulnerable. Sometime after 3:00 a.m. they hopped on Hancock's coach and slipped away to safety in Woburn, about five miles distant.[6]

The day began to dawn as a British advance force of two hundred men under Major John Pitcairn approached Lexington on the road to Concord. An anxious colonial drum roll sounded, and "about seventy-seven" militia men formed with rifles at Lexington Green, under their commander, Captain John Parker, a veteran of the French and Indian War.[7] The odds were overwhelming—professional British soldiers holding an almost three-to-one advantage over rag-tag farmers and blacksmiths—and, in testimony later, Parker insisted he merely ordered the militia to meet on the Common to decide a course of action. There was to be no confrontation, he said, "unless they should insult or molest us," and as soon the vanguard of his Majesty's troops appeared in their front, "I immediately ordered our Militia to disperse, and not to fire."[8]

But fire, someone did.

The identity of the man whose gunshot set off the Revolutionary War is unknown to history. Each side blamed the other for shooting first. One militia member said he heard a British officer yell, "throw down your Arms ye Villains, ye Rebels!" and then "fire, by God, fire,"[9] but it just as easily could have been a trigger-happy Lexingtonian, jangled by nerves, unable to contain himself. What is known for certain is that once the shot rang out, frothing redcoats surged forward in a rampage, killing eight militia and wounding ten. Several Americans fired back in a rush of adrenaline but did almost no damage, inflicting light wounds on two soldiers and grazing the side of Pitcairn's horse. The Battle of Lexington was over in a brief flash of muzzles. It was said that the British gave three quick shouts of triumph before quickly reforming their units and marching on to Concord, undeterred.[10]

Colonial couriers ran into a tangle of misfortunes as they went about their dangerous work, sounding alarms. Revere was captured and briefly detained by a British patrol, and Dawes fell off his horse while

Figure 4.1. Statue of Captain John Parker at Lexington. *(Author photo)*

barely avoiding arrest. But a third man, Samuel Prescott, ventured forward in the cauldron to warn Concord of the British approach. Militia units and "minute men" from the nearby towns of Lincoln, Bedford, and

Acton raced in to provide support and—given the chance to prepare by Prescott's warning—took up positions on high ground above the town and the North Bridge. Mindful of orders not to fire first, they watched and waited with thumping heartbeats.

British troops fanned out across the area in search of suspected military stores but came up empty-handed (most had been moved elsewhere or cleverly hidden). A probing unit of 120 men searched a farm belonging to the Concord militia colonel, James Barrett, but uncovered only a few random items. Perhaps hoping to spread a message of terror, redcoats in the town set fire to a pile of artillery carriage parts they had found, sending plumes of smoke skyward. Frantic local militia mistook the smoke as blatant arson, fearing for their homes and shops, especially when sparks set a townhouse ablaze. "Will you let them burn the town down?" one man screamed, pleading for action.[11]

On such quirks of fate does history hinge. Colonial troops—now four hundred strong—began to advance on the North Bridge, muskets loaded. One historian called it "the first time that an American force, under orders, with a clear command structure, took the field in an offensive capacity." Indeed, a British soldier recalled, "they began to march by divisions down upon us from their left in a very military manner." The royal invaders were aghast. They never imagined such temerity from untrained "rabble." Soon, three British shots rang out, followed by a volley; two Americans were killed, and four others were wounded.[12]

Unlike at Lexington, however, the colonials held their ground, firing back with determination and precision. The chilling cry—"Fire! For God's sake, fire!"—marked the first time in history that American soldiers were ordered to shoot at British troops. Twelve of His Majesty's soldiers were hit, three of them killed, and if that was an escalation that no one could have imagined hours earlier, an even more shocking development was the sight of British professionals *retreating* from mere militia. "We were obliged to give way," one of them said, "then run with the greatest precipitance."[13]

Gage's men now had to navigate a treacherous eighteen-mile gauntlet back to Boston. Militia and minutemen from towns across the region—Reading, Chelmsford, Billerica, Framingham, Sudbury, Woburn,

Watertown, Medford, Dedham, Lynn—poured in along the route to make the journey as miserable as possible. Alternating between ambushes and stand-up firefights, they harassed the British every step of the way, including clashes as Meriam's Corner, Elm Brook Hill, Menotomy, and a return engagement at Lexington (known as "Parker's Revenge"). As many as four thousand colonials reported for action during the day, more than offsetting British reinforcements and stunning the redcoat leaders.

The butcher's bill of battle was sobering. The Americans suffered 49 killed, 41 wounded, and five missing for a total of 95 casualties. British losses were even worse, almost triple: 73 killed, 174 wounded, and 26 missing for a total of 273. Brigadier General Hugh Early Percy sorted through the carnage and was almost inconsolable as he came away with a new, grudging respect for the colonials. "Whoever looks upon them as an irregular mob will find himself much mistaken," Percy wrote. "They have men amongst them who know very well what they are about. . . . For my part, I never imagined they would have attacked the King's troops or have the perseverance I found in them."[14]

And yet it was one of victors, militia man Noah Parkhurst of Lincoln, fresh off the first armed combat of his life, who saw the uncertain future more clearly than most. "Now the war has begun," he said, "and no one knows when it will end."[15]

* * *

Although a second meeting of the Continental Congress was already scheduled for May, the stakes had now been raised beyond anyone's imagination. News of bloodshed at Lexington and Concord, and the accompanying British retreat, had galvanized moderates and radicals in an unexpectedly common cause. Almost overnight, they found themselves running a war.

"The impious War of Tyranny against Innocence has commenc'd in the Neighborhood of Boston," moderate John Dickinson wrote in anger. "What human Policy can divine the Prudence of precipitating Us into these shocking Scenes? Why have We been so rashly declared Rebels?" He warned the king and his ministers that the Americans were a united, resolved people.[16]

Back in September 1774, when delegates traveled from twelve colonies to their first meeting in Philadelphia, a curious citizenry showed up to support them along the way, shaking hands and slapping backs. Now, however, the pulse had changed dramatically. Connecticut militia units came out to march with New England delegates as they made their way south, providing security, giving it the feel of a grand procession. Momentum picked up as they crossed into New York City, "led by a battalion of 800 men and cheered on by welcoming throngs." Similar scenes met those coming from Virginia and North Carolina, as "we were constantly meeting Armed men to Escort the delegates . . . on their Way." In Baltimore, local militia men were startled when George Washington and other southern delegates stopped briefly to review the troops.[17]

By the time groups from Massachusetts, Connecticut, New York, and New Jersey arrived together on the outskirts of Philadelphia, they were met "by about Two Hundred of the principle Gentlemen on Horseback with their Swords Drawn." Hancock and Samuel Adams rode in an open, four-wheeled carriage, and a lengthy stream of smaller horse-drawn carriages, carrying men who were about to become famous, followed closely behind. "Thus rolling and gathering like a Snowball," wrote Silas Deane of Connecticut, "we approached the City, full of people, [with] the crowd as great as New York, the Bells all ringing and the air rent with Shouts and huzza's."[18]

They got down to business on May 10, with forty-six delegates from eleven colonies in attendance (those from Rhode Island and Georgia were still in transit, along with several stragglers). Peyton Randolph led the powerful Virginia contingent, which again included Washington, Richard Henry Lee, and Patrick Henry. Massachusetts had the Adams cousins, Thomas Cushing, Robert Treat Paine, and the newly elected Hancock. Pennsylvania's delegation was bolstered by the presence of Benjamin Franklin, who was back on home soil after a long-term stay in England. When Dr. Lyman Hall joined the group a few days later, he became the first resident of the colony of Georgia to attend a congressional session, although a full Georgia delegation would not arrive until the fall.[19]

The meeting site had been moved a few blocks down Chestnut Street, from Carpenters' Hall to the larger and grander Pennsylvania State House. They gathered in the Assembly Room on the first floor, a reasonably comfortable space for the fifty-plus delegates, about forty feet square, with tall windows on two sides for ample sunlight. Randolph presided from a low platform at the front of the room, sitting in a high-backed chair. Modest work tables, covered in green cloth, were arranged in a semicircle to face him, with seating assignments broken down by regions and colonies (although no formal seating chart has ever been found). Behind the building was the State House Yard, "an open public green the size of a city block and enclosed the whole way around by a seven-foot brick wall," where delegates could relax, stretch their legs, and hold important private conversations.[20]

Colonial assemblies had issued instructions to their delegations a few months earlier, providing parameters for the decisions they could make in Philadelphia. Typical was the edict from Massachusetts, empowering delegates to support measures only "for the recovery and establishment of American rights and Liberties, and for restoring harmony between Great-Britain and the Colonies." The directives were written between December and March—*before* Lexington and Concord—but there could be no doubt that reconciliation remained the goal as Congress opened its daily sessions in mid-May.[21]

In reality, much had changed with the Lexington gunfire. On May 11, Hancock read a letter from the Massachusetts assembly that effectively changed the course of American history. It called the "Establishment of an Army indispensably necessary" and announced a plan to raise 13,600 men for that purpose, while asking for additional troops from New Hampshire, Rhode Island, and Connecticut. Massachusetts knew it was risking censure from others by jumping ahead of the Continental Congress, but "the sudden Exigency of our public Affairs precluded the possibility of waiting for your directions." Creating an army was "the only mean left to stem the rapid Progress of a tyrannical Ministry." Counterproductive as this sounded, it might be the only way to restore peace while remaining part of the British Empire.[22]

There also were unsettling rumbles beyond Massachusetts. On May 9, the day before Congress convened, an independent New England militia had seized British fortifications at Fort Ticonderoga in upstate New York and overrun redcoats at nearby Crown Point. On May 15, with British troops reportedly headed to New York City, Congress advised New Yorkers to be in a "constant readiness for protecting the inhabitants from insult and injury." At the same time, they were warned that armed conflict should result only if the British commit hostilities or invade private property. Everyone on both sides was walking a very fine line.[23]

The first of Rhode Island's two delegates arrived in Philadelphia on May 15, giving Congress representatives from thirteen colonies. Two days later, Congress resolved itself into a Committee of the Whole for "consideration of the state of America," a momentous and potentially divisive task. Richard Henry Lee of Virginia set the tone by proposing to raise a colonial army, but John Rutledge of South Carolina wanted certain questions answered before moving forward to a vote. "Some other points must be settled," Rutledge said, "such as do we *aim at independency*? Or do we only ask for a restoration of rights and putting us on our old footing."[24]

The raw nature of the questions rattled many congressmen. No one, it seemed, was ready to push American independence in a public or legislative forum. Robert R. Livingston of New York agreed with Rutledge that the goal of any armed resistance had to be clearly defined. John Dickinson tried to thread a strategic needle while calling for both a "Vigorous preparation for War" and "a further plan for a reconciliation if it is possible." Debate sizzled for more than a week, but it was difficult to reach a unified plan on reconciliation in the midst of combat; there were so many variables, so many clashing opinions. By the end of the month, they had decided that yet another petition would be sent to King George III, professing a "most ardent wish for the restoration of . . . harmony" but seeking a just regard "for the undoubted rights and true interests of these colonies."[25]

A major change in leadership took place on May 24, when Randolph was called back to Virginia to lead the colonial assembly (local jurisdictions still taking precedence in many minds over a makeshift "national" body). Hancock was named the new president by a unanimous vote. The arrival of prominent personalities such as Franklin and Hancock during this brief period in spring 1775 had an enormous effect on the legislative body gathered in Philadelphia. Another influential addition came in mid-June, when the Virginia assembly chose the young attorney Thomas Jefferson to fill Randolph's vacated seat—bringing Franklin, Hancock, Jefferson, Lee, and the Adams cousins together as a group for the first time.[26]

* * *

An informal army made up of men from several colonies was already gathering in Boston "for the general defense of the rights of America."

On June 2, a letter from the Massachusetts assembly urged Congress to provide operational oversight of those troops to "more effectually answer the purpose designed."[27]

The pace of the dispute with England was about to change. Quickly.

The next day, a historic day—June 3, 1775—Congress voted to borrow money to purchase gunpowder for the "Continental Army," the first time that the term appeared in the official records. Within two weeks it called for companies of expert riflemen to be formed in Pennsylvania, Maryland, and Virginia and sent to Boston to join the infantry. The enlistment form committed each man to service "as a soldier in the American continental army, for one year, unless sooner discharged." A committee was assigned to draft and propose army regulations, led by the military veteran from Virginia, George Washington.[28]

Washington received a far more demanding task on June 15, when he was appointed to command the new American army.[29] A footnote in the *Journals of the Continental Congress* identified Thomas Johnson of Maryland as the delegate who nominated Washington, but it was John Adams who claimed credit for himself years later. An account from Adams's autobiography, written in the early 1800s, was so compelling that it came to be accepted as the story of Washington's nomination, especially given the lack of detail in congressional reports. Adams wrote:

I walked with Mr. Samuel Adams in the State house Yard, for a little Exercise and fresh Air, before the hour of Congress. . . . I am determined this Morning to make a direct motion that Congress should adopt the Army before Boston and appoint Colonel Washington Commander of it. . . . I had no hesitation to declare that I had but one Gentleman in Mind for that important command, and that was a Gentlemen from Virginia who was among Us and very well know to all of US, a Gentleman whose Skill and Experience as an Officer, whose independent fortune, great Talents and excellent universal Character, would command the Approbation of all America, and unite the cordial Exertions of all the Colonies better than any other Person in the Union.[30]

It should be noted, however, that Adams contradicted himself in 1815, writing in a letter that Washington was "nominated by Mr. Johnson of Maryland."[31]

Though the vote was unanimous, Washington was not without opposition for the top army post. Some New Englanders favored Artemas Ward of Massachusetts, who commanded the colony's militia and was already on duty near Boston. President Hancock also had his eye on the job. But the Adams cousins and many others knew that this could not be seen as an all–New England effort if they were to obtain widespread support from north to south. Washington's selection had as much to do with geographical balance as it did his own military résumé.

That is why Washington took a decidedly humble tone when addressing Congress on June 16 to accept the position. "Tho' I am truly sensible of the high Honour done me, in this Appointment," he said, "yet I feel great distress, from a consciousness that my abilities and military experience may not be equal to the extensive and important Trust. However, as the Congress desire it, I will . . . exert every power I possess in their service, and for support of the glorious cause."[32]

Washington could not have known that the cause was under attack once again in Boston. On June 17, at about the same time Congress formally approved his commission, veteran British soldiers made three assaults against inexperienced patriots on the hills of Charlestown peninsula. The Americans held their ground until running out of ammunition during the third attack, but they managed to inflict massive casualties on His Majesty's startled troops. The victorious British lost 1,054 in killed, wounded, and missing at the Battle of Bunker Hill—a staggering figure, almost 40 percent of those engaged. "The success is too dearly bought," British general William Howe grumbled. Patriot casualties numbered just four hundred, although one of those killed was Joseph Warren, president of the provincial assembly and a rising star in the revolution.[33]

Word of the battle did not reach Philadelphia until June 22, but the impact on Congress was immediate. In rapid fashion over the next week, it appointed eight brigadier generals to serve under Washington; ordered that blankets and other necessities be provided for all troops; appropriated $2 million for the "defence of America"; recommended that New York recruit and pay more of its own soldiers; advised Pennsylvania to form eight companies of riflemen into a battalion; considered a probe of Canadian territory from Fort Ticonderoga and Crown Point; and, finally, on June 30, approved formal articles of war against the mother country.[34]

There were sixty-nine articles in all, creating rules of operation and discipline for the army. It was done out of necessity, Congress said, because "His Majesty's most faithful subjects in these Colonies are reduced to a dangerous and critical situation, by the attempts of the British ministry to carry into execution, by force of arms, several unconstitutional and oppressive acts of the British parliament." Accordingly, any actions taken in self-defense were not only necessary but "an indispensable duty."

A committee was assigned to review the articles and have them published as soon as possible.[35]

* * *

Fascinated with documents that announced their intentions to the world, the delegates approved two more in summer 1775. One was a justification for taking up arms against England. The other was a petition begging the king to intervene.

Contradictory as those messages may have seemed, they allowed Congress to grope for answers while seeking peace through the barrel of a gun.

"A Declaration of the Causes and Necessity of Taking Up Arms" was assigned on June 23 to a five-man committee that included John Rutledge, Benjamin Franklin, and John Jay. Their task was to produce a document "to be published by General Washington, upon his arrival at the camp in Boston," describing the need for armed resistance. Rutledge spent the better part of two days composing the first draft, but it was deemed insufficient by the others, who found "much fault-finding and declamation, with little sense of dignity." On June 26, Congress then added two more distinguished writers to the committee—John Dickinson and its newest member, Thomas Jefferson, who had taken his seat only a few days earlier.[36]

The reputation of Jefferson's masterly pen was well known by the time he reported to Congress on June 21. He had written the vibrant "Summary View of the Rights of British America" in 1774, taking on the king in print for the first time, and his timely arrival in Philadelphia made him a logical choice to explain America's stance. Alas, when Dickinson read Jefferson's draft sometime during the last week of June, he disagreed with several points, crossing out words and making edits. The headstrong Jefferson rejected those changes, so Dickinson took it on himself to produce an extensively rewritten version. Congress then debated Dickinson's draft "by paragraphs," and it was ultimately approved, after several more edits, on July 6.[37]

Many years later, after their legacies had been well established—Jefferson as the author of the Declaration of Independence, Dickson as the curmudgeon who argued against it—Jefferson claimed that his original draft about the necessity for taking up arms was "too strong for Mr. Dickinson," saying "[h]e still retained the hope of reconciliation with the mother country, and was unwilling it should be lessened by offensive statements."[38] A careful analysis, however, shows that to be untrue. Historian Pauline Maier contends that Dickinson had "made Jefferson's draft stronger, more assertive, even threatening."[39] Many modern-day Americans caught up in the Jefferson mystique would be stunned to read his thoughts on reconciliation in early July 1775, before they had fully evolved.

Even while laying out the causes for war that summer in the starkest of terms, Jefferson wrote:

> But that this our declaration may not disquiet the minds of our good fellow subjects in all parts of the empire, we do further assure them that we mean not in any wise to affect that union with them in which we have so long & so happily lived & which we wish so much to see again restored.[40]

The document's purpose was to assure the army that its cause was justified, and it was Dickinson who made the most compelling case. Americans, he said, had been faced with choosing between "an unconditional submission to the Tyranny of irritated Ministers, or Resistance by Force. The latter is our Choice." As for the growing but still unspoken threat of dissolving their union, Dickinson wrote that England "has *not yet* driven us into that desperate Measure" (emphasis added). It was the first time that independence was implied so strongly in a formal message from the colonists to the Crown.[41]

The list of grievances ranged from a relentless stream of taxes to a campaign of aggression that raised the "Indignation of a virtuous, loyal, and affectionate People." Though John Adams was unsure that a declaration was needed, he liked the general tone of their work. "This day has been spent in debating a manifesto setting forth the causes of our taking up arms," he wrote to a friend on July 5. "There is some spunk in it."[42]

Adams was less impressed with the other significant document from this period, known (and often derided) as the Olive Branch Petition to the king. It dated back to May 25, when Congress pondered whether a "humble and dutiful petition [should] be presented to his Majesty," seeking a "most desirable reconciliation." Two days of debate followed, with Dickinson arguing on behalf of the proposal and Adams leading the opposition. Adams, cranky as ever, thought they were wasting their time.[43]

An early draft of notes for Dickinson's speech carried the cumbersome title of "Arguments in Congress in Favour of a Reconciliation & sending over persons to lay the Colonies at the Feet of his Majesty and pray(ing) for Peace." He worried that a full-scale war would be damaging to both parties and thought a properly written petition could calm the king's fears of independence. Dickinson planned to do so by pledging an unabashed loyalty to George III, including "our Attachment to his person, Family and Government—our Love to our Parent State—our Readiness & Willingness . . . to support, maintain & defend the Interests & Rights of his Majesty."

He also played on racial insecurities, warning of "The Danger of Insurrection by Negroes in Southern Colonies" and "Incursions of Canadians & Indians upon the Northern Colonies."[44]

Adams rose immediately to counter Dickinson on behalf of the dissenters. If King George III had not acted on their first petition in the fall, why would he change his mind *now*, on a second but similar petition? Unfortunately, Adams kept no notes of his speech that day—he spoke off the cuff, as usual, and wrote of it only sparingly, years later, in his autobiography. "The motion was introduced and supported by long speeches," he recalled. "I was opposed to it, of course, and made an opposition to it in as long a speech as I commonly made." John Sullivan of New Hampshire also railed against the proposal, but Adams curiously stepped out to the State House Yard in the middle of Sullivan's speech to conduct unrelated business. At that point, Dickinson stormed out after him.

According to Adams:

> He broke out upon me in a most abrupt and extraordinary manner; in as violent a passion as he was capable of feeling, and with an air, countenance and gestures, as rough and haughty as if I had been a school-boy and he the master. He vociferated, "What is the reason, Mr. Adams, that you New England men oppose our measures of reconciliation? There now is Sullivan, in a long harangue, following you in a determined opposition to our petition to the King. Look ye! If you don't concur with us in our pacific system, I and a number of us will break off from you in New England, and we will carry on the opposition by ourselves in our own way."[45]

(Written in the early 1800s, Adams's account is the only one that exists of this encounter. It is doubtful, however, that Dickinson would have used the phrase "our pacific system," given that he also wrote the declaration for taking up arms, served in the local militia, and went on to fight in the Revolutionary War.)

Congress had many other issues to deal with as May turned to June and did not even get around to appointing a committee to write the petition until June 3. Members again included Rutledge, Franklin, and Jay—an impressive roster—but Dickinson was the committee's conscience and did much of the composition. Editing was postponed for several weeks while he dealt with other matters, and it was not until early July that delegates took a vote on Dickinson's final draft.

The core message was summarized in its second-to-last paragraph: "We, therefore, beseech your Majesty that your royal authority and influence may be graciously interposed to procure us relief from our afflicting fears and jealousies . . . and to settle peace through every part of your dominion." Once approved on July 5, it was signed by all forty-nine delegates in attendance, including Adams, R. H. Lee, and other radicals, gritting their teeth for the sake of unanimity. "It must be proposed," Adams conceded the next day. "We can't avoid it."[46]

Despite that accommodating public face, however, Adams fumed in private. He considered the petition to be a "measure of imbecility" that "embarrassed every exertion of Congress" and sought, ultimately, "to obtain decisive declarations *against* independence."[47] He groused about the absurdity of preparing for war while extending Dickinson's olive branch. Later that month, in a letter to his friend, James Warren, he made his anger personal when he wrote that a "piddling Genius, whose Fame has been trumpeted so loudly, has given a silly Cast to our whole Doings." There was no doubt that he meant Dickinson.[48]

The caustic schoolyard reference might have remained hidden for years had the letter not been intercepted by British authorities. It was reprinted in several newspapers for the express purpose of embarrassing Adams and driving a public wedge between him and Dickinson. Publicity from the stolen letter turned out to have little impact on congressional action that summer—with the petition and other documents behind them, the delegates looked forward to a much-needed recess—but it damaged what was left of the Adams-Dickinson relationship for the rest of the revolutionary era. Adams realized as much the next time he encountered his rival on Chestnut Street.[49]

"We met, and passed near enough to touch elbows," Adams wrote. "He passed without moving his hat or head or hand. I bowed, and pulled off my hat. He passed haughtily by. The cause of his offense is the letter, no doubt. . . . We are not on speaking terms nor bowing terms for the time to come."[50] (There was something oddly poetic that the two men would do verbal battle again when the crucial independence vote came to the floor a year later.)

In the meantime, Congress appointed Richard Penn of Philadelphia to carry the Olive Branch Petition across the ocean. Penn was a native of England and the former acting governor of Pennsylvania, and it was thought he would be viewed by the Crown as an acceptable colonial courier. Penn's ship departed on July 11, heading for Bristol and then London, where he would team up with American agent Arthur Lee to attempt to get an audience with—and, more important, a response from—King George III.[51]

CHAPTER 5

"Open and Avowed Rebellion"

THE KING OF ENGLAND DID NOT LIKE WHAT HE WAS HEARING IN THE
late spring and early summer of 1775. As news of the firefights at Lexington and Concord reached London, he gasped at the insolence of his
American colonists and pondered possible solutions to this odious revolt.

"I cannot help being of the opinion that with firmness and perseverance, America will be brought to submission," he wrote to Lord Dartmouth in early June. He continued:

> If not, old England will perhaps not appear so formidable in the eyes
> of Europe as at other periods, but yet will be able to make her rebel-
> lious children rue the hour they cast off obedience. America must be a
> colony of England or treated as an enemy. Distant possessions standing
> upon an equality with the superior state [are] more ruinous than being
> deprived of such connections.

Long before others would reach the same conclusion, the king saw only
two possible results: surrender or separation. There could be no other out-
come for subjects in a faraway land who dared to challenge the authority
of the Crown—and he did not seem to favor one extreme over the other.
His views came together in an angry, rambling letter on July 1, 1775,
when he wrote to another minister that "no situation can ever change
my fixed resolution, either to bring the colonies to due obedience to the
legislature of the mother country or to cast them off!"[1]

What no one in London knew at the time was that matters in America had spun wildly out of the king's control. It was mid-July when word arrived of the pyrrhic British victory at Bunker Hill, marred by the stain of one thousand casualties—including ninety officers killed and wounded at the hands of raw colonial volunteers. George III and his court were so shaken that they approved a massive military buildup, designed to place twenty thousand troops in America by April 1776—more than doubling the current force. In addition to hiring foreign mercenaries to fight on England's behalf, there was hope that homegrown privateers could assist the military by disrupting colonial trade on the high seas.[2]

Such was the royal mind-set when an eager but oblivious Richard Penn set foot in London on August 14, carrying with him the Olive Branch Petition. A note had been sent in advance to the colonial agent, Arthur Lee, declaring that if the "Administration be desirous of stopping the Effusion of British blood, the opportunity is now offered to them." The team of Penn and Lee dutifully forwarded a copy of the petition to Lord Dartmouth on August 21, but the secretary of state for the colonies was inconveniently out of town for two weeks. By the time they hand-delivered the original version in early September, the king had already made up his mind.[3]

Specifically, on August 23, King George issued a proclamation "for suppressing Rebellion and Sedition," taking direct aim at the Continental Congress. While conceding that some had been misled "by dangerous and ill-designing Men," the king accused them of proceeding to "open and avowed rebellion" by "traitorously preparing, ordering and levying War against Us." He targeted not just the usual miscreants in Massachusetts but, for the first time in public, all thirteen American colonies. In what amounted to an informal declaration of war, George III called on the British military "to exert their utmost Endeavors to suppress such Rebellion, and to bring the Traitors to Justice."[4]

Penn and Lee bided their time until September 1, "the first moment that was permitted us," and only then presented the petition to Dartmouth in person. To the surprise of almost no one, it was quickly and firmly rejected. "As His Majesty [would] not receive it on the throne," Dartmouth told them the next day, "no answer would be given."[5] The document that offered the last great hope for reconciliation between England and America would not be considered, or even viewed.

* * *

The Second Continental Congress called a five-week recess from August 1 to September 5. Delegates had worked virtually nonstop for twelve weeks—six days a week, ten to twelve hours a day, a grueling pace under any circumstance—but a need for rest was only one of the motivating factors.

Congressional leaders thought delegates should return home to gauge the reaction of local assemblies since the outbreak of war. As Samuel Adams put it in a letter to his wife, "the arduous Business that has been before Congress [has] added to the Necessity and Importance of . . . attending their respective Conventions." It struck them that no one in Congress had been able to receive feedback in person after shots were fired at Lexington and Concord. As an aside, Adams said that he did not mind escaping Philadelphia for New England during the decidedly "sultry month of August."[6]

Delegates would not return to the State House until early September, but a few kept up brisk correspondence during the break, sharing updates, exchanging ideas, and refusing to let momentum fade. (Given what would happen over the next year, historian Jack Rakove still found it "astonishing that men responsible for directing a civil war should vote a recess of five weeks").[7] One of the most active was Jefferson, whose pen was rarely idle during the time he served in Congress. An August 25 letter to his loyalist cousin, John Randolph, captured the conflicting sentiments that even Jefferson felt less than a year before the Declaration of Independence.

Jefferson's thoughts on revolution were a work in progress. Though he regretted that Randolph soon would be leaving his native Virginia for England, the young congressman saw a glimmer of hope in the journey. "Looking with fondness toward a reconciliation with Great Britain," he wrote. "I cannot help hoping you may be able to contribute towards expediting this good work." To achieve that goal, Randolph would have to help debunk the notion that "we are cowards and shall surrender at discretion to an armed force. The past or future operations of the war must confirm or undeceive them." But Jefferson got around to the heart of his personal conundrum in the next-to-last paragraph of the letter from Monticello:

> [I] would rather be in dependence on Great Britain, properly limited, than on any nation upon earth, or than on no nation. But I am one of those too who rather than submit to the right of legislating for us assumed by the British parliament, and which late experience has [shown] they will so cruelly exercise, would lend my hand to sink the whole island in the ocean.[8]

Travel issues and a fondness for home cooking prevented Congress from resuming its work by the assigned date of September 5, but enough delegates had returned by September 13 to get things underway. The most encouraging news was that Georgia had finally sent a full delegation—in response, it said, to the "alarming and critical situation of affairs upon the Continent of America."[9] Much of the business at the start of this second session focused on the necessary tasks of funding, feeding, and supplying the fledgling army. These included everything from procuring cannons to buying gunpowder, ordering medicine, collecting shirts and pants, and delivering "any number not exceeding twenty thousand good plan double-bridled musquet locks."[10]

The most significant legislative action came on October 18, when New Hampshire asked for advice "with respect to our administering of Justice, and regulating our civil police." John Adams saw it as a grand opportunity to urge a colony to create its own government. It was no coincidence, then, that radical stalwarts Adams and Richard Henry Lee maneuvered their way onto the committee assigned to answer New Hampshire's request. By November 4, after considerable haggling with moderates, the committee recommended that leaders there "call a full and free representation of the people, and that the representatives, if they think it is necessary, establish such a form of government as, in their judgement, will best produce the happiness of the people." South

Carolina promptly asked for and received a similar directive, and other colonies, including Virginia, were soon to follow.[11]

Emotions were rising now among the radical faction, and with good reason. In late October, reports of the king's provocative August speech made it across the ocean and were published in local newspapers. Even moderate members now found themselves accused by their beloved monarch of treason in the form of "open and avowed rebellion." If that weren't enough, Richard Penn reported to Congress on November 9 that the Olive Branch Petition had been rejected without so much as a glance from George III.[12]

Disillusioned as he may have been by this sudden turn of events, John Dickinson mounted a new campaign to counter the growing momentum for independence. Less than a week after the New Hampshire news broke, he wrote fiery instructions for the Pennsylvania delegation to address the "present critical & Alarming State of public Affairs." Dickinson was adamant about "obtaining a Redress of Grievances" to repair the union between England and America, but he sought to avoid any action from Congress that would hinder reconciliation. Accordingly, Pennsylvanians were to "dissent from and utterly reject any propositions, should such be made, that may cause or lead to a Separation from our Mother Country, a Change in the Form of Government, or the Establishment of a Commonwealth."[13]

Delaware, New Jersey, and Maryland were among those who fell into line, backing Pennsylvania and renouncing separation from England.[14]

Less than a year before declaring independence, the Continental Congress still was deeply divided.

* * *

On October 26, 1775, while Americans squabbled among themselves, King George III traveled in a grand procession from St. James's Palace to the Palace of Westminster, surrounded by opulence that was unimaginable in the colonies. In advance of a much-anticipated speech to Parliament, the king prepared comments to build support for his plan to subjugate the rebels.[15]

In the most impactful oration of his sixty years on the throne, George III proclaimed in the starkest terms that he would summon all the powers of empire to "put a speedy end to these disorders by the most decisive exertions." In doing so, he planned to forcibly impress on misguided Americans that "to be a subject of Great Britain, *with all its consequences*, is to be the freest member of any civil society in the known world" (emphasis added). These were heartening words to the majority in both houses who were frustrated by the loss of blood and treasure in the unnatural six-month war, but they stunned and emboldened many colonists—disavowing the notion that reconciliation was possible and clearing the way for revolution in 1776.

The king opened with a flourish, charging that "gross misrepresentations" from "traitorous leaders" had led to "a system of opinions repugnant to the true constitution of the colonies, and to their subordinate relation to Great Britain." They had, as a result, formed an army, proposed a naval force, seized the public revenue and assumed governmental duties of their own accord, while offering only "vague expressions of attachment to the Parent State . . . whilst they were preparing for a general revolt." The underlying goal of these actions had become so clear to His Majesty that he spoke of it in a formal speech for the first time: "The rebellious war now levied is become more general, and is manifestly carried on for the purpose of establishing an independent empire."

The thought of it galled him. Failing to crush the rebellion, allowing these traitors to succeed, would be a mortifying affront to the Crown and the empire. "The object is too important," he said, "the spirit of the British nation too high, the resources with which God hath blessed her too numerous, to give up so many Colonies which she has planted with great industry, nursed with great tenderness, encourage with many commercial advantages, and protected and defended at much expence."[16]

The monarch and his cabinet had privately committed to increasing their force in America to twenty thousand men by April 1776, and had replaced Thomas Gage with William Howe as commander of the army.[17] Now, however, he made his intentions public, announcing major increases in both land and naval forces, while noting, almost as an afterthought, that "I have received the most friendly offers of foreign

Figure 5.1. King George III. *(Wikimedia Commons)*

assistance." That last bit of news set off rampant panic when word of the speech reached America in early January. The specter of specially hired troops from other countries ravaging the countryside in support of the British army sent shivers up colonial spines.

It mattered little that he couched those remarks with his own version of an olive branch, offering "tenderness and mercy" to those who professed a renewed allegiance to the Crown.[18]

Parliament met immediately after the king's speech to debate its merits, hearing spirited dissent from small pro-American factions in both houses, before voting overwhelmingly to approve. The final tally was 176–72 in the House of Commons and 76–33 in the House of Lords. What would haunt many of them for years to come, however, was a series of questions posed by the Earl of Shelburne, a critic of the king's harsh language toward the colonists. "How comes it that the colonies are charged with planning independency?" Shelburne asked. "Who is it that presumes to put an assertion contrary to fact, contrary to evidence. . . . Is it their intention, by thus perpetually sounding independence in the ears of the Americans, to lead them into it?"[19]

(It is one of the reasons that, years later, when someone asked John Adams who was most responsible for the American Revolution, he answered "King George III.")[20]

Back in the colonies, meanwhile, two separate and unrelated actions by British surrogates added to the tumult. Little more than a week before the king addressed Parliament, colonists learned that the British navy had attacked, bombed, and burned the town of Falmouth, Massachusetts (now Portland, Maine). Then, in early November, Lord Dunmore, the royal governor of Virginia, offered freedom to any American slave who joined him to fight against their masters.[21] Colonists quivered.

The Royal Navy had received orders that fall "to proceed as in the case of actual rebellion against such of the sea port towns and places . . . in which any troops shall be raised or military works erected." It was October 16 when Lieutenant Henry Mowat posted the following warning to citizens of Falmouth:

After so many premeditated Attacks on the legal Perogatives of the best of Sovereigns.... And in place of a dutiful and grateful return to your King and Parent state; you have been guilty of the most unpardonable Rebellion.... Having it in orders to execute a just Punishment on the Town of Falmouth ... I warn you to remove without delay the Human Species out of the said town; for which purpose I give you the time of two hours.[22]

Mowat was persuaded to wait until the next day before unleashing a ruthless bombardment that reduced the town to a "smoldering ruin." Resistance from shell-shocked citizens was nonexistent. By late November, Congress issued a report that the king's naval commanders had "burned and destroyed the flourishing and populous town of Falmouth, and have fired upon and much injured several other towns within the United Colonies," victimizing "hundreds of helpless women and children." These were deemed attacks unworthy of "civilized nations" and added to a sense of growing colonial rage.[23]

Lord Dunmore of Virginia had his own plan to resist rebellion (part of which was moving his own headquarters to the safety of a British warship). In November, seeking to bolster loyalist forces and thwart colonial momentum, he issued a proclamation to recruit slaves and other disaffected Americans to the loyalist cause. Dunmore called for "all indentured servants, Negroes or others [to join] his Majesty's troops, as soon as may be, for more speedily reducing this colony to a proper sense of their duty, to his Majesty's crown and dignity." Roughly three hundred Black men signed up within a month, creating the "Royal Ethiopian Regiment" and stoking fears of a wider slave uprising. Though these troops achieved little success on the battlefield, the psychological impact on Virginians and other southerners was palpable. Historian Merrill Jensen believed Dunmore's proclamation "did more to convert many Virginians to the idea of independence than all acts of Parliament since the founding of the colonies."[24]

* * *

Much of the critical activity in Congress during the final months of 1775 took place behind the scenes. John Adams was particularly busy, sketching out a preliminary model for colonial governments before anyone else had given it much thought.

Adams had been part of the committee advising New Hampshire and South Carolina to "establish such a form of Government as in their judgement will best produce the happiness of the people, and most effectually secure peace and good order."[25] But what exactly did that mean? How would it be accomplished? No one knew for certain until Adams put pen to paper in a private letter to Richard Henry Lee on November 15, laying out his earliest plan for three branches of government and a rigid separation of powers. It was the precursor to a more comprehensive document he produced in spring 1776, titled *Thoughts on Government, Applicable to the Present State of the American Colonies*—a published pamphlet that had a profound impact on his congressional peers.

Back in 1775, however, Adams was just getting started. His initial effort did not include broader views of the purpose of government, and it lacked detail on many essential functions, such as forming militia and providing for the education of youth. But Adams was specific about a three-branch model—legislative, executive, and judicial—and noted that "it is by balancing each of these Powers against the other two, that the Effort in humane Nature towards Tyranny, can alone be checked and restrained and any degree of Freedom preserved in the Constitution." He listed eleven principles, ranging from public voting procedures to the appointment of officers and magistrates, and somehow believed that only one month would be necessary to "accomplish a total Revolution in the Government of a Colony." Lee, reading all this—even in preliminary form—was wide-eyed.[26]

It was also during this period that Thomas Jefferson made his irrevocable move toward revolutionary fanaticism. In another letter to his cousin, John Randolph, on November 29, 1775, Jefferson wrote, "Believe me Dear Sir there is not in the British empire a man who more cordially loves a Union with Gr. Britain than I do. But by the god that made me I will cease to exist before I yield to a connection on such terms as the

British parliament propose and in this I think I speak the sentiments of America."

Jefferson had no idea that he would soon articulate the sentiments of all America for all time, but his late November missive to Randolph offered a window into his evolving mind-set. Referencing the king, he wrote, "to undo his empire he has but one truth more to learn, that after colonies have drawn the sword there is but one step more they can take. That step is now pressed upon us by the measures adopted as if they were afraid we would not take it." It was now only a matter of time, he believed, until recalcitrant moderates joined them in the cause, even if much work remained for the radical caucus. "We want neither induce-ment nor power to declare and assert a separation," Jefferson said. "It is will alone that is wanting, and that is growing apace under the fostering hand of our king."[27] With a final dagger, he characterized George III as "the bitterest enemy we have."

The official stance of the Continental Congress was far more cautious in the final months of 1775. Delegates were understandably unnerved by the king's charge of rebellion in his August speech, and Congress on November 13 appointed a committee to respond to "sundry illegal min-isterial proclamations that have lately appeared in America." Committee members Lee (Virginia), James Wilson (Pennsylvania), and William Livingston (New Jersey) spent two weeks working on a draft before presenting it on November 29 for debate by the full body. Considerable editing followed, paragraph by paragraph, an often-cumbersome process, until Congress approved a final declaration on December 6, addressing "this unhappy and unnatural controversy, in which Britons fight against Britons, and the descendants of Britons." Even while defending their rights and denying the authority of Parliament, they insisted that they were *not* in rebellion and still remained loyal to the king.[28]

George III and Parliament would not hear about this last-ditch declaration for months, but it was unlikely that their minds would have changed. They lashed out once more in late November, when Lord North proposed the Prohibitory Act—which, true to its antagonistic name, cut off "all manner of trade and commerce" with the thirteen colonies and ruled that all American ships and cargoes were to be "forfeited to

his Majesty" as though they were "the ships and effects of open enemies."[29] In short, the colonies were no longer under the Crown's protection. They were now enemies—vulnerable, as one historian put it, to
"legalized piracy." The king signed the act into law on December 22, and
when word finally reached Congress weeks later, John Hancock quipped
that it "bodes no good" because "making all our Vessels lawful Prize don't
look like a Reconciliation."[30]

The final day of the year also brought distressing news from the
northern battlefield. Colonials venturing boldly into Canada had captured Montreal by mid-November, but a joint force under generals Richard Montgomery and Benedict Arnold was repulsed with heavy losses at
the Battle of Quebec City on December 31. British troops killed Montgomery, wounded Arnold, and shattered American momentum. It was
clear by New Year's Eve 1775 that this shocking revolutionary warfare—
whatever its goal in the future—would be a long, hard slog for both sides.

CHAPTER 6

The Ninth of January

THE MATCH THAT LIT THE AMERICAN REVOLUTION BECAME A BLOW-
torch in the second week of 1776.

It was sometime in the afternoon of Monday, January 8 that two
unexpected news items arrived at the State House in Philadelphia. The
first was especially jarring to southern delegates—Lord Dunmore's loyalist troops in Virginia had attacked the port city of Norfolk—but the
second trumped all other congressional business that day. A copy of the
king's incendiary October speech made it across the ocean from London,
branding the colonists as rebels and accusing them, for the first time, of
seeking independence.[1]

Mortified moderates huddled and sprang into action. The next day,
James Wilson of Pennsylvania moved that Congress declare "their present Intentions respecting an Independency, observing that the King's
Speech directly charged Us with that Design." Wilson was backed by
John Dickinson, who made notes to "assure his Majesty that he is mis-
inform'd concerning the Intentions of his faithful subjects in America"
and that "these Colonies do not wish to change or alter the Forms of
Government subsisting in them at the Commencement of the present
unhappy Controversy." But Samuel Adams objected on behalf of the
radicals, believing they were already on dangerous ground because of the
December statement denying rebellion. "The motion alarmed me," he
said. "I thought Congress had been explicit enough."[2] Adams and others
managed to have the process tabled for more than a month, and when

Wilson offered an updated proposal in mid-February, it gained such little backing from the full body that it was "in consequence, dropped."[3]

There was a clear reason why some minds had changed in the interim. On January 9, the same day as Wilson's original motion, a new and provocative pamphlet, *Common Sense*, was published in Philadelphia. The author, unidentified at the time, turned out to be a recent arrival from England named Thomas Paine, whose background of failure in most aspects of life—including, but not limited to, business and marriage—belied the power of his written words. Until that day, arguments for independence found their strength in the erudite language of English and Scottish philosophers (and, frankly, in the legalese of lawyers such as John Adams). But Paine wrote in a raw, searing, street-wise style that dazzled the gritty masses from Massachusetts to Georgia. He branded the king "the Royal Brute of Britain"; railed about a system of "British barbarity"; warned moderates that it was "truly farcical" to support reconciliation because "reconciliation and ruin are nearly related" and added, in a purposefully condescending tone, "there is something very absurd in supposing a continent to be perpetually governed by an island."[4]

Paine came to America in November 1774, armed only with a letter of recommendation from the colonial agent in London (who happened to be Benjamin Franklin). He found employment as editor of the monthly *Pennsylvania Magazine* in Philadelphia, but it was not until fate led him to the print shop of Robert Bell on Third Street that he left his mark on history. The original edition on January 9 was such a sensation that other printers sought his business, producing multiple versions, and within three months an astounding 150,000 copies had been sold throughout the colonies. The happy coincidence of great timing was not lost on the radicals. In addition to reports of the king's October speech, Congress learned in early January that a large British fleet "was seen at Sea with 5000 troops on Board," which, true or not, sounded the alarms of invasion.[5] *Common Sense* became a rallying cry for revolution.

At a time when most Americans were loathe to vilify the king in public, Paine launched a bare-knuckled royal assault. He waited only until the second paragraph of his "Introduction" to charge that "the good people of this country are grievously oppressed" by George III and

Parliament. He went on to charge that the fatal flaw of English government was "monarchial tyranny in the person of the king" and warned that "the king is not to be trusted without being looked after, or in other words, that a thirst for absolute power is the natural disease monarchy." Equally problematic was the system of hereditary succession, which Paine judged to be an insult to society and posterity—and, in particular, to common men like himself. "One of the strongest natural proofs of the folly of hereditary right in kings is that nature disapproves it," he wrote, "otherwise she would not so frequently turn it into ridicule by giving mankind an *ass for a lion*."[6]

Paine's views became more extreme over time. He no doubt harbored contempt for British rule when he traveled to America late in 1774, but, as happened with Jefferson, it took the epoch-making events of 1775 to turn him from advocate to revolutionary. The key point for Paine was the dual attack on Lexington and Concord. "No man was a warmer wisher for reconciliation than myself before the fatal nineteenth of April 1775," he wrote, "but the moment the event of that day was made known, I rejected the hardened, sullen tempered Pharoah of England forever."[7] In retrospect, *Common Sense* was almost a year in the making, with Paine's ire stoked by each monarchial indiscretion.

But what would happen once the break from England was made? What kind of system could possibly govern the colonies? Paine had some ideas (even while allowing that "government in its best state is but a necessary evil"). There would be a single-house Continental Congress with at least 390 members, and no fewer than 30 from each colony. Provincial assemblies would meet once a year and oversee domestic issues, subject to the authority of Congress. Laws could only be passed with a three-fifths majority of the continental body. This was a vague and perhaps naïve plan, offering only "hints," as Paine admitted, of what an American government might someday be.[8] It was the weakest part of his pamphlet, and the one most open to ridicule. John Adams groused a few months later that "this Writer has a better Hand at pulling down than building."[9]

But Paine's intended audience, the regular folks in the countryside—farmers, mechanics, bakers, blacksmiths, and artisans—were not so focused on intricate details of governmental theory. His promise of a

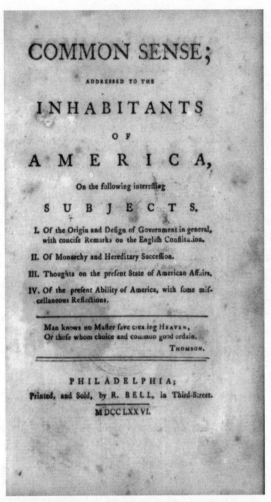

Figure 6.1. Thomas Paine's provocative pamphlet, *Common Sense*, published in January 1776, helped inspire the American Revolution. *(Wikimedia Commons)*

brighter future for the entire continent electrified them. Keep in mind that much of what had happened behind the closed doors of Congress in Philadelphia was still unknown to average colonial residents early in 1776. Paine spoke to them directly, forcefully, in language they understood, offering tantalizing peeks at a new life that was possible only with the bold, decisive act of independence:

The sun never shined on a cause of greater worth . . . we have every opportunity and every encouragement before us, to form the noblest purest constitution on the face of the earth. We have it in our power to being the world over again. A situation, similar to the present, hath not happened since the days of Noah until now. The birthday of a new world is at hand.[10]

Sales of his pamphlet soared at a rate never before seen on the continent. Members of Congress who favored separation purchased extra copies and sent them back home to constituents in an unofficial but effective marketing push. Samuel Ward of Rhode Island wrote to his brother that *Common Sense* "ought surely to be distributed throughout all the Colonies if it was even at the public Expence."[11] William Tudor, judge advocate general of the army, told John Adams that it was "read with great Avidity" and said the concepts put forth "astonish, convince and please Us." Tudor wondered if Adams himself, or perhaps the esteemed Franklin, had been the author, but Adams denied any credit. "I am as innocent of it as a babe," he said. "I could not reach the Strength and Brevity of his style, nor his elegant Symplicity, nor his piercing Pathos." In later years, Adams—driven by omnipresent vanity—tried to deny the impact of *Common Sense*, saying it espoused ideas that were already making the rounds, and trashing Paine's feeble plan for constitutional government. Yet in spring 1776, with independence fever on the rise in the colonies, he conceded that it had been "a very meritorious Production."[12]

One passage near the end of Paine's work garnered little notice at the time, but it turned out to be the most prescient of all:

Were a manifesto to be published and despatched to foreign courts, setting forth the miseries we have endured, and the peaceful methods we have ineffectually used for redress . . . that, not being able, any longer, to live happily or safely under the cruel disposition of the British court, we had been driven to the necessity of breaking off all connections with her . . . such a memorial would produce more effect to this Continent than if a ship were freighted with petitions to Britain.[13]

* * *

Not that independence was a given in January 1776. Far from it.

Despite the popularity of *Common Sense*, a significant part of the population still sought reconciliation with England, especially in the moderate middle colonies, where pride in British heritage was strongest. Congress found itself bogged down because several delegations were under strict orders from assemblies back home to reject all talk of separation. Legislatively, at least, there was no clear path forward for either side.[14]

Most troubling was a list of instructions prepared by the Maryland convention and sent to its delegates at Philadelphia in early January. They were forbidden to "assent to any proposition to declare these Colonies independent of the Crown of Great Britain," and that if Congress made such a decision, they were to report back to Maryland immediately. At the same time, "desirous as we are of peace with Great Britain on safe and honourable terms," Maryland troops were to "join with the other Colonies in such military operations as may be judged proper and necessary for the common defence, until such a peace can be happily maintained."[15] Reconciliation was the goal, even if it took gunfire and casualties to make the point.

As far back as the start of the Second Continental Congress in May 1775, Delaware's delegates were told to "studiously avoid . . . everything respectful or offensive to our most gracious sovereign." Pennsylvania's assembly issued orders in November to "dissent from and utterly reject any propositions . . . that may cause or lead to a separation from our mother country, or a change in the form of this government." New Jersey followed Pennsylvania's lead with almost identical language in early January, as Governor William Franklin, Benjamin's son, and a staunch British loyalist, said it was his opinion that most residents were opposed to independence.[16] Even in small pockets of New England such as Portsmouth, New Hampshire, delegates to that colony's convention were advised to act with "the greatest caution, calmness and deliberation," and to avoid any hints "that we are aiming at independency, which we totally disavow."[17]

(For his part, Samuel Adams read the Portsmouth instructions and said he was furious because it "discovers a Timidity which is unbecoming a People as oppressed and insulted as they are." These were fascinating times.)[18]

Letters and documents from moderate congressmen during this period reflect the passion of their antiseparation cause. Shortly after hearing of the king's October speech, John Jay said it was "ungenerous and groundless" to call independence the goal. Dickinson hoped His Majesty could be "so graciously inclined to institute some Method that may have a Tendency to bring the present Contest to a perfect and lasting Accommodation."[19] The ever-optimistic James Duane expected to receive "important Intelligence from England" at any moment, which, he said, would "Fix the Fate of America." Duane wanted to return home to New York for a few weeks but told fellow delegate Robert Livingston that he could not bring himself to do so under the circumstances. "If Parliament should offer [reasonable?] Terms of Conciliation," he wrote, "I should never forgive myself for being absent on so great and interesting an Occasion."

Duane and others were energized because the arrival of a young Scottish nobleman, Lord Drummond, offered hope for a diplomatic situation, but Drummond's role was not sanctioned by the Crown, and, despite meetings with Duane, Jay, Wilson, and William Livingston (who also were acting on their own), nothing came of it. The stalemate continued.[20]

* * *

John Adams spent almost the entire month of January 1776 at home in Massachusetts, which is not to say he was idle.

Tireless as ever, dedicated almost to a fault, he resumed his seat on the Massachusetts Council, attended sixteen council sessions, volunteered for committee work, dined with George Washington at army headquarters, and sat in on several informal councils of war. When the general asked for advice, Adams gave it. But at one point he reminded Washington that "you are vested with full power and authority to act as you shall think for the good and welfare of the service."[21]

In his free time—some of which apparently remained—Adams continued his work on an outline of American government. He had jotted preliminary thoughts in a letter to Richard Henry Lee in November, but his wife and closest advisor, Abigail, thought far too many questions were left unanswered. "If we seperate from Brittain, what Code of Laws will be established?" she asked him in a written response. "How shall we be governed so as to retain our Liberties? Can any government be free which is not adminstred by general stated Laws? Who shall frame these Laws? Who will give them force and energy?"

In closing, she added, "I feel anxious for the fate of our Monarchy or Democracy, or what ever is to take place."[22]

Adams took it to heart, as he always did when Abigail wrote or spoke. One can imagine him scrawling ideas on scraps of paper during breaks in the Massachusetts Council in January, embracing some concepts, eliminating others. In time this would lead to his epic *Thoughts on Government* in April 1776, requested by several colonies as a foundation of their state constitutions. For now, however, it was a work in progress, developed in private for the most part—away from prying British eyes.

Adams went public only once in those early days of 1776. It was under the guise of a document endorsing newly appointed magistrates at regional courts throughout Massachusetts, titled, "A Proclamation of the General Court," on January 19. But Danielle Allen, a modern-day scholar at Harvard University, believes the proclamation written by Adams had a purpose far greater than justifying legal operations in one New England province. It was, in essence, a blueprint for the Declaration of Independence.

"It begins with exactly the same sort of ideas," Allen said. "Every step along the way in this proclamation is a step taken in the Declaration of Independence as well. This was a document that Massachusetts generated—again, Adams drafted it—at the point when they were establishing new political institutions for themselves. So it was part of this project of constituting new governments for the states. . . . Massachusetts had just rearranged their political institutions, and to support that rearrangement, and to prepare the people for self-government, they decided to make this proclamation.

"It's an extraordinary text."[23]

Indeed, the first two paragraphs presented ideas that were eerily similar to those contained in the Declaration six months later:

> The frailty of human Nature, the Wants of Individuals, and the numerous Dangers which surround them, through the Course of Life, have in all Ages, and in every country impelled them to form Societies and establish Governments.
>
> As the Happiness of the People is the sole End of Government, So the Consent of the People is the only Foundation of it, in Reason, Morality and the natural Fitness of things; and therefore every Act of Government, every Exercise of Sovereignty, against, or without, the Consent of the People, is Injustice, Usurpation, and Tyranny.[24]

The final product from Congress in July would include far more elegant language, but the basic foundation was the same. The "Course of Life" became the "Course of human events." The "Consent of the People" became the "consent of the governed." Governments were either "established" or "instituted," depending on one's choice of words. The purpose of government was to ensure "Happiness" or, at least, the "pursuit of Happiness." And Americans had been "impelled" to take action because of British "Tyranny" and "Usurpation[s]."[25]

Historians at the National Archives, reviewing the proclamation for their Founders Online research project, found themselves in agreement with Allen, noting that "[Adams's] first eight paragraphs read more like a preamble to a declaration of independence than a plea for acceptance of appointed magistrates."[26]

Adams also hammered home the importance of a separation of powers among the legislative, executive, and judicial branches, laying them out in a well-defined order. It was a precursor of his influential *Thoughts on Government* in April and another likely influence on Jefferson's work.

But did Jefferson ever read the Massachusetts proclamation from January 1776? No evidence exists to suggest that he did. Historians are certain, however, that he drew on the concepts of several contemporary writers as he undertook his historic work. Jefferson admitted years later that his goal was "not to find out new principles, or new arguments, never before thought of, not merely to say things which had never been said before, but to place before mankind the common sense of the subject."[27] Jefferson and Adams both served on the five-man congressional committee to draft the Declaration of Independence, and the two men worked side by side, sharing ideas, and probably discussing the structure of the document in advance.

"We don't know for a fact, but I'm pretty confident he would have had Adams' proclamation," Allen said. "Adams was on the committee. The vocabulary of this proclamation shows up in the Declaration of Independence. I think its's pretty good wager that, indeed, Adams gave Jefferson a copy."[28]

Adams left Massachusetts for Philadelphia in late January, returning to Congress to reunite with the pro-independence group. Discussions on exactly how to proceed gained traction once Adams resumed his seat at the State House on February 9. He spent the next few days consulting with colleagues to decide which items deserved precedence and which required more time to mature. It was sometime around February 15 that Adams formalized their plan with an astounding diary entry titled "Memorandum of Measures to be Pursued in Congress."

There were fifteen ideas in all, ranging from "An Alliance to be formed with France and Spain" to "Money to be sent to the Paymaster, to pay our Debts." Some focused specifically on the war effort, including "Forces to be raised and maintained in Canada and New York. St Lawrence and Hudson Rivers to be secured."

Carrying over unexpectedly to a second page—not quite an afterthought, but certainly not a priority at that point—was the No. 14 item on the list: a "Declaration of Independency."[29]

Adams believed that something as combustible as revolution had to have a strong foundation, and he wanted to move forward in an orderly, almost deliberate fashion before declaring independence. The people probably weren't ready to make the break—not now, not yet. But unanticipated actions in England and elsewhere got in the way of his systematic plan.

* * *

In a year of hugely consequential dates for the American colonies, there was no expectation that February 27 would be one of them. Congress went about its routine daily business, approving travel for a member of the clergy, setting dates for the election of mid-level officers, accepting various committee reports, and facilitating the payment of bills. Ho hum. Later that afternoon, however, Robert Morris of Pennsylvania obtained the first copy of the Prohibitory Act, which had just arrived in Philadelphia from England. Shocking in length and toxicity, it prohibited all trade with the colonies, encouraged the seizure of American ships and cargo, threatened the use of foreign mercenaries against the Continental army, and—in the course of forty-five rambling and often redundant clauses over sixteen pages filled with small print—placed the colonists outside the Crown's protection.

Congressional eyes bulged as they read in disbelief. Richard Smith of New Jersey, one of the body's most avid diarists, found himself at a momentary loss for words, other than to note the following: "The Bill is very long & cruel."[30]

Radicals reacted with fury, led, of course, by John Adams, who referred to the act by several demeaning names—"the restraining Act, or prohibitory Act, or piratical Act, or plundering Act"—but added, "I think the most apposite is the Act of Independency. It makes us independent in Spight of all our supplications and Entreaties." Richard Henry Lee agreed, finding it "curious to observe that whilst people here are disputing and hesitating about independency. The court by one bold act of Parliament . . . [has] already put the two countries asunder." Supporters of reconciliation were stunned by the seemingly endless spate of negative news. Even Morris, who was born in England and still sought ties to the mother country, could see the weakening state of loyalist opposition. "[The] burning of towns, seizing our Ships, with numerous acts of wanton barbarity & Cruelty perpetrated by the British Forces has prepared Men's minds for an Independency, that were shock'd at the idea a few weeks ago," he wrote.[31]

The Prohibitory Act was part of a chain reaction of events in February and March that slowly built support for breaking with England. One of the most significant came on March 3, when the Committee of

Secret Correspondence in Congress assigned Connecticut's Silas Deane to travel to France as its representative. Although Deane would have some cover as a merchant doing business in Paris, it was the first risky attempt to engage with a foreign power. "On your arrival in France, you will for some time be engaged in the business of providing goods for the Indian trade," Deane was told. "This will give good countenance to your appearance in the character of a merchant, which we wish you naturally to retain among the French, in general, it being probably that the court of France may not like it should it be known publickly that any agent from the Colonies is in that country." While there, Deane was to make vital connections on a personal level "and furnish us with such information as may be important."[32]

Several weeks later, adding to the international intrigue, Congress voted to send a three-man delegation to Canada in an effort to persuade residents there to become the fourteenth colony. That the mission would be led by Franklin, the best-known American in the world, underscored the significance of their task. Instructions delivered to Franklin on March 20 were unambiguous: "You are to repair to Canada and make known to the people of that country the wishes and intentions of the Congress with respect to them." Franklin would be accompanied on the trip to Montreal by two respected Marylanders, Samuel Chase and Charles Carroll.[33]

There were two enormous challenges facing these men as they departed Philadelphia. One was that a makeshift American army under Benedict Arnold and Richard Montgomery had already invaded Canada and taken Montreal before being repelled at Quebec late in 1775. Serious losses during that campaign, including the death of Montgomery, compelled them to fall back into a siege of the city. Congress tried to dance around this awkward situation by advising its commission to "represent to them that the arms of the United Colonies [had been] carried into that province for the purpose of frustrating the designs of the British court against our common liberties." The other challenge was that the delegation's key member, Franklin, was seventy years old and possibly unable to endure an arduous 450-mile trip over difficult terrain in the frigid early spring. (Indeed, along the way, he wrote, "I begin to apprehend that I have undertaken a Fatigue that at my Time of Life may prove to be too much for me.")[34]

Taken together, however, the missions assigned to Deane and Franklin between March 2 and March 20 signaled a new phase of the clash with England. Reaching out to a foreign country, albeit secretly, and trying to recruit more British subjects to the American cause were brazen maneuvers that would have been unthinkable even three months earlier. Radicals in Congress rejoiced—and that was before news of a sensational battlefield development made it to Philadelphia. Couriers riding from Boston brought reports that the mighty British military had gathered belongings, dumped supplies, loaded large transit ships, and prepared to evacuate that city on March 17, ceding control to the American rebels.

* * *

The rag-tag colonial army had conducted a siege of Boston after Massachusetts militia men chased the British from Concord on April 19, 1775. George Washington took command that summer, and the army's ranks grew; however, discipline was lacking, and odds of making an attack seemed slim. The British were trapped by land but controlled the waterfront and had no problem resupplying themselves. Other than sporadic raids, the two sides did little more than stare each other down for almost a year.[35]

The equation changed, finally, in March 1776, when Washington's men managed to haul heavy cannons to the top of Dorchester Heights, commanding the city and making the British position untenable. The state of colonial artillery up to that point was abysmal, but these were the captured British guns that Colonel Henry Knox had miraculously dragged from Fort Ticonderoga on muddy forest roads, across frozen lakes and over the Berkshire Mountains, covering three hundred miles in fifty-six days. Washington wanted to attack at once but settled on a more conservative plan to draw the British out of their fortifications and pummel them with a strout defensive stand. Secrecy and speed were essential in placing the guns. The effort was to begin after dark on March 4 and be completed by dawn on March 5, the sixteenth anniversary of the Boston Massacre.[36]

Washington used some of his artillery to distract the British with strategic bombardments on the nights of March 2, 3, and 4. The noise (as well as a clever plan to wrap the cannons' wheels in straw) muffled the intense work at Dorchester Heights on March 4. At first light the next morning, British officers were dumbfounded. A London newspaper reported that the cannons "were all raised during the night, with an expedition equal to that of the genie belonging to Aladdin's wonderful lamp. From these hills, they commanded the whole town." Local legend has it that an embarrassed General William Howe blurted out, "My God, these fellows have done more work in one night than I could make my army do in three months."[37]

Howe was determined to make an attack anyway, but the combination of bad weather and objections from subordinates over the next few days convinced him otherwise. The colonial position looked impregnable, they said, and the British were achieving no real purpose in holding Boston indefinitely. It took days to prepare an orderly departure for that large a force, but on March 17—St. Patrick's Day—Howe and his men were ready to pull out. The floating procession of more than one hundred ships carried eleven thousand soldiers and loyalists out of the harbor and into the sea, on their way to the temporary safe haven of Halifax in Canada.[38]

Bostonians whooped it up in the short term. Timothy Newell, a local politician and church deacon, wrote in his diary entry for March 17 that "they all embarked about 9 o'clock and the whole fleet came to sail. . . . Thus was this unhappy distressed town (thro' a manifest interposition of divine providence) relieved from a set of men whose unparalleled wickedness, profanity, debauchery and cruelty is inexpressible."[39] An army staff officer watching from Dorchester Heights gloated that "the Pirates all abandoned their Works in Boston and Charlestown and went on board their Ships." He added, in a letter to John Adams, "I think the flight of the British Fleet and Army before the American Arms must have a happy and very important effect on the great Cause we are engaged in. I wish it may stimulate the Congress to form an American Government *immediately*."[40]

Congress still was not ready for that type of action, and some wondered if the day would ever come. But less than a week after the British retreat, the oft-divided governmental body came together in a cheeky response to the Prohibitory Act. A series of resolves passed on March 23 approved the use of private ships and crews to prey on British shipping, seeking to "make reprisals upon [our] enemies and otherwise annoy them."[41] Congress even drew up formal commission papers, granting to these *privateers* the right "by force of arms to attack, seize and take the ships and other vessels belonging to the inhabitants of Great Britain."[42] It was another step of unprecedented aggressiveness that made reconciliation nearly impossible.

A combination of all these factors caused colonial spirits to soar to new heights as the momentous month of March drew to a close. Deane and Franklin left on their foreign missions; British soldiers retreated in disgrace to Halifax; and swashbuckling privateers were now unleashed without restraint against British merchant ships on the high seas. Congress was so thrilled with Washington's performance that it presented him with a golden medal and an official letter of thanks in the aftermath of the British pullout. Perhaps delegates didn't realize that the enemy would regroup over the next few months for an attack on New York City:

> Those Pages in the Annals of America will record your Title to a conspicuous Place in the Temple of Fame, which shall inform Posterity that under your Directions, an undisciplined Band of Husbandmen, in the Course of a few Months, became Soldiers . . .
>
> Accept, therefore, Sir, the Thanks of the United Colonies, unanimously declared by their Delegates, to be due to you, and the brave Officers and Troops under your Command, and be please to communicate to them this distinguished Mark of the Approbation of their Country.[43]

It was April 2, 1776. The praise was well deserved, but Washington knew better than anyone that there was much more work to be done.

CHAPTER 7

The Fifteenth of May

MASSACHUSETTS AND VIRGINIA HAD DOMINATED THE INDEPENDENCE movement for the past two years, but it was outreach from a less prominent colony that convinced John Adams to formalize his thoughts on government in spring 1776.

Two North Carolina delegates, William Hooper and John Penn, were called home from Philadelphia to attend the Fourth Provincial Congress in late March. The purpose of the assembly was fourfold: to raise new regiments for the army, reorganize the local militia, authorize more bills of credit, and—most dramatically—draft a colonial constitution. Mindful of that final goal, Hooper and Penn each sought out Adams for suggestions.[1]

Adams could barely contain his glee. "If I was possess'd of Abilities equal to the great Task you have imposed upon me, which is to sketch out the outlines of a Constitution for a Colony," he said, "I should think myself the happiest of Men in complying with your Desire." In truth, Adams had been pondering the matter for months, at least as far back as November 1775, but his work advanced more quickly following the publication of Thomas Paine's *Common Sense* in January. In a letter to his wife on March 19, Adams wrote "although I could not have written any Thing in so manly and striking a style, I flatter myself I should have made a more respectable Figure as an Architect, if I had undertaken such a Work."[2]

Now he had his chance. Adams wrote separate letters to the two Carolinians, which he described as "copies" (although one was two hundred words longer than the other), and it is clear that Hooper and Penn shared them with other delegates before heading south on March 27. George Wythe of Virginia and Jonathan Dickinson Sergeant of New Jersey were so intrigued that they called on Adams for copies of their own. He complied, of course, but made each version slightly different, adding words and phrases, editing and rewriting as he went. Wythe's letter had an additional one thousand words, and Sergeant's was even longer, "enlarged and amplified a good deal." When his friend Richard Henry Lee wanted a fifth copy, Adams was so weary that he sent along the same language he'd written for Wythe.

It was this Lee/Wythe version that was published in pamphlet form as *Thoughts on Government* and put on sale to the public in Philadelphia on April 22.[3]

Adams was displeased with the quality of his work, calling it rough and even crude in places, but he understood the impact it might make on American history. In the second paragraph of his letter to Penn in late March, he said:

> It has been the Will of Heaven, that We should be thrown into Existence at a Period, when the greatest Philosophers and Lawyers of Antiquity would have wished to have lived: a Period, when a Coincidence of Circumstances, without Example has afforded to thirteen Colonies at once an opportunity of beginning Government anew from the Foundation and building as they choose. How few of the human Race, have ever had an opportunity of choosing a System of Government for themselves and their Children? How few have ever had any Thing more of [a] Choice in Government than in Climate?[4]

Adams offered more detail than any of his previous musings on governmental structure, but the foundational pillars were the same:

- a clear separation of powers among the executive, legislative, and judicial branches;
- an elected "Governor," who would fill the executive role;

- a two-house legislature, which pleased him in that it differed dramatically from Paine's proposal;
- a wholly independent judiciary; and
- an unspoken but evolving system of checks and balances.

These were part of his grand vision for a republican form of government, drawing of its power from the people, in stark contrast to the hereditary monarchy they had known all of their lives.

The makeup of the legislature was essential to the Adams plan. One house, a "Representative Assembly," would be elected by public vote and serve as "an exact portrait of the people at large." Governmental balance would come from a second house, a smaller and distinct "Council" of perhaps thirty members, elected by the larger assembly. Each legislator would serve for a maximum of three years. Once both houses were seated, they would come together and elect a governor for a one-year term.

Also included were a "militia law" and a clause calling for the "liberal education of youth."

Historian Joseph Ellis reminds us that Adams at the time was proposing an outline of government "at the state, not the national level." Adams knew it could not be a one-size-fits-all format and wanted each colony to take his ideas and adapt them to local and regional needs. But "if a Continental Constitution should be formed," Adams wrote, "it should be a Congress, containing a fair and adequate Representation of the Colonies, and its authority should sacredly be confined to these cases: war, trade, disputes between Colony and Colony, the Post-Office, and the unappropriated lands of the Crown, as they used to be called." Colonies were the focus at the moment, however; a national plan would have to wait.[5]

Adams consented to his *Thoughts* being published, but he insisted that it be done anonymously as a "Letter from a Gentleman to His Friend." Despite his well-known vanity, he was not yet ready to risk his reputation among the masses in the face of such uncertainty. The public version even ended with the author's awkward request to keep his name out of sight, for this feeble attempt, if it should be known to be mine, would oblige me to apply to myself those lines of the immortal John Milton, in one of his sonnets:

> I did but teach the age to quit their clogs
> By the plain rules of ancient Liberty
> When lo! a barbarous noise surrounded me,
> Of owls and cuckoos, apes, asses and dogs.[6]

The delegates who received his letters kept their word about his identity (at least briefly), but they did not understand Adams's reticence; they were energized by his call to action. Hooper and Penn reached the provincial congress at Halifax, North Carolina, on April 15, after a trip of nineteen days, to find that the body had already been radicalized toward separation. Indeed, on April 12, North Carolina became the first colony to "empower" its delegates to vote for independence if such a motion were made. Armed with the Adams letters and backed by the power of the Continental Congress, Hooper and Penn were appointed to the committee to draft a colonial constitution. Penn wrote to Adams on April 17 that "a total separation is what [the people here] want. Independence is the word most used. . . . We are endeavoring to form a Constitution as thought necessary to exert all powers of Government, [and] you may expect it will be a popular one."[7]

This is not to suggest that *Thoughts on Government* was received throughout the colonies with widespread acclaim. There was plenty of opposition, including from prominent colleagues in Congress. Virginia's Carter Braxton led the naysayers, mocking the very concept of republican government, calling it a recipe for failure at best and outright disaster at worst. "The best of these systems exist only in theory, and they were never confirmed by experience," Braxton claimed. "I do not recall a single instance of a nation who supported this form of government for any length of time, or with any degree of greatness, which convinces me . . . that the principle contended for is ideal and a feature of warm imagination."[8]

Sneering at Adams and his cohorts but fearing the momentum of their movement, Braxton added, "The best opportunity in the World [is] being now offered them to throw off all Subjugation & embrace their darling Democracy, [and] they are determined to accept it."[9]

* * *

There was a steady stream of jolting news, almost on a daily basis, as the calendar turned to May.

On May 4, tiny Rhode Island took the bold step of *declaring its own independence* from England. The colony's general assembly passed a resolution charging King George III with "forgetting his dignity . . . and entirely departing from the duties and Character of a good king . . . endeavoring to destroy the good people of this colony, and of all the United Colonies, by sending Fleets and Armies to America." Later that day, Rhode Island gave its delegates approval to join with other colonies in all measures necessary "to annoy the common enemy" and ensure American rights."[10]

On May 6, Virginia's Fifth Revolutionary Convention heard its call to order in Williamsburg, with many delegates bringing instructions to push for independence. Radical leader Patrick Henry said he was "roused by the now apparent spirit of the people, as a pillar of fire."[11]

That same day, May 6, Richard Henry Lee received alarming news that thousands of foreign mercenaries were heading to America to reinforce the British army. According to a newspaper report from Ireland, these included "Hessians, Hanoverians, Mechlenburghers, Scotch Hollanders & Scott Highlanders, with some British Regiments." Their destinations were not certain, Lee told an associate, but options were said to be "N. York, New England, Canada, and 2 expeditions more South." It was a reminder that the threat of war and possible destruction could never be far from colonial minds.[12]

May 10 brought a different approach in Massachusetts, where the colony's delegates to Congress were already free to vote on independence as they pleased. The Massachusetts assembly wanted to come out even stronger "in favour of independency," emphasizing the depth of support among residents at the local level. Instructions went out to towns across the province, calling for meetings to consider the topic in public settings. Specifically, inhabitants were asked that if the "United Colonies" indeed declared independence, would they "solemnly engage with their Lives and Fortunes to Support Congress in the Measure." The concept spread to other colonies, including Virginia and Maryland, and, by that summer, there were at least ninety locally inspired "declarations" of independence.[13]

All of this served as a prelude to the much more seismic actions of the Continental Congress in Philadelphia between May 10 and May 15, when clashes between the radical and moderate factions reached a boiling point. Congress periodically formed into a Committee of the Whole to "take into farther consideration the state of the United Colonies," and during one of these sessions in early May, Adams and Lee proposed a resolution advising colonial assemblies about creating their own governments. It was approved without much fanfare on the afternoon of May 10:

> Resolved,
>
> That it be recommended to the respective assemblies and conventions of the United Colonies, where no government sufficient to the exigencies of their affairs have been hitherto established, to adopt such government as shall, in the opinion of the representatives of the people, best conduce to the happiness and safety of their constituents in particular, and America in general.[14]

At first glance, given the legalese and potential loopholes ("where no government sufficient to the exigencies"), the language did not seem so radical. Congress, after all, had been providing such advice when asked by individual colonies since fall 1775, and Adams's own *Thoughts on Government* had been circulating for almost three weeks. The stunning part was that the resolution passed with near unanimity, including support from the leading moderate at the State House, John Dickinson. One theory is that Dickinson refused to object because he thought Adams and Lee had boxed themselves in with excess verbiage. His own colony of Pennsylvania, for instance, would not be affected because it already had a government "sufficient to the exigencies of their affairs."

But there were other influential factors at work behind the scenes. On May 1, an attempt to radicalize the Pennsylvania assembly by adding more pro-independence members had been defeated at the ballot box. Dickinson's faction again won the day. What they did not anticipate, however, was that on May 8, Thomas Paine, writing under the pseudonym "Forester," savaged the election in the *Pennsylvania Journal* and called for the overthrow of Pennsylvania's government. "Our present condition is alarming," he wrote. "We are worse off than other provinces. . . . The House of Assembly in its present form is disqualified from such business." The timing of the Adams-Lee proposal, then, was not merely coincidental. It addressed all of the colonies with sweeping language, but Pennsylvania was an important, and most likely specific, target.[15]

Dickinson responded by making a horrible miscalculation on the afternoon of Friday, May 10. Aware that Congress had appointed a three-man committee to craft a preamble to the resolution—led by Adams, of all people, and including Lee—he nonetheless left town that weekend for his property in Delaware. Dickinson vanished from Philadelphia for ten vitally important days. When Congress reconvened on Monday, May 13, Adams presented an explosive preamble that was *three times longer* than the resolution it introduced. He likely sought some input from committee colleagues Lee and Edward Rutledge, but there is little doubt that he was the primary author of a de facto declaration of independence.

> Whereas his Britannic Majesty, in conjunction with the lords and commons of Great Britain, has, by a late act of Parliament, excluded the inhabitants of these United Colonies from the protection of his crown; And whereas, no answer, whatsoever to the humble petitions of the colonies for redress of grievances and reconciliation with Great Britain, has been or is likely to be given; but, the whole force of that kingdom, aided by foreign mercenaries, is to be exerted for the destruction of the good people of these colonies; And whereas, it appears absolutely irreconcileable to reason and good Conscience, for the people of these colonies not to take the oaths and affirmations necessary for the support of any government under the crown of Great Britain, and it is necessary that the exercise of every kind of authority under the said crown should be totally suppressed, and all the powers of government exerted, under the authority of the people of the colonies, for the preservation of

internal peace, virtue and good order, as well as for the defence of their lives, liberties and properties, against the hostile invasions and cruel depredations of their enemies; therefore, resolved.[16]

Wow.

Seizing the moment, Adams had ventured far beyond the mundane language of a resolution that was already approved. His document marked the first time that Congress directly accused the king of governmental malfeasance—by excluding the colonists from his protection, by refusing to answer their petitions, and, perhaps worst of all, by sending foreign mercenaries to contribute to their destruction. Accordingly, Adams said, authority from the king should be "totally suppressed," with powers of government being transferred to "the people of the colonies." He sharpened the edges of those words as he wrote, coming very close to a point of no return.[17]

It touched off two days of "much heat and debate" in Congress.[18] James Duane of New York spoke first. Leading the moderates in Dickinson's absence, Duane opened by reading instructions from his provincial assembly, which barred New York delegates from voting for independence (and, thus, from voting for the preamble). But his main point was that Congress did not have the authority to advise individual colonies on *any* form of government. "You have no right to pass the Resolution—any more than Parliament has," he barked. "[You] ought not to determine a Point of this sort, about instituting Government."

Duane was reminded that Congress had *already* passed the resolution, and that the topic in question today was the Adams preamble. That flustered him, at least briefly, but he still could not understand why a preamble was necessary, and why the process had moved so quickly, almost to the point of being rammed through. "Why all this Haste?" Duane wondered. "Why this urging? Why this driving?—Disputes about Independence are in all the Colonies. What is this owing to, but Indiscretion?"[19]

Many others rose to speak with differing perspectives. Thomas McKean of Delaware thought the preamble might help broker "harmony" with England but also fretted about foreign mercenaries "coming to destroy Us. . . . I do think WE shall lose our Liberties, Properties and Lives too, if We do not take this Step." Samuel Adams reiterated many of the key points of the preamble and wondered how colonists had put up with the king and Parliament as long as they had. James Wilson of Pennsylvania, a Dickinson protégé, asked why they couldn't at least postpone a vote on the longer preliminary text. "Will the Cause suffer much if this Preamble is not published at this Time?"[20]

There would be no postponement. Congress proceeded with the vote on May 15, even though the Maryland delegation walked out in protest that day and members from Georgia had not yet arrived. (Maryland's instructions forbade its delegates to "assent to any proposition" on independence and ordered them to return home if such a proposal were made, which they did). The final tally never was reported in official congressional records, but Carter Braxton of Virginia wrote a few days later that the preamble carried "I think by 6 to 4," with one abstention. Divisiveness reigned. Tempers simmered.[21]

The closeness of the vote could not dampen John Adams's enthusiasm. On the afternoon of May 15 he wrote to a friend in Massachusetts: "This Day the Congress has passed the most important Resolution that ever was taken in America."[22] Two days later, he contemplated his own place in history and engaged in more than a little bragging in a lengthy letter home to Abigail. "When I consider the great Events which are passed, and those greater which are rapidly advancing, and that I may have been instrumental of touching some Springs, and turning some small Wheels, which had had and will have such Effects, I feel an Awe upon my Mind which is not easily described."

Adams conceded for the first time that the sheer speed of events over the past few weeks had changed his mind about the timeline for separation. He no longer believed that forming a confederation of colonies or creating foreign alliances were necessary predecessors to independency. "[Great Britain] has at last driven America to the last Step, a compleat Seperation from her, a total absolute Independence, not only of her Parliament but of her Crown, for such is the Amount of the Resolve of the 15th." The author of the preamble now saw an America ready to take its place on the world stage as a self-governing, fully functional international power. "I have Reason to believe that no Colony, which shall assume a Government under the People, will give it up," Adams wrote. "There is something very unnatural and odious in a Government 1000 Leagues off. An whole Government of our own Choice, managed by Person who We love, revere and can confide in, has charms in it for which Men will fight."[23]

But Adams was not the only member of Congress putting pen to paper in the aftermath of the May 15 vote. There was a constant flow of letters coming from Philadelphia to colleagues and constituents back home, carrying either exciting or deflating news, depending on one's political persuasion. Moderates wrote haltingly, in fretful tones. Livingston said it "had occasioned a great alarm here, & the anxious folk are very fearful of it being attended with many ill consequences." Braxton noted that it "falls a little short of independence" but agreed it was "an alarming occasion," calling the preamble "not altogether candid nor true." Duane, writing to John Jay in New York, advised caution regarding a change in the "present mode" of government. "Let us see the Conduct of the middle Colonies before we come to a Decision. It cannot injure us to wait a few weeks . . . for this trying Question will clearly discover the true principles & the Extent of the Union of the Colonies."[24]

Radical members came closer to celebration as they enclosed copies of the preamble with their letters. Caesar Rodney of Delaware told his brother that "[m]ost of those here who are Termed the *Cool Considerate Men* think it amounts to a declaration of Independence." Oliver Wolcott of Connecticut predicted that "[a] Revolution in Government . . . is about to take Effect. May God grant a happy establishment of it, and security to the Rights of the People." Stephen Hopkins of Rhode Island thought it would "not be long before the Congress will throw of all connection as well in name as in substance with Great Britain, as one thing after another seem gradually to lead them to such a step." He was convinced that most colonies would very soon form new governments, as the resolution suggested and the preamble supported.[25]

But no one was more effusive than Adams, who wrote on May 20: "Every Post and every Day rolls in upon Us Independence like a Torrent." Georgia's delegates had finally arrived, he said, with "unlimited

Power" to vote for separation. North Carolina had pledged its support, and several others were starting to come around. Virginia's intention to form a new government was confirmed by numerous letters, all of which "breath[e] the same spirit." Pro-independence Pennsylvanians had even rallied in the rain at the State House Yard, an "entertaining Maneuver," conducted with "great order, Decency and Propriety," and noted warily by their foes. He also knew that his cousin, Samuel, was working behind the scenes to effect a change of government in Pennsylvania.[26]

There was one more important action in mid-May that few seemed to notice at the time. Thomas Jefferson rode back into town on May 14, resuming his seat at the Continental Congress for the first time since the turn of the year. Stressful family matters had kept him home in Virginia for five months; his wife, Martha, was ill, and his mother, Jane, suffered a stroke and died on March 31. Jefferson wanted to stay there even longer, caring for Martha and working on the colony's new constitution, which he considered to be of more importance than anything happening in Congress. "It is a work of the most interesting nature, and such as every individual would wish to have his voice in," he said. "In truth it is the whole object of the present controversy." Alas, Jefferson was needed in Philadelphia.[27]

* * *

May 15, 1776, was an extraordinary day in Virginia as well. Sometime that afternoon, the colony's Fifth Revolutionary Convention instructed its delegates in the Continental Congress to propose American independence.

The convention had opened at Williamsburg a week earlier with 132 delegates in attendance (including a twenty-five-year-old rising star from Orange County named James Madison). Debate on independence was held, but the only sticking point was whether this most powerful colony should make a declaration of its own, as Rhode Island had done, or try to lead a group effort in Congress. In the end, the members settled for making a proposal on behalf of all the colonies.[28]

Resolved,

That the Delegates appointed to represent this Colony in General Congress be instructed to propose to that respectable body to declare the United Colonies free and independent States, absolved from all allegiance to, or dependence upon, the Crown or Parliament of Great Britain; and that they give the assent of this Colony to such declaration, and to whatever measures may be thought proper and necessary by the Congress for forming foreign alliances, and a Confederation of the Colonies, at such time and in the manner as to them shall seem best: Provided that the power of forming Government for, and the regulations of the internal concerns of each Colony, be left to the respective Colonial Legislatures.[29]

It would take almost two weeks for the resolution to reach the State House in Philadelphia, and another week and a half for Richard Henry Lee to make the motion in Congress, but the convention in Williamsburg had done its job on May 15, pushing the unwieldy process along.

Taken in the context of history, John Adams found the coincidence of timing astounding. "Is it not a little remarkable," he wrote to a friend in Virginia in early June, "that this Congress and your Convention should come to Resolutions so nearly Similar, on the Same day?"[30]

* * *

Reaction to news from other fronts ran the gamut of emotions for delegates at the State House that month. Reports from Benjamin Franklin's commissioners in Canada were distressing at best. The American war effort against the British had stalled there because of limited manpower, ravages of smallpox, and a chronic lack of supplies and funds. Odds of recruiting Canada as another British territory to oppose the empire—in effect, a fourteenth colony—were now all but nonexistent. "Until the arrival of money, it seems improper to propose the federal union of this province with others," Franklin wrote, "as the few friends we have here will scare venture to exert themselves in promoting it until they see our credit recovered and a sufficient army arrived."[31]

Word that fresh British troops and German hirelings had arrived to fortify Canada was enough to convince the commissioners to advise an American withdrawal. On May 6, they wrote to Congress that "if hard money cannot be procured and forwarded with dispatch to Canada, it would be advisable, in our opinion, to withdraw our army & fortify the passes on the lakes to prevent the enemy, & the Canadians, if so inclined, from making irruptions into & depredations on our frontiers." With no money available or forthcoming, the American venture into Canada soon fell apart. The seventy-year-old Franklin—forlorn and wracked with pain, suffering from boils, gout, and swollen limbs that would impair him for months—started his grueling trip back to Philadelphia on May 11. Even Benedict Arnold, who had helped lead the charge into Canada in 1775, thought it best to pull out and "secure our own country before it is too late."[32]

It was at about the same time that Congress learned of England's expanding plans to crush the colonial military. Confirming earlier reports, John Hancock wrote to the Massachusetts assembly on May 16 that "by the best Intelligence from Europe it appears That the British Nation have proceeded to the last Extremity, and have actually taken into Pay a number of foreign Troops; who, in all probability, are on their Passage to America at this very Time." He called for greater diligence throughout the colonies and asked that reinforcements be sent to Boston as soon as possible, because "our Enemies may, as far as we know, be at our very Door." Now more than ever, local militias were put on high alert.[33]

Five days after Hancock's letter, Congress received copies of the treaties King George III had signed to obtain more than sixteen thousand foreign troops. A continental soldier who was captured and taken to London had been allowed to return to America following his release in late March. In one of the greatest clandestine efforts of the war, he made it to Philadelphia with smuggled documents sewn into his clothing. "And tho Searched at Halifax two or three times," Caesar Rodney wrote, "he brought undiscovered a Number of Letters and Newspapers to the Congress, by which we are possessed of all their plans for the destruction of America." These included agreements with the Duke of Brunswick for 4,084 troops; with the Landgrave of Hesse Cassel for 12,000; and with the Count of Hanau for 668. A committee of five was appointed with instructions to consider "an adequate reward" for the soldier and have the treaties published in newspapers, spreading the word.[34]

Congress also learned in late May that the king had rejected a petition from the City of London asking for a negotiated peace. English moderates were outraged by the use of foreign mercenaries and sought "the most solemn, clear, distinct and unambiguous specification of those just and honourable terms" for a settlement with the colonies. Alas, George III was in no mood to compromise. He deplored "the miseries which a great part of my subjects in America have brought upon themselves by an unjustifiable resistance to the constitutional authority of the kingdom" but vowed that he would back off only when the rebellion ended and authority was reestablished. Otherwise, he said in a statement, "I will invariably pursue the most proper and effectual means" to bring them to subjugation.[35]

In the midst of all this, General George Washington was called to Philadelphia to meet with Congress about the state of the war. Hancock wrote to Washington in New York on May 16, advising that "you should embrace the earliest opportunity of coming . . . to consult with Congress upon such Measures as may be necessary for carrying on the ensuing Campaign." Washington arrived on May 23, setting foot in the State House for the first time in almost a year and reuniting with former colleagues, as gleefully reported by Philadelphia newspapers. Generals Horatio Gates and Thomas Mifflin accompanied him in initial meetings about the military situation in Canada and efforts "as shall be taken to secure the frontiers."[36]

The main purpose of Washington's trip, however, was to plot overall strategy for the war. He met with the full Congress for parts of two days on May 24 and May 25, but the large group process was so unwieldy that a more narrowly focused committee was formed, with one delegate from each colony, to ensure balanced representation. John Adams, Richard Henry Lee, James Wilson, and Robert R. Livingston were among the members. They filed their report a few days later, outlining plans for the defense of New York, New England, and the "Southern Colonies"; confirming the need for an additional twenty-five thousand militia to help fend off British attacks; approving the appointment of more brigadier generals; demanding the punishment of spies found in any of the army's camps; and calling for an "animated address" to "impress the minds of the people with the necessity of their now moving forward to save their country, their freedom and property."[37]

A committee led by Thomas Jefferson and Samuel Adams produced the address, which, while repeating familiar charges, sought to motivate its audience by declaring that "[u]niting firmly, resolving wisely, and acting vigorously, it is morally certain we cannot be subdued."[38]

The tenor of congressional meetings took on new energy after May 27, when news of Virginia's resolution on independence reached Philadelphia. Washington's brother, John, had been an alternate delegate at the Virginia Convention in Williamsburg, and the general wrote that "I am very glad [you] have passed so nobble a vote, with so much unanimity." As Washington sounded out various congressmen on the subject, however, he worried that moderates might have enough strength to slow down or even derail the process. He complained to his brother that "many Members of Congress . . . are still feeding themselves upon the dainty food of reconciliation . . . it is but too obvious that it has an operation upon every part of their conduct, and is a clog to their proceedings."[39]

Distracted by other issues, Washington may not have sensed that a change was already underway in Pennsylvania, where delegates were still forbidden to vote for independence. The May 10 resolution about forming colonial governments and the May 15 preamble about breaking from England had led to a series of rowdy public meetings, culminating on May 20 at the State House Yard, where four thousand angry Philadelphians gathered to voice their opinions in a downpour. They loudly condemned the Pennsylvania assembly, denounced its instructions against independence, and called for a provincial convention "for the express purpose of establishing a new government on the authority of the people only." It was stunning in both its passion and ferocity. A transition of that sort might still take several months, but for the first time there was hope that this very reluctant colony might align itself with others in their radical move toward independence.[40]

In retrospect, the American Revolution was at its tipping point when Washington set off on his return trip to New York on June 4, 1776. The military situation was precarious, with tens of thousands of British and foreign troops preparing to assault the Continental army. The political framework was unsettled, as Congress continued to mull the independence question with no clear consensus. Hancock recognized as much when he wrote to the assemblies of six northern colonies, some of whom had yet to fully commit to independence, challenging their patriotism with his own sense of desperation: "Our Affairs are hastening fast to a Crisis; and the approaching Campaign will in all Probability determine for ever the Fate of America," he told them. "[It is] on your Exertions at this Critical Period, together with those of the other Colonies in the Common Cause, that the Salvation of America now evidently depends."[41]

CHAPTER 8

The Seventh of June

ANY THOUGHT OF ACHIEVING INDEPENDENCE IN A SERIES OF ORDERLY steps, as John Adams once hoped, was no longer feasible by early June 1776.

England's growing military presence, the king's oppressive edicts, and stubborn opposition from moderate American delegates had combined to skew the revolutionary time line.

Adams noted the new reality in a rambling letter to Patrick Henry in Virginia on June 3. "I fear We cannot proceed Systematically, and that We shall be obliged to declare ourselves independent States before We confederate, and indeed before all the Colonies have established their Governments," he wrote. "It is now pretty clear that all these Measures will follow one another in a rapid Succession, and it may not perhaps be of Importance which is done first."[1]

Congress devoted much of its time to war matters in the first week of June, but members were keenly aware of Virginia's resolution and wondered when it would be brought to the floor. They discussed it often in small groups—either "out of doors" in the State House Yard, or at the City Tavern on Second Street, where many of them gathered after legislative sessions. Radicals were encouraged when the staunchly moderate Robert Morris began to backpedal and reassess his views, dazed by the king's response to the London petition on reconciliation. "I confess I never lost hope . . . until I saw this Answer, which in my opinion breathes Death & Destruction," Morris wrote on June 5. "Everybody sees it in the same light, and it will bring us all to one way of thinking, so that you may soon expect to hear of New Governments in every Colony, and in conclusion a Declaration of Independency." Despite some changing hearts, however, delegates from five colonies were still banned from supporting independence—Morris's home province of Pennsylvania, as well as New York, New Jersey, Delaware, and Maryland.[2]

With South Carolina's delegation said to be wavering, radicals faced the specter of a 7–6 vote for independence, embarrassingly indecisive and hardly the stuff of world-changing revolution.

Troubling as that was, they didn't have the luxury of time. Many believed the only option was to forge ahead and force the issue in Congress. Despite this, the official records for Friday, June 6 gave no hint of any change in agenda, with delegates handling military and financial issues, including the reimbursement of soldiers for expenses incurred while tracking down two escaped parolees.[3] But a series of back-channel conversations made it clear to the radical faction that Richard Henry Lee would make the momentous motion the following day.

Samuel Adams was the first to put it in writing, albeit without firm details, in a note he sent that night to a friend in Massachusetts:

> Tomorrow a Motion will be made, and a Question, I hope, decided, the most important that was ever agitated in America.[4]

* * *

June 7, 1776, one of the most significant dates in U.S. history, began with a collective yawn in Philadelphia.

Congressional delegates dealt with a steady stream of issues that, almost 250 years later, seem absurdly inconsequential. They approved the payment of damages to Charles Walker of New Providence after the Continental navy had taken his ship and cargo of imported wood. They addressed resolutions from the convention of South Carolina regarding several battalions of troops raised for the colony's defense. They considered complaints about the quality of gunpowder produced by Oswald Eve's mill and appointed a three-man committee to identify the problem. Only then, after most of their other business had been transacted, did

Richard Henry Lee rise from his seat to propose American independence on behalf of the Virginia legislature.[5]

The scion of one of his colony's most prominent families, Lee was the ideal delegate to take this historic step. He had long been a proponent of separation from England and worked closely with fellow radicals John and Samuel Adams to achieve that end while bridging a political divide between northern and southern colonies. By his physical appearance, Lee also added a touch of drama to the proceedings. He wore a black silk glove on his left hand to cover injuries sustained in a hunting accident and was known to gesticulate with it at appropriate intervals to make crucial points.[6]

Now more than ever, the effect was mesmerizing.

Resolved,

That these United Colonies are, and of right ought to be, free and independent States, that they are absolved from all allegiance to the British Crown, and that all political connection between them and the State of Great Britain is, and ought to be, totally dissolved.

That it is expedient forthwith to take the most effectual measures for forming foreign Alliances.

That a plan of confederation be prepared and transmitted to the respective Colonies for their consideration and approbation.[7]

John Adams seconded the motion. Many of his colleagues then fell silent for long moments, pondering the impact of what was now before them.

The wording of Lee's proposal was not identical to the Virginia resolution, raising questions as to whether he had rewritten it on his own accord (or perhaps with help from Adams, Thomas Jefferson, or both). No answer was given, but it mattered little because the content and spirit were the same; if anything, the motion was clearer and stronger than the original. One fascinating addition to the final version was a specific phrase lifted from Parliament's Declaratory Act in 1766, which said the colonies "are, and of right ought to be" subordinate to the Crown. Lee's clever use of tactical plagiarism was intended as a verbal punch to the gut of the legislative leaders of the empire.[8]

Figure 8.1. Richard Henry Lee. *(Wikimedia Commons)*

Curiously, Congress put off discussion until the following day, advising delegates to "be enjoined to attend punctually at 10 o'Clock in order to take the same into consideration." The one-day delay never was explained, beyond a note from Jefferson that they were "obliged to attend at that time to some other business." Indeed, records show they wrapped up their session on June 7 by debating a series of punishments for a New Jersey couple accused of counterfeiting congressional bills of credit, calmly insisting that miscreants make "satisfaction to such persons as have been injured by taking the said counterfeit bills."[9] Independence would have to wait at least a few more hours.

Lee's motion became the primary topic on Saturday, June 8, when Congress resolved itself into a Committee of the Whole, meaning it could operate under informal rules to facilitate debate—and do so without keeping official records. Fortunately for history, Jefferson compiled his own contemporaneous notes over the summer and fall, which, while somewhat written from memory, give us "an extraordinarily graphic account of the debates and proceedings" during this period and are probably the best single source of information about the move toward independence. Jefferson reported that the delegates debated well into the evening on Saturday, took a much-needed rest on Sunday, and then resumed their deliberations with renewed energy on Monday, June 10.[10]

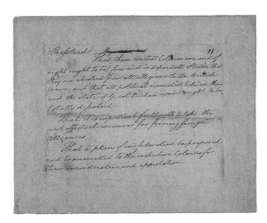

Figure 8.2. The resolution for American independence, in Lee's handwriting, presented to Congress on June 7, 1776. *(National Archives)*

Opposing the motion were John Dickinson and James Wilson of Pennsylvania, Robert R. Livingston of New York, and Edward Rutledge of South Carolina. Jefferson was gentle in his assessment of their work, refusing to criticize; he accused them only of pressing for a delay. "Tho' they were friends to the measures themselves and saw the impossibility that we should ever again be united with Gr. Britain," he wrote, "they were against adopting them at this time."[11] But notes taken by Dickinson in advance of speeches on June 8 and 10 tell a starkly different story of the moderates' counterattack. "The Sense of America as exprest is for Reconciliation," Dickinson wrote. "What Evidence have We of a contrary Sense? . . . Do not let Us turn our Backs on Reconciliation till We find it a Monster too dreadful to approach."[12]

Dickinson and his cohorts believed that residents in many colonies were not yet ready to support independence. Congress, they said, should defer "taking any capital step till the voice of the people drove us into it . . . without them, our declaration could not be carried into effect." They pointed to the negative reaction of colonies such as Maryland and New York to the preamble on May 15, indicating that they "were not yet ripe to bidding adieu to the British connection." A bit more time was going to be needed to fully gauge support for the American cause.

There was immense risk in moving too quickly on this potentially devastating proposal. At least five delegations had not even been empowered to vote for independence, and "if such a declaration should now be agreed to, these delegates must now retire & possibly their colonies secede from the Union." That statement alone sent chills through the State House. Congress could not afford to take any action that would cause defections and sap its strength—which, in turn, would make foreign alliances almost impossible to attain. In the meantime, colonial assemblies in Pennsylvania, New Jersey, and Delaware were preparing to meet and possibly rewrite instructions for their delegates. Why not wait a few weeks to hear the results?[13]

Jefferson did not quote the individual speakers by name, but historians believe that Dickinson was the chief strategist and likely the lead spokesman at those early June sessions. His copious notes included passages that could have been used almost verbatim to counter the radicals on the debate floor: "What Mortal can tell with Certainty that it will not be our best Interest to be reconciled with G.B.? It will depend on the Terms. They are yet unknown. . . . It will be a bargain to procure the aid & naval protection of G.B. We may purchase it perhaps at a reasonable price . . . would we be so unreasonable as to reject it?"[14] Dickinson was a formidable advocate with the persuasive skills of a brilliant trial lawyer, and he seemed to enjoy the chance to match wits with his chief rival on the radical side, John Adams.

Adams was joined by his usual partners, Lee and George Wythe, to speak on behalf of the motion. They fought back against the moderates by claiming that Lee's proposal of June 7 was not nearly as extreme as Dickinson had made it sound. "The question was not whether, by a declaration of independence, we should make ourselves what we are not," they said, "but whether we should declare a fact that already exists." The king had declared independence *from* the colonists by waging war for fourteen months and placing them outside of his protection. Why would anyone want to wait much longer to make it official?

Regarding foreign support, they argued that France or Spain would never commit to helping the colonies while they still belonged to the British Empire; only by breaking ties with the king and Parliament could such alliances be achieved. "A declaration of independence alone could render it consistent with European delicacy for European powers to treat with us, or even to receive an Ambassador from us." The radicals also acknowledged the staggering odds they faced on the battlefield, making it imperative to move quickly and decisively before the losses piled up: "The present campaign may be unsuccessful, & therefore we had better propose an alliance while our affairs wear a hopeful aspect."[15]

Both sides scored points but seemed to change few minds during a full day of sparkling oratory on June 8. Rutledge estimated that the unofficial tally remained the same when Congress adjourned in the early evening, with six colonies still unwilling or unable to vote for independence. At 10:00 p.m., he wrote to his friend and fellow moderate, John Jay, in New York, informing him that "This Congress sat till 7 o'clock this Evening on Consequence of a Motion of R. H. Lee's resolving ourselves free & independent States. The Sensible part of the House opposed the

Motion. . . . They saw no Wisdom in a Declaration of Independence, nor any Purpose to be answer'd by it." But others in his faction were not so sure. Dickinson sent a frantic note to another moderate Pennsylvania delegate, Thomas Willing, asking him to resume his seat at the State House as soon as possible; they needed strength in numbers. At the same time, Livingston and other New York members alerted their colonial assembly that "[we] here expect that the question of Independence will be very shortly agitated in Congress. Some of us consider ourselves as bound by our instructions not to vote on that question, & all wish to have your sentiments thereon."[16]

Sunday, June 9 was a day off for Congress, giving everyone a break and delighting most delegates, who were understandably exhausted. Not so for John Adams. He kept up his work at a frenzied pace, holding private meetings, twisting arms, probing allegiances, and composing at least three letters to friends in Massachusetts. One of these, in particular, written to William Cushing (a future justice of the U.S. Supreme Court), summed up his mind-set on the eve of what Adams thought might be the definitive vote on American independence.

> Objects of the most Stupendous Magnitude, Measures in which the Lives and Liberties of Millions, born & unborn are most essentially interested are now before Us. We are in the very midst of a Revolution, the most compleat, unexpected, and remarkable of any in the History of Nations. A few Matters must be dispatched before I can return. Every Colony must be induced to institute and perfect Government. All the colonies must confederate together, in some Solemn Compact. The Colonies must be declared free and independent States, and Ambassadors must be Sent abroad to foreign Courts, to solicit their Acknowledgement of Us, as Sovereign States, and to form with them . . . commercial Treaties of Friendship and Alliance. When these Things shall be once well finished . . . I shall think that I have answered the End of my Creation.[17]

Congress went back into session on Monday, June 10 and, after dealing with several small matters related to the army, including the appointment of a deputy paymaster general in the eastern department, resolved itself again into a Committee of the Whole to resume the debate. Much of the same ground was covered by many of the same speakers, with Dickinson and Adams leading the way. Had a vote been taken that afternoon, independence likely would have passed by one or two votes—a decidedly weak message for the "country" and the world. But Adams knew that several moderate colonial assemblies were meeting to review their instructions on independence, and he sought at this crucial moment to embarrass them with a taunt: "The conduct of some colonies from the beginning of this contest [gives] reason to suspect it was their settled policy to keep to the rear of the confederacy, that their particular prospect might be better in the worse event."[18] One can only imagine the tension in the room.

Surprisingly, it was Edward Rutledge who helped them avoid another frustrating split decision. He proposed that Congress should postpone the vote on independence for "3 Weeks to a Month" to allow certain hesitant colonies to clarify their positions. The full body agreed, but only by a slim 7–5 margin, setting the new date as July 1 for the final vote. In the meantime, to avoid losing any time, they were to appoint a committee "to prepare a declaration . . . in case the Congress agree thereto."[19]

Given the importance of what was taking place, it is remarkable that the American public was still being kept in the dark, wholly unaware of the congressional action. Newspaper reports were nonexistent, and random rumors gained little traction. Delegates were still sworn to secrecy—out of fear for their safety, as much as anything else—and only a few broke the rules by revealing details in private letters. Hancock was deliberately coy when he wrote to Washington in New York on the night of June 10, wrapping his hints in the most general terms possible: "We have been two Days in a Committee of the Whole deliberating on three Capital Matters, the most important in their Nature of any that have yet been before us."[20] Washington had been in Philadelphia just a few days earlier and no doubt was able read between the lines.

But it was Massachusetts delegate Elbridge Gerry who violated all the terms of their secrecy agreement when he wrote to James Warren of his colonial assembly the next day, June 11, with a message full of detail, vigor, and snarky comments. Aside from Jefferson's notes, it is the only contemporary, unvarnished description of the June 10 decision by a sitting member of Congress in Philadelphia:

> Yesterday after a long debate the question of independence was postponed until the first [of] July, in order to give the assemblies of the middle colonies an opportunity to take off their restrictions and let their delegates unite in the measure. In the interim will go on plans for confederation and foreign alliance.
>
> If these slow people had hearkened to reason in time, this work would have long ere now been completed, and the disadvantage arising from the want of such measure been wholly avoided; but Providence has undoubtedly wise ends in coupling together the vigorous and the indolent; the first are retarded but the latter are urged on, and both come together to the goal.[21]

* * *

Delegates went back into session at 9:00 a.m. on Tuesday, June 11, and, despite the weighty matter of independence hanging over them, promptly focused on twelve unrelated matters. The first committee to be formed that day was one tasked with determining how much to pay the secretary of Congress for his services. Prominent on the agenda was a meeting with leaders of the Six Nations Indian confederacy, to whom the delegates pledged friendship for "as long as the sun shall shine and the water runs." Otherwise, they read aloud letters from army officers, including Washington; approved payment for an Indian translator; referred several items to the Committee of Prisoners; and ordered regiments from several colonies to march to the defense of New York City. It was only after all other matters were completed—and probably sometime in the mid-afternoon—that Congress got around to choosing the committee to prepare the declaration.[22]

The "Committee of Five," as it came to be known, was an impressive, well-balanced group made up of John Adams of Massachusetts, Roger Sherman of Connecticut, Robert R. Livingston of New York, Benjamin Franklin of Pennsylvania, and Thomas Jefferson of Virginia. They offered regional diversity in that two were from New England, two were from the middle colonies, and one was from the South. The inclusion of Livingston was noteworthy because he had spoken strongly for delaying independence in the debates of June 8–10. But the full body believed it had selected a proper slate of candidates, with Jefferson, the brilliant writer, receiving the most votes and Adams placing second, followed by Franklin and the others.[23]

The most striking omission was that of Richard Henry Lee, the Virginia provocateur who made the historic motion on June 7. Lee's pro-independence bona fides were well known by all in Congress. Adams tried to explain his absence in later years by saying that Lee was excluded because of a perceived conflict with another Virginian, Benjamin Harrison, but records from the period do not support Adams's claim. Lee and Wythe were already planning to leave for Virginia on June 13 to take part in writing that colony's constitution, which they considered to be a far more important duty. In addition, Lee had recently received "distressing intelligence that his lady was dangerously ill."[24]

Lee's presence was much desired by the vaunted Virginia assembly. Longtime friend George Mason had written to him from Williamsburg on May 18, "I need not tell you how much you will be wanted here on this Occasion. . . . We cannot do without you. . . . At all Events, my dear Sir, let us see you here as soon as possible." Lee's decision to leave for home was reached no later than June 2, when he wrote to another colleague that "I hope to be in Virga. in 10 or 12 days."[25] Though it is largely forgotten today, this was a significant pivot point in U.S. history. If Lee had been convinced to stay in Philadelphia, he almost certainly would have been part of the committee, and—inasmuch as he would have filled Virginia's quota—Jefferson would have been assigned other duties. Someone else, perhaps Adams, or Lee himself, would have written the Declaration of Independence. Fate sometimes turns in dramatic ways on otherwise mundane daily decisions.

With the declaration committee now in place, Congress wasted little time in turning its attention elsewhere. Committees still were needed to address the other items in Lee's resolution—foreign alliances and a confederation of colonies—and it became clear that everyone would have to pitch in. This was no time to specialize. Adams and Franklin were joined by Dickinson as part of a five-man committee chosen on June 12 "to prepare a plan of treaties to be proposed to foreign powers." One man from each colony then was named to a much larger group assigned to "prepare and digest the form of a confederation to be entered into between these colonies." Members included Sherman and Livingston from the declaration committee, as well as Dickinson, Rutledge, and Samuel Adams.[26]

Interestingly enough, John Adams thought the most important assignment he received that week came on June 13, when he was voted as chairman of the five-man Board of War and Ordnance to oversee all aspects of the war. Secrecy for this committee was considered so imperative by the full body that Adams and the others—Sherman, Rutledge, Wilson, and Harrison—were required to take and sign the following oath:

> I [name] do solemnly swear that I will not, directly or indirectly, divulge any matter or thing which shall come to my knowledge as [a member] of the board of war and ordnance for the United Colonies, established by Congress, without the leave of said board of war and ordnance, and that I will faithfully execute my said office, according to the best of my skill and judgement. So help me God.[27]

Those pledges took on an added degree of solemnity on June 14, when rumors reached the State House that British ships were sailing up the Delaware River toward Philadelphia. Congress wasted no time in approving the delivery of "such a quantity of [gun] powder as shall seem necessary" to troops defending the colony. Reminders of potential attacks were everywhere.[28]

* * *

Rutledge's proposal to delay the vote on independence gave several colonies just enough time to reconsider or enhance their views. Movement began in Connecticut within a few days.

On June 14, Connecticut's assembly gave explicit instructions for its delegates to "declare the United American Colonies free and independent States" and to "give the assent of this Colony to such Declaration when they shall judge it expedient." Virginia's resolution was the tipping point.

Connecticut's governor thanked the "ancient and patriotick Colony of Virginia" for being bold enough to "point out some ways and means to extricate ourselves and countrymen from those unprovoked oppressions." That made it easier for others to fall in line.[29]

Indeed, both New Hampshire and Delaware changed their instructions the next day. New Hampshire's assembly referenced the "last probable resource to get rid of their unprovoked tyranny" when approving its delegates to "join with other Colonies in declaring the thirteen United Colonies a free and independent State" (interestingly, New Hampshire was the only colony to use the singular "State"). Delaware's language wasn't quite as overt, but it called for a new government for the protection and happiness of residents and supported approving other measures to promote the liberty of America.[30]

The heretofore moderate New Jersey assembly also reversed course with a series of startling actions in mid-June. Most notable was the arrest of its loyalist governor, William Franklin, who was described as "a virulent enemy to his country and a person who may prove to be dangerous." Hearing news of the governor's demise, a local assemblyman wrote to John Adams: "We are passing the Rubicon, & our Delegates in Congress first of July will vote [for independence]." Radicals continued their work on multiple fronts, and by June 22, New Jersey had formed a new government, elected a new slate of delegates to Congress, and empowered those delegates to vote for separation "if you shall judge it necessary and expedient."[31]

Pennsylvania's transition was even more fascinating—and more complex. Much of that was because its assembly held its meetings in the State House, just one floor above the Continental Congress (with Dickinson scurrying up and down the steps between the two bodies). Moderates still were in control of the assembly, but their iron-clad grip had been pried open by the May 15 preamble. As a defensive measure, members agreed to soften their stance on independence and rewrite instructions in a desperate attempt to calm the opposition and retain power: "The Situation of public Affairs is since so greatly altered, that we now think ourselves justifiable in removing the Restrictions laid upon you."

Approved on June 8, the new instructions allowed Pennsylvania's delegation to "concur with the other Delegates" in forming foreign alliances and adopting other measures in support of American liberty. But the words *independence* or *separation* were not mentioned, and the language was far too lukewarm to appease the howling critics. The assembly adjourned on June 14 and never would meet again. "The timid and trimming politics of some men of large property here have almost done their business for them," John Adams crowed in a celebratory letter. "They have lost their influence and grown obnoxious."[32]

In the meantime, a rival Provincial Conference was called, with a twofold purpose: to declare independence and start the process of drafting a new Pennsylvania constitution. Members read aloud the May 15 preamble, chided the current government for being "not competent to the exigencies of our Affairs," and drew up a fresh set of instructions for delegates in Congress. These included a statement of "our willingness to concur in a vote of the Congress declaring the United Colonies free and independent States."[33]

The amount of change over a two-week period was dizzying. By June 24, eleven of the thirteen colonial delegations had either been formally encouraged to support independence or given the latitude to vote as they saw fit. Of those eleven, South Carolina, Pennsylvania, and Delaware still were wild cards whose votes could go either way, depending on which delegates showed up at the State House on any given day. But Maryland and New York were the only remaining holdouts.

"That we are divorced [from England] is to me very clear," Adams wrote on June 22. "The only Question is concerning the Proper time for making an explicit Declaration in Words. Some People must have Time to look around them, before, behind, on the right hand, and on the left, then to think, and after this to resolve. Others see at one intuitive Glance into past the future, and judge with Precision at one. But remember you can't make thirteen Clocks Strike precisely alike, at the Same Second."[34]

* * *

Members of the committee to write the "explicit Declaration" likely met for the first time on the evening of June 11, shortly after Congress had adjourned for the day. We never can be certain of the details of this critical period because they kept no formal records of their proceedings. Much of the popular narrative was stitched together years later, based on reminiscences from Adams and Jefferson in the 1800s, when both were old men with foggy memories and conflicting agendas.

"Piecing together the story demands sifting through contradictory clues with the care of a shrewd detective," historian Pauline Maier wrote. "Indeed, a good part of the story involves evaluating evidence."[35] It does not help that Franklin, Sherman, and Livingston wrote almost nothing (or at least nothing insightful) about the roles they played.

One astonishing discovery is that Franklin, despite all the reverence accorded him in history, had very little impact on the committee. Sidelined by a painful case of gout after returning from Quebec, he was not a participant in early meetings or strategy sessions; he does not appear to have been directly involved until June 21, ten days into the process, when Jefferson sent him the draft, asking for his input. On the same day, Franklin wrote to Washington: "I am just recovering from a severe Fit of the Gout, which has kept me from Congress and Company almost ever since you left us [in early June], so that I know little of what has pass'd there, except that a Declaration of Independence is preparing." As late as June 26, two days before the committee completed its work, he told a colleague: "I hope in a few days to be strong enough to come to town & attend my Duty in Congress."[36]

Patrick Spero, a scholar at the American Philosophical Society Library in Philadelphia, which was founded by Franklin in 1743, confirmed that Franklin was homebound for several weeks because of his affliction. "He eventually retired to a friend's house outside of Philadelphia to try and recover, and he was, for a period of this time, unable to attend, most likely, the actual committee meetings," Spero said. "So Franklin was not an active participant in the committee in the sense of, if it met, Franklin was there. But Jefferson reached out to him at least once, possibly twice, to get his advice on how the declaration was shaping up."[37]

Jefferson credited him with at least five small edits to the draft, and there is circumstantial evidence that Franklin was the member who inserted the epic phrase "self-evident" in the preamble.[38] But when their meetings began on June 11, and for much of the next two and a half weeks, the "Committee of Five" became a somewhat smaller detachment of four.

The account of how Jefferson came to write the draft has been muddled over the years by discordant tales from the participants. According to the notes he compiled later in 1776, Jefferson explained it in the simplest terms: "The committee for drawing the declaration of Independance desired me to prepare it. I did so." He told much the same story in the 1820s, adding only that the committee "unanimously pressed on myself alone to the make the draft."[39] Accurate as those assertions may have been, however, it was a much more expansive narrative from Adams in 1805 that became the most widely accepted and repeated version. Rich in detail and fanciful in delivery—which enchanted historians—it claimed that he, Adams, had selected and encouraged Jefferson to write the Declaration:

> The Committee had several meetings, in which were proposed the Articles of which the Declaration was to consist, and minutes made of them [to guide the writer]. The Committee then appointed Mr. Jefferson and me, to draw them up in form and cloath them in a proper Dress. The Sub Committee met, and considered the Minutes, making such Observations on them as then occurred; when Mr. Jefferson desired me to take them to my Lodgings and make the Draught. This I declined, and gave several reasons for declining. 1. That he was a Virginian and I a Massachusettsian. 2. that he was a southern Man and I a northern one. 3. That I had been so obnoxious for my early and constant Zeal in promoting the Measure, that any draught of mine would undergo a more severe Scrutiny. 4thly and lastly that would be reason enough if there were no other, I had a great Opinion of the elegance of his pen, and none at all of my own. I therefore insisted that no hesitation should be made on his part.[40]

Adams seemed to have forgotten that in 1779, only three years after the Declaration, when his memory was sharper, he wrote: "We appointed Jefferson a sub-committee to draw it up." There was no mention of Adams *also* being on the subcommittee. It stands as the best, most persuasive evidence that Jefferson was the committee's first choice as draftsman all along, as Jefferson had said in 1776, and continued to say into the 1820s.[41]

What has become increasingly apparent to students of the revolution is that none of the committee members, including Jefferson—and certainly not Adams—thought the Declaration would become the most hallowed document in American history. It was just another item on their lengthy "to-do" list in mid-June 1776. Separation from England would not even be declared for several weeks; the British were beefing up their forces and preparing an attack on New York; and each of the committee members was tasked with numerous other time-consuming assignments. Adams still was expected to lead the debates in Congress, and he considered his roles with the committee on foreign treaties and the Board of War and Ordnance to have much greater impacts on the cause. It was only decades later, when he saw Jefferson being hailed as the revered author of independence, that Adams began to regret not taking the assignment for himself. Jealousy got the best of him, and his "recollections" changed.

"The golden haze that eventually enveloped the Declaration had not yet formed" in 1776, historian Joseph Ellis wrote. "Its subsequent significance was lost on all the participants, Jefferson included. All assumed that more important business was going on elsewhere, either in our committees meeting in Philadelphia or, in Jefferson's case, down in Williamsburg. What became the great creative moment was perceived by all concerned as a minor administrative chore."[42]

CHAPTER 9

The Twenty-Eighth of June

BY EARLY JUNE, THOMAS JEFFERSON HAD MOVED TO THE SECOND FLOOR of a three-story house at the southwest corner of Seventh and Market Streets, about two blocks from the State House and away from the bustle of the city. Accompanied by his fourteen-year-old enslaved servant, Bob Hemings, he brought along a portable writing box and a small wooden desk that he designed himself, spending much of his time in the front parlor, where he "wrote habitually." The work included three draft versions of a constitution for Virginia, various committee reports, private letters home, official correspondence, and, for a time in the second full week of that month, the Declaration of Independence.[1]

It was a scene Jefferson could not have fathomed only ten months earlier. Writing to his cousin, John Randolph, on August 25, 1775, he hoped "for a restoration of our just rights" but wished above all for "a return of the happy period when . . . I may withdraw myself totally from the public stage and pass the rest of my days in domestic ease and tranquility, banishing every desire of afterwards ever even hearing what passes in the world."[2] Now he was front and center as wordsmith of an insurgency that would redefine global politics for centuries to come.

At first glance, it appears that Jefferson had a full seventeen days to complete his assignment—from June 11, when the committee appointed him, to June 28, when it was submitted to Congress for review—which would have been a leisurely pace for a writer of his skill. But he did the work with astounding speed, and it is possible that he completed the first draft as early as Friday, June 14. John Adams would later recall that

Jefferson "in a day or two produced to me his Draught." Hyperbolic as that sounds, especially coming from Adams, circumstantial evidence shows that he was not far off in his assessment.[3]

Jefferson had planned all along to share copies of his draft with Adams and Benjamin Franklin, "requesting their corrections, because they were the two members of whose judgements and amendments I wished most to have the benefit before presenting it to the Committee."[4] Adams saw it first and carefully wrote out his own copy, preserving the text for in its early developmental stages. Jefferson probably showed his draft to Adams on Saturday, June 15; that is when Congress tasked him to write two reports regarding the military campaign in Canada, which were due to the full body on Monday. Those lengthy and very detailed accounts took up parts of eleven pages in the *Journals of the Continental Congress*, and would have occupied nearly all of his time that weekend, including Sunday, June 16, the only day off for members. It is important to note that Jefferson was named to two more committees that month—one on June 20, the other on June 24—and had several other assignments while he was also writing the Declaration. He did not operate in a vacuum.[5]

There were many reasons why Jefferson was able to write as quickly as he did, even in this hectic political environment. Much of it was the ability to draw from his own substantive work over the past two years, when his thoughts on American grievances grew and crystalized. He had authored the acclaimed "Summary View of the Rights of British America" in 1774 and wrote a draft of "A Declaration of the Causes and Necessity of Taking Up Arms" for the Second Continental Congress in 1775. Most recently—in a frenzied three-week period starting on May 23—he produced three drafts of a proposed Virginia constitution, two of which had preambles that excoriated King George III. By happy coincidence, he also saw a copy of Virginia's new Declaration of Rights, drafted by George Mason, which was published in a Philadelphia newspaper on June 12. That language was fresh in his mind and probably at his fingertips as he hunched over the writing box in his parlor at Seventh and Market.[6]

Jefferson's main role was to justify independence for the colonies. His message had to be persuasive enough to convince multiple audiences—Congress itself, the American public, European powers, the rest of the world—that such a break was reasonable, viable, defensible, and virtually unavoidable. Doing so required a lengthy series of charges against the king, which Jefferson could conveniently lift and reformat from his previous writings, including the Virginia drafts. But he also sought a higher, more eloquent purpose in the opening two paragraphs, intending to create "an expression of the American mind, and to give to that expression the proper tone and spirit called for by the occasion."[7]

In early draft form, the first paragraph set Jefferson's tone with dignity and grace:

> When in the course of human events it becomes necessary for a people to advance from that subordination in which they have hitherto remained and to assume among the powers of the earth the equal & independent station to which the laws of nature & of nature's god entitle them, a decent respect to the opinions of mankind requires that they should declare the causes which impel them to the change.

The wording of that introduction would be edited slightly and tightened up for the final version—Adams, Franklin, the committee and Congress all had their say—but readers could already sense the impact of what was to follow. It had become "necessary" in the "course of human events" that the causes should be declared and made public out of "a decent respect to the opinions of mankind." This was no longer an inner-family squabble with ancestral British brethren over taxation and legislative rights but, rather, the bold assumption of an "independent station . . . among the powers of the earth." It was the forthright and unambiguous language of revolution.[8]

The second paragraph, often known as the preamble, took it one step further with a series of majestic assertions about American liberty (even if Jefferson could not have imagined how it would still resonate centuries later). Similarly, this early version had yet to undergo a full editing process, but even its roughest form, with assorted excess words and phrases, laid out the foundation pillars of U.S. democracy in clear, emphatic terms:

> We hold these truths to be sacred & undeniable, that all men are cre-
> ated equal & independent, that from that equal creation they derive
> their rights inherent & inalienable, among which are the preservation
> of life, & liberty & the pursuit of happiness; that to secure these ends,
> governments are instituted among men, deriving their just powers from
> the consent of the governed; that whenever any form of government
> shall become destructive of these ends, it is the right of the people to
> alter or to abolish it, & to institute new government, laying its foun-
> dation on such principles & organizing its powers in such form, as to
> them shall seem most likely to effect their safety & happiness.[9]

Whew. It was a long but extremely powerful sentence, invoking the dual
tenets of freedom and equality, confirming the people's "right" to form
a new government with the "consent of the governed." Careful editing
by Jefferson's colleagues would soon make it leaner and more evocative,
especially when "sacred & undeniable" were replaced by the now iconic
"self-evident" truths. The two phrases that would endure for all time
were "all men are created equal" and the gently edited "life, liberty and
the pursuit of happiness," both sacred elements of the American creed.
Contrary to modern mythology, however, Jefferson was not treading on
new ground in the preamble; he was merely encapsulating thoughts that
had been published many times before, and were often bandied about in
the late eighteenth century.

John Locke, the revered British philosopher of the Enlightenment
era, had addressed the natural rights of life, liberty, and property in
his *Second Treatise on Government* (1689), making a lasting impression
on many Americans. Specifically, Locke wrote that, since men were
"all equal and independent, no one ought to harm another in his life,
health, liberty or possessions."[10] James Wilson, the moderate delegate
from Pennsylvania, opined in 1774 that "[a]ll men are by nature equal
and free; no one has a right to any authority over another without his
consent." And John Adams, in his provincial proclamation of January 19,
1776, stated with great fervor that "[a]s the Happiness of the People is
the sole End of Government, So the Consent of the People is the only
Foundation of it."[11]

All of those thoughts were likely in Jefferson's head, but it is reasonable to assume that he was most deeply affected by Mason's draft of the Virginia Declaration of Rights, published in the *Pennsylvania Gazette* on June 12, the same day he began his work. It began by stating the following:

> All men born equally free and independant, and have certain inherent natural rights, of which they cannot, by any compact, deprive or divest their posterity; among which are the enjoyment of life and liberty, with the means of acquiring and possessing property, and pursuing and obtaining happiness and safety.[12]

Mason's draft also declared that "all power is vested in, and consequently derived from the people," and that "government is, or ought to be, instituted for the common benefit, protection and security of the people."[13] The language of the Declaration of Independence is eerily similar—almost uncomfortably so to the modern reader—but what Jefferson did in reframing those epic words was not considered plagiarism at the time. Writers in the 1700s were encouraged to borrow liberally from others and engage in the "creative adaptation of pre-existing models," one scholar said, "with the highest praise going to "imitations whose excellence exceeded that of the examples that inspired them."[14] Peter Onuf, a renowned Jefferson expert from the University of Virginia, noted that he was merely probing the common "complaints of the day," collaborating with colleagues in the "pre-revolutionary, patriotic public sphere."[15]

Most fascinating to historians was the small but impactful editorial change from "sacred & undeniable" to "self-evident," the source of which is still shrouded in mystery. Scholars often attribute this to Franklin, although there is no direct evidence to support that assertion, and no citations confirm it. Jefferson gave Franklin credit for five other changes in the document, but notably did not do it here; Franklin, for his part, never claimed it; and Adams was uncharacteristically silent on the subject. Perhaps they did not think it was very important at the time—unable to grasp what it would mean to Americans in the future, and focused more intently on the charges against the king.[16]

The case for Franklin is made most persuasively by his biographer, the preeminent historian Walter Isaacson. "The most important of his edits was small but resounding," Isaacson wrote. "He crossed out, using the heavy backslashes that he often employed, the last three words of Jefferson's phrase, 'We hold these truths to be sacred and undeniable' and changed them to the words now enshrined in history: 'We hold these truths to be self-evident.'" Curiously, though, these iconic "heavy backslashes" do not appear on any of the other changes credited to Franklin, where words are merely crossed out with a straight line.

But Isaacson believed that he drew on a theory developed by Scottish philosopher David Hume (who happened to be Franklin's good friend) that certain truths are "self-evident by virtue of reason and definition." The few other edits that Jefferson credited to Franklin were similar in purpose, brevity, and style. At one point later in the draft, when Jefferson railed at King George III for sending foreign mercenaries to America to "deluge us in blood," Franklin changed it to, simply, "destroy us." In another place, "subject them to arbitrary power" was rewritten to read "reduce them under absolute Despotism."[17]

It is worth noting that John Adams's copy of the draft, which he made very early in the process—certainly before Jefferson's June 21 outreach to Franklin—already included the change from "sacred & undeniable" to "self-evident." This adds another confusing element to the Declaration's timeline. Had Jefferson made the change on his own, since writers constantly edit their own work? Could Adams have been responsible? Did those two men discuss it and make a joint decision? Or did Jefferson reach out to the homebound Franklin sometime *before* that June 21 note? Was Franklin really the father of "self-evident" in the Declaration? We can never know for certain.[18]

Regardless of how it happened, the soon-to-be-historic alteration was made well before the committee presented Jefferson's draft to Congress on June 28. It gave the preamble more strength and verve, allowing him to set up the much longer second section of the Declaration, the litany of charges against the king. Jefferson conceded that "governments long established should not be changed for light & transient reasons" but sought to expose "unremitting injuries and usurpations" that enabled

England to establish "an absolute tyranny" over the colonies (which he now identified as "states").

"To prove this," he wrote, in one of the sublime transitional paragraphs in American history, "let facts be submitted to a candid world."[19]

* * *

Whether the candid world was ready or not, the facts came fast and furious from Jefferson's pen.

He was most comfortable with this accusatorial section, since he had been outlining grievances against the king and Parliament for the previous two years. He had, in fact, spent the previous three weeks sketching out multiple drafts of a proposed Virginia constitution, including many of the same complaints presented in much the same way. Jefferson refined them as he wrote, modeling the Virginia preamble on England's 1689 Declaration of Rights, which was written to oust King James II in favor of new sovereigns William and Mary. By the time he got around to his latest congressional assignment, Jefferson was already an expert in the admittedly nasty business of announcing revolution.[20]

The list of charges in the final version of the Declaration of Independence is often ignored by most modern readers of the document, who are drawn instead to its soaring language about equality and natural rights. But this was by far *the* most important segment to Congress in 1776. Historian Robert Parkinson of Binghamton University reminds us to view it as "fundamentally a political document with pressing aims: it had to clarify a confusing military conflict, distinguish friends from enemies, inspire armed resistance, and garner sympathy (and aid) from European powers." The case for independence had to be clear and compelling, and that case could be made only with a potent series of indictments against the king.[21]

Jefferson did not select his charges haphazardly. Scholars have noticed a method to the way he assembled them—"thematically," as Parkinson says, and increasing in seriousness and emotion as he went along. Most shocking to contemporaries was Jefferson's singular focus on King George III as his target, instead of Parliament, the first time that had happened in a formal congressional document. It is true that Jefferson challenged the king in his "Summary View" in 1774, but that was an unofficial essay presented to the Virginia legislature. Congress's other petitions, including the "Olive Branch" and the "Declaration of Causes," were intended only to *inform* His Majesty of Parliament's oppressions. The dramatic change in strategy likely was made at the committee's first meeting, when Jefferson, Adams, Robert R. Livingston, and Roger Sherman discussed and debated the best ways to achieve their goals.[22]

In the earliest surviving version of his draft, Jefferson made twenty-five charges against the king. Over the next few weeks, Adams, Franklin, the committee, and Congress would add, delete, edit, tweak, prod, and massage these into a final total of twenty-seven, but the overall tone was the same.[23] They were arranged in order to attack the king's executive power; his support for legislation passed by "others," meaning Parliament; and his blatant acts of war and cruelty. A review of Jefferson's drafts of the Virginia constitution shows that he had been fleshing out the same list of charges for weeks, and aside from a few additions, he essentially repurposed them in slightly different language.

The first group of charges was the least persuasive, and almost deliberately vague. He began by claiming that "his present majesty" has "refused his Assent to Laws, the most wholesome and necessary for the public good" (it was not far off from the Virginia draft, which accused the king of "putting his negative on laws the most wholesome & necessary for the public good"). Jefferson built his case slowly, sometimes referring to local issues that would have been unfamiliar to most Americans at the time. The charge that "he has called together legislative bodies at places unusual, uncomfortable & distant from the depository of their public records" likely was a favor to John Adams, who groused that the king once moved the Massachusetts assembly from Boston to Cambridge. Few of these would have been enough, on their own, to break from an empire or inspire young men to take up arms.[24]

The second section was far more specific and aggressive, drawn from acts imposed by Parliament over the past decade, including the Declaratory Act, the Coercive Acts, and the very recent Prohibitory Act. The monarch was culpable, Jefferson said, because "he has combined with others" in "giving assent to their pretended acts of legislation." Notable on the list were "quartering large bodies of troops among us . . . cutting off our trade with all parts of the world . . . imposing taxes on us without our consent . . . [and] suspending our own legislatures & declaring themselves invested with power to legislate for us in all cases whatsoever." The language was stark and clear enough that colonists from New Hampshire to Georgia could nod their heads and understand.[25]

But it was not until the third group of charges that Jefferson served up the red meat of revolution. The king not only had "plundered our seas, ravaged our coasts, burnt our towns & destroyed the lives of our people" but also was at this time "transporting large armies of foreign mercenaries to compleat the works of death, destruction and tyranny." This was followed by the racially charged accusation that "merciless Indian savages" had been incited to attack colonial settlements on the frontier. Jefferson apparently saw it as a guileful precursor to the last of his original charges—the longest and, by far, the most controversial—laying blame for the transatlantic slave trade at the feet of King George III.

The king, he said, had violated "the most sacred rights of life & liberty in the persons of a distant people . . . captivating & carrying them into slavery in another hemisphere." This was considered "piratical warfare . . . the warfare of the CHRISTIAN king of Great Britain, determined to keep open a market where MEN should be bought & sold." The hypocrisy is mind-boggling, because Jefferson willingly owned more than six hundred enslaved people in his lifetime, including four hundred at his sprawling plantation, Monticello. Could that possibly be the *king's* fault? Jefferson's reliance on slavery for his livelihood was undoubtedly behind a final, vengeful passage in the charge: "he is now exciting those very people to rise in arms against us . . . paying off former crimes committed against the *liberties* of one people, with crimes which he urges them to commit against the *lives* of another."[26]

The large group of editors would have to decide whether that wording remained in the official version.

* * *

With the list of charges completed, Jefferson now had to wrap up his draft before presenting it to Adams, Franklin, and the committee. The transition to this final section began with a scathing critique of the British people for failing to support the colonial cause.

Jefferson opened with his long-held (though hardly justifiable) belief that the New World had been settled at the "expence of our own blood & treasure," unassisted by the "wealth or the strength of Great Britain." Colonists never would submit to being ruled by Parliament from London, he said, but when the prospect of self-government in the colonies was proposed, "our British brethren . . . [became] deaf to the voice of justice." Moreover, Americans in 1776 were indignant that soldiers of their "common blood" were being sent across the ocean to enforce submission with bullets and cannon balls, aided by thousands of foreign mercenaries. "We might have been a free & a great people together," Jefferson said, "but a communication of grandeur & of freedom it seems is below their dignity." Circumstances called for breaking all ties and bidding "our everlasting Adieu!"[27]

That left only one more paragraph, the all-important declaratory conclusion. Jefferson was blunt in his approach, announcing that "the representatives of the United States of America in General Congress assembled . . . reject and renounce all allegiance to the kings of Great Britain." It was the first time that the name of the new country was used in a public forum, but the shock value of that revelation did not detract from the overall message. Americans, Jefferson said, would now "utterly dissolve & break all political connection . . . between us & the people and parliament of Great Britain." In doing so, they "assert and declare these colonies to be free and independant states," assuming the power to "levy war, conclude peace, contract alliances, establish commerce, & to do all other acts and things which independent states may of right do."

This was revolutionary fervor at its best, flowing from the pen of an idealistic thirty-three-year-old lawyer and plantation owner from Virginia who had returned to Congress only one month earlier (and who, if he had his way, would have been back at the colonial convention in Williamsburg, working on Virginia's constitution). In a closing sentence, meant to underscore the devotion of radical congressmen who knew they were committing treason against the Crown, Jefferson wrote: "And for the support of this declaration we mutually pledge our lives, our fortunes & our sacred honour."[28] It was magnificent, passionate language.

Precise details of the Declaration's editing process over the next few weeks are lost to history, although there are tantalizing clues. If we assume, as is reasonable, that Jefferson completed the draft by Saturday, June 15, when he received his next assignment from Congress, it is likely that he presented his copy to Adams that same day, asking for preliminary comments. There also is circumstantial evidence that Adams, Jefferson, and two other committee members—Roger Sherman and Robert R. Livingston—met the following week for group editing work.

That information comes from the note Jefferson sent to the home-bound Franklin on the morning of Friday, June 21, while Franklin was still recovering from his case of gout. An illuminating piece of Declaration history, it went undiscovered for centuries until scholar Julian P. Boyd published it for the first time in 1950, in the first volume of the *Thomas Jefferson Papers*. Passing along his draft of the Declaration with preliminary edits made by Adams and others, Jefferson wrote:

> The inclosed paper has been read and with some small alterations approved of by the committee. Will Doctr. Franklin be so good as to peruse it and suggest such alterations as his more enlarged view of the subject will dictate? The paper having been returned to me to change a particular sentiment or two, I propose laying it before the committee tomorrow morning, if Doctr. Franklin can think of it before that time.[29]

June 21 was the same day that Franklin wrote to George Washington, telling the general that his condition had "kept me from Congress and Company" for more than two weeks, and that he knew little "except that a Declaration of Independence is preparing." Five days later, on June 26, Franklin messaged another colleague that he hoped to "be strong enough to come to town & attend my Duty in Congress" in a few days.[30]

Several reasonable conclusions can be drawn from these exchanges:

- From the tone of the Jefferson and Franklin notes, it is clear that Franklin had not attended any committee meetings in person, and would not be able to do so before the draft was due in Congress on June 28.

- Franklin likely hadn't seen the draft before this.

- The committee had met *at least* twice—an initial meeting, when it gave Jefferson his assignment, and an editing meeting, where it made alterations and suggested changing "a sentiment or two."

- The four other members of the committee were scheduled to meet again the next day, Saturday, June 22, which was an off-day for Congress (as was Sunday, June 23—more time for editing).

- Jefferson placed great value in Franklin's opinion, because of his wisdom, international experience, and "enlarged view of the subject."

Given that Adams had made a very early copy of the draft, scholars have been able to gauge when edits were made in the two weeks between June 15 and June 28, when it went to Congress. Two scholars, in particular—Boyd and Gerard W. Gawalt of the Library of Congress—led the way in this intricate research, comparing copies, including a heavily edited version that Jefferson later called his "Original Rough Draught," and a one-page fragment of an even earlier draft that Boyd found in 1947. They determined that fifteen changes were made by the time of the Adams copy, and an additional thirty-two before June 28, for a total of forty-seven during the committee editing period.[31]

Most of these were minor in nature—tweaking words or phrases, smoothing out rough edges, and adding clarity. Some were undoubtedly made by Jefferson himself, and some would have been verbal suggestions from the others during meetings, which Jefferson then applied to his draft. In a letter to James Madison in August 1823, when Jefferson was eighty years old, he included a copy of the committee draft "with the corrections of Doctor Franklin and mr Adams interlined in their own hand writings." Five of these changes were credited to Franklin, two to Adams. "I then wrote a fair copy," Jefferson recalled, "reported it to the Committee, and from them unaltered to Congress."[32]

Specific edits by Sherman and Livingston never were identified.

Figure 9.1. A romanticized image of (l–r) Benjamin Franklin, John Adams, and Thomas Jefferson reviewing Jefferson's draft of the Declaration of Independence. Although Franklin and Adams helped edit the Declaration, there is no evidence that they met with Jefferson at the same time. *(Wikimedia Commons)*

The most famous of the early changes was "self-evident," which had been inserted in the preamble by the time of the Adams copy in mid-June. But another alternation that still resonates with modern-day Americans was the addition of a more profound religious component in the second paragraph. Human rights that originally were said to be granted "from that equal creation" now became rights that were "endowed by their Creator," a stronger and more spiritual assertion.[33]

There also was a seemingly random flip-flop of "inalienable" (in Jefferson's original version) and "unalienable" (in the Adams version). Both spellings of the word were acceptable in 1776.[34]

Jefferson was pleased with the result as the late June deadline approached, having considered and approved all the changes made by the committee. His next objective was to deliver the document to Congress by June 28, the last Friday of the month, giving members a full two days to review it before their scheduled vote on independence on Monday, July 1.

* * *

Delegate Samuel Chase of Maryland returned to the State House on June 11 after his unsuccessful trip to Canada with Franklin, but he did not remain in Philadelphia for long. He soon headed home to Annapolis to agitate for independence in one of the last two holdout colonies. John Adams wrote to Chase on June 17 to apply pressure from afar, informing him that the Delaware, Pennsylvania, and New Jersey delegations were now free to vote for independence, and that once-reticent New Jersey had chosen five new delegates to Congress, "all independant Souls."[35]

Maryland's assembly knew that Congress had set the vote for July 1, and that several of its own counties supported a break from England. Provincial leaders hoped to temporarily recall their delegates from Philadelphia for a brief convention, but not "without first having obtained an order that consideration of the questions of Independence, foreign alliance, and a further Confederation of Colonies" be postponed until they returned.[36] That request was promptly denied. "We should have been happy to have obliged your Convention and your Delegates," Adams told Chase, "[b]ut it is now become public in the Colonies that those Questions are to be brought on the first of July."[37]

It is now become public in the Colonies. Tension mounted, as Americans waited for a verdict on their future. Maryland relented on June 28, giving in to the irrepressible surge of momentum, announcing that it had withdrawn its old instructions and empowered its delegates "to concur with the other United Colonies, or a majority of them, in declaring the United Colonies free and independent States." Chase was so excited that he rushed out of the Annapolis meeting to send a note to Adams. "I am at this Moment from the House to procure an Express to follow the Post with an Unanimous Vote of our Convention for *Independence*, etc. etc.," he wrote. "See the glorious Effects of County Instructions. Our people have fire if not smothered. . . . *Now for a government.*"[38]

June 28 also marked the final formal meeting of Congress before the vote for independence. It began the day by approving payments of $750 and $117 to individual residents who provided lumber and plated iron for the war effort. It received the credentials for five new delegates from New Jersey and heard instructions to join in declaring the colonies "independent of Great Britain." It approved a report from the Board of War to build a fort on the Delaware River and handled several other administrative items on the agenda. Only then, after the obligatory daily business had been completed, did Jefferson step forward to present the historic document.

He brought a clean "fair copy" of the heavily edited rough draft for Congress to peruse. The official records address this event in the most matter-of-fact way possible, noting that "the committee appointed to prepare a declaration brought in a draught, which was read." Jefferson offered no more detail in his autobiography, writing only that "I reported it to the house on Friday the 28th of June when it was read and ordered to lie on the table."[39] No one ever recorded who read the draft to the delegates. Was it Jefferson? The author would have been an obvious choice, given his grasp of the issues and language, but Jefferson was a reluctant public speaker, even among colleagues and friends. Adams once called him "a silent member" of Congress and said he had "never spoken in public; during the whole Time I sat with him in Congress I never heard him utter three Sentences together."[40] The reader of the declaration that day must not have been Adams, because he never mentioned it in any of his later writings (and surely would have taken credit had he done it), and there is no evidence that Franklin even attended the June 28 session. Despite the impact of the moment we can never know for sure.

Moderates realized there was no turning back once this written proposal for breaking with England was officially introduced at the State House. New York was the only colony that had not given its delegates the freedom to vote for independence; the most they could hope for now was another delay to disrupt the process. On Saturday, June 29, an off-day for Congress, while some members took their first heart-pounding look at the committee draft, Edward Rutledge of South Carolina sent a desperate request to fellow moderate John Jay, who was attending the provincial congress in New York:

> I write this for the express Purpose of requesting that if possible you will give your Attendance in Congress on Monday next. I know full well that your Presence must be useful at New York, but I am sincerely convinced that it will be absolutely necessary in this City during the whole of the ensuing Week. A Declaration of Independence, the Form of a Confederation of these Colonies, and a Scheme for a Treaty with foreign Powers will be laid before the House on Monday. Whether we shall be able effectually to oppose the first, and infuse Wisdom into the others will depend in a great Measure upon the Exertions of the Honest and sensible part of the Members. I trust you will contribute in a considerable degree to Effect the business and therefore I wish you to be with us. . . . You must know the importance of these Questions too well not to wish to be present while they are debating.[41]

But Jay did not return, preferring to remain in New York and deal with matters there, including preliminary work on a new colonial constitution. The moderates were on their own. There would be no last-minute reinforcements as Rutledge, John Dickinson, and the others plotted their final, pertinacious stand.

CHAPTER 10

The Second of July

LEST ANYONE FORGET, THERE ALSO WAS A WAR GOING ON.

On June 28, the same day the committee laid its draft on independence before Congress, an advance guard of British ships was spotted off the coast of Long Island. These were the 113 vessels with nine thousand troops that had left Halifax under General William Howe three weeks earlier—the vanguard, as it turned out, of a full-fledged royal invasion. Another three thousand soldiers soon would sail north from Charleston, South Carolina (where they had attempted, unsuccessfully, to bomb that city into submission), and twenty thousand more were on the way from England on gun-laden ships of war under the command of Howe's brother, Admiral Richard Howe. Standing in opposition to this formidable armada was George Washington's raw and mostly undisciplined force of perhaps ten thousand.[1] "I am hopeful . . . that I should get some reinforcements," Washington wrote in a blatant hint to Hancock on June 29. "Be that as It may, I shall make the best disposition I can of our Troops in order to give them a proper reception, and to prevent the ruin and destruction they are meditating against us."[2]

Delegates to Congress knew their lives would be in danger if the British ever reached Philadelphia, but there was no sign of wavering as the July 1 vote approached. They had come too far and risked too much to turn back now. Private letters from two members of the North Carolina delegation, both written on June 28, offer rarely seen insight into this nerve-wracking period. John Penn predicted: "The first day of July will be remarkable; then the question relative to Independence will be ajitated

and there is no doubt but a total seperation from Britain will take place."
Joseph Hewes, a latecomer to the independence movement, added, "On
Monday the great question of Independancy and Total Seperation from
all political intercourse with Great Britain will come on; it will be carried
I expect by a great Majority and then I suppose we shall take upon us a
New Name."[3]

Perhaps more than any other delegate, John Adams felt the pressure
of what was about to take place. Early on the morning of July 1, he wrote
to a colleague in Georgia that the "greatest Debate of all" was going to be
held, and that "this day or Tomorrow is to determine its fate." Members
had time to examine Thomas Jefferson's draft over the weekend, reading
and digesting it for themselves, and one of them, Josiah Bartlett of New
Hampshire, judged the Declaration to be "a pretty good one." But Adams
knew there were holdouts on the moderate side, and it would take even
more persuasion before any ballots were cast.[4]

Given the impact of this vote on the country and the world, it is
astounding that Congress did not take up the topic immediately when
President John Hancock struck the gavel on July 1. The first order of
business involved a series of fourteen letters related to the war effort,
three of them from General Washington himself and two from Benedict Arnold. Delegates also approved a payment of $6,000 to a Virginia
resident for services rendered and heard instructions from the Maryland
convention, freeing its representatives to vote for independence. It was
probably sometime just before noon that they took into consideration
"the resolution concerning independency."[5]

Congress again resolved itself into a Committee of the Whole to
avoid a full account of the proceedings. It would be an informal debate,
with members encouraged to speak and disagree freely. As expected, John
Dickinson of Pennsylvania rose first to make a final, impassioned plea
for delay. Adams had described him on their first encounter in 1774 as
"a shadow; tall but slender as a reed; pale as ashes," and the look was
even more pronounced by the summer of 1776; however, Dickinson was
a worthy adversary, firm in his convictions, often unmoved by public
opinion. He spoke this day "with great Ingenuity and Eloquence," Adams
said, "and in a speech of great Length . . . he combined together all that

had been before written in Pamphlets and Newspapers and all that had from time to time been said in Congress by himself and others."[6]

Dickinson did not write out his speech, but two sets of notes he used for reference are preserved on six pages in the *Journals of the Continental Congress* (volume 5). They reveal a stubborn advocate for his cause who had reached the conclusion the cause was hopelessly doomed. "The Consequences involved in the Motion now lying before You are of such Magnitude that I tremble under the oppressive Honor of sharing in its Determination," he said. "My Conduct this Day, I expect, will give the finishing Blow to my once too great and . . . now too diminish'd Popularity."

Dickinson saw a dark future in binding "ourselves to an eternal Quarrel with [Great Britain] by a Declaration of Independence." He did not believe that aid from foreign powers was forthcoming, and without it any long-term resistance was futile. "The War will be carried on with more severity," he warned, "burning towns, letting loose Indians on the Frontiers." A better course would be to settle internal disputes over land boundaries and other matters before making a long-shot attempt at foreign aid. "Why not wait will [we are] better prepar'd?" Why move to destroy "a House before We have got another?" To do otherwise would be to "brave the Storm in a Skiff made of Paper."[7]

The room fell silent as Dickinson finished, resuming his seat with the Pennsylvania delegation. One can imagine him slumping in the chair, exhausted, seemingly resigned to defeat. Adams waited for someone else to take the floor, either in support or response, repeating the arguments that "had been repeated and hackneyed in that Room before a hundred Times," but all that followed was a long, uncomfortable pause. Sensing, finally, that there would be no other alternative, Adams himself rose to speak.[8]

Unlike Dickinson, he had no notes to guide him. The topic was so familiar, the emotion so engrained, that he could make his case without any formal preparation. Looking back on it years later, Adams recalled: "I began by saying that this was the first time of my Life that I had ever wished for the Talents and Eloquence of the ancient Orators of Greece and Rome, for I was very sure that none of them ever had before him a

Figure 10.1. John Dickinson. *(Wikimedia Commons)*

question of more Importance." He probably used a line from an earlier letter, saying, "We are in the midst of a Revolution, the most compleat, unexpected and remarkable of any in the History of Nations." He may have referenced the defiant preamble he wrote for Congress in mid-May. Nature added sound effects, with rain falling and thunder crashing outside. Then he, too, returned to his seat.

Unfortunately for Adams, the newly elected delegates from New Jersey did not reach the State House until the last moments of his speech. Unaware of all that had been said in Congress over the past six months, they asked him to repeat the arguments he had just made at length on the State House floor. Adams objected, saying he was not an actor or gladiator who entertained audiences, and an awkward stalemate ensued until Edward Rutledge intervened once again. The moderate member from South Carolina reminded Adams that no one else in Congress could match his passion, or his command of the facts on independence. Relenting, finally, out of respect, Adams "summed up the Reasons, Objections and Answers, in as concise a manner as I could, till all the New Jersey Gentlemen said they were satisfied."[9]

Other delegates then stood to speak in response, although no record was made of what was said, or by whom (they were still resolved into a Committee of the Whole). Scholars have determined that the debate lasted for "nine hours without interruption" until a straw vote was taken to gauge the mood. Proceeding by candlelight in the darkness—adding a surreal, almost mystical backdrop—each delegation polled its members. The format called for one vote per colony.[10]

To the surprise of many, four of the thirteen colonies still did not support independence. The preliminary tally was 9–2–1–1—nine for, two against, one deadlocked, and one abstaining. Had it been official, the resolution would have passed comfortably, overwhelmingly—*nine* clocks striking at once—but it was not the united front they hoped to project.

New York's delegation had yet to receive new instructions, so its abstention was fully expected, and understood. But South Carolina and Pennsylvania were still stubbornly in the "no" column, and little Delaware was deadlocked, unable to vote one way or the other.[11]

The Pennsylvania vote was especially intriguing—four delegates against the resolution and three in support. Dickinson was joined by fellow moderates Robert Morris, Thomas Willing, and Charles Humphreys in casting the "no" ballots. Voting for the measure were Benjamin Franklin, John Morton, and, surprisingly, the heretofore moderate James Wilson. Wilson, a longtime Dickinson ally, had spoken harshly against independence in the June 8–10 debates. Now, against all odds, he had switched sides.[12]

South Carolina seemed firm in its opposition, with Rutledge at the helm. Empowered to vote for independence by his assembly back home, he nonetheless wrote in early June that "[n]o Reason could be assigned for pressing into this Measure, but the Reason of every Madman, a [show] of our Spirit."[13] But Rutledge *had* intervened with Adams on New Jersey's behalf earlier in the day, and some thought this was a sign that he was softening under pressure. It was, at the very least, a glint of hope.

Delaware's case was even more promising. Its two-man delegation had split the vote—Thomas McKean for, George Read against—but a third member, Caesar Rodney, who supported independence, was said to be riding the eighty miles from Dover on horseback through the night, determined to be in Philadelphia the next morning.[14]

The tension at the State House was thick, unyielding. Adams paced and wiped his brow. What should they do now? As delegates huddled in small groups, debating options, it was Rutledge who put the "country" first and found a solution. "Mr. Rutledge of S. Carolina then requested the determination might be put off to the next day," Jefferson wrote, "as he believed his colleagues, tho' they disapproved of the resolution, would then join in it for the sake of unanimity."[15]

It would have been unthinkable even one day earlier: Rutledge, the last-minute hero of independence.

They were not there yet, but they were getting closer.

* * *

The official congressional records of Tuesday, July 2, 1776, are almost comically benign.

Delegates reviewed four letters from military officers, one from the council of Massachusetts Bay, and one from the paymaster general on weekly accounting matters.

When the great resolution on American independence was introduced at about mid-morning, Congress reported only that it was "agreed to."

Agreed to!

Record-keepers at least had the good sense to include the first sentence of Richard Henry Lee's proposal from June 7, that "these United Colonies" were now "Free and Independent States," and all political connections between them and Great Britain were now "totally dissolved." But their small piece of earth-shattering news was sandwiched in among other daily business, as though they were trying to hide it. No explanation was given. No mention of the vote was made.[16]

Fortunately for history, Adams, Jefferson, Thomas McKean, and others fleshed out the details over time.

The first delegates to arrive at the State House that morning noticed two empty chairs at the Pennsylvania table—chairs where John

Dickinson and Robert Morris usually held court. What could it possibly mean? Were those two moderate leaders *not going to vote?*[17]

Shortly after Hancock called the meeting to order, Caesar Rodney came bursting through the State House door in mud-spattered boots and spurs, after riding all night through the rain. Once described by John Adams as "the oddest-looking man in the world . . . tall, thin and slender as a reed," Rodney was a welcome sight to the radical faction when he took the third seat at Delaware's table.[18]

Back now in a full legislative session, the delegates readied their votes as Secretary Charles Thomson called the role.

As expected, the same nine colonies who supported independence on July 1—Connecticut, Georgia, Maryland, Massachusetts, New Hampshire, New Jersey, North Carolina, Pennsylvania, and Rhode

Figure 10.2. The Assembly Room at the Pennsylvania State House (now Independence Hall), where Congress voted for independence, then edited, approved, and signed the Declaration. *(Author photo)*

Island—were back in the "yes" column on July 2. But that is where the similarities ended.

Delaware broke its deadlock when Rodney cast the decisive vote. South Carolina did a complete about-face, following Rutledge's lead in the quest for unanimity. Pennsylvania changed course with the surprising voluntary absences of Dickinson and Morris, who decided it was no longer prudent to impede progress and stayed home. Even with New York abstaining, the final tally for independence was 12–0–1.[19]

And so it was finished, the deed done, history made. Implausible as it many have seemed only one day earlier, twelve of the thirteen clocks had struck at precisely the same time.[20]

Delegates who led the way deserved a moment to reflect on what they accomplished, perhaps even to celebrate, but Adams and his colleagues knew there was no time for frivolity; toasts at the City Tavern would have to wait. The official records said they began at once to review the "declaration on independence," but, after a few hours, lacking the time to assess it fully, they postponed that work for one more day. Congress closed by approving disciplinary action against two officers by the Marine Committee before adjourning until 9:00 a.m. on July 3.[21]

There was no plan for a public announcement about the vote on independence, but word leaked out almost immediately. The *Pennsylvania Evening Post* rushed the unexpected late-breaking news onto the fourth and final page of its July 2 edition, inserting one sentence below a military recruiting notice and just above an advertisement offering two ships for sale. Without the benefit of a headline, it reported the following: "This day the CONTINENTAL CONGRESS declared the UNITED COLONIES FREE and INDEPENDENT STATES." A young artist named Charles Willson Peale was one of many to record it word for word in his diary. Delegate Elbridge Gerry of Massachusetts wrote to a colleague back home that "the Facts are as well known at the Coffee House of the City as in Congress," and as if to prove that point, the *Pennsylvania Gazette* published news of the vote on July 3 (albeit in a one-sentence item on page 2, noting that it had happened "yesterday").[22]

The self-imposed vow of secrecy at the State House was being ignored by some members, and no one defied the policy more than John

Adams, who, on July 3, sent two letters of remarkable detail to his wife, Abigail, in Massachusetts.

"Yesterday the greatest Question was decided which ever was debated in America, and a greater perhaps never was or will be decided among Men," he wrote in the first letter. "A Resolution was passed without one dissenting Colony. . . . It is the Will of Heaven that that two Countries should be sundered forever. . . . You will see in a few days a Declaration setting forth the Causes which have impell'd Us to this mighty Revolution, and the Reasons which will justify it in the Sight of God and Man."[23]

Adams took a brief pause to collect his thoughts before picking up his pen again. His second letter included an eerily prescient prediction of how Americans of the future would celebrate their independence:

> The Second Day of July 1776 will be the most memorable Epocha in the history of America. I am apt to believe it will be celebrated by succeeding Generations as the great anniversary Festival. It ought to be commemorated as the Day of Deliverance by Acts of Devotion to God Almighty. It ought to be solemnized with Pomp and Parade, with Shews, Games, Sports, Guns, Bells, Bonfires and Illuminations from one End of this Continent to the other from this Time forward forever more.[24]

* * *

There was another, more disturbing development on July 2. Many more British ships reached the waterways around New York, threatening the very independence that Congress had just approved.

Washington wrote Hancock to confirm that it was the remainder of Howe's fleet from Halifax, now totaling more than one hundred ships in all. On the evening of July 2, he said, "fifty of them came up the Bay and Anchored on the Staten Island side." Washington could not be sure of their intentions but was "extremely apprehensive" that they might round up livestock and supplies in an effort to "ravage that part of the country." He begged Hancock to solicit the state militias for more troops.[25]

Congress had been worried enough about the military situation to take action of its own, even before receiving Washington's update. It instructed the Committee of Safety in Pennsylvania to send as many troops as could be spared to Monmouth County in New Jersey, and asked several Pennsylvania counties to send "batallions and companies as fast as raised" to Philadelphia, which soon might be a target of attack. Similar requests went out to Maryland and Delaware for militia reinforcements at multiple sites. Pennsylvania also was asked to ship a supply of flints for rifles to the troops defending New York.[26]

Washington at this point had never led his inexperienced army in combat (he was not yet present at Bunker Hill, and the year-long defense of Boston was a siege). But he sensed that they were rattled by the presence of enemy troops nearby, and a word from their commander might help rouse passion and stiffen resolve. Accordingly, although he had not yet heard Congress's decision on independence, he took it upon himself to issue his own declaration on July 2, under the bland title of "General Orders," one of the great, if overshadowed, documents of the revolutionary era.

Washington wrote:

> The time is now near at hand which must probably determine whether Americans are to be Freemen or Slaves. . . . The fate of unborn Millions will now depend, under God, on the Courage and Conduct of this army—Our cruel and unrelenting Enemy leaves us no choice but a brave resistance, or the most abject submission; this is all we can expect—We can therefore resolve to conquer or die. . . . The Eyes of all our Countrymen are now upon us, and we shall have their blessings, and praises, if happily we are the instruments of saving them from the Tyranny mediated against them. Let us therefore animate and encourage each other, and shew the whole world that a Freeman contending for Liberty on his own ground is superior to any slavish mercenary on earth.[27]

That same day, five British warships approached American forts on a probing mission, keeping their distance but projecting massive power. Washington was confident that General Howe would wait for the arrival of his brother's fleet from England before organizing an attack, but he was proud to see "an agreeable spirt and willingness for Action seem to animate and pervade the whole of our Troops." His men had raced to their posts in an encouraging show of defiance. Within a day or two, the Congress in Philadelphia would give them even more motivation.[28]

* * *

Beginning in the afternoon of July 2, delegates spent parts of the next three days editing the draft of the Declaration submitted by the committee.

Most of the work took place on Wednesday, July 3, when the largest block of time was set aside for that purpose, but even then, Congress addressed six other business matters before resolving again into a Committee of the Whole for "farther consideration" of the document.[29]

It was an astonishing feat of group editing, achieved under immense pressure by strong-willed men with distinct, often-divergent views. The committee had made forty-seven changes to the original language before submitting its draft to Congress, but those were relatively minor tweaks of language, and were agreed to, or at least accepted by, Jefferson. The full body of delegates took a harsher editing approach. They made another thirty-nine revisions, removing or altering about 20 percent of the draft and shortening it by about four hundred words.

Jefferson was beside himself, but that was the natural pride of a writer shining through; most scholars believe that Congress improved the draft. He had, after all, written with uncommon haste for such a weighty document, completing his first draft within a few days. This also was at a time when he preferred to be back in Virginia, working on that colony's constitution, which he considered to be "the whole object of the present controversy." The declaration assignment had been something of consolation prize.[30]

No one knows which delegates spoke up during the editing process, or who was responsible for the changes; no credit ever was given. They were understandably gentle with the first two paragraphs but still made a few small edits to the legendary preamble. The phrase "inherent and inalienable rights" became "certain inalienable rights" (soon changed to "unalienable," perhaps inadvertently by the printer, since both forms of the word were acceptable). Excess language was deleted in several places. Also in this section, "expunge" was changed to "alter" and "unremitting" injuries and usurpations became "repeated" injuries and usurpations. The editors were serious about examining every sentence, every word, which is why the process lasted through the morning of July 4. It was so precise that, at one point, "neglected utterly" became "utterly neglected."[31]

On several occasions, Congress softened Jefferson's most extreme charges, knowing that they would be reviewed and critiqued by "a candid world." Pointed phrases such as "a faith yet unsullied by falsehood" did not survive to the final version. And yet with one of his rants against the king, the delegates made the language even stronger, more damning. Whereas Jefferson complained that George III was transporting large armies of foreign mercenaries to "complete acts of death, desolation and tyranny," Congress added that it was "scarcely paralleled in the most barbarous ages" and "totally" unworthy of the head of a civilized nation.[32]

The two biggest and most controversial changes came near the end of the document. No serious observer could give credence to Jefferson's ridiculous claim that King George III was responsible for the Atlantic slave trade, laid out in a fierce diatribe of 261 words. Almost all of it was deleted; the only vague reference to Black slavery in the final version was a seven-word sentence about "domestic insurrections." Congress also could not endorse Jefferson's long, rambling, vindictive paragraph about their ancestral "British brethren," keeping some elements but cutting it by more than half, from 348 words to 117.[33]

The delegates *did* manage to include a reference to Lord Dunmore's slave uprising, but they camouflaged it by jamming two racially charged grievances into one. The king, they said, "has excited domestic insurrections among us, and has endeavoured to bring on the inhabitants of our frontiers, the merciless Indian Savages, whose known rule of warfare is an undistinguished destruction of all ages, sexes and conditions."[34]

Jefferson never could understand why his passage on the slave trade was omitted. Writing years later, he was only too happy to review the matter and spread the blame around. The main culprits, he said, were the colonies of "South Carolina and Georgia," who never restrained their importation of slaves, and, in fact, wanted that commerce to continue. But he also assailed "our northern brethren," who owned relatively few slaves yet "felt a little tender under those censures" because they "had been pretty considerable carriers of them to others."[35] Adams, a strident opponent of slavery, thought that Jefferson's attack on the slave trade was a possible first step on the road to abolition. He was "delighted" with Jefferson's draft, "especially that concerning Negro Slavery, which though I knew his Southern Brethren would never suffer to pass in Congress, I certainly would never oppose."[36]

But this was not the time. The delegates' goal was to declare independence, and if a true debate over slavery would impede that progress, Adams and the others would put it aside for another day. They also knew that any direct mention in their nation's inaugural document would be mocked in England and across the world for its naked hypocrisy. So out it went.

Congress was more measured in its work on the penultimate paragraph about the British people. While cutting some of Jefferson's most outlandish allegations, including that America was settled without any help from Great Britain, it preserved the sharp tone of others. The British had tried, through repeated acts of their legislatures, "to extend an unwarrantable jurisdiction over us" and remained stubbornly "deaf to the voice of justice and consanguinity." As a result, despite the ties of "our common kindred," Americans were left with no other option than to "hold them, as we hold the rest of mankind, Enemies in War, in Peace Friends."[37]

That brought them at long last to the decisive final paragraph, where they would tie it all together and declare independence. Much of Jefferson's language and all of his spirit were preserved in the final version. The delegates insisted, however, that the precise wording of Richard Henry Lee's resolution be included, providing vital context in their announcement to the world: "That these United Colonies are, and of right ought to be, free and independent States, that they are absolved from all allegiance to the British Crown, and that all political connection between them and the State of Great Britain, is and ought to be totally dissolved." It was only at that point that they could sit back for a moment and admire their splendid handiwork.

All but Jefferson, that is. He was despondent.

No writer likes to be edited in private, much less in a cacophonous group setting, where every point is analyzed and debated. Jefferson believed that they had impaired his work and weakened it considerably, especially the passages about the slave trade and the British people. "The pusillanimous idea that we had friends in England worth keeping terms with still haunted the minds of many," he wrote, bitterly. "For this reason those passages which conveyed censures on the people of England were struck out, lest they should give them offence."[38]

Jefferson's agony was apparent to all, especially Benjamin Franklin, the oldest member of Congress, who was sitting next to him and "perceived that I was not insensible to these mutilations." Franklin tried to cheer him up with a fanciful story from his past. Years ago, a friend who was a hat-maker had made a sign for his new shop, announcing, "John Thompson, Hatter, makes and sells hats for ready money," with a small drawing of a hat. When Thompson asked friends for their advice, however, each suggested removing a word or phrase for clarity until all that remained was the name "John Thompson" and the image of the hat. The lesson, Franklin said, was that while editing can be painful, it is always necessary and often useful. Jefferson gritted his teeth and nodded (although he stubbornly sent several copies of the committee's draft to friends, always believing it to be superior).[39]

Many others knew that Congress did exceptional work, taking a draft that was already a "pretty good one" and making it better, clearer, more defensible. To do so while British troops were pouring into New York, hoping to destroy the Continental army and march on Philadelphia, made it all the more remarkable. "It is difficult to imagine any modern-day legislature performing an editing task of this magnitude and scope," wrote historian Joseph Ellis, "and it is impossible to imagine it being done as well."[40] As had become its custom, however, Congress made a most understated entry in the official records. The secretary wrote only that "[t]he Declaration being read again, was agreed to."

If a formal vote was taken, no one mentioned it. It was almost as though they felt the serious business had happened two days earlier, on July 2, when they passed Lee's resolution on independence.[41]

Multiple delegates wrote letters about the voting on July 1 and 2, but it is curious that only two of them mentioned independence in letters on July 4. Abraham Clark of New Jersey said he had no news and only touched on the possibility that they would support "the Declaration now on the Anvil." It was left to Caesar Rodney of Delaware to break the code of silence, announcing in a letter to his brother: "We have now Got through with the Whole of the declaration and Ordered it to be printed, so that You will soon have the pleasure of seeing it."[42]

Adding to the mystery, no one recorded exactly what time the Declaration was approved on July 4. Jefferson later said it was "in the evening," but the general consensus of scholars is that it happened in the late morning, which is confirmed, at least circumstantially, by the official records. There were sixteen other points of business that day listed *after* the Declaration was passed.

One of them tasked the drafting committee with having the document printed. Indeed, once a clean "fair copy" of the edited Declaration was written out by hand, Adams and the others had it delivered that evening to John Dunlap's print shop at the corner of Second and Market Streets, with an order for several hundred printed copies.[43]

CHAPTER 11

The Ninth of July

THE PROPRIETOR OF THE UNOBTRUSIVE PRINT SHOP A FEW BLOCKS from the State House was no stranger to the revolution.

John Dunlap was a founding member of the First Troop of Philadelphia City Cavalry in 1774 and went on to serve with his unit (under Washington, no less) in the battles of Trenton and Princeton. But it was at his print shop, not on the battlefield, that the Irish immigrant found his way into American history, setting the type and printing the first several hundred copies of the Declaration of Independence on the night of July 4, 1776.[1]

It is not known who wrote out the fresh, updated copy that Dunlap used as his guide. Perhaps it was the congressional secretary, Charles Thomson, or his assistant, Timothy Matlack, who had outstanding penmanship, but it had to be done very quickly, after three days of heavy editing. Regrettably, that copy has not survived. Dunlap worked diligently overnight and into the morning of July 5, producing an estimated two hundred broadside prints of a document titled "A DECLARATION by the REPRESENTATIVES of the UNITED STATES OF AMERICA, in GENERAL CONGRESS assembled." A line added at the top of the page read "IN CONGRESS, July 4, 1776," enshrining that date in the minds of Americans for all time. (Twenty-six of these original "Dunlap broadsides" are known to exist.)[2]

This earliest printed version of the Declaration was not *hand-signed* by anyone, despite enduring myths to the contrary. Confusion has arisen over the years because the bottom of the document said it was "Signed by ORDER and in BEHALF of the Congress," but that is followed only by the typeset names of President John Hancock and Secretary Thomson. Even after making the decisive break from England, the full body still was taking matters deliberately—one step at a time.[3]

Their next task was to go public with the news. Indeed, one of the last acts of the editing process called for Congress to "solemnly PUBLISH and DECLARE" independence on behalf of "the good People of these Colonies." Members arranged for printed copies of the Declaration to be sent to colonial assemblies, conventions, committees, and counsels of safety, asking that it be proclaimed "in each of the United States, and at the head of the army" in as timely a manner as possible. But the limits of eighteenth-century communication meant it would take days and probably weeks to reach governments as far away as New Hampshire and Georgia.[4]

Hancock composed letters to the various state leaders on July 5 and 6. He tweaked some of the wording as he went, often to address a specific local issue, but the letter he sent to the New Jersey Convention on July 5 was fairly representative of his message, and it included the following passage:

> I do myself the Honour to enclose, in Obedience to the Commands of Congress, a copy of the Declaration of Independence, which you will please to have proclaimed in your Colony, in such Way and Manner as you shall judge best. The important Consequences resulting to the American States from this Declaration of Independence, considered as the Ground & Foundation of a future Government, will naturally suggest the Propriety of proclaiming it in such a Mode, as that the People may be universally informed of it.[5]

Two members of Congress also sent letters of their own, probably without Hancock's knowledge. New Jersey delegate Abraham Clark wrote to a commander in the state's militia: "I enclose a Declaration of Congress, which is directed to be Published in all the Colonies, and Armies, and which I make no doubt you will Publish in your Brigade." Loose-lipped Elbridge Gerry of Massachusetts, always eager to be the bearer of good

Figure 11.1. John Dunlap of Philadelphia printed the first version of the Declaration of Independence on July 4–5, 1776. Copies of these "Dunlap broadsides" were sent to General George Washington and each of the state assemblies, informing Americans that the break had been made. *(Wikimedia Commons)*

news, told a colleague back home: "I have the pleasure to inform you that a determined resolution of the delegates of some of the colonies to push the question of independency has had a most happy effect." Gerry reported that New York's delegation had abstained but predicted it would soon come around to make the vote unanimous.[6]

Additional letters went out from Hancock on July 6, including one to army headquarters that was the most important of all. Continental soldiers had been serving for more than a year with no objective beyond the vague and uninspiring "restoration of rights within the empire." The Declaration of Independence turned what had been a second-rate civil war into a major international conflict that raised the possibility of a new world order, but only if they could be successful in defeating the powerful British in battle. Addressing General Washington in New York, Hancock wrote, in part:

> The Congress, for some Time past, have had their Attention occupied by one of the most interesting and important Subjects that could possibly come before them, or any other Assembly of Men. . . .
>
> [F]ully convinced that our Affairs may take a more favourable Turn, the Congress have judged it necessary to dissolve the Connection between Great Britain and the American Colonies, and to declare them free and independent States; as you will perceive by the enclosed Declaration, which I am directed to transmit to you, and to request you will have it proclaimed at the Head of the Army.

Hancock added that they were sending ten thousand flints for muskets from the Pennsylvania Committee of Safety and reminded Washington that militia troops from Pennsylvania, Delaware, and Maryland were on their way to the New York area, where British forces were gathering.[7]

Even in the glow of independence—barely two days after it had been declared in print for the first time, thanks to Dunlap—Congress was unremittingly focused on the war.

* * *

The first residents of Philadelphia to learn that the Declaration had been approved and printed were the few readers of the German-language *Pennsylvanischer Staatsbote* on July 5. The dominant English-language newspapers in the city did not publish on Fridays, creating an opening for *Staatsbote*'s publisher, Heinrich Miller, a fierce advocate of colonial rights. The paper's translated account read that "[y]esterday the honorable

Continental Congress declared the United Colonies free and independent states. The declaration is now in press in English; it is dated July 4, 1776, and will be published today or tomorrow."[8]

The *Pennsylvania Evening Post* remained a step ahead of its other competitors by publishing the first full copy of the Declaration in its July 6 edition. The text took up all of the front page and part of the second, but it appeared without any introduction or context, and was followed immediately by advertisements for the sale of two ships and a "[q]uantity of very fine TIMOTHY HAY . . . A FEW Hogsheads and Barrels of JAMAICA SUGAR of the best quality." Rival Philadelphia newspapers, including Dunlap's, followed with their own copies over the next few days.[9]

Congress scheduled the first formal public reading for July 8 at the State House Yard. It was election day for the new Provincial Convention, ensuring that a boisterous crowd of politically active patriots would be milling about the city.[10] One paper, *Dunlap's and Claypool's American Daily Advertiser*, ran an announcement in large type that morning that "THIS DAY at Twelve o'clock the DECLARATION of INDEPENDENCE will be PROCLAIMED at the State House," and news spread quickly by word of mouth. The timing coincided with the congressional lunch break, no doubt by design, giving John Adams and others a chance to witness a surreal revolutionary scene.

Colonel John Nixon of the Pennsylvania Committee of Safety had the honor of reading the Declaration from a wooden stage at the back of the building. *Dunlap's Maryland Gazette* reported that dignitaries "went in procession to the State-House, where the Declaration of Independency of the UNITED STATES of AMERICA was read to a very large number of inhabitants of the city and county, which was received with general applause and heart-felt satisfaction." Adams noted that militia battalions paraded on the common and fired a celebratory salute of thirteen guns, while "the Bells rung all day, and almost all night. Even the Chimers, Chimed away." Supporters celebrated the news by ripping down royal imagery from public places and throwing the king's coat of arms into a bonfire.[11]

(Several historians believe that there actually was an earlier public reading of the Declaration on July 4, the same day it was approved—in the State House Yard, no less—but those accounts are based on three sources who wrote or spoke from memory many years after the fact. One was a boy who was ten years old in 1776 and another was a girl who was fourteen. A third mention is found in one paragraph of a 423-page autobiography by Charles Biddle, a Pennsylvania statesman who served in the revolution, although his grandson, who edited and published the book in 1883, said that Biddle, too, had "written from memory" and that it was probably done "not earlier than 1802." Two of these accounts reported that "very few respectable people" were present near the State House that day, leading some to believe that it was not the same event as July 8. But it is difficult to fathom that a July 4 public reading of the Declaration of Independence would not appear in any letters or diaries in summer 1776, would not be mentioned by any members of Congress, and would not be reported by any of the competitive Philadelphia newspapers. While the possibility of an earlier reading cannot be discounted, it is likely that those reports from memory are part of the "golden haze" that came to surround the Declaration in later years—the notion that everything of importance happened on the Fourth of July.)[12]

There also were public readings on July 8 in the nearby cities of Easton, Pennsylvania, and Trenton, New Jersey, proof that Hancock's letters from three days earlier had spurred local officials to action. The Easton ceremony was led by a handsomely dressed column of local militia marching with "drums beating and fifes playing," while a large group of spectators "gave their hearty assent with three loud huzzas." At Trenton, the Declaration was followed by a reading of the state's new constitution to loud acclaim. A local newspaper reported that "the people are now convinced of what we ought long since to have known, that our enemies have left us no middle way between perfect freedom and abject slavery."[13]

It is both curious and noteworthy that the most muted response during this period came from Thomas Jefferson himself. Still smarting about massive edits to the draft he submitted to Congress, Jefferson made a clean copy of his work "as originally framed" and sent it to Richard

Henry Lee in Virginia, along with the final edited version. "You will judge whether it is the better or worse for the critics," he wrote. (Perhaps to appease his colleague, Lee replied two weeks later, saying, "I wish, sincerely, as for the honor of Congress, as for that of the States, that the Manuscript had not been mangled as it is"). While most Americans applauded the official congressional product, Jefferson always believed that his work was better and continued to write about it well into the 1800s.[14]

Congress also faced the challenge of alerting foreign governments about the historic break. It was especially crucial to get word to France, a British nemesis and the most likely potential ally. The Secret Committee of Correspondence, led by Benjamin Franklin and Robert Morris, composed a letter on July 8 to its agent in Paris, accompanied by the first copy of the Declaration to be sent across the ocean. Another congressional committee would soon recommend a treaty of mutual commerce between the two countries, but the Court of France first had to be formally informed that the colonies had split from England and King George III. Franklin and Morris wrote:

> With this you will receive the Declaration of the Congress for a final separation from Great Britain. It was the universal demand of the people, justly exasperated by the obstinate perseverance of the Crown in its tyrannical and destructive measures, and the Congress were very unanimous in complying with that demand. You will immediately communicate the piece to the Court of France, and send copies of it to the other Courts of Europe. It may be well also to procure a good translation of it into French, and get it published in the Gazettes.[15]

The letter was lost at sea before it could be delivered, and a follow-up attempt would not arrive in Paris until mid-November, when news of the Declaration was already well known from newspaper reports, but it offers a tantalizing window into congressional thinking in the frantic and unprecedented days of early July.[16]

* * *

The vote for independence on July 2 had not been unanimous because New York's delegation abstained—still waiting for instructions from its new colonial assembly.

That situation changed a week later, after the assembly had moved under pressure to White Plains, about thirty miles from New York City.

The sight of British ships off Staten Island jangled nerves and caused a panic. Assembly members called a recess on June 30 and did not reconvene at their new site until July 9. New York's delegates in Philadelphia did not know this when they sent an urgent letter on the morning of July 2, reporting that "[t]he important Question of Independency was agitated yesterday" and was to be decided that day at the State House. They wanted to know how to respond if the vote went overwhelmingly for independence:

> Difficulties . . . will arise should Independency be declared . . . every Colony (ours only excepted) having withdrawn their former instructions, and either positively instructed their Delegates to vote for Independency; or concur in such a vote if they should find it expedient. . . . We wish therefore for your earliest Advice and Instructions whether we are to consider our Colony bound by the Vote of the Majority in Favour of Independency.[17]

By July 9, however, Hancock's letter announcing the Declaration had arrived and superseded it; independence had been declared, supported by every colony but one. The provincial body knew it was time for action, racing through some obligatory housekeeping matters before referring the Declaration to a five-man committee led by John Jay. Jay had long been a moderate voice, both at home and in Philadelphia, seeking some sort of reasonable reconciliation with England, but he and his committee knew they had no other option but to approve, especially now with British troops poised to strike New York. By early afternoon they recommended its adoption.[18]

Jay wrote the formal resolution, dated July 9 in the name of the "Convention of the Representatives of the State of New York." Its tone was more dutiful than celebratory, hedged with regret and differing in style from all the others. "While we lament the cruel necessity which has rendered that measure unavoidable," he wrote, "we approve the same, and will, at the risque of our lives and fortunes, join with the other colonies in supporting it." The updated vote made it 13–0 for independence, achieving the desired unanimity, even if it was a few days late.[19] (Centuries later, in 1996, an official of the New York Historical Society told the *New York Times* "we don't really belong with that group on the Fourth" when promoting an exhibit titled *July 9, 1776: New York's Independence Day*.)[20]

But not all New Yorkers supported the new stance. Chief among the naysayers was a loyalist delegate to Congress, John Aslop, who fired off a bitter response when word of the July 9 resolution reached Philadelphia a week later. "As long as the door was left open for a reconciliation with Great Britain," Aslop wrote, he was willing to work to achieve that end. "But as you have . . . by that declaration closed the door of reconciliation, I must beg leave." Undaunted, the New York assembly accepted his resignation and moved on.[21]

July 9 also was the day that Washington had the Declaration read to his troops in New York. It was a transformative moment for the army, changing its role from a mere defense of rights to an all-out war for American independence. Strangely enough, Washington's daily list of orders began with a report that two deserters would receive thirty-nine lashes, followed by news that Congress had approved one chaplain for each of the army's regiments. In the fifth paragraph he got around to announcing that the Declaration would be read at 6:00 p.m. "with an audible voice" before several brigades assembled on the Commons.[22]

Washington expected the reaction to be electric, and it was—in part because, as one officer said, British soldiers were "constantly in view, upon and at Staten Island." The general thought it served as "fresh incentive to every officer, and soldier, to act with Fidelity and Courage, as knowing that now the peace and safety of his Country depends . . . solely on the success of our arms." Cheers rang out as residents joined clamorous soldiers in a triumphant march down Broadway, creating a public spectacle. At Bowling Green, the massive equestrian statue of King George III was violently yanked from its pedestal and "laid prostrate in the dirt" according to one newspaper account, "the just dessert of an ungrateful tyrant." Shattered pieces of lead were gathered up and made into bullets for the army, in the hope that they would one day "assimilate with the brains of our infatuated adversaries."[23]

The rarely celebrated "Ninth of July" had changed New York for all time.

* * *

Back in Philadelphia, the work of political revolution continued.

Congress still had to deliver on the two other goals of the June 7 motion for independence: forming foreign alliances and creating a plan of confederation among the colonies. Committees had been working since mid-June, digging into the complex, often confounding details. It did not take long for members to learn that the gallant, exhilarating act of declaring independence was only the beginning of the long, pockmarked road toward nationhood. Starting on July 2 and confirmed on July 4, they were faced with the even more challenging task of building a new government from scratch.[24]

John Adams described the scene in a typically rambunctious letter to his wife on July 11. He wrote that Congress was daily "employed in political Regulations, forming the Sentiments of the People of the Colonies into some consistent System, extinguishing the Remainders of Authority under the Crown . . . gradually erecting and strengthening governments . . . turning their Thoughts upon the Principles of Polity and the Forms of Government . . . and [framing] a limited and defined Confederacy for the united Colonies." It was hectic, exhausting work, with barely a moment to rest and none at all to reflect. Adams thought of asking for a leave of absence, but he knew there were still too many issues after only nine days of independence. What form would their government take? When, and exactly where, would the British military strike? How would foreign governments react to the Declaration?

Adams stayed.[25]

The committee on confederation delivered a draft to Congress on July 12, titled the "Articles of Confederation and Perpetual Union." It would take more than a year for the articles to be debated and approved, and almost five years until they were ratified by the states, but the foundation of this first organized U.S. government was laid during this period in early July 1776. Regrettably (again), we do not know exactly how the process unfolded. Scant evidence is available beyond several early drafts of the articles by John Dickinson; brief mentions in letters by committee members Josiah Bartlett and Edward Rutledge; and one entry in Dickinson's notes for his July 1 speech on independence at the State House. Scholars believe, however, that most of the substantial writing was done between June 12 and July 1, at which point the more pressing issue of the vote on independence took over.[26]

The job before them—forging a governmental union that was acceptable to all thirteen colonies—could not be easily achieved. Bartlett wrote as early as June 17 that "some difficulties have arisen" and "I fear it will take some time before it will finally be settled." Rutledge thought the early draft would not pass without substantial revisions and decried "the Idea of destroying all Provincial Distinctions, making everything . . . bend to what they call the good of the whole." Specifically, he feared the dominance of New England states. Dickinson, for his part, complained that "the Committee on Confederation dispute almost every Article—some of us totally despair of any reasonable Terms of Confederation."[27]

Their work was interrupted for several days by the vote on independence, but Jefferson picked up the story in his notes a few weeks later. After the draft was submitted on July 12, Congress resolved itself into a Committee of the Whole on July 22 to take it "under consideration." Heated debates were held over a number of months, including whether each state should have one vote on legislation, or whether voting should be done proportionally, by population (it ended up being one vote per state). Clashes over many other issues were fiercely contested and took more than a year to resolve. A final edited version was not approved by Congress until November 15, 1777, and the Articles of Confederation were not ratified by the states until March 1, 1781, creating the first true national government in American history. But the crucial early work had been done in June and July 1776, when the thought of independence was fresh and raw.[28]

Adams led the way on the other key goal of the June 7 motion, "to take the most effectual measures for forming foreign alliances." It had been part of his to-do list as far back as February, when he listed as "an Alliance to be formed with France and Spain" as one of his objectives for the year. By April he had narrowed the focus to France, a longtime British rival still reeling from its loss in the French and Indian War. Adams thought a well-defined treaty of commerce "would admit France into an equal participation of the benefits of our commerce; would encourage her Manufactures, increase her Exports of the Produce of her Soil . . . [and] raise her from her present deep humiliation, distress and decay." That, in his mind, would be ample compensation for acknowledging America's independence on the world stage.[29]

Franklin, Dickinson, and Morris were members of the committee, but it was Adams who single-handedly set the course of American diplomacy for the next century. At this early stage of nationhood, he wanted nothing more than a commercial alliance, with no military or diplomatic ties. Sensitive to committing too much, too soon, Adams feared that a more wide-ranging agreement "might embarrass Us in after times and involve Us in future European Wars." Although that would change out of necessity in the near future, it was the backbone of the proposal he placed before Congress late that summer.[30]

His "Plan of Treaties" was submitted to Congress on July 18 and was approved, with only limited revisions, on September 17, as a model of early legislative success.[31]

* * *

It was less than two weeks after the vote for independence that Lord Richard Howe's massive fleet with twenty thousand men arrived in Long Island Sound. Howe's July 12 landing tempered American euphoria just as it was spreading to other colonies.

Determined to flaunt his naval superiority, Howe sent two ships sailing up the Hudson River past overmatched and under-drilled U.S. defenses in a teasing, defiant show of strength. He knew that once he teamed up with his brother, General William Howe, and welcomed some other arrivals, they would have a force of more than thirty thousand British regulars and Hessian hired hands to petrify the ragged continentals.[32]

Surely, Lord Howe thought, Washington saw the folly of further resistance.

That explains a letter he wrote on July 13 announcing that he and his brother had been named peace commissioners by King George III. It was Howe's way of offering Washington a path to end their awkward war. "I trust that a dispassionate consideration of the King's benevolent intentions may be the means of preventing the further Effusion of Blood," he wrote, "and become productive of Peace and lasting Union between Great Britain and America." Howe suggested that they meet in person "as near to the Town of New York as will be most for your accommodation."[33]

The tone was consistent with the Howe brothers' long-held view of American colonists; they did not despise them, or even consider them as enemies (at least at first). Both men supported colonial liberties while serving in Parliament before the war, and the Howe family was touched that the Massachusetts Assembly funded a monument at Westminster Abbey to honor another brother, George, who was killed during the French and Indian War. The Howes accepted their assignment to put down the rebellion under the condition that they also had authority to negotiate a settlement, but they were under strict orders not to treat the Americans as equals.[34]

Army officials rejected Howe's letter because of a technicality; it was addressed to "George Washington Esqr., &c, &c, &c," with no mention of his military position or title. Washington's indignant aide told Howe's courier that no such person existed, sneering that "all the World knew who Genl. Washington was since the Transactions of last Summer." The courier was taken aback. "Lord Howe will lament exceedingly this affair," he said, "as the letter is quite a civil nature and not a military one . . . and that he had come with great powers." Howe also regretted not arriving "a little sooner"—meaning before the Declaration of Independence, which had caught the British by surprise.[35]

Washington undoubtedly approved and even orchestrated the rejection; he wrote to Hancock the next day, saying, "I deemed it a duty to my Country and my appointment to insist upon that respect which in any other than a public view I would willingly have waived." A second letter from Richard Howe, addressed in the same manner to "Esqr., &c,

&c, &c," also was turned down. The stalemate lasted until a third British courier asked if the general would receive an in-person visit from William Howe's adjutant, Lieutenant Colonel James Patterson—which Washington, after some consideration, and perhaps to send his own message, accepted.[36]

Patterson opened the July 20 meeting at Washington's New York headquarters by assuring him that the Howes did not mean to "derogate from the Respect or Rank of General Washington." Only the "Goodness and Benevolence of the King" had led him to appoint them as "his Commissioners to accommodate this unhappy Dispute," and it might be too good of an opportunity for the Americans to pass up. Washington narrowed his eyes and glared. He believed that the Howes had little power beyond granting pardons and could do so only if his troops put down their arms. "Those who have committed no Fault want no Pardon," the general said. "We are only defending what we deem our indisputable Rights."[37]

One American observer said Patterson seemed "as awestruck as if before something super-natural."[38] But if the British officer was fairly startled—and he was—his reaction paled in comparison to that of Lord Howe, who received a letter the same day from his old friend Benjamin Franklin.

Franklin knew Howe from his many years of service as the American agent in London and worked for much of that time to achieve a closer bond between England and the colonies. Now, however, Franklin's views had changed entirely. If all Howe had to offer after more than a year of bloody warfare was "Pardons upon Submission," which is as it seemed, Franklin told him, "it must give your Lordship Pain to be sent so far on so hopeless a Business." Then he became even more graphic, more intense.

> Directing Pardons to be offered the Colonies, who are the very Parties injured, expresses indeed that Opinion of our Ignorance, Baseness, and Insensibility which your uninform'd and proud Nation has long been pleased to entertain of us; but it can have no other Effect than that of increasing our Resentment. It is impossible we should think of Submission to a Government, that has with the most wanton Barbarity and

Cruelty, burnt our defenceless Towns in the midst of Winter, excited the Savages to massacre our Farmers, and our Slaves to murder their Masters, and is even now bringing foreign Mercenaries to deluge our Settlements with Blood. These atrocious Injuries have extinguished every remaining Spark of Affection for that Parent Country we once held so dear.[39]

Franklin went on for seven paragraphs, at one point even advising Howe to "relinquish so odious a Command, and return to a more honourable private Station." Knowing full well that it was not a practical, or even possible, solution, he concluded the letter with thoughts on England's call to arms. "I am persuaded cool and dispassionate Posterity will condemn to Infamy those who advised it," Franklin wrote, "and that even Success will not save from some degree of Dishonour those who voluntarily engag'd to conduct it."[40]

Washington and Franklin had sent the message in their own styles. There would be no need for peace commissioners.

* * *

Congress was so busy in the second and third weeks of July that one significant nation-building feat was overshadowed. That came on Friday, July 19, when members realized they had to update the printed Declaration that was already making the rounds.

John Jay's letter about New York's vote of approval had arrived in Philadelphia four days earlier. Focused on matters of more immediate importance, Congress didn't get around to reacting in any formal way until the morning of July 19. Its sixth order of business that day called for the Declaration to be "fairly engrossed on parchment" and given a new title: "The *unanimous* declaration of the thirteen United States of America. Afterward, it would "be signed by every member of Congress," although a date for the signing was still undetermined.

The original title on July 4 had been "A DECLARATION by the REPRESENTATIVES of the UNITED STATES OF AMERICA, in GENERAL CONGRESS assembled." That was the version that appeared in Dunlap broadsides and was sent to state leaders following the 12–0–1 vote. No one outside of Congress would even see the updated heading until 1777, and some contemporary Americans probably never noticed the difference, but this new claim of unanimity, made possible by New York's vote, was a far more potent message for the country and the world.

To have the document "fairly engrossed" meant that it would be written out by hand, beautifully, formally, and in distinctive letters. The assignment went to master calligrapher Timothy Matlack, a clerk for Secretary Thomson, whose job included selecting the animal skin as parchment and gathering the iron gall ink. Like other early contributors to the printing of the Declaration, Matlack added his own editorial flourish (all of these early editions, starting with Jefferson's draft, vary slightly in capitalization and punctuation, since there was no such thing as a style guide). Given his place in the timing of the rollout, Matlack's version became the most memorable, the most famous in American history—what most people today consider *the* Declaration.

Matlack was quite busy himself during this period; he recently was elected to the Pennsylvania Constitutional Convention, would soon join the Philadelphia Council of Safety, and served with a local militia unit, the fifth battalion of riflemen. That is part of the reason he took his time with the crucial task and did not submit it to Congress until the end of July. Historians at the National Archives described his work as painstakingly "laying out the text on parchment, determining the margins and space between the lines, and calculating the space that would be needed at the bottom of the document for signatures." He used almost the entire width of the parchment for his text and left about one-quarter of the page blank at the bottom for members to sign.[41]

Matlack's unique flair for style and capitalization was evident at the top. The first line, identifying place and date ("IN CONGRESS, July 4 1776") was followed by the reformatted title, "The unanimous Declaration of the thirteen united States of America." He went with "unalienable" instead of Jefferson's original "inalienable" and used series of long dashes to indicate paragraphs, conserving space. As a result, the text of this iconic version appears in one large block, as opposed to the more traditional style of spacing preferred by the printer Dunlap.[42]

The unique challenge faced by Matlack was the need to preserve space for signing—and the timing of his late July work is indisputable proof that the Declaration was *not* signed on July 4, as many Americans still believe (and as even Jefferson and Adams mis-remembered later). Further evidence is found in a July 9 letter from Adams to delegate Samuel Chase in Maryland, with Adams writing that "as soon as an American Seal is prepared, I conjecture the Declaration will be Subscribed by all the Members, which will give you the opportunity you wish for, of transmitting your Name, among the votaries of Independence." Adams was, in fact, named to a committee on July 4 to create an American seal, but nothing was submitted until late August and a seal was not adopted for six years, so it had no effect on the signing. Congressional records show that the members did not begin to sign Matlack's parchment until early August, and, even then, contrary to modern mythology, not everyone signed on the same day.[43]

CHAPTER 12

The Second of August

DAY BY DAY, WEEK BY WEEK, DEPENDING ON THE DISTANCE FROM PHIL-adelphia, news of independence spread throughout the country.

State leaders distributed copies of Dunlap broadsides as soon they arrived—in New Jersey first, then in Maryland, Connecticut, Rhode Island, and beyond. Newspapers in six states had published the Declaration by July 16, when Salem's *American Gazette* was the first to do it in Massachusetts, beating its Boston rivals by one day. But almost a full month had passed before South Carolinians could read the full text in Charleston's *South-Carolina and American General Advertiser* on August 2.[1]

Mayors and local councils held readings of the Declaration before large public gatherings, with patriotic rituals to suit the occasion. Militia units marched in town squares and fired thirteen-gun salutes to honor the fledgling nation. At Portsmouth, New Hampshire, on July 16, the *New Hampshire Gazette* reported that "the pleasing countenance of the many Patriots present spoke a hearty concurrence in this interesting measure, which was confirmed by three Huzzas, and all conducted in peace and good order."[2] At other locales, including Boston, however, crowds became so aroused that they tore down the King's Arms and other royal symbols, stomping them into pieces or setting them ablaze.

Boston's event on July 18 began when the Declaration was read from the balcony of the State House to an audience that included "the Committee of Council, a number of the honorable House of Representatives, the Magistrates, Ministers, Selectmen and other Gentlemen of Boston

Figure 12.1. The Declaration of Independence was read at a public ceremony in Boston on July 18, 1776. Similar events were held in towns around the country. *(Wikimedia Commons)*

and neighboring towns." Two regiments of Continental soldiers then lined up in thirteen distinctive groups on the north side of King Street, and two artillery detachments fired their cannons thirteen times, for "the number of American States United." Later that evening, after six patriotic toasts were made (and consumed), "the King's arms, and every sign with any resemblance of it, whether lion and crown, pestle and mortar and crown, heart and crown, &c., together with every sign that belonged to a Tory, was taken down, and . . . made a general conflagration."[3]

John Adams had no access to Boston papers while he was serving in Philadelphia, but his wife wrote that "every vestige" of the king "from every place it appeared" was ripped away and burned amid loud shouting in the street. "Thus ends royal Authority in this State," Abigail Adams declared, "and all the people shall say Amen."[4]

In retrospect, the most striking aspect of these 1776 celebrations is that the document itself was the focal point. In an era long before "breaking news" and in-depth analysis, the formal public reading of those thirteen hundred words was the way most Americans learned of their independence. It is especially intriguing that newspaper accounts made no mention of the Declaration's now-famous preamble, with its self-evident truths of life, liberty, and the pursuit of happiness; those concepts already were well known and accepted, expressed by numerous other writers (including George Mason in the recent Virginia Bill of Rights). Instead, the twenty-seven charges against the king drew great interest as they were laid out in public for the first time. Using the charges as justification, virtually every story honed in on the cogent phrase of the day—the thirteen colonies had rejected the British monarchy to become "free and independent states."

Independence fever spread as the broadsides reached other destinations. On July 22, in Worcester, Massachusetts, "the bells were set a ringing and the drums a beating . . . after which the Declaration of Independence of the United States was read to a large and respectable body, who testified their approbation by repeated huzzas." The King's Arms, "an odious signature of despotism," were pulled down and mangled. Thirteen shots rang out to rousing cheers. The evening then concluded with a whopping twenty-five toasts—among them, "May the Freedom and Independency of America endure till the sun grows dim with age, and this earth return to Chaos."[5]

Despite reports of "decency and order" at most events, some developed harsher, more vindictive, even racial tones. On July 22 in Huntingdon, New York, newly independent Americans tore the name "George III" from a flag, then used some scraps to fashion an effigy of the monarch—with "its face black like [Lord] Dunmore's Virginia regiment, its head adorned with a wooden crown, and its head stuck full of feathers, like . . . Savages" as the *New-York Journal* reported. The makeshift King George III figure was promptly "hung on the gallows, exploded and burnt to ashes." And that was *before* they drank thirteen toasts.[6]

It took several weeks for the Declaration to reach the southern states. The *Virginia Gazette* in Williamsburg published an extract in its July 19 edition, but there was not enough time to set the full text in type; instead, it ran the next day. An outdoor reading followed on July 25 "at the Capitol, the Courthouse, and the Palace, amidst the acclamations of the people." South Carolina did not have its first printing until August 2 or its first reading on August 5 "before a vast concourse" of onlookers in Charleston.[7]

Georgia's assembly was gathered in Savannah on August 10 when John Hancock's letter with the broadside finally arrived. After nodding approval in a closed-door meeting, members arranged for three public readings that day: in the square at the Assembly House; at the Liberty Pole, where troops "discharged their field pieces and fired in platoons"; and at the Trustees Gardens, with even more artillery punctuating the news.

For good measure, patriotic Georgians held a mock funeral for the king near the steps of the courthouse, witnessed by "a greater number of people than ever appeared on any occasion before in this province." The formal proclamation at "interment" was ruthlessly fitting for the moment:

> Forasmuch as George The Third, of Great Britain, hath most flagrantly violated his coronation oath, and trampled upon the constitution of our country, and the sacred rights of mankind, we therefore commit his political existence to the ground, corruption to corruption, tyranny to

the grave, and oppression to eternal infamy; in sure and certain hope that he will never again obtain a resurrection to rule over these United States of America.[8]

* * *

One of the greatest events in American history was the signing of the Declaration of Independence, but no one outside of Congress knew that it happened when it did.

For the record, it was August 2, 1776—at least for forty-nine of the fifty-six signers.

Seven other delegates signed *after* that date.[9]

Confusion has reigned almost since the time of the signing, fueled by the delegates' need for secrecy after breaking with England. The first mention of a potential signing process does not even appear in the congressional records until July 19, following word of New York's delayed vote. That is when Congress called for an updated version of the July 4 document to be "engrossed" on parchment, and, once it was completed, "signed by every member." Timothy Matlack's work clearly took the better part of two weeks, because it was not until August 2 that Congress led its private daily record with the understated news: "The declaration of independence being engrossed and compared at the table was signed (by the members)."[10]

That was it. No fanfare. No celebration. No leaks to the local gazettes or even in letters home—the best indication of all that a cone of silence prevailed. Historian David McCullough, in his biography of John Adams, noted with some bemusement that "to judge what was in the newspapers and the correspondence of the delegates, the signing never took place."[11]

There can be no doubt about why they were silent: a clear and persistent fear that their lives were now in danger. Dr. Herbert Frieden- wald, who wrote a deeply researched history of the Declaration in 1904, thought the intention was "to protect for a time the members who sub- scribed their names to an act that would have rendered them liable for trial by treason, if the revolution had been suppressed by the British gov- ernment." As for the month-long delay in signing, however, Friedenwald

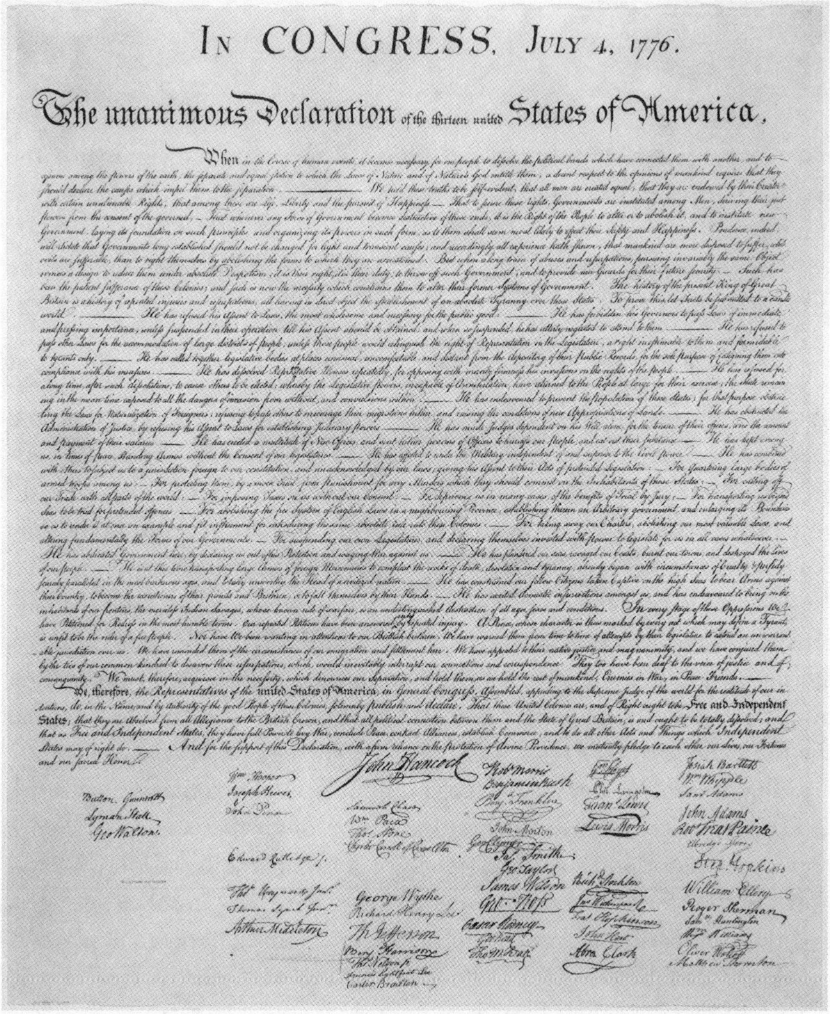

IN CONGRESS, JULY 4, 1776.

The unanimous Declaration of the thirteen united States of America.

Figure 12.2. The updated "unanimous" Declaration of Independence, in the handwriting of Timothy Matlack, which delegates started to sign on August 2, 1776. The original signed version has faded over time; this is a facsimile created in the nineteenth century. *(Wikimedia Commons)* had a different theory. "To but a few men did the actual act of signing assume the large importance that it has since attained," he wrote. "The unanimous adoption of the Declaration was the important event, the signing a mere final touch, an after-thought."[12]

In fact, of all the letters written by delegates in July 1776, only three even broached the *possibility* of signing—and then just barely, before moving on to other topics. On July 5, Samuel Chase, who had gone home to Maryland to rally support for independence, wrote to John Adams, asking, "How shall I transmit to posterity that I gave my assent?" Adams responded on July 9 that once an American Seal was prepared, "I conjecture the Declaration will be subscribed by all the Members, which will give you the opportunity you wish for." Fellow delegate Elbridge Gerry, who left Philadelphia due to ill health following the vote, wrote to Adams from Massachusetts on July 21, "Pray subscribe for me the Declaration of Independence if the same is to be signed as proposed."[13]

Nonetheless, Jefferson stubbornly claimed to the end of his days that the signing happened on July 4. He insisted that once their debates on language had finished on the "evening" of the "4th," the Declaration was "reported by the [committee], agreed to by the house, and signed by every member present except Mr. Dickinson." Alas, there are inexplicable fissures in Jefferson's account. Most members agreed that the Declaration was approved on the morning of July 4, not the evening. While it is true that Dickinson never signed, neither did other members who were there that day. The New York delegates who signed the Declaration could not possibly have done so on July 4 because their colony had not yet freed them to vote. Perhaps most stunningly, eight men who signed were not even elected to Congress until *after* July 4.[14]

Thomas McKean of Delaware, who was present on July 4 but left soon afterward to serve in the war, did not sign until sometime after January 1777—and perhaps not until 1781.[15]

And while Jefferson later speculated that a paper version of the Declaration was signed by delegates on July 4—only to be followed one month later by the signed parchment version—no supporting evidence has ever been found. According to Friedenwald, Jefferson deftly changed his story after being "driven into a corner" by facts. Moreover, he said, congressional secretary Charles Thomson had "carefully preserved . . . all the other documents of importance to which signatures are attached," and it was inconceivable that Thomson would "have allowed an original of such value to have been destroyed."[16] Most historians debunk Jefferson's claim.

So what do we know of the fifty-six men who "affixed their signatures" to the most famous document in American history? How did it happen? Who signed when?

Here is a rundown of highlights:

- Eight delegates who were present in Philadelphia in early July did not sign the Declaration. They included Dickinson, the leading opponent, and Robert R. Livingston of New York, who served on the Declaration's drafting committee.[17]

- Another opponent, Robert Morris of Pennsylvania, who, like Dickinson, absented himself from the July 2 vote, changed his stance and signed the Declaration on August 2. "Altho the Councils of America have taken a different course from my Judgements & wishes," Morris wrote in late July, "I think an individual that declines the Service of his Country because its Councils are not comfortable to his Ideas makes him a bad Subject; a good one will follow if he cannot lead."[18]

- Congress did not take daily attendance, but it is believed that forty-nine of the fifty-six signers were present at the State House on August 2.

- Seven men who eventually signed the Declaration were not in Philadelphia on August 2. For instance, Richard Henry Lee, who had formally proposed independence in early June, did not return from Virginia until August 27. Other "late" signers included Gerry of Massachusetts, McKean of Delaware, George Wythe of Virginia, Lewis Morris of New York, Oliver Wolcott of Connecticut, and Matthew Thornton of New Hampshire. All but McKean had signed by early November.

- As mentioned earlier, eight of the signers were not elected to Congress until after July 4, including five members of the revamped Pennsylvania delegation. These newcomers were Benjamin Rush, George Clymer, James Smith, George Taylor, and George Ross (all from Pennsylvania); William Williams (Connecticut); Charles Carroll (Maryland); and Thornton (New Hampshire). Thornton was not elected until September and did not report to Philadelphia until November 4; nonetheless, because of the July 19 edict that the Declaration would "be signed by every member of Congress," he asked for, and was granted, permission to sign.

- John Rogers of Maryland was the only delegate who voted for independence on July 2 but did not sign the Declaration. Conversely, George Read of Delaware was the only delegate who voted against independence and still signed the document.[19]

President John Hancock was the first to sign on August 2, centering his large, stylish script at the top of the space left by Matlack (but there is no evidence that he did it to make it easier for the king to "read my name without spectacles," as is often alleged). For the record, the king never saw the parchment version anyway; he learned of American independence through news reports and the earlier Dunlap broadside. Forty-eight other delegates then signed by state, in six uneven columns, south to north, with Georgia on the far left and four New England states on the far right. Although this was clearly done in groups—by design—the individual states were not identified, making it look like a disorganized jumble to the untrained eye.[20]

The seven men who signed after August 2 then had to fit their names into the space that remained. Fortunately for four of them—Gerry (Massachusetts), McKean (Delaware), Morris (New York), and Wolcott (Connecticut)—there was room at the end of their states' list of delegates. Conversely, the two Virginians, Wythe and Lee, signed at the top of their delegation because colleagues had left an opening there. But Thornton of New Hampshire was forced by space limitations to sign at the bottom of *Connecticut's* group.[21]

The desire for secrecy was such that no one outside of the State House would see the names for more than five months. It was not until January 18, 1777, that Congress ordered "an authenticated copy of the Declaration of Independency, with the names of the members of Congress subscribing the same, [to] be sent to each of the United States, and that they be desired to have the same put upon record." At the time, there were fifty-five signatures on the parchment, all but that of Thomas McKean, who was off fighting the Revolutionary War. The first printing that contained McKean's name as the fifty-sixth signatory did not appear until 1782, leaving historians uncertain as to when he actually signed.[22]

Any doubt that the signers did not immediately grasp the meaning of their actions is dispelled by a letter that Benjamin Rush wrote to John Adams in 1811. After remembering "the solicitude and labors, and fears, and sorrows and sleepless nights of the men who projected, proposed, defended and Subscribed the declaration of independence," Rush went on to ask, "Do you recollect the pensive and awful silence which pervaded the house when we were called up, one after another, to the table of the President of Congress, to subscribe what was believed by many at the time to be our own death warrants?"[23]

Still awestruck after all those years, Rush knew the answer in advance. Those who were there that day would *never* forget.

* * *

General William Howe was the first British official in America to send word of independence to England. A July 8 letter to Lord George Germain included a one-sentence announcement—"I am informed that the Continental Congress have declared the United Colonies Free and Independent States"—but, given the time it took for transatlantic travel, Howe's matter-of-fact description did not reach London until August 10.

Multiple copies of the Dunlap broadside soon followed, to be passed along to influential newspapers and magazines.

The *London Chronicle* published the full text of the Declaration of Independence in its August 15 edition. The *St. James's Chronicle*, also of London, followed the next day but added a stunning bit of editorial chutzpah, deleting all direct references to the king. In the second paragraph, for instance, the paper changed "The history of the present king of Great Britain" to "The present history of Great Britain." Afterward, every mention of "he" in the list of charges against the king was replaced by "it"—placing focus on the country and its government, not the esteemed monarch.[24]

Monthly magazines also joined the parade of distributors, albeit with different styles. The *London Magazine* and the *Universal Magazine* published excerpts that did not include any of the charges. The *Gentleman's Magazine* printed the full text without comment, but, on a later page, added, "Whether these grievances were real or imaginary, or whether they did or did not deserve a parliamentary inquiry, we will not presume to decide."[25] One edition of the *Scots Magazine* was defiant enough to go on the attack, however, mocking the Americans and picking apart pieces of the Declaration's preamble.

> All men, it is true, are equally created, but what is this in the purpose? It certainly is no reason why the Americans should turn rebels, because the people of G. Britain are their fellow creatures, i.e., are created as well as themselves. . . . They therefore have introduced their self-evident truth, either through ignorance, or by design, with a self-evident falsehood. . . . These [gentlemen] assume to themselves an unalienable right of talking nonsense.[26]

Several editions of the *Kentish Gazette* kept up the anti-American barrage. One account said colonial complaints against the king were based on an "absurd" foundation. "There must be something more substantial behind this curtain of phantom," the *Gazette* wrote. "What this something is, time has discovered to the whole world to be nothing more or less than a formed plan of independence." The paper went on to claim that "the common people of America," who, until recently, "trembled and recoiled at the idea of independence," had been led astray by "artful Priests and Demagogues" in Congress.[27]

But there were occasional pro-American voices that rose in support. A weekly paper in London, called, appropriately, *Crisis*, defended colonial rights, assailed monarchial rule, and warned English citizens to be just

THE YEAR THAT MADE AMERICA

as concerned for liberty as their overseas counterparts. After publishing the Declaration on August 24, *Crisis* endorsed it as the clarion call "of the brave, free, and virtuous Americans, against the most dastardly, slavish and vicious tyrant that ever disgraced a Nation." For its part, the *Gazette* even allowed a Welsh preacher, Dr. Richard Price, to advocate for independence. He accused the British of acting "like mad parents" and, instead of relaxing "our authority" as the colonies grew and matured, "we have carried it to the greatest extent and exercised it with the greatest rigour. No wonder then, that they have turned upon us, and obliged us to remember that they are not children."[28]

Still, most British publications were disdainful of the Declaration, and anger simmered as it spread from town to town. Writers saw it as a vain attempt to justify treason through the most outrageous public means, using vacant phrases such as "created equal" and, especially, "pursuit of happiness," whatever that might have meant. Mostly, though, they denounced the colonists as ungrateful subjects who took the vast and incomparable blessings of the British Empire for granted. If a thorough beating on the battlefield was what it took to get their point across, the prevailing attitude was "so be it."

It is not known if Lord Germain presented his copy of the Dunlap broadside to King George III. Regardless, the king would have been aware of the Declaration by at least by third week of August, given the speed of news reports and public reprintings. What is noteworthy (and revealing of his condescending attitude) is that he chose not to respond immediately, making no formal comment until late October, even though he had judged the colonists to be "in rebellion." It was as if he knew his supporters and underlings, as well as friendly newspapers, would mount a fierce counterattack on his behalf.[29]

(It also should be mentioned that if the king *had* seen the Declaration, it would have been one of the early broadside editions printed on July 4–5, and not the later "unanimous" version. Accordingly, he would have seen only the typeset names of Hancock and Thomson at the bottom, not the famed collection of handwritten signatures made on or after August 2.)

Two of the king's most avid supporters published blistering pamphlets that fall to taunt the Americans and disparage the Declaration. One was John Lind, a London barrister and political activist who sought a seat in Parliament; the other was Thomas Hutchinson, a Boston native and former royal governor of Massachusetts who left for England in 1774, never to return. Both made cases that colonial independence was based on flimsy pretenses, laid out in tepid, indefensible language by foolish, misguided traitors.[30]

Lind, in his *Answer to the Declaration of the American Congress*, was delighted that the king had not responded quickly. "Easy as it were, and fit as it may be, to refute the calumnies contained in that audacious paper," he wrote, "it could not be expected that his Majesty or his Ministers should condescend to give an answer." That was because the Declaration was an "insult to everyone who bears the name of Briton." Lind then dissected the charges by challenging all claims of tyranny and usurpation. The purpose, he said, was to erase any stain "which the false accusations of the rebellious Congress may have thrown on the character of a Prince, so justly entitled to the love of his subjects, and the esteem of foreign nations."[31]

Hutchinson's work began as a letter to Philip York, the second Earle of Hardwick, who was "utterly at a loss to what facts many parts of the Declaration of Independence published by the Philadelphia Congress referred, and . . . wished they had been more particularly mentioned." The former governor set out to examine the list of grievances, bringing unique perspective to the task—he had, after all, dealt with the Boston Massacre and Boston Tea Party during his time there, and knew both John and Sam Adams.

Writing in a pamphlet titled *Strictures upon the Declaration of the Congress at Philadelphia in a Letter to a Noble Lord*, Hutchinson tried to refute the charges, one by one. He believed they presented no justification for rebellion but offered only "false and frivolous reasons in support of it." The colonies had been so intent on declaring independence, he said, that even "if no Taxes or Duties had been laid upon" them, other issues "would have been found for exception to the authority of Parliament." In other words, Americans had been so deceived by dishonest leaders and clever rabble-rousers that this attempt to break from England was inevitable, even without valid reason.

Hutchinson added:

> They have . . . fully avowed these principles of Independence, by declaring they will pay no obedience to the Laws of the Supreme Legislature . . . and have endeavoured to persuade such as they called their British Brethren to justify the Rebellion begun in America; and from thence they expected a general convulsion to the Kingdom. . . . These expectations failing, after they had gone too far in acts of Rebellion to hope for impunity, they were under *necessity* of a separation, and of involving themselves . . . in the distressed of horrors of war against the power from which they revolted.[32]

Both sides were dug in, determined, defiant—the British no less than the Americans, as Lind and Hutchinson showed. Regardless of one's viewpoint, pro or con, all that remained was to decide it on the battlefield.

* * *

The British military buildup continued in and around New York with no clear hint of action.

George Washington was puzzled.

The steady influx of enemy troops led him to predict on August 7 that "an attack is now . . . expected which will Probably decide the Fate of America," but the lack of any movement over the next two weeks gave him pause. What where the British doing? What did it mean? "The reason of this is incomprehensible to me," Washington wrote to his cousin, Lund, on August 19. "There is something exceedingly misterious in the conduct of the Enemy."[33]

It turned out that the Howe brothers were playing the long game simply because they could. Supremely confident and certain of eventual victory, there was no reason to force an attack before some recently arrived Hessian mercenaries had a chance to rest after their transatlantic trip. The invading force now numbered thirty-two thousand troops in all—twenty thousand British veterans, eight thousand Hessians—and seventy warships bristling with firepower gave them undisputed control of the harbor. The Howes held out hope that this disparity in military strength might convince Washington to begin the peace talks he had rejected in July—perhaps now, before the first shot was fired.[34]

But finally, on August 22, with the defiant Americans refusing to stand down, General William Howe gave the signal, and the British army began to move.

In broad daylight, several hundred transport ships carrying fifteen thousand battle-tested soldiers were rowed across the Narrows from Staten Island to the beach at Gravesend Bay. They came ashore, observed but uncontested, at the southwestern corner of Long Island, the vanguard of the first major military attack since the Declaration of Independence. Within a few days there would be more additions, mostly Hessians, building the force to twenty thousand. The British advantage in manpower was so prodigious that even after Washington hustled two groups of largely untrained militia to Long Island, increasing his total to ninety-five hundred, Howe had an edge of more than two to one. (More than half of Washington's army was still back in Manhattan, where he supposed, incorrectly, that the main attack would come.)[35]

Sensing the gravity of the moment, Washington used his General Orders the next day to give the army a pep talk—his formal way of stiffening resolve on what seemed like the eve of battle. "The Enemy have now landed on Long Island, and the hour is fast approaching, on which the Honor and Success of this army, and the safety of our bleeding Country depend," Washington wrote. "Remember, officers and Soldiers, that you are Freemen, fighting for the blessings of Liberty."

But if honor and patriotism were not enough inspiration, he added, "It is the General's expresses orders that if any man attempt so skulk, lay down or retreat without Orders he be instantly shot down as an example."[36]

The Americans had taken up defensive lines on Gowanus Heights and Brooklyn Heights, designed to handle frontal assaults while inflicting massive casualties, but they had somehow failed to protect a road to the east, Jamaica Pass. The British saw this opening and pounced. A group of generals—Howe, Henry Clinton, and Charles Cornwallis—led ten thousand soldiers on a flanking movement through the pass on August 27, swamping the American positions and unhinging the Gowanus Heights line. Inexperienced militia panicked at once, abandoning their posts and scurrying to the safety of forts on Brooklyn Heights.

Several American units *did* fight fiercely, including the First Maryland Regiment, which faced its baptism of fire in a gallant rearguard action, allowing others to retreat. The cost, unfortunately, was severe. "My God," exclaimed Washington, watching from a hill above, "what brave fellows I must this day lose!"

The battle was over by early afternoon. Casualty figures were imprecise, but modern estimates are that that both sides suffered between three hundred and four hundred killed and wounded. Perhaps most devastating for the Americans was the loss of up to one thousand prisoners, including General John Sullivan, a former member of Congress. After assessing the damage and gathering as much intelligence as possible, Washington saw that he and his men were dangerously hemmed in on three sides with their backs to the East River, still facing possible annihilation.[37]

It was fortunate for the future of the United States that William Howe had other ideas. Whether he could have ended the revolution by destroying the shell-shocked Continental army with one more assault on Brooklyn Heights can never be known. American general Israel Putnam believed that Howe "had our whole army in his power. . . . Had he instantly followed up his victory, the consequences to the cause of liberty must have been dreadful." But Howe was content to hold his position and hunker down for a siege. He did not want to risk severe losses with a frontal attack on the Heights, even if it were successful—to do so would be "criminal"—and he believed that the one-sided contest on August 27 might persuade the trapped Americans to resume peace talks and end this imperial nonsense.[38]

Washington considered several options, all of them bad. Surrender was out of the question, and fighting another battle here on the same ground, against the same troops, seemed pointless. What about retreat? He found the thought distasteful but could see no better solution to save the army, and when a council of war endorsed the idea two days later, he set out to make it happen. Doing this from a fixed position against a vastly superior opponent was daunting, however—requiring precise planning, cooperative weather, and more than a little luck.

But it all fell into place. On the pitch-black night of August 29, a regiment of Massachusetts fishermen and seamen ingeniously commandeered boats and ferried almost nine thousand Continental troops across the river to Manhattan, and temporary safety. An escaping soldier remembered that "we were strictly enjoined not to speak, or even cough. All orders were . . . communicated to men in whispers." It helped, certainly, that the winds had changed in their favor, but the most fortuitous quirk of fate was that Admiral Richard Howe, who commanded the waterways, failed to notice the movement (he was immersed in a dinner discussion with high-ranking American prisoners, including General Sullivan). Even when dawn broke on August 30, threatening the passage of the last few units, a dense fog appeared in a "peculiar providential occurrence" to cover their retreat.[39]

Legend has it that Washington was the last man to step into the last boat on the Long Island side, an inspirational image for his troops. The next day, August 31, on the cusp of a new phase of the war, his General Orders framed their near-disastrous experience in terms meant to both encourage and provoke:

> The General hopes the several officers, both superior and inferior, will now exert themselves, and gloriously determine to conquer, or die— From the justice of our cause—the situation of the harbour, and the bravery of her sons, America can only expect success—Now is the time for every man to exert himself and make our Country glorious, or it will become contemptable.[40]

The British view was harsher, of course, even condescending and sneering. The Americans had run away from the fight this time, proficient in retreat, but they could not elude the king's men for long. General James Grant had led some of the troops in the attack on Gowanus Heights and reveled in their "field day" against a blundering, overmatched foe.

"If a good bleeding can bring those Bible-faced Yankees to their senses," Grant wrote to a colleague a few days after the battle, "the fever of independency should soon abate."[41]

CHAPTER 13

The Twenty-Fifth of December

CONGRESS WAITED ANXIOUSLY FOR NEWS FROM THE BATTLEFIELD. ON August 20, a pensive Thomas Jefferson wrote to a friend in Virginia, "We have been in hourly expectation of the great decision at New York, but it has not yet happened." More than a week passed with no word from the front, making for a taut, solemn mood as they went about their daily business. On August 30, three days after the battle—and one day after George Washington's escape—John Adams wrote to Abigail: "The Two Armies on Long Island had been shooting at each other for this whole Week past, but We have no particular Account of the Advantages gained or Losses suffered, on either side."[1]

News did not arrive until August 31, when Washington apologized to John Hancock for the delay. It was caused, he said, by "extreme fatigue," because "for Forty-Eight Hours preceding . . . I had hardly been off my Horse and never closed my Eyes." The general glossed over details of the battle, perhaps believing that a lengthy description of their retreat was admission enough of what occurred. The closest he came to conceding the disastrous result was when he said the army suffered "from 700 to a Thousand killed and taken."

But it was a sentence in the third paragraph of his report that grabbed the attention of many in Congress. Washington announced not only that General John Sullivan, a former delegate from New Hampshire, had been captured by the British but also that Lord Richard Howe was sending Sullivan to Congress with a message. "Genl Sullivan says Lord Howe is extremely desirous of seeing some of the Members of Congress, for which purposes he was allowed to come out and communicate . . . what was passed between him & his Lordship," Washington told Hancock. "I have consented to his going to Philadelphia."[2]

Washington's report was presented to the full body as the first order of business on September 2; the congressional journal said it explained, among other things, the reasons for "quitting Long Island." Howe's proposal then took up much of the day on September 3. In the message delivered by Sullivan, he offered to meet with several members of Congress at a place of their choosing to reach a negotiated compromise before more lives were lost. Howe said that obtaining "full powers" to do so from the king had "[d]elayed him near Two months in England and prevented his arrival at this place before the Declaration of Independency."

It was the same approach he had tried with Washington in mid-July, but with the same flawed foundation—as Adams and others soon recognized. His Lordship made clear that he could only meet with representatives as "private Gentlemen," not as formal members of Congress; he was forbidden to engage them as leaders of an independent nation while attempting to lure them back into the empire. Expecting some pushback, but hopeful that defeat on Long Island had rattled American confidence, Howe sought to assure them that if "they found any probable Ground of an Accommodation, the authority of Congress must be afterwards Acknowledged, otherwise the Compact would not be Compleat."[3]

Thus began debates over several days as to how to respond to Howe's overture. Adams, as might be expected, harrumphed throughout. He accused his former colleague, Sullivan, of being "a duck decoy, whom Lord Howe has sent among us to seduce us into a renunciation of our independence" and at one point whispered to Benjamin Rush that he wished "the first ball that had been fired on the day of the defeat of our army had gone through [Sullivan's] head." Adams was against sending emissaries to Howe, as were Rush, George Ross of Pennsylvania, and John Witherspoon of New Jersey, believing it would show weakness. But it was Witherspoon, not Adams, who gave the definitive speech on their behalf at a full session of Congress on September 5.

The Presbyterian minister took to the State House pulpit and cut through the convoluted vagaries of Howe's language, charging that the

British wanted nothing less than "absolute, unconditional submission." Despite appearing to offer an olive branch after whipping Washington's army, Howe had "uniformly avoided any circumstance that can imply we are anything else but subjects of the king of Great Britain, in rebellion." Witherspoon said it was clear now that British leaders—and the admiral, in particular—had had no intention of ever acknowledging American independence. As a result, entering into "any correspondence with him in the manner now proposed is actually giving up, or at least subjecting to a new consideration, the independence which we have declared."[4]

It is doubtful that anyone in Congress thought a session with Howe could bring an end to the conflict, but many felt the offer should be accepted nonetheless—considering it "necessary in the eye of the public to satisfy them that we are always ready to hear anything that will restore peace to the country." Edward Rutledge spoke in support of a motion to meet with Howe, as did Thomas Lynch of South Carolina and Thomas Stone of Maryland, and their opinion carried the day, with one key distinction. Congress, on behalf of a free and independent nation, could not "send any of its members to confer with his lordship in their private characters" but would agree to send a committee "to know whether he has the authority to treat with persons authorized by Congress for that purpose . . . and what that authority is."[5]

It was brilliant political maneuvering. In order to avoid an endless series of letters back and forth, Howe was forced to accept.

The next day, September 6, Congress voted for a three-man team, led by John Adams (New England) and Benjamin Franklin (middle states). Rutledge and Richard Henry Lee garnered an equal number of votes to represent the south, but a second ballot gave the edge to Rutledge. The delegates set off from Philadelphia on September 9 to meet with Howe near his headquarters on Staten Island. It was on this trip that Adams and Franklin were forced to share a bed and got into a jovial debate on whether it was healthier to sleep with windows open or closed. Perhaps by seniority, Franklin—the open window advocate—prevailed. "The Doctor then began [a] harangue upon Air and cold and Respiration and Perspiration," Adams said, "with which I was so much amused that I soon fell asleep, and left him with his Philosophy together."[6]

It was much more serious business on September 11 when they reached Perth Amboy, New Jersey, for a short ride across the channel on a red-and-gilt barge sent by his lordship. Howe offered one of his own officers as a volunteer hostage to guarantee that the men would return safely, but Adams and Franklin thought the idea preposterous. "Gentlemen, you make me a very high Compliment," a startled Howe said when he walked down to greet them, seeing that the officer had returned. "And you may depend on it, I will consider it as the most sacred of Things." But other than a few polite exchanges at the start—especially when Franklin, who knew Howe from his many years in London, introduced Adams and Rutledge—the meeting went downhill quickly.[7]

"Is there no way of treading back this Step of Independency, and opening the door to a full discussion?" Lord Howe asked, according to notes taken by his secretary, Henry Strachey.

No, there was not.

The two sides could not even agree on the status of the American delegation. Howe insisted that he had no power to "consider the Colonies in the light of Independent States" and therefore "could not confer with them as a Congress . . . could not acknowledge that Body which was not acknowledged by the King." The Americans wondered why they were wasting their time. Desperate to find some common ground, Howe said he was pleased to consider them "private Gentlemen of Influence in the Colonies," but could do so only with another, concurrent label: "British subjects." Adams, in particular, recoiled with horror. "Your Lordship may consider me in what light you please, and indeed, I should be willing to consider myself, for a few moments, in any character which would be agreeable," he said, "except that of a British Subject."[8]

It had reached a point where further talk was pointless. If Howe thought that America's commitment to independence was shattered by the drubbing on Long Island, he was badly mistaken. "His Lordship then saying that he was sorry find that no Accommodation was likely to take place," Adams wrote, "he put an end to the Conference." It is noteworthy, in retrospect, that Howe bid the three men a polite farewell as they prepared to cross the water to New Jersey, keeping his promise of safety to the end. Years later, Adams would learn that his had been one of the names on a list of Americans to be hanged for treason if a settlement had been reached.[9]

For now, though, all eyes focused on a war that would extend throughout the winter—and probably, both sides knew, for years. One of Howe's staffers looked on the Americans with disdain as they headed back to an uncertain future. "They met, they talked, they parted," he wrote, "and now nothing remains but to fight it out against a set of the most determined hypocrites and demagogues, compiled of the refuse of the colonies, that ever were permitted by Providence to be the scourge of a country."[10]

* * *

The military situation was tenuous. The Americans had somehow escaped Long Island, but now they were under threat in Manhattan as the Howes resumed offensive operations after the foiled peace conference.

At a council of war on September 12, Washington's officers voted 10–3 to rescind a plan to defend New York City. "I am fully convinced that it cannot be done," Washington wrote to Hancock, "and that an attempt for that purpose . . . might & most certainly would be attended with the consequences fatal and alarming." With support from a large majority, the council "not only determined a removal of the Army prudent but absolutely necessary."[11]

Unaware of this decision, the Howes opened a full-fledged assault on September 15. It started with a massive bombardment by five warships, clearing the way for four thousand British and Hessian soldiers to storm the shore at Kip's Bay, on the southeast side of Manhattan. The few Americans left there to cover the retreat promptly turned and ran. While no one could blame them, it caused a panic among other troops who, until that point, had been moving in orderly fashion toward Harlem Heights, on the northern part of the island. "The demons of fear and disorder seemed to take full possession of all and everything that day," one of them said.[12]

Washington's troops *did* fight well a few days later in a skirmish at Harlem Heights—surprising the British and briefly raising spirits—but the odds were stacked against them. Backed by a demonstrably superior force—one that had already shoved the Americans from Long Island to upper Manhattan—the Howe brothers issued their own proclamation on September 19, hoping to undermine the resistance:

> Although Congress . . . have disavowed every purpose of reconciliation not consonant with their extravagant and inadmissible claim of Independence, the King's Commissioners think it fit to declare that they are equally desirous to confer with his Majesty's well-affected subjects, upon the means of restoring publick tranquillity, and establishing a permanent union with every Colony as a part of the *British* Empire . . . it is recommended to the inhabitants at large to reflect seriously upon their present conditions and expectations, and judge for themselves whether it be more inconsistent with their honour and happiness to offer up their lives as a sacrifice to the unjust and precarious cause in which they are engaged, or return to their allegiance [and] accept the blessings of peace.[13]

The proclamation did not have much immediate tangible effect—it was published only in loyalist newspapers in New York and New Jersey—but it was reflective of the Howes' continuing strategy of trying to win hearts and minds with limited war.[14]

Washington was safe for now on Harlem Heights, but the state of his dwindling army was wretched at best. He needed more men, more supplies, better medical care, and far more discipline to keep his units intact, limit desertions, and prevent the Declaration from being symbolically torn to shreds. In an alarming letter to Hancock on September 25, he wrote that "we are now . . . upon the eve of another dissolution of our Army" and "unless some speedy and effectual measures are adopted by Congress, our cause will be lost." Pay for soldiers was feeble; there was overreliance on militia; and a stricter from of rules and regulations (including approved punishment for violations) was absolutely essential.[15]

What he did not know was that Congress already had taken steps to address those problems, shaken by the news from Long Island. On September 16, John Adams and the Board of War proposed ambitious plans that were adopted by the full body over the next several days. Congress offered $20 and one hundred acres of land for any man enlisting for the duration of the war. Harsher punishments were approved for violations ranging from insubordination to sleeping on guard duty (with occasional use of the motivational word *death*, lest anyone doubt how serious they were). Most vitally, at least from Washington's perspective, eighty-eight new battalions were to be raised by the states, with each state expected to fill a quota—fifteen battalions each for Massachusetts and Virginia, twelve for Pennsylvania, six for South Carolina, and one for Georgia.[16]

Unfortunately for Washington, this organized increase in troops never happened; the "country" was so young and unstructured that Congress lacked authority to impose recruiting standards on "free and independent states." Nonetheless, the attempt to do so under extreme circumstances was not lost on the commanding general. It convinced him that the leaders in Philadelphia understood his dilemma and still were committed to the cause despite constantly distressing news from the battlefield.[17]

A much more impactful decision on the fate of the revolution came on September 26, when Congress elected Jefferson and Franklin to join Silas Deane as commissioners to the court of France. The goal was to form a diplomatic alliance with England's fiercest rival to add heft to the American cause. Jefferson declined, having already returned to Monticello to care for his wife, who was in ill health (his rejection letter mentioned "circumstances very peculiar in the situation of my family"). Jefferson was replaced in this crucial post by Arthur Lee, Richard Henry Lee's brother, who had served as colonial agent in England before the war.[18]

Back in New York, meanwhile, the two armies glared at one another across Harlem Heights, creating a maddening and almost inexplicable lull for several weeks—"as quiet as if they were a thousand miles apart," one man wrote. But by mid-October, when General William Howe put his troops in motion for a flanking movement, the Americans decided to pull out. At a council of war on October 16, Washington's officers voted overwhelmingly, 16–1, to evacuate northern Manhattan, leaving New York City to the British. Two days later, the bedraggled Continental army began its trudge across King's Bridge to the temporary safety of White Plains in Westchester County, about eighteen miles away.[19]

It was the beginning of a long, disjointed, but tactically effective journey that would lead him across New Jersey and into Pennsylvania by the end of the year.

* * *

The Declaration of Independence had reached London by early August, but it was not until October 31 that King George III spoke about it in public. The tone of his annual speech to both houses of Parliament was equal parts outrage and condescension.

The king seemed astonished, saying that "my colonies" and "my unhappy people" had not yet "recovered from delusion" and resumed their happy lives as British subjects. He blamed Congress, of course:

> So daring and desperate is the spirit of [their] leaders, whose object has always been dominion and power, that they have now openly renounced all allegiance to the crown, and all political connection to this country; they have rejected, with circumstances of dignity and insult, the means of conciliation held out to them under the authority of our commission, and have presumed to set up their rebellious confederacies for independent states. If their treason be suffered to take root, much mischief must grow from it.

Fortunately, he said, "my officers" and the "troops in my service" appeared to have the rebellion well in hand. Recent victories in Canada and on Long Island had seriously degraded the insurgency and burnished the image of British military might. The king's goal now was to restore "the blessings of law and liberty" to his American subjects while bringing their misguided leaders in Congress and the army to justice. Despite the "strongest hopes of the most decisive good consequences," however—and he likely swallowed hard—"we must, at all events, prepare for another campaign."[20]

The fall campaign was nearing its end as he spoke. The Americans suffered more setbacks in a three-week period between October 28 and November 19—losing battles at White Plains and Fort Washington in New York before abandoning Fort Lee in New Jersey. Developing plans on the fly, reacting to circumstances while seeing more desertions, Washington kept his men on the move. The short-term goal was little more than the survival of the army. Hustling from post to post, staying one step ahead of the enemy, inflicting casualties where possible but avoiding fights in an open field, his strategy was minimalist—and wholly defensive. Perhaps he could frustrate the British, or, at the very least, wear them out.

Conversely, one of Howe's soldiers, feeling invincible after a steady stream of victories, claimed that the American army "is broken all to pieces, and the spirit of their leaders . . . is also broken." Many overconfident colleagues shared the same conclusion: "It is well nigh over for them."[21]

The American retreat through New Jersey began in earnest on November 21. Washington and his troops crossed the Acquackononk Bridge over the Passaic River and headed south toward Newark and New Brunswick. Their next stop was Trenton—just across the Delaware River from Pennsylvania, and about thirty miles from Philadelphia. A British force under Charles Cornwallis took up the pursuit on November 25, with orders to chase the Americans at least as far as New Brunswick. In this classic military game of cat and mouse, he would then check in with Howe for further instructions.[22]

Cornwallis reached New Brunswick on December 1 and called a halt, as was planned. On the same day, about twenty-five miles to the southeast, Washington made plans to cross from Trenton into Pennsylvania. "It being impossible to oppose them with our present force with the least prospect of success," he wrote to Hancock, "we shall retreat to the west side of [the] Delaware . . . where it is hoped we shall meet a reinforcement sufficient to check their progress." Washington told one of his colonels to gather as many boats, oars, and poles as possible "for the purpose of Carrying over the Troops & Baggage in [the] most expeditious Manner."[23]

Inexplicably, Cornwallis remained in place for six days, giving Washington a rare chance to plan and move as he pleased. Most of his soldiers had crossed over to Pennsylvania by December 7, followed by the commanding general early the next morning. An advance guard of

British and Hessian troops was finally sent out from New Brunswick to track them; it reached Trenton on December 8—a very close call that Cornwallis would later come to regret. Fortunately for Washington, the British brought no boats to attempt an immediate river crossing, and after exchanging a few shots, which did little damage, both sides settled in to plot their next moves.[24]

Reporting to Hancock on December 9, Washington wrote that "the Security of Philadelphia should be our next Object." He guessed, correctly, that the city was now in a state of upheaval, with the British barely thirty miles away. A local paper referenced "very good intelligence that the British intend to make a push for Philadelphia," and Richard Henry Lee of Virginia, the fire-breathing patriot who had proposed independence in June, acknowledged that there was "much alarm." Lee and other delegates to Congress, fearing they would be hung for treason as traitors if Philadelphia fell, decided to temporarily move their base of operations one hundred miles away to Baltimore (Congress would meet there from December 20, 1776, until February 27, 1777).[25]

As it turned out, Congress's retreat was unnecessary. By December 13, William Howe had decided to call off the chase and suspend operations until the following spring, "the weather having become too severe to keep the field." Winter camps were set up across northern New Jersey and New York, with Howe himself settling into comfortable quarters in New York City. A scant force of about fifteen hundred Hessians was left behind to hold Trenton and keep an eye on the Americans.

Howe's decision marked a turning point in the war, which had thus far been absurdly one sided. He may not have known it at the time, but the Americans were at their weakest point since the start of the conflict. Many enlistments expired on December 1; desertions from the army were rampant; General Charles Lee, a senior commander, was taken prisoner on December 12; and even more enlistments were up at the end of the year. Since late November, hundreds of New Jersey residents had signed oaths of allegiance to the Crown, pledging "peaceful obedience" and receiving "free and general pardon[s]." But even in what seemed like the final desperate days of the American cause, the impact of this sudden respite at Trenton was something the Howe brothers never could have imagined.[26]

* * *

As the author of *Common Sense* in January 1776, British immigrant Thomas Paine did as much as anyone to inspire the American public to revolution. But Paine was not content to let his pen do the talking. He signed up for military service, spent three months in the Pennsylvania militia, and, by the fall of that year, volunteered as an aide-de-camp to Washington's brilliant young subordinate, General Nathaniel Greene.

Paine joined Greene at Fort Lee in New Jersey before it was abandoned, working to boost morale and passing out copies of his work to discourage desertion. But even as Paine accompanied the troops on their glum retreat, Greene and others saw him slipping away for moments here and there to jot a few lines in his journal. It seemed odd behavior under the circumstances. Little did anyone know that he was working on another essay at a time when the American spirit was at its lowest ebb since Howe came ashore at Long Island.[27]

Over time it would be a series of thirteen essays over seven years, but the first one, written in December 1776, would supersede *Common Sense* in some ways. Titled "The American Crisis," it was published in the *Pennsylvania Journal* on December 19, stoking passion among the public and catching Washington's attention on the west bank of the Delaware. It soon would be printed widely in pamphlet form. The opening lines—among the most vivid in American history—were meant to rejuvenate the "Spirit of '76" at a pivot point for the country and the army:

> These are the times that try men's souls. The summer soldier and the sunshine patriot will, in this crisis, shrink from the service of their country; but he that stands by it now, deserves the love and thanks of man and woman. Tyranny, like hell, is not easily conquered; yet we have this consolation with us, that the harder the conflict, the more glorious the triumph. What we obtain too cheaply, we esteem too lightly.[28]

Legend holds that Washington had Paine's words read to his troops a few days later, although there is no supporting evidence to confirm it. Undoubtedly, however, copies of the essay were passed through the army's ranks and made a deep impression.[29] Inspiration from any source was welcomed at this point as Washington and his officers planned one of the most daring raids of the war. Defying the odds and military convention, American soldiers would slip across the Delaware under cover of darkness on Christmas night to attack the unsuspecting Hessians.

As far back as September, Washington thought it would take "brilliant stroke" to save the revolution. By mid-December, with defeats piling up, he was willing to pin his hopes on a "lucky blow" (as he wrote on December 14 to the governor of Connecticut). Other officers were of the same mind, scrambling for options as Christmas approached. Washington's adjutant general, Joseph Reed, wondered about the chance for "a diversion" or even "something more" at Trenton. "I will not disguise my own Sentiments that our Cause is desperate & hopeless if we do not take the Opp[ortunity] . . . at present to strike some Stroke," Reed wrote on December 22. "Our Affairs are hastening fast to Ruin if we do not retrieve them by some happy Event."[30]

Washington finalized the plan at a dinner meeting on Christmas Eve. He and Nathaniel Greene would lead the main force of twenty-four hundred across the Delaware at McConkey's Ferry after the sun had set on Christmas night. Once across, hopefully by midnight, they would split into two columns and march nine miles to Trenton to surprise the Hessians before dawn.

Weather played havoc with the timing—a nasty, frigid blend of rain, sleet, and wind—and they were three hours behind when the last group came ashore. A daylight attack might jeopardize the mission, but Washington had come too far to turn back now. With the fate of their country at stake, the Americans swooped into Trenton at 8:00 a.m. on December 26 and overwhelmed the startled Hessians with "passions easier conceived than described." The fight was over in less than an hour; U.S. troops killed twenty-one, wounded ninety, and captured *nine hundred*, while suffering only four casualties of their own.[31]

The impact on the revolution, and American history, was incalculable, but Washington did not stop there. He seized the moment to persuade some of his troops to stay past the end of their enlistments and added more recruits to the cause. They clashed with British regulars at Trenton on January 2, wiggled out of a potential trap that night, and then defeated another British force at the Battle of Princeton on January 3. In the ten days since Christmas Eve, they had found their footing and turned the war—and the world—upside down.

"A few days ago, [the Americans] had given up the cause for lost," a British loyalist groused in the wake of Washington's crossing. "But their late successes have turned the scales, and now they are all liberty mad again."[32]

* * *

Congress was meeting at its temporary home in Baltimore when news arrived of Trenton and Princeton. On January 7, a committee led by Robert Morris wrote to Washington, stating, "We waited with Impatience to learn the consequence of your late movements and have been highly gratifyed." Though still hesitant to return to Philadelphia—Congress would remain in Baltimore through the third week of February—the unexpected battlefield success had revived its sagging confidence and lightened the mood. The committee told Washington that the success of his army was "beyond expectation . . . only the beginning of more important advantages" and would likely have "the most important publick consequences." Hancock, in a private letter, added, "I entertain the most pleasing Expectation that our Affairs will henceforth assume a better Complexion."

So emboldened was Congress that, within a few weeks, it chose to make a historic move of its own.[33]

In the six months since the Declaration had been approved, the American public saw only the Dunlap broadside version—printed on July 4–5, before New York had voted, and containing only the typeset names of Hancock and Charles Thomson. Copies of these early "Dunlaps" were sent to all the states, and, eventually, to England and around the world. But no one outside of Congress had seen the later Matlack parchment, with its fifty-five handwritten signatures; no one even knew it existed. The names were kept private through the fall and early winter to ensure their personal safety.

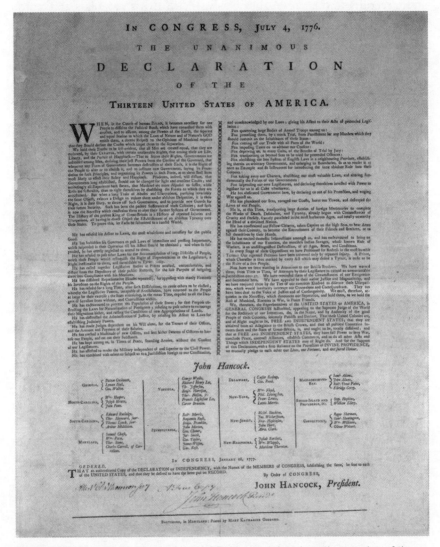

Figure 13.1. Mary Katharine Goddard of Baltimore printed another version of the Declaration in January 1777. This "Goddard broadside" marked the first time that Americans learned the names of the signers. *(Wikimedia Commons)*

The public's understanding began to change, however, on January 18, 1777, an otherwise uneventful Saturday, when Congress ordered

> [t]hat an authenticated copy of the Declaration of Independency, with the names of the members of Congress subscribing the same, be sent to each of the United States, and that they be desired to have the same put on record.[34]

Congress had no immediate access to Dunlap's printing press, but it had been doing business for several weeks with a prominent Baltimore printer, Mary Katharine Goddard. As publisher of the local *Maryland Journal*, Goddard had run the text of the Declaration in the July 10 edition, and her dual role as the city's postmaster led to direct connections with members of Congress. Her task here was historic on many fronts. It was the first time that the public would learn the names of the signers; the first time it would see the updated title ("The *Unanimous* Declaration of the Thirteen United States of America"); the first time a woman would do the printing; and the first time a copy was meant for preservation (as Congress would soon instruct the states).[35]

It took Goddard less than two weeks to complete her work. On January 31, Hancock sent the following letter to each of the thirteen states, accompanied by a copy of the new "Goddard broadside":

> As there is not a more distinguished Event in the History of America, than the Declaration of her Independence—nor any that in all Probability, will so much excited the Attention of future Ages, it is highly proper that the Memory of that Transaction, together with the Causes that gave Rise to it, should be preserved in the most careful Manner that can be devised. I am therefore commanded by Congress to transmit to you the enclosed Copy of the Act of Independence with the List of several Members of Congress subscribed thereto and to request, that you will cause the same to be put on Record, that it may henceforth form a Part of the Archives of your State, and remain a lasting Testimony of your approbation of that necessary & important Measure.[36]

Now the world would know.

Goddard recorded the names of fifty-five signers, set in type and arranged by state, with the exception of President Hancock, who was centered at the top. The lone omission was Thomas McKean of Delaware, who was serving in the army and would add his name later. In the absence of any formal published list, Goddard may have referenced the original Matlack parchment to determine who had signed, and in which order; it remained in possession of Congress and likely was transported to Baltimore for safety when the group moved.

Another stark departure from Matlack was an additional name, little known to history, appearing in small type at the bottom of the page. Tucked in below the signers, but clear enough for the British to see, it read, simply, "Baltimore, in Maryland: Printed by MARY KATHA-RINE GODDARD."[37]

There was no turning back for any of them now, Mary included.

CHAPTER 14

Forgotten Document?

THE DECLARATION OF INDEPENDENCE HAD DONE ITS JOB BY EARLY 1777—announcing the break with England, describing the reasons in detail, and spreading the news to a "candid world."

From that point forward, however, the American people *forgot about it*, putting their fate in the hands of the army and waiting for word from the front. Historians of the revolutionary era have marveled at this for years.

"Considering how revered a position the Declaration of Independence later won in the hearts and minds of the American people," Pauline Maier wrote, "their disregard for it in the earliest years of the new nation verges on the incredible."[1]

Anniversary celebrations happened, of course, but they were sporadic, and randomly planned. Americans lionized the act of independence, the rejection of monarchy, the assumption of self-government—but not the document that laid out the reasons. Rarely after the summer of 1776 was the full text of the Declaration read aloud in public settings. One historian found that these former British subjects focused instead on "their own state constitutions and the promise of liberty contained within them."[2]

Indeed, the first anniversary event in Philadelphia on July 4, 1777, took place almost by accident. As John Adams wrote to his daughter, Nabby, "the thought of taking notice of this day was not conceived until the second of this month, and it was not mentioned until the third." Nonetheless, Congress gave itself a day off from running the war to enjoy

221

"a festivity and ceremony becoming the occasion." (Just one year after writing that July 2 would be "the most memorable Epocha in the history of America," Adams had acceded to public opinion that July 4 was "the anniversary of American Independence").[3]

Toasts were made, bells were rung, and ships of the Continental navy lined up in the river in a splendid patriotic display. President John Hancock and other members of Congress clambered aboard the frigate *Delaware* and were saluted by thirteen shots from naval cannons. North Carolina delegate Thomas Burke wrote that a Hessian band captured at Trenton six months earlier "performed very delightfully, the pleasure not being a little heightened by the reflection that they were hired by the British Court for purposes very different from those to which they were applied." Congress hosted a fine dinner, after which militia companies from Maryland and North Carolina paraded through the streets to boisterous cheers. The *Pennsylvania Evening Post* concluded, "Thus may the fourth of July, that glorious and every memorable day, be celebrated through America by the sons of freedom, from age to age, till time shall be no more. Amen and amen."[4]

No one mentioned the Declaration.

Similar celebrations were held that day in Boston, Portsmouth, Providence, and Charleston, where seventy-six cannons saluted the year of independence. Flags flew from all vessels in Charleston harbor, and festivities peaked with a candlelight illumination on the streets. In most villages and towns, however, and even in some camps of George Washington's army, the date passed without much notice. It apparently "occurred to very few people that the anniversary ought to be celebrated," one historian wrote, "until they read in the papers of celebrations [in other communities]."[5]

The mood in many locales varied from year to year in the late 1770s, depending on the pace of the war and the proximity of enemy troops. Congress even had to flee Philadelphia for a second time in 1777, not long after the magic of the first anniversary.

Closing in on the capital city on September 11, a British force under William Howe defeated Washington at Brandywine Creek, about thirty miles away. General Nathaniel Greene fought an effective rearguard action, allowing many U.S. troops to escape to safety, but Howe succeeded in clearing a path to Philadelphia. Within a week, Congress resolved that "[w]hereas the city of Philadelphia, notwithstanding the brave existence of the American army, may possibly . . . be, for a time, possessed by the enemy's army . . . it may be essential to the public welfare that Congress should adjourn to some place more remote than this city from the scene of action, in order that deliberations may be conducted without inter-ruption." Delegates fled seventy miles to Lancaster, Pennsylvania, by September 27 and another twenty-five miles to York by September 30, settling in at the York Court House for a lengthy stay.[6]

It took almost nine months, until mid-June 1778, for Washington to send word that Philadelphia was back in American hands; the British, learning of an alliance between the United States and France, had pulled out to consolidate their forces in New York and prepare for the new threat.[7] On June 24, cautious congressional leaders determined it was safe enough to pack up their belongings in York and return to Philadelphia. That same day, mindful of the approaching anniversary—and feeling more patriotic than ever—the relieved delegates issued the following order:

> That a committee of three be appointed to take proper measures for a public celebration of the anniversary of independence at Philadelphia on the 4th day of July next, and that they be authorized and directed to invited the President and Council and Speaker of the Assembly of Pennsylvania, and such other gentlemen and strangers of distinction as they shall deem proper. . . . Resolved that Congress will, in a body, attend divine worship on Sunday, the 5th day of July next, to return thanks for the divine mercy in supporting the independence of these States and that the chaplains be requested to officiate and to preach sermons suited to the occasion.[8]

Cloaked as it was in language of a government decree, this was at least the informal beginning of the Fourth of July tradition in the United States. The *Pennsylvania Packet* reported a few days later about a joyous event hailing "the glorious Anniversary of the Independence of Amer-ica by the Honourable Congress." Thomas McKean described "elegant entertainment and a fine band of musick" and mentioned "[t]he firing of a vast number of cannon." At army headquarters in New Jersey, Washington called for his troops to "adorn their hats with Green-Boughs" to make the best appearance possible; as a reward, and to ensure a spirited bash, he promised to serve double rations of rum to each man.[9]

And so it went for several years as the war effort ebbed and flowed. The first formal state recognition of a July 4 holiday came in 1781, when the Massachusetts legislature ordered that preparations be made "for celebrating the anniversary of the Independence of the United States." Several years later, Boston's town meeting voted to forego its annual remembrance of the date of the Boston Massacre (March 5, 1770) and replace it with July 4, noting "the important and happy effects . . . which already have and will forever continue to flow from the Auspicious Epoch." By the middle of the decade, momentum had progressed to the point that Congress invited guests from France, Spain, and the Netherlands to a July 4 gala in Philadelphia.[10]

If any of these celebrations included public readings of the Declaration, however, no one referenced it. There was no talk of the glorious preamble, no hint of self-evident truths, no recitation of the charges against the king. "It took some time for the Declaration of Independence to matter in American life," historian Jonathan Gienapp said. "That might seem difficult to believe since it is regarded as the nation's foundational text containing its governing creed. Yet, for well over a decade after it was written, it was largely forgotten and ignored. Americans celebrated the break with England but not the now-famous document that justified why."[11]

Then, in 1783 and 1787, two new documents trumped the Declaration in legal power.

* * *

The death knell for the British war effort came in October 1781, when General Charles Cornwallis surrendered his army to American and French troops at Yorktown. American legend holds that a British band played "The World's Turned Upside Down," but even if that story is apocryphal (which is likely), the impact of the surrender to forces from both sides of the Atlantic was *real*. When word finally reached London in late November, an astonished Lord North slapped his forehead and declared "Oh God, it's all over. It's all over."

England, for all its military might, was tired and drained after six years of war with the rebellious colonists; few significant inroads had been made since the first shots were fired at Lexington in April 1775. Losses were significant, the treasury was battered, and much of the British public opposed more needless fighting. Accordingly, on March 5, 1782, Parliament passed a bill authorizing peace negotiations in Paris. Lord North resigned ten days later and was eventually replaced by a more progressive leader in Lord Shelburne.[12]

The original American peace delegation included John Adams, Benjamin Franklin, and Thomas Jefferson. If Jefferson had not declined the post, having recently rejoined Congress after a two-year stint as governor of Virginia, the same three men who helped start the revolution would have had a hand in ending it. As it happened, Adams and Franklin were joined by John Jay and, much later in the process, Henry Laurens, in what probably still ranks as the greatest diplomatic team in American history. They gained concessions that were not even fathomable when the First Continental Congress met in Philadelphia nine years earlier.[13]

It was Jay who did much of the hard-knuckle negotiating as talks became serious that fall (Franklin, at age seventy-six, suffered from gout and other maladies, and Adams was bogged down in the Netherlands). The New York attorney had made an interesting and crucial pivot since his earliest sessions of Congress, when he promoted moderate views and sought reconciliation. Now Jay demanded that England acknowledge America's independence as the foundation of any agreement. Without it, he said firmly, they could not and would not move forward.[14]

Jay and Adams communicated often while Adams was in the Netherlands to complete a treaty of commerce. "My opinion coincides with yours as to the Impropriety of treating with our Enemies on any other than equal footing," Jay wrote on September 1. "We have told [British negotiator Richard] Oswald so, and he has sent an Express to London to communicate it, and require further Instructions." Later that month, Jay informed Adams that Oswald had permission "to treat of peace with the

Commissioners of the United States of America." It was a giant step forward for the Americans, but talks remained so delicate that Adams was advised to "say nothing of this till you see me."[15]

Jay prepared the first draft of a peace treaty in early October. By the time Adams reached Paris later that month, Jay and Franklin had made progress on numerous fronts. Aside from independence, key issues were America's boundaries (north of Florida, south of Canada, and, significantly, west to the Mississippi River); fishing rights off Newfoundland; outstanding debts; and treatment of American "loyalists." The three Americans met for long hours with Oswald and another British negotiator, Henry Strachey, well into November, debating, prodding, and hammering out details. Laurens, who had been recuperating in the south of France, joined the team in late November.[16]

The result of all this negotiating was one of the most important documents in U.S. history—the "Preliminary Articles of Peace"—signed on November 30, 1782.[17]

It was "preliminary" out of necessity, because Britain had unresolved issues elsewhere in Europe. The American commissioners reported to Congress that their hard-won articles would be "inserted in a definitive Treaty as soon as the Terms between the Crown of France & Great Britain shall be agreed on." The news reached London on December 3. Two days later, King George III informed Parliament that after "finding it indispensable to the attainment of [peace]," he had offered to declare the colonies "Free and Independent States"—the exact wording Richard Henry Lee used in his independence resolution of June 7, 1776.[18]

"It is come finally to this," an exultant Franklin wrote.

The "Definitive Treaty of Paris" was signed on September 3, 1783, at the Hôtel d'York on rue Jacob. American signatories were Adams, Franklin, and Jay, in alphabetical order (with Laurens briefly absent again). The king's newest representative, David Hartley, signed on behalf of England.[19] Artist Benjamin West proposed to make a "Peace of Paris" painting, featuring key figures for both sides, but the British negotiators refused the offer, perhaps embarrassed by all the empire had lost. As a result, West's incomplete work features only Adams, Franklin, Jay,

Laurens, and Franklin's grandson, William Temple Franklin, who served as the commissioners' secretary.[20]

The formal treaty included ten articles, but the most meaningful for the Americans was "Article 1st":

> HIS BRITANNIC MAJESTY acknowledges the said UNITED STATES, viz. New-Hampshire, Massachusetts Bay, Rhode-Island & Providence Plantations, Connecticut, New-York, New Jersey, Pennsylvania, Delaware, Maryland, Virginia, North Carolina, South Carolina & Georgia, to be free sovereign & Independent States; that he Treats with them as such, and for himself his Heirs & Successors relinquishes all Claims to the Government Propriety and Territorial Rights of the same & every Part thereof.[21]

The ideas proposed in the Declaration of Independence seven years earlier had been contested on the field of battle, debated at the negotiating table, and now, finally, attained. The revolution was over. America was free.[22]

* * *

On July 5, 1776, one day after the Declaration was approved, John Hancock told the states that it should be "considered as the Ground & Foundation of a future Government."[23] But that was a stretch.

The Declaration justified the reasons for a new government, serving up bold claims of unalienable rights and touting "consent of the governed," but it had no power to apply those ideas, much less enforce them. Instead, a second document, called the Articles of Confederation, was conceived in 1776 and ratified in 1781, establishing a "league of friendship" among thirteen disparate states that were feeling their way on the world stage.[24]

By 1786, its flaws were evident. The central government had little authority, could not impose taxes on the public, and lacked a chief executive officer. The economy was in tatters, inflation was outrageous, and the depressed condition of business caused farmers in western Massachusetts

Figure 14.1. John Adams and Benjamin Franklin were part of the American negotiation team for the Treaty of Paris, which formally ended the Revolutionary War. Artist Benjamin West's painting is incomplete because the British delegation refused to sit for his work. From left to right are John Jay, John Adams, Benjamin Franklin, Henry Laurens, and William Temple Franklin. *(Wikimedia Commons)*

to rebel. It was at this point that a young, headstrong delegate from Virginia put forth a proposal for the "supremacy of national authority."[25]

By late summer 1786, James Madison and other "nationalistic" politicians from five states—Virginia, Delaware, Pennsylvania, New Jersey, and New York—met at Annapolis, Maryland, to trade ideas and consider their options. The original purpose was to address the regulation of commerce, but talks soon extended to other areas. On September 14, John Dickinson, now representing Delaware, wrote a letter to Congress claiming that there were "important defects in the system of Federal Government," which, under closer examination, "may be greater and more numerous" than had been realized. As a result, Madison's small group advised that it may essentially tend to advance the interests of the Union to procure the concurrence of other States, in the appointment of Commissioners to meet at Philadelphia on the second Monday in May next, to take into consideration the situation of the United States, to devise such further provisions as shall appear to them necessary to render the constitution of the Federal Government adequate to the exigencies of the Union.[26]

The thought was shocking enough that Congress waited until February before referring it to a "grand committee" of twelve appointees. After meeting for a full week to debate strategy and ponder implications, the committee reported that it "entirely [agreed] with them as to the inefficiency of the federal government and the necessity of devising" additional provisions. Its members approved moving forward with the convention.

The full body agreed on February 21, but with several contingencies. Congress called for a convention to begin on May 14 for the "sole and express purpose of *revising* the Articles of Confederation." After completing their work in a matter of weeks, the specially selected delegates would report back on "alterations and provisions therein." It was clear to everyone involved that Congress had endorsed only adjustments to the text, not a massive overhaul, and certainly not a complete rewrite.[27]

That was enough of an opening for Madison. There were not enough delegates for a quorum on May 14 (and would not be until May 25), but Madison and like-minded cohorts from Virginia and Pennsylvania used those early days to coalesce and plot strategy, concocting a plan that would do much more than amend the Articles. Their most consequential meeting came on May 16 at the home of Benjamin Franklin, attended by Madison, George Washington, George Wythe, Robert Morris, James Wilson, and other power brokers. The mere presence of Franklin and Washington brought exceptional gravitas to their national government agenda.[28]

(For the record, revolutionary stalwarts John Adams and Thomas Jefferson were serving as diplomats overseas, and John Jay, who signed the Treaty of Paris, was tied up as secretary of foreign affairs—none took part in the "Constitutional Convention").[29]

The formal convention began on May 25, after representatives from nine states had arrived in Philadelphia. It remained in continuous session until September 17, with the exception of two brief adjournments (including one of two days for the July 4 holiday). Twelve states would eventually send delegates, all but Rhode Island, which feared a "conspiracy" to overthrow the government. George Mason of Virginia wrote to his son: "The Eyes of United States are Turned upon this Assembly, and their Expectations raised to a very anxious Degree. May God grant that we may be able to gratify them, by establishing a wise and just government."[30]

There was patriotic symmetry as the fifty-five delegates met in the same Assembly Room at the State House where the Declaration of Independence was approved. Their first official act was a rare unanimous vote—Robert Morris nominated Washington as president, and the revolutionary hero took his post while reminding colleagues of "the novelty of the scene of business." After making a vow of secrecy, members went on to establish rules and consider the potential for sweeping change. By the time Edmond Randolph of the Virginia delegation took the floor on May 29, "decrying the evils that had befallen the country," it was apparent that this would not be a mere revision of the Articles after all.[31]

The radicals had seized control of the convention. Their "Virginia Plan" called for a strong national government with three branches designed to balance and check one another. Debates continued for four months on a wide range of topics, including style and substance, the method of representation, the powers and mode of the election of the executive, and the future of chattel slavery.[32] But the underlying tone was set on May 30 when the following resolution was made:

> That in order to carry into execution the design of the States in forming this convention, and to accomplish the objects proposed by confederation . . . a national government should be established consisting of a supreme Legislative, Executive and Judiciary.[33]

The Virginia Plan called for proportional representation in Congress, meaning that the number of delegates from each state would be determined by population. Smaller states balked and wanted equal representation for all. A compromise plan, often credited to Connecticut, offered proportional representation in the House of Representatives and equal representation in the Senate. The "Connecticut Compromise" was passed on July 16, but only by the slimmest of margins—5–4, with one state deadlocked (just ten delegations were present that day). As in the case for independence, consensus was not easily achieved, and unanimity seemed out of reach.[34]

After several months of heated argument and angst, the convention on July 23 appointed a five-person Committee of Detail to "prepare and report a Constitution." A recess was called from July 27 to August 5 for the committee to do its work and present a preliminary draft. The full body then took the next five weeks to hammer and mold the draft constitution into something that most found, at the very least, acceptable.[35]

Monumental decisions were reached. The new chief executive would be elected not by popular vote but by a politically expedient process called an electoral college. A Bill of Rights, sought by a minority of voices, would not be included at the start for the moment. Slavery was enshrined because delegates could not reach a solution for this immoral, contradictory issue (it was coldly determined that each enslaved person would be counted as three-fifths of a person for taxation and representation purposes).

In the first week of September, yet another committee was formed to polish the final draft of the U.S. Constitution. Three of those appointed to the "Committee of Style and Substance" were Madison, Alexander Hamilton of New York, and Gouverneur Morris of Pennsylvania, a powerful triumvirate.[36] Precise details of their work were not recorded, but Morris seems to have taken the lead, outshining his more famous colleagues, adding linguistic flair and refining the powerful preamble so familiar to Americans today:

> **We the People** of the United States, in Order to form a more perfect Union, establish Justice, ensure domestic Tranquility, provide for the common defense, promote the general Welfare, and secure the

Blessings of Liberty to ourselves and our Posterity, do ordain and establish this Constitution for the United States of America.[37]

Madison gave Morris full credit "for the *finish* given to the style and arrangement," writing years later that "a better choice could not have been made, as the performance of the task shows."[38]

It was in this way that the promise of the Declaration was transformed into a functioning national government. Thirty-nine of the forty-two delegates present at the State House on September 17, 1787, signed the Constitution, and it was ratified less than a year later when New Hampshire became the ninth state to confirm. There were objections in those early years over the lack of a "Bill of Rights"—Jefferson even complained about it from overseas—but that was remedied in 1791, when the first ten amendments, featuring freedom of speech and the right to bear arms, were added.[39]

None of the Constitution's framers, including Franklin, agreed with every aspect of the finished product—"I confess I do not entirely approve," he said—but, given the vast diversity of opinion rendered during four months of wild debate, the old sage was astounded "to find this system approaching so near to perfection as it does." Grudging compromise for the good of the country had done the trick. In a speech at the close of the convention in 1787, Franklin told his colleagues, "I think it will astonish our enemies, who are waiting with confidence to hear that our councils are confounded like those of the builders of Babel, and that our States are on the point of separation. . . . Thus, I consent, sir, to this Constitution because I expect no better, and because I am not sure that it is not the best."[40]

* * *

The revival of the Declaration of Independence began with the dawn of partisan politics in the 1790s.

On one side were George Washington, John Adams, and the Federalists, believing in strong national government as affirmed by the Constitution. On the other were Thomas Jefferson and the Anti-Federalists, also known as Republicans, who championed states' rights and feared the encroachment of northern business interests.

Absurd as it seems now, this pitted the Constitution *against* the Declaration, with warring factions using them as props in heated arguments. It was especially true after most Republicans learned *for the first time* about Jefferson's role in writing the Declaration. As one scholar noted, "Jefferson became one of the leaders of the opposition party to the administration of George Washington, and Jefferson's Republican supporters began celebrating him as the author."[41]

The question of authorship had never been raised in public since the Declaration was approved on July 4, 1776. Aside from congressional delegates and some friends back in Virginia, few Americans knew at the time that Jefferson was the primary draftsman. It was not until well into the 1780s that word began to spread, slowly at first. In May 1783, a minister's speech in Hartford teased the notion that "Jefferson . . . poured the soul of the continent into the monumental act of independence," stopping just short of a major news break.[42] Jefferson followed by dropping hints of his own in a letter to a Paris newspaper in August 1787.

Jefferson was serving as minister France when he read an account that gave John Dickinson credit for American independence—according to the *Journal de Paris*, it was Dickinson who had "set her free." Properly indignant, Jefferson sketched out a letter to the editor on the same day, giving his own detailed report of the independence process. "I was on the spot," he declared, "and can relate to you this transaction with precision." He did so in an elaborate fourteen-sentence paragraph before calming down and deciding not to send it; the letter went unpublished and was only discovered years later in Jefferson's papers.[43]

The story of Jefferson's involvement continued to leak, however—across the country and around the world—including on July 4, 1789, when a group of Americans in Paris delivered a written tribute to his residence. "As this is the anniversary of our Independence," they wrote, "the sensations of pleasure are much increased from the idea that we are addressing ourselves to a man who sustained so conspicuous a part in the immortal transactions of that day—whose dignity, energy and eloquence of thought and expression added a peculiar lustre to that declaratory act which announced to the world the existence of an empire." It was evident by then that a growing number of Americans had come to view Jefferson as the Declaration's sole author.[44]

Federalism prevailed during the presidential administrations of Washington and Adams, (1789–1801), but, even during this period, both parties jostled for control of Fourth of July celebrations—and, with it, the Declaration. Historian and author Shira Lurie described this odd competition as a joint "civics lesson," with each side promoting its vision of America's future on the most patriotic day of the year.

"Control over the Fourth of July becomes very, very important, especially as this partisan battle heats up," Lurie said. "For the Federalists, they're advancing an interpretation of the American Revolution that's in the past. They are saying the revolution is now over, and its promises were achieved with the Constitution . . . the final triumph of the patriot cause. For the Republicans, the revolution is ongoing. It's a struggle first against the British, and now, in this new order, to ensure that Americans remain free, that the government does not revert back to tyranny, or monarchy, or both. They are very interested in kind of rekindling the 'Spirit of '76' and keeping the 'Spirit of '76' alive."[45]

Federalist celebrations made few references to the Declaration and none at all to Jefferson. Newspapers reported that toasts were raised to Washington and Adams amid other "Federal festivity." No mention was made of the deep anti-British roots of the revolution because of efforts to expand trade relations with their former oppressors. The Republicans, meanwhile, held regular readings of the Declaration, "the original object of the public Anniversary" from the pen of "the immortal Jefferson." One Republican paper said the Declaration was "not to be celebrated merely as affecting the separation of one country from the jurisdiction of another; but as being the result of a rational discussion and definition of the rights of man, and the end of civil government."[46]

Jefferson's victory in the 1800 presidential election finally tipped the balance of power to the Republicans. It was the first time in American history that executive leadership passed from one party to the other, and it ushered in a new era of acrimony with the defeated Federalists. As the Fourth of July approached in 1801, a Philadelphia newspaper wrote: "It will be amusing to perceive how rarely the Declaration of Independence will be read . . . to the Old Tories." A later account noted that "the festival was celebrated with the accustomed gladness by the republicans," while cowardly Federalists "were invisible." In 1803, a Federalist paper in New York was accused of "openly censuring" the reading of the Declaration as "hostile to the British government."[47]

The pro-Republican *Independent Chronicle* even charged the following:

> You have from a malignity of heart towards Mr. Jefferson and the Republicans of America, from a hatred to republicanism itself, and from an unnecessary and groundless antipathy to the French Revolution, improved the hour which has been sacredly devoted to the memory of our national birth, for the purposes of degrading all the principles which produce our glorious Revolution.[48]

The Federalists fired back with fury. In addition to praising Washington and Adams, the purpose of their very public campaign was to diminish Jefferson's role in writing the Declaration. They stated, correctly, that the vote for independence came on July 2, not July 4, and that Adams, who was part of the Committee of Five, "must have had his voice in the instrument." Federalist writers revealed that ideas in the founding document had been "borrowed" or "compiled" from others, including philosopher John Locke, and mocked their Republican opponents for "pretend[ing] that Mr. Jefferson is entitled almost exclusively to the credit."[49] More than twenty-five years after the Declaration was approved, the two sides still pawed the turf and sneered at one another.

But the Federalist Party began to fade following the War of 1812 and soon ceased to exist as a viable political organization. It was clear by the end of the 1816 election, when James Monroe trounced Rufus King by 68 points, that Republicanism had endured and prevailed. Even when a new party system was formed in the 1820s and 1830s, upending and reshaping U.S. politics, both Jacksonian Democrats and Whigs sought to adopt and absorb Jefferson's legacy. As a result, the Declaration reclaimed its place as the icon of American freedom, revered in new ways by a modern generation, and Jefferson was ensconced in history as its singular, unquestioned "author."[50]

That part of the battle was over.

CHAPTER 15

Adams vs. Jefferson

T<small>HE SURPRISINGLY BITTER PERSONAL FEUD BETWEEN</small> J<small>OHN</small> A<small>DAMS AND</small> Thomas Jefferson grew out of the partisan politics of the 1790s. It escalated during the election of 1796, when Adams defeated Jefferson for the presidency, and reached a breaking point in the election of 1800, when Jefferson unseated Adams (and Adams refused to attend the inauguration). At one point in the early 1800s, these two former friends from the founding generation did not speak for eleven years.[1]

Their U.S. political careers began cordially enough in the first George Washington administration, with Adams serving as vice president and Jefferson as secretary of state. Washington was the unanimous choice for president in 1789, named on all sixty-nine electoral ballots, and Adams finished a strong second with thirty-four (each elector cast two ballots).[2] Alexander Hamilton was named secretary of the treasury, Henry Knox secretary of war, and John Jay chief justice of the Supreme Court. Jefferson then returned from his post as minister to France to become chief foreign policy advisor, completing what seemed to be an independence-era Hall of Fame.[3]

The convergence of big names did not work out so well in practice. Washington retained Adams's loyalty but rarely sought out his advice, reducing him to a sideline role. Jefferson battled with Hamilton over just about every issue imaginable. A disciple of strict Federalist principles, Hamilton advocated strong central government and even stronger ties with England; his pet project was a national financial system centered on a national bank. Jefferson opposed almost of all of it, defended states' rights, championed Republican values, and carried pro-French sympathies that frustrated Hamilton and the others. Heads butted often. Tempers flared.[4]

The tipping point for Jefferson likely came in spring 1793, after Washington and Adams were elected to a second term. Faced with choosing sides in an overseas war between England and France, Washington issued a Proclamation of Neutrality on April 22, pledging to "pursue a conduct friendly and impartial toward the belligerent powers." Jefferson could not understand the lack of support for his French colleagues and saw no purpose in continuing in his role. He wrote a resignation letter on July 31, hoping to "retire to scenes of greater tranquility from those which I am every day more and more convinced that neither my talents, tone of mind, nor time of life fit me." Although he was convinced to stay on until the end of the year, Jefferson made it official on December 31, telling the president "my propensities to retirement [are] daily more & more irresistible."[5]

Adams tried to remain respectful of his friend in public, but thought the decision was best for all involved, given their divergent views on policy. "Jefferson went off yesterday, and a good riddance of bad ware," he wrote on January 6, 1794. "I hope his Temper will be more cool and his Principles more reasonable in Retirement than they have been in office."[6]

Predictably, however, Jefferson's "retirement" did not last long. Political parties were forming, and battle lines were being drawn as word spread that Washington might leave office after two terms. As early as 1790, a visiting French diplomat had seen great potential in a Jefferson candidacy. "It appears certain at present that [Adams] will never be President," he wrote, "and that he will have a very formidable competitor in Mr. Jefferson, who, with more talents and knowledge than he, has infinitely more the principles and manners of a republican." Washington's farewell address in September 1796 cleared the way for the first contested presidential election in American history, with Vice President Adams and private citizen Jefferson as the lead combatants.[7]

Adams never was a strong party man, but he was, in his core beliefs, a Federalist. Jefferson stood for the new opposition, the Republicans. Adding to the drama, the convoluted election system called for each party to nominate two national candidates, with the top vote-getter becoming president, the runner-up vice president. One could imagine a potentially awkward mix of a Federalist president and Republican vice president, pitting one against the other, perhaps inviting sabotage—something Adams saw in advance. "It will be a dangerous Crisis in public affairs," he wrote in January 1796, "if the President and Vice President should be in opposite Boxes."[8]

That is exactly what happened. Following a rancorous campaign that saw both sides mount furious attacks—another first in U.S. politics—Adams squeaked out a close victory in the 1796 election with 71 votes to Jefferson's 68. Federalist Thomas Pinckney finished third with 59. As vice president and presiding officer of the Senate, it was Adams who counted the ballots and somewhat clumsily announced in February 1797 that "John Adams" was the new president, with Jefferson, his chief rival, as vice president.[9]

There was hope in the countryside that these two pillars of the revolution could govern together in bipartisan spirit. For his part, Adams was pleased to hear that Jefferson would accept the number 2 role as evidence "of his friendship for me—and of his Modesty and Moderation." Jefferson confided to James Madison that he had "no feelings which would revolt at a secondary position to Mr. Adams," especially since "he has always been my senior from the commencement of our public life, and the expression of the public will being equal, this circumstance ought to give him the preference." Indeed, a reunited partnership seemed imminent.[10]

Those chances were even more likely when Jefferson composed a pre-inaugural letter to Adams from Monticello:

> The public and the public papers have been much occupied lately in placing us in a point of opposition to each other. I trust with confidence that less of it has been felt by ourselves personally . . .
>
> I devoutly wish you may be able to shun for us this war by which our agriculture, commerce and credit will be destroyed. If you are, the glory will be all your own; and that your administration may be filled with glory and happiness to yourself and advantage to us is the sincere

wish of one who, though, in the course of our voyage through life, various little incidents have happened or been contrived to separate us, still retains for you the solid esteem of the moments when we were working for our independence, and sentiments of respect and affectionate attachment.[11]

But three days later, just as the new year turned, Jefferson hesitated. He sent a copy of the letter to his Republican friend, Madison, asking if anything he had written "should render the delivery of it ineligible in your opinion."[12] It was a fateful pause. Madison's objections damaged any hope of the two men working together. "Considering the possibility that Mr. A's course of administration may force an opposition to it from the Republican quarter," he wrote, " . . . there may be real embarrassments from giving written possession to him of the degree of compliment and confidence which your personal delicacy and friendship have suggested."

The letter never was sent.

For the record, Adams's Federalist friends were no more interested in a governing coalition than Madison (and a discordant tone was struck that continues in American politics to this day).[13]

In March 1797, around the time of the inauguration, the new president and vice president saw each other for the first time in three years. Jefferson had decided by then that the leader of the opposition party should not take an active part in the administration's affairs. Adams knew it was unlikely that Jefferson would accept an appointment to a peace commission to France, but he made the offer anyway—and then hoped that Madison, with Jefferson's encouragement, might fill the role instead. When both men declined out of party loyalty, any chance of bipartisanship was dead in the water.

From that point on, according to Jefferson, the president never "said one word to me on the subject, or ever consulted me as to any measures of the government."[14]

Adams's main achievement as president was avoiding all-out war with France, but he never came close to matching his feats of the 1770s; he was far better as a revolutionary than a chief executive officer. His four-year term in office is remembered mostly for the Alien and Sedition

Acts, which cracked down on immigration, enabled deportation, and criminalized criticism of the government. Passed and signed in the midst of a war environment, they nonetheless stirred up fierce opposition and helped lead to the president's downfall.[15]

The election of 1800 again featured four candidates, two from each party—Adams and Charles Cotesworth Pinckney for the Federalists, Jefferson and Aaron Burr for the Republicans. Adams and Jefferson drew much of the attention in what one author called "a contest of personal vilification surpassing any presidential election in American history." Adams was deemed a monarchist and a heretic, Jefferson an atheist and a French intriguer. Adams faced opposition from within his own party, led by Hamilton, who identified "great and intrinsic defects in his character." There was talk that he would create an American dynasty by having one of his sons marry a daughter of King George III. Meanwhile, one newspaper wrote that if Jefferson were elected president, "murder, robbery, rape, adultery, and incest will be openly taught and practiced, the air will be rent with the cries of the distressed, the soil will be soaked with blood, and the nation black with crimes."[16]

The result of the election defied predictions and stunned both parties. Republicans Jefferson and Burr *tied* for the top spot with 73 votes each, well ahead of Adams, who had 65 (Pinckney finished fourth with 64). Article II, Section 1 of the Constitution called for the House of Representatives to intercede in the "unlikely" event of an electoral tie. After six days and thirty-six ballots, Jefferson eked out a victory to become the third president of the United States, with Burr in the VP role. Republicans took power for the first time.[17]

Even in defeat, however, Adams had two more salvos to fire before leaving office. He promoted his secretary of state, John Marshall, to chief justice of the U.S. Supreme Court, ensuring that a Federalist would lead one of three branches of government under Jefferson. Then, on inauguration day, March 4, 1801, Adams left the capital at 4:00 a.m., departing eight hours before his former friend took the oath of office. "Sensible, moderate men of both parties would have been pleased had he tarried until after the installation of his successor," one correspondent wrote. "It certainly would have had a good effect."[18]

Jefferson went on to serve two terms and is regarded as one of the most successful presidents in U.S. history (he is generally ranked in the top ten, often in the top seven). His Louisiana Purchase in 1803 nearly doubled the size of the country, and the Lewis and Clark Expedition of 1804–1806 helped spark massive western expansion. Jefferson's tenure also was the start of a twenty-four-year "Virginia dynasty" in the White House, with fellow Republicans Madison (1809–1817) and James Monroe (1817–1825) as immediate successors. It ended, ironically, only when Adams's son, John Quincy Adams, won the presidency in 1824.[19]

* * *

Private citizen Adams was on his way to Massachusetts when the new president wrote to him on March 8, 1801.

Jefferson enclosed an unopened letter addressed to Adams, offering "the high homage of his high consideration and respect." Adams answered on March 24, writing that the letter dealt, sadly, with the funeral of his son, Charles, who had died recently at the age of thirty. Adams signed off by adding, "I See nothing to obscure your prospect of a quiet and prosperous Administration, which I heartily wish you."[20]

The two men did not see each other or write again for eleven years.

Their mutual friend, Dr. Benjamin Rush, was stunned and appalled by the unnatural feud. He regarded Adams and Jefferson as the "personification of the American Republic" and saw value to the country in some sort of reunion, especially after Jefferson left office in 1809. But it was not easy. All of his early attempts failed. By 1811, an exasperated Rush tried to use nostalgia as a hook, telling Jefferson: "When I consider your early Attachment to Mr. Adams, and his to you, when I consider how much the liberties & Independence of the United States owe to the Concert of your principles and labors . . . I have ardently wished a friendly and epistolary intercourse might be revived between you before you take a final leave of the Common Object of your Affections."[21]

Still, there was nothing.

The decisive break came purely by chance in summer 1811, when a Virginian named Edward Coles, private secretary to President Madison, paid a visit to Adams in New England. In the midst of their extensive talks on U.S. history over two days, Adams blurted out, "I always loved Jefferson, and still love him." Coles carried the news back to Monticello, where Jefferson was startled—and deeply touched. "This is enough for me," he told Rush in a letter, "to revive towards him all the affections of the most cordial moments of our lives. Why should we be separated by mere differences of Opinion in politicks, Religion, philosophy or anything else? His Opinions are as honestly formed as my own."[22]

Rush seized the moment and dashed off a note to Adams. It was the thawing of relations he had always imagined, embraced at the same moment by the two feuding founders. Left unresolved was how they would break the ice after all those years, but Rush encouraged Adams, as senior statesman, to write the first letter. He sought to nullify any pushback with a patriotic pep talk:

> Fellow labourers in erecting the great fabric of American independence!—Fellow Sufferers in the Calumnies of falsehoods of party rage!—Fellow heirs Of the gratitude, and Affection of posterity!—and Fellow passengers in a stage that must shortly convey you both into the presence of a Judge with whom the forgiveness and love of enemies is the condition of Acceptance—embrace—embrace each Other!—Bedew your letters of reconciliation with tears of Affections and joy.[23]

Adams took the bait.

On January 1, 1812, at the dawn of a new year and new era, he wrote to his old friend at Monticello. As a special personal gift, he sent along two volumes of lectures prepared by his son, John Quincy—"One who was honoured in his youth with some of your Attention and much of your kindness." Adams offered updates on other members of his family "you formerly knew," including his only daughter and her husband. He concluded by saying, "I wish you Sir many happy New Years and that you may enter the next and many succeeding Years with as animating Prospects for the Public as those at present before Us."

Jefferson answered on January 21. "A letter from you calls up recollections very dear to my mind," he wrote. "It carries me back to the times when, beset with difficulties and dangers, we were fellow laborers in the same cause, struggling for what is most valuable to man, his right of self-government." Jefferson noted with sorrow that so few of the Declaration's signers were still alive, "not more than half a dozen on your side of the Potomack, and, on this side, myself alone." His calculations were off—ten of the signers remained in 1811—but the point was well taken. Years were passing. Time was short.[24]

There were thirteen letters exchanged that first year, and more than 150 between 1811 and their deaths in 1826. The busiest year was 1813, when they wrote a combined thirty-five times.[25] Despite their cordiality, however, the two old oaks clung stubbornly to different philosophies of government. "In the Measures of Administration I have neither agreed with you or Mr. Madison," Adams wrote on May 1, 1812. "Whether you or I were right Posterity must judge." A renewal of their debates in this far less caustic forum seemed to inspire the former rivals.

"You and I ought not to die before We have explained ourselves to each other," Adams wrote on July 15, 1813—but whether that was achieved to satisfaction of either, no one knows for sure. Probably not.[26]

It did not matter to Rush. He saw the mere act of reconciliation, which he alone had forced, as his parting gift to American posterity. Jefferson agreed with Adams that no one could properly write the history of the revolution, "except perhaps its external facts," but their letters during this period offered clues and context to flesh out the story for future historians. The good doctor had achieved his goal.

"I rejoice in the correspondence which has taken place between you and your old friend Mr. Jefferson," Rush wrote to Adams early in 1812. "I consider you and him as the North and South Poles of the American Revolution. Some talked, some wrote, and some fought to promote and establish it, but you and Mr. Jefferson *thought* for us all."[27]

* * *

The most famous image of Adams and Jefferson together in the same setting hangs today in the rotunda of the U.S. Capitol.

Commissioned from artist John Trumbull in 1817, the painting, *Declaration of Independence*, depicts a popular but heavily romanticized version of the nation's founding.

For years, many Americans thought it captured the "signing" of the Declaration on July 4 at Independence Hall (there are many sources that still describe it that way). In reality, what Trumbull did was reimagine the moment on June 28, 1776, when Jefferson, Adams, and the committee presented their draft to the Second Continental Congress.[28]

The idea for the painting grew out of a meeting between Jefferson and Trumbull in Paris in the 1780s. Trumbull, son of the longtime governor of Connecticut—and briefly an aide-de-camp to George Washington in 1775—explained that he hoped to paint a series of battles from the revolution. Jefferson thought it was a fine concept but suggested the Declaration as another compelling topic. He even offered hastily done sketches of the Assembly Room in Philadelphia to prod Trumbull along.[29]

Trumbull had studied under Benjamin West, the famed artist, and used West's image of the Treaty of Paris as the model. He began with a small painting of the drafting committee showing its work to Congress, then spent years crafting likenesses of forty-seven delegates who served that summer. A U.S. Capitol historian notes that Trumbull "decided not to attempt a wholly accurate rendering of the scene; rather, he made his goal the preservation of the images of the Nation's founders. He excluded those for whom no authoritative image could be found or created." That explains why men who did not sign the Declaration, such as John Dickinson and Robert R. Livingston, are included in the painting, but fourteen others who *did* sign are missing. One study determined that only thirty-one of the forty-three delegates present in Congress on June 28 made it into the painting.[30]

Trumbull depicts Jefferson presenting the draft to President John Hancock at the front of the room. Jefferson is flanked by Adams and Franklin, with fellow committee members Livingston and Roger Sherman behind them. Adams, in particular, strikes a bold and determined pose, hand on hip, one knee slightly bent. Most of the other delegates are seated side by side in a pleasant, orderly arrangement—the kind that certainly never happened within those walls that summer.

To prepare for public display in 1818, the small image was repurposed on a much larger canvas, twelve feet by eighteen feet. Trumbull insisted that John Adams and many of his family members join him for a special unveiling at Boston in November. Curmudgeonly as ever, Adams warned Trumbull about inaccuracies in advance—"Let not our posterity be deluded with fictions under the pretense of poetical or graphical license"—and wondered why such a dramatically large size was necessary ("The dimensions . . . appear vast"). But when the painting was shown at several sites across the country, including Faneuil Hall, it generated huge audiences and widespread public acclaim.[31]

Adams's son, John Quincy, who was secretary of state when the painting came to Washington, saw positive aspects despite its obvious flaws. He knew that no single image by a third-party artist could possibly capture the founding moment. "I am glad that you have seen Trumbull's picture of Independence," he wrote to his father shortly afterward, boosting his spirits. "I rejoice that the Picture has been painted, as a collection of likenesses taken from life, of the founders of the greatest Nation this Ball of Earth has seen or will see."[32]

The younger Adams made an even more important gesture in 1820 when he arranged for a Washington engraver, William J. Stone, to produce an official facsimile of the Declaration. The original parchment copy made by Timothy Matlack in 1776 was starting to fade after forty-plus years because of rough handling and exposure to sunlight. John Quincy feared further damage to the iconic text and wanted to preserve it for all time. Stone's engraving, made on copperplate, is the clear, sharp, black-on-white version printed in textbooks and familiar to most Americans today.[33]

It took Stone almost three full years to complete his work. A modern government document says: "The Stone Declaration of Independence captured much of the original document's artistry before it deteriorated to its present condition. Before photography, documents like the Declaration . . . could be produced in only a few ways: by hand tracing, using a mechanical device like a pantograph, or wetting an original document and lifting a small amount of ink from it." It is not known, however, which process the engraver used.[34]

Stone sold the facsimile version to the U.S. State Department in 1823. John Quincy Adams and his staff ordered two hundred copies,

Figure 15.1. John Trumbull's painting, *Declaration of Independence*, is displayed at the U.S. Capitol. It is a romanticized recreation of the moment when the Committee of Five delivered its draft to Congress in Philadelphia on June 28, 1776. Committee members are (l–r) John Adams, Roger Sherman, Robert R. Livingston, Thomas Jefferson, and Benjamin Franklin. *(Wikimedia Commons)*

distributing them to a series of dignitaries—including two each to the only surviving signers of the Declaration—Adams, Jefferson, and Charles Carroll. Also receiving two copies were President James Monroe, Vice President Daniel Thompkins, former president James Madison, and the Marquis de Lafayette. Others went to the Senate, the House of Representatives, the White House, the Supreme Court, and "the governors and legislatures of the states and territories, and to universities and colleges in the United States."[35]

The Stone engraving added to the luster and legacy of the Declaration in the early 1820s and became the basis for all future facsimiles.

* * *

Adams and Jefferson returned to the subject of independence on several occasions in the 1820s, often encouraged by others to recount the story. Adams was eight-five years old at the start of the decade, Jefferson seventy-seven. Their years were whisking by.

One of the most intriguing inquiries came to Adams in 1822 from his former secretary of state, Timothy Pickering. An unrepentant Federalist, Pickering was piecing together an account of the spring and summer of 1776, particularly in regard to declaring independence. The act was so "distinguished," he said, that "the most particular history of that transaction will probably be sought for; not merely as an interesting curiosity, but to do substantial justice to the abilities and energies of the leaders in that great measure." In part, he wondered how someone as young as Jefferson was picked to lead the drafting committee.

Pickering laid out the story as he knew it the time, drawn mostly from available "public journals." Could Adams provide further details or more insight? As his eight-paragraph letter went on, however, it was clear that Pickering had another motive. He was preparing either an article or an oration about the Declaration, and he doubted whether the document—or Jefferson himself—deserved such hallowed status.

"After all," Pickering wrote, "it does not contain many new ideas . . ."

> It is rather a compilation of facts & sentiments stated and expressed during the preceding eleven years. . . . The great merit of any compilation consists in the lucid and forcible arrangement of the matter. The reported declaration [as submitted by the committee] was evidently enfeebled by its redundancies—Yet there is no end of the praises of Mr. Jefferson as the *author* of the declaration of independence—If he had been the author of our independence itself, he could hardly have been more eulogized—I have thought it desirable that the real facts in this case should be ascertained."[36]

Adams responded four days later. Much to Pickering's dismay, there was extensive praise of Jefferson and his work.

Jefferson "came into Congress in June 1775 and brought with him a reputation for literature, science, and a happy talent for composition," Adams said. "Writings of his were handed about, remarkable for the peculiar felicity of expression. Though a silent member in Congress, he was so prompt, frank, and explicit upon Committees . . . that he soon seized upon my heart." Adams then repeated the story, first told in the early 1800s, that he personally selected Jefferson to write the first draft (no one ever confirmed this, but the tale was so compelling that it became an accepted part of history).

Adams recalled seeing Jefferson's draft for the first time and being "delighted with its high tone, and the flights of Oratory with which it abounded." That included his condemnation of the slave trade, which he knew "his Southern Brethren would never suffer to pass." There were "other expressions which I would not have inserted if I had drawn it up," but he decided not to object because "Franklin and Sherman were to inspect it afterwards." After all that, however, the eighty-six-year-old Adams fell into Pickering's trap.

"As you justly observe," he wrote, "there is not an idea in it, but what had been hackney'd in Congress for two years before."[37]

Pickering's eyes widened; that was confirmation enough. He adapted those comments into a rousing Independence Day speech at Salem, Massachusetts, in July 1823. Pickering's tone was upbeat and respectful—even overtly patriotic—but he stunned the audience by claiming "it appears that this celebrated paper was a compilation of facts and sentiments stated and expressed in some preceding years, by those who wrote and vindicated the rights of the colonies." He went on to claim that edits made by Congress had "manifestly improved" it.[38]

News of Pickering's speech reached Monticello in a matter of weeks. Jefferson pondered it briefly before making his only comments in a private letter to James Madison on August 30, 1823.

He gave his old friend the benefit of the doubt. "I should . . . say that, in some of the particulars, Mr. Adams's memory has led him into unquestionable error," Jefferson wrote. "At the age of 88, and 47 years after the transaction of independence, this [memory] is not wonderful." Jefferson conceded that he, too, suffered from failing recollections, but he had the advantage of "written notes, taken by myself on the spot." Indeed, Jefferson had contemporary notes from 1776, many of them jotted that summer and fall, and he used them as a guide to tell his slightly different version of the story decades later.[39]

He did not dispute the claim that much of the language had been "hackney'd" for years. "I only know that I turned to neither book or pamphlet while writing it," Jefferson wrote. "I did not consider it as any part of my charge to invent new ideas altogether & to offer no sentiment which had ever been expressed before." (He was thinking along those same lines two years later when he said, "it was intended to be an expression of the American mind").[40]

But Jefferson did not stop with his thoughts on the Declaration. He interrupted his own storytelling to heap effusive praise on his Massachusetts colleague. "No man's confident & fervid addresses, more than Mr Adams's, encouraged and supported us thro' the difficulties surrounding us, which, like the ceaseless action of gravity, weight on us by night and day," Jefferson wrote. Moreover, it was Adams who "supported the declaration with zeal & ability, fighting fearlessly for every word of it" on the floor of Congress.[41]

If a "little lapse of memory" had resulted years later, so be it.

It was the final, definitive olive branch from one old rival to the other.

* * *

Adams and Jefferson exchanged only three short letters in 1826, the last year of their lives. Both men were ill, deteriorating quickly.

On March 25, Jefferson wrote that his grandson, Thomas Jefferson Randolph, would soon be visiting Boston, and "would think he had seen nothing were he to leave it without having seen you." Randolph delivered the letter in person on April 17, prompting Adams to write that it was "consoling" to have it come from "your grandson" himself. Adams added one brief comment about public affairs ("pretty much as usual") before signing off with "My love to all our family, and best wishes to all your health."[42]

It was the last either man heard from one another.

Both were invited to the fiftieth anniversary of American independence in Washington on July 4, 1826, but their feeble conditions would not allow it. Jefferson wrote to organizers on June 24 to express his regret for declining. "It adds sensibly to the sufferings of sickness to be deprived by it of a personal participation in the rejoicings of that day," he wrote.

"Let the annual return of this day forever refresh our recollection of [our] rights, and an undiminished devotion to them."[43]

His last wish was to survive until the day that made him famous. Late on the night of July 3 at Monticello, Jefferson awoke briefly and asked, "Is it the Fourth?" Told that it soon would be, he said, "Ah, just as I wished."

He faded in and out of consciousness on the morning of July 4, "murmuring" at one point about the Revolutionary Committee of Safety, acting as though he were writing another epic text. Jefferson took his last breath at about 1:00 p.m., dying with his eyes open.[44]

Six hundred miles to the north, John Adams faced a similar fate. Sometime in the late afternoon, bed-ridden and struggling to breathe, he stirred himself awake to whisper, "Thomas Jefferson survives." His thoughts were on Jefferson in his final moments, wondering if his old friend had bested him again. Shortly after 6:00 p.m., Adams, too, fell silent and followed Jefferson in death.[45]

The odds that this would happen to these two giants of history on the fiftieth anniversary of American independence were too absurd to calculate. Many in the country saw it as "visible and palpable" evidence of "Divine favor" at work. Eulogies were held across the country, with one orator saying, "the superstitious saw it as miraculous, and the judicious saw in the event the hand of Providence."[46] But it was left to a loquacious future senator from Massachusetts named Caleb Cushing to sum it up best for posterity.

"For one such man to die on such a day would have been an event never to be forgotten," Cushing said. "But for them, on the anniversary of the day when the nation was born, and on its fiftieth anniversary, too, to quit the scene of their earthly honors as it were in company—oh, never, never shall the lapse of ages or the annals of time disclose a parallel."[47]

Figure 15.2. Thomas Jefferson wrote the inscription for his own tombstone, leading with what he considered to be his greatest achievement: "Author of the Declaration of American Independence." The tombstone sits in the family graveyard at Monticello. *(Author photo)*

CHAPTER 16

"Four Score and Seven Years"

THE FIRST PERSON WHO TRIED TO CAPITALIZE ON THE PROMISE OF THE Declaration of Independence was Prince Hall, a free Black resident of Boston. He was a different kind of revolutionary.

Hall saw the Declaration as a pivot point in history and adopted some of its language in a petition to the Massachusetts legislature in January 1777. Advocating freedom on behalf of seven enslaved colleagues, he wrote that they had an "inalienable right to that freedom, which the great Parent of the Universe hath bestowed equally on all Mankind" (and especially in this "land of Liberty"). Hall's petition did not succeed, but the passion of his quest rattled viewpoints in the region; six years later, in 1783, the Massachusetts Supreme Judicial Court declared slavery unconstitutional.[1]

A much more expansive group effort came in 1848, when a first of-its-kind Women's Rights Convention was held in Seneca Falls, New York. More than three hundred women and men crowded into Wesleyan Chapel over two sweltering days in mid-July to hear a "Declaration of Sentiments," asserting gender equality—outlined by activist Elizabeth Cady Stanton, modeled closely on the Declaration of Independence, and eventually signed by one hundred attendees, including abolitionist Frederick Douglass.[2]

(Had he been alive at the time, John Adams would have understood. His wife, Abigail, advised him in spring 1776 to "[r]emember the Ladies, and be more generous and favourable to them than your ancestors. Do not put such unlimited power into the hands of the Husbands. . . . If particular care and attention is not paid to the Ladies, we are determined to foment a Rebellion, and will not hold ourselves bound by any Laws in which we have no voice or Representation.")[3]

The proposals from Seneca Falls were too new and bold to have any immediate impact, but the convention is viewed by many as the birthplace of American feminism. Stanton and her coauthor, Mary Ann M'Clintock, altered the language of the Declaration to make their points with a style and verve never attempted before. "We hold these truths to be self-evident that all men *and women* are created equal," they wrote. "The history of mankind is a history of repeated injuries and usurpations on the part of man toward woman, having in direct object the establishment of absolute tyranny over her. To prove this, let fact be submitted to a candid world."

They went on to list sixteen charges, mimicking Jefferson's style against the king and leading with "[h]e has never permitted her to exercise her inalienable right to the elective franchise."[4]

The document was ratified on July 20 after an unexpectedly heated debate on the right to vote; some in attendance weren't willing to go that far. Sixty-eight women and thirty-two men agreed to sign it by the end of the day (although, remarkably, Stanton's husband, Henry, was one who did not). The *North Star*, an abolitionist newspaper published by Douglass in Rochester, New York, carried a full account the next week, under the large, stark headline "The Rights of Women." Douglass wrote that if "government is only just which governs by the free consent of the governed, there can be no reason in the word for denying to woman the exercise of the elective franchise, or a hand in making and administering the laws of the land." Like Stanton and M'Clintock, he leaned on the same principles and language the founders had espoused.[5]

"By tying the complaints of women to the most distinguished political statement the nation had made, [Stanton] implied that women's demands were no more or less radicals than the American Revolution," historian Linda Kerber wrote. "They were, in fact, an implicit fulfillment of the commitments already made" in the Declaration.[6]

In both cases, for the first time in American history, leaders from underserved communities took Jefferson's words and claimed them for themselves.

* * *

Frederick Douglass escaped from slavery in Maryland in 1838 to become one of the country's most vigorous and revered abolitionists. Blessed with a deep, baritone voice and a flair for evocative oratory, Douglass—at his unrepentant best—was scathing in his criticism of America's hypocrisy over freedom and bondage.

As such, he revered the Declaration of Independence but had no use for the Fourth of July.

Those two conflicting views came to a head in summer 1852, when the Ladies' Anti-Slavery Society in Rochester tapped Douglass to give a speech on Independence Day. The first hint that it might be something different came when he changed the date to July 5. The day's events began smoothly enough, with a prayer and public reading of the entire Declaration, before Douglass strode confidently, almost defiantly, to the podium. The thirty-page script he prepared did not have a formal title, but it came to be known in history as: "What to the Slave Is the 4th of July?"[7]

Douglass knew he would be pushing boundaries that even the six hundred abolitionists in his audience—mostly white, and mostly patriotic—might find revolting. He disarmed them at first with an overly humble apology about "my limited powers of speech" and followed with praise of the founding fathers. "The signers of the Declaration of Independence were brave men . . . statesmen, patriots and heroes," Douglass said. "It does not happen to a nation to raise, at one time, such a number of truly great men." But he changed his tone abruptly, as if on cue, reminding them that the holiday they celebrated was not for everyone—and certainly not for him.

Eyebrows arched.

This was "*your* National Independence," Douglass sneered, "*your* political freedom," achieved by "*your* fathers" (emphasis added). There was an entire race of American residents, some of them free men, who were not included. "The Fourth [of] July is yours, not mine. You may rejoice, I must mourn . . . pardon me, allow me to ask why am I called to speak here today? What have I, or those I represent, to do with your national independence?"

It all was working up to the most momentous passage of his speech.

> What, to the American slave, is your 4th of July? I answer, a day that revels to him, more than all the other days in the year, the gross injustice and cruelty which he is the constant victim. To him, your celebration is a sham; your boasted liberty, an unholy license; your national greatness, swelling vanity . . . your prayers and hymns, your sermons and thanks-givings, with all your religious parade, and solemnity, are, to him, mere bombast, fraud, deception, hypocrisy. . . . There is not a nation on earth guilty of practices, more shocking and bloody, than are the people of these United States, at this very hour.[8]

Douglass went on for fifteen more pages of text, chastising the country for its lip service to freedom and equality. It was only near the end that he softened his focus and shifted into an upbeat final message. "I do not despair of this country," Douglass said. "There are forces in operation which must inevitably work the downfall of slavery. . . . I, therefore, leave off where I began, with hope . . . drawing encouragement from the Declaration of Independence, the great principles it contains, and the genius of American institutions."[9] When he finished and stepped back from the podium, the largely white audience had gotten over its initial shock and responded with a "universal burst of applause."[10]

There was a much different atmosphere ten years later, when Douglass spoke before a crowd of two thousand at rural Himrod's Corner, New York, on July 4, 1862. The American Civil War was now in its second full year, and white men from northern states were fighting and dying on far-away battlefields to determine the fate of the Union. President Abraham Lincoln's war to end the rebellion offered no guarantee of success, but Douglass saw an astounding shift in attitude and national purpose. It was no longer just "your" fathers anymore, but "*our* fathers" . . . "*this* national anniversary" . . . "*our* Generals" . . . "*this* great republic." The transition

Figure 16.1. Frederick Douglass gave an impactful speech in 1852, titled "What to the Slave Is the 4th of July?" *(Wikimedia Commons)*

was complete when he added, "We are now continuing the tremendous struggle which your fathers, *and my fathers*, began eighty-six years ago."[11]

Less than three months later, on September 22, 1862, following victory at the Battle of Antietam, Lincoln issued the preliminary Emancipation Proclamation, freeing all slaves in rebelling southern states. It shifted the war from a fight to save the Union to a clash over slavery and a new birth of freedom for all Americans, something that Douglass, the brilliant and audacious former slave, had helped to bring about in his own way.

* * *

Other than Thomas Jefferson and John Adams, no president had a deeper connection to the Declaration of Independence than Abraham Lincoln. No one drove that narrative harder than Lincoln himself.

"I have never had a feeling politically that did not spring from the sentiments embodied in the Declaration," he said in a speech at Independence Hall in February 1861.[12]

The connection likely stemmed from his teenage years in Springfield, Illinois, when Lincoln received his first copy of William Grisham's *History of the United States*. Grisham's book, published in 1821, carried the Declaration in its entirety and called on readers to "demonstrate by our actions 'That all men are created equal; that they are endowed by their Creator with certain unalienable rights; that amongst these are life, liberty and the pursuit of happiness." Lincoln devoured it; looking back, one can see him starting on a path that would lead to national politics, the presidency, and the Gettysburg Address.[13]

The impact was clear by 1838, when Lincoln, a twenty-eight-year-old member of the Illinois state legislature, spoke at the Young Men's Lyceum in Springfield. In a speech titled "The Perpetuation of Our Political Institutions," he focused on the threat of rising social disorder on American freedoms. "Let every lover of liberty . . . swear by the blood of the Revolution, never to violate in the least particular, the laws of the country," Lincoln said. "As the patriots of seventy-six did to the support of the Declaration of Independence, so to the support of the Constitution and Laws, let every American pledge his life, his property, and his sacred honor." Four years later, speaking at a local temperance convention, he touched on similar themes. "Of our political revolution of '76, we are all justly proud. . . . In it was the germ that vegetated, and still is to grow and expand into the universal liberty of mankind."[14]

Lincoln also was influenced by Mason L. Weems's heavily romanticized biography on George Washington, *The Life of Washington*, published in 1800. It was the book responsible for many long-held Washington myths that still persist today, including chopping down a cherry tree and never telling a lie (one reviewer called it "eighty pages of as entertaining and edifying matter as can be found in the annals of fanaticism and absurdity"). Just as absurdly, Weems's version of the founding claimed that all five members of the committee to draft the Declaration—Jefferson, Adams, Benjamin Franklin, Robert R. Livingston, and Roger Sherman—were asked to compose separate drafts. When they reconvened a few days later, Jefferson read his version first, to loud and unanimous approval. "It had the honour to give such complete satisfaction, that none other was read," Weems wrote.[15]

That began the deification of Jefferson in Lincoln's mind—a sense of hero worship that continued for the rest of his life. Studying Jefferson's writing at every opportunity, he adopted his language and ideas in speeches, letters, and inaugural addresses, often quoting him directly, almost always defending him. "The principles of Jefferson are the definitions and axioms of free society," Lincoln wrote in 1859, a year before running for president. "But soberly, it is now no child's play to save the principles of Jefferson from total overthrow in this nation."[16]

For Lincoln and most Americans at the start of the 1850s, the preamble took precedence over all other aspects of the Declaration. Almost eighty years after the revolution, there was no more need to obsess over British tyranny or the real and imagined vices of the king. Much of the other wording was irrelevant by now, intended for ancient issues already achieved. What endured over time was the vivid second paragraph, increasing in meaning and power—in particular, the self-evident truth that all men are created equal.

Lincoln saw it as an essential ally in 1854, when slavery was the topic again. Senator Stephen A. Douglas of Illinois had marshaled a bill through Congress, the Kansas-Nebraska Act, allowing residents of new territories to determine for themselves whether slavery should be allowed. This idea of "popular sovereignty" appalled Lincoln, who believed that the act's effect—negating the Missouri Compromise—would give pro-slavery activists a stronger foothold. It was a turning point in the life of this former congressman who had willingly left the public stage.

"From 1849–1854, I practiced law more assiduously than ever before," Lincoln wrote, admitting, "I was losing interest in politics, when the repeal of the Missouri Compromise aroused me again."[17]

Douglas was on a public relations tour of Illinois when he scheduled a three-hour speech in Peoria on October 16, 1854, extolling the virtues of repeal. Lincoln, who was present, rose immediately to refute him. The two men were not yet opposing candidates for political office, but their stances on this vital moral issue could not have been more extreme. A modern historian judged Lincoln's speech to be "the most comprehensive expression of [his] political thought and statesmanship on slavery . . . a multifaceted critique of the institution on moral, political, legal, and historical grounds."[18] To no one's surprise, he referenced the Declaration on several occasions.

Lincoln said the "declared indifference" of popular sovereignty was actually "covert *real* zeal" for the spread of slavery. He attacked human bondage as a "monstrous injustice" that "enables the enemies of free institutions" to taunt Americans as hypocrites. He ranted that otherwise reasonable men were now in "an open war with the very fundamental principles of civil liberty, criticizing the Declaration of Independence." He was aghast, emboldened, and energized.

He had no solution for the overall issue of slavery, Lincoln conceded. "If all earthly power were given me, I should not know what to do as to the institution." But if it could not be stopped altogether in the 1850s, it could at least be restrained in the territories. The Compromise had achieved that, at least in part, before Douglas and the Congress repealed it, and now more work was required. In its absence, the written words of a slaveholder—Jefferson—could fill the void. Lincoln said:

> Let us re-adopt the Declaration of Independence, and with it, the practices and policy, which harmonize with it. Let north and south—let all Americans—let all lovers of liberty everywhere—join in the great and good work. If we do this, we shall not only have saved the Union; but we shall have so saved it, as to make, and to keep it, forever worthy of the saving. We shall have so saved it, that the succeeding millions of free happy people, the world over, shall rise up, and call us blessed, to the latest generations.[19]

Four years later, the two men faced off again in a race for Douglas's U.S. Senate seat, engaging in a series of debates made famous by oratorical fire. The foundational issues of slavery and popular sovereignty remained the same.

On July 9, 1858, in Chicago, Douglas left no doubt as to where he stood. "I am opposed to negro equality," he said. "[T]his government of ours is founded on the white basis. It was made by the white man, for the benefit of the white man. . . . I am opposing to taking any step that recognizes the negro man or the Indian as the equal of the white."[20] Lincoln took it all in before countering with vigor the next night.

He opened by reciting the preamble's claim of equality for all. "This is the electric cord of the Declaration that links the hearts of patriotic and liberty-loving men everywhere, that will link those patriotic hearts as long as the love of freedom exists in the minds of men throughout the world," Lincoln said. "I should like to know if taking this old Declaration of Independence, which declares that all men are equal upon principle and making exceptions to it, where will it stop?" Attendees answered with loud shouts that it should not be altered or refuted. "Let us stick to it, then," he said. "Let us stand firmly by it."[21]

They renewed their verbal sparring at Springfield, Illinois, on July 17, promoting different versions of the same themes.

From Douglas: "Remember that at the time the Declaration was put forth, every one of the Thirteen Colonies were slaveholding colonies—every man who signed the Declaration represented slaveholding constituents."

From Lincoln: "I adhere to the Declaration of Independence. If Judge Douglas and his friends are not willing to stand by it, let them come up and amend it. Let them make it read that all men are created equal except negroes. Let us have it decided whether the Declaration of Independence, in this blessed year of 1858, shall be thus amended."[22]

There were many other issues beyond slavery, of course, and Douglas, with the power of incumbency, won reelection to his seat, but Lincoln made a substantial impression on the national stage. The rivalry that began four years earlier would play out once more in a much more fateful contest for the presidency in 1860.

* * *

In spring 1859, private citizen Lincoln was invited to travel to Boston for a festival honoring Jefferson's birthday. His schedule did not permit it, but the letter he sent to decline the invitation gave his most eloquent view of the Declaration's draftsman:

> All honor to Jefferson—to the man who, in the concrete pressure of a struggle for national independence by a single people, had the coolness, forecast and capacity to introduce in a merely revolutionary document, an abstract truth, applicable to all men and all times, and so to embalm it there, that to-day, and in all coming days, it shall be a rebuke and a stumbling-block to the very harbingers of re-appearing tyranny and oppression.
>
> Your obedient servant,
> A. LINCOLN[23]

The letter was reprinted often in Republican papers, forging, at least in theory, an unbreakable link between the two men in the eyes of Republican voters.

The party nominated Lincoln for president in 1860, with a platform that called for "maintenance of the principles promulgated in the Declaration of Independence and embodied in the federal Constitution."[24] He went on to defeat Douglas and two other candidates in one of the most fractured results in American history. Revealingly, Lincoln got no votes in ten of the eleven states that would make up the Confederacy and only miniscule support (1.1 percent) in Virginia.[25] Fearing for the future of slavery and disruption of its economy because of a Lincoln presidency, South Carolina became the first state to secede from the Union in December 1860.

Six other states had seceded by the time the president-elect began his trip east toward Washington, DC, in late winter 1861.[26] On February 22, the anniversary of Washington's birthday, his PR-savvy aides scheduled a flag-raising ceremony at Independence Hall. Lincoln was genuinely moved by his first visit to the birthplace of the Declaration, touring the Assembly Room and walking in the footsteps of Jefferson and Adams. "You have kindly suggested to me that in my hands is the task of restoring peace in our distracted country," Lincoln said. "I can say in return that all the political sentiments I entertain have been drawn from the sentiments which originated, and were given to the world from this hall. . . . I have often pondered over the dangers which were incurred by the men who assembled here and adopted the Declaration of Independence. . . . It was that which gave promise that in due time the weights should be lifted from the shoulders of all men, and that all should have an equal chance."[27]

And yet Lincoln made it clear in his first inaugural address on March 4, 1861, that he had no immediate plans to end slavery in the south. "I have no purpose, directly or indirectly, to interfere with the institution of slavery in the States where it exists," he said. "I believe I have no lawful right to do so." Near the end of his speech, he touched on the "momentous issue" of a potential civil war and tried his best to calm the nerves of southern citizens. "The Government will not assail you," Lincoln pledged. "You can have no conflict without yourselves being aggressors. . . . We are not enemies, but friends. We must not be enemies."[28]

Those words mattered little south of the Mason-Dixon line. The Confederacy of seceding states fired on federal troops at Fort Sumter, South Carolina, on April 12, 1861, starting a war that lasted for four years and cost more than seven hundred thousand lives. Despite overwhelming advantages in manpower and equipment, Lincoln's Union army suffered repeated defeats in the first year of anguished combat. It was not until victory at the Battle of Antietam at Sharpsburg, Maryland, in September 1862 that the president changed the course of the war and American history with one dramatic stroke of his pen.

The Emancipation Proclamation freed all slaves in rebelling states and—not insignificantly from a war perspective—allowed Black troops to join the army. It was issued in preliminary form on September 22, 1862, five days after Antietam, and went into effect on January 1, 1863. But Lincoln still needed to have victories on the battlefield, and major Union setbacks at Fredericksburg, Virginia, in December 1862 and Chancellorsville, Virginia, in May 1863 undercut his authority. It was not until the first week of July 1863 that the momentum turned in a big way.

Union troops defeated Robert E. Lee's army in the three-day Battle of Gettysburg in Pennsylvania, crushing Pickett's Charge on July 3 and

Figure 16.2. Abraham Lincoln helped raise a flag at Independence Hall on February 22, 1861, the anniversary of George Washington's birthday. This occurred shortly before Lincoln's inauguration as president. *(Wikimedia Commons)*

forcing Lee to retreat. One day later, Confederate troops surrendered to Ulysses S. Grant at the strategic river port city of Vicksburg, Mississippi. News of successive victories around the anniversary of independence sparked massive celebrations across the war-weary north. In Washington on July 7, a group of gleeful serenaders at the White House even demanded a few words from the president. Though he was not prepared for a formal speech, Lincoln acquiesced by giving one of the most poignant (if underappreciated) addresses of his life:

> I do most sincerely thank Almighty God for the occasion on which you have called. How long ago is it?—eighty odd years—since on the Fourth of July for the first time in the history of the world a nation, by its representatives, assembled and declared as a self-evident truth that "all men are created equal." That was the birthday of the United States of America. Since then, the Fourth of July has had several peculiar recognitions.
>
> The two most distinguished men in the framing and support of the Declaration were Thomas Jefferson and John Adams—the one having penned it and the other sustained it most forcibly in debate—the only two of the fifty-five who [signed] it being elected President of the United States. Precisely fifty years after they put their hands to the paper it please Almighty God to take both from the stage of action. This was indeed an extraordinary and remarkable event in our history. Another President (James Monroe), five years after, was called from this stage of existence on the same day and month of the years . . .
>
> Now, on this last Fourth of July just passed, when we have a gigantic Rebellion . . . in a succession of battles . . . the cohorts of those who opposed the declaration that all men are created equal, "turned tail" and run.

Lincoln halted after only a few minutes. He had not yet given the topic enough thought, and this was neither the time nor the setting to broach its broader context. "Gentlemen," he said, "this is a glorious theme, and the occasion for a speech, but I am not prepared to make one worthy of the occasion."[29] That would come a few months later, at an event to honor the fallen heroes at Gettysburg.

Officials there planned to dedicate a new national soldiers' cemetery on November 19, 1863. The keynote speaker would be Edward Everett of Massachusetts, one of the nation's premier orators, but Lincoln was asked, "as Chief Executive of the nation," to "set apart these grounds to their sacred use by a few appropriate remarks." When the day arrived, Everett delivered a thunderous two-hour address before Lincoln stepped forward to close the event, almost as an afterthought. Over the course of a scant 272 words, he realigned the national creed with a masterclass of oration that is still regarded as the greatest speech in American history.

Lincoln began by addressing the country's birth with remarkable specificity. It was no longer "eighty odd years" ago, as he had said four months earlier in Washington. It was "four score and seven years." Eighty-six years. Dating to 1776.

America did not begin with the Battle of Lexington and Concord in 1775. It did not begin with the Constitution of 1787. It began, instead, when Jefferson, Adams, and other members of the Second Continental Congress approved and signed the Declaration of Independence. Now, thanks to the immortal words of his Gettysburg Address, it would be embedded even deeper in history for future generations:

> Four score and seven years ago our fathers brought forth on this continent, a new nation, conceived in Liberty and dedicated to the proposition that all men are created equal. Now we are engaged in a great civil war, testing whether that nation, or any nation so conceived, and so dedicated, can long endure.

He made sharp, uplifting points in ten beautifully crafted sentences: that men who fell in battle here did not die in vain; that a "new birth of freedom" was still possible for the country; and that "government of the people, by the people, for the people, shall not perish from the earth."[30] Brevity was part of its grandeur. The speech was so short that photographers did not have a chance to capture even one image of Lincoln at the podium. A reporter from Philadelphia approached him afterward to ask, in all seriousness, "if that was all."

"Yes, for the present," the president said.[31]

The war continued for two more years, but Lincoln's words echoed down through the ages (by contrast, no one remembered anything Everett said). Even after he was struck down by an assassin's bullet on April 15, 1865, six days after Lee surrendered to Grant, his impact on the country, and the spirit of democracy, endured. It is safe to say that, other than Jefferson and Adams, and possibly Benjamin Franklin, no one did more to promote the ideals of American independence than Lincoln. His love for it was genuine, forged in the cauldron of political strife—not something that happened by chance on one magical day at Gettysburg in November 1863.

As historian Garry Wills noted in his book *Lincoln at Gettysburg*, "Lincoln was able to achieve the loftiness, ideality, and brevity of the Gettysburg Address because he had spent a good part of the 1850s repeatedly relating all the most sensitive issues of the day to the Declaration's supreme principle. If all men are created equal, they cannot be property." It was almost as though he had written the words himself.[32]

* * *

The words of the Declaration of Independence have remained vivid and purposeful since Lincoln's day, adapted to protests for women's suffrage, civil rights, labor causes, and many others. In many of these cases, activists sought to "seize the Declaration, make it their own, and if necessary rewrite it to make explicit how it could extend to people who felt marginalized or excluded." Nineteenth-century examples included "The Working Man's Declaration of Independence" and "The Declaration of the Rights of the Women of the United States." On July 4, 1892, the farmers' alliance declared independence from the two-party system and started its own (ill-fated) party, the People's Party.[33]

The Declaration and Fourth of July celebrations also had influence across the ocean, including in, of all places, England (which would have made Jefferson shudder). On July 4, 1918, nearing the end of World War I, Winston Churchill, then the British minister of munitions, said "a great harmony exists between the spirit and language of the Declaration of Independence and all we are fighting for now."[34] Several months later, representatives of twelve countries in the Mid-European Union traveled to Independence Hall to debate and sign the Declaration of Common Aims, creating a short-lived alliance in the cradle of America's birth.[35]

One of the most remarkable and ironic uses of Jefferson's language came in 1945, when Vietnamese leader Ho Chi Minh declared his country's independence from France. Speaking to a massive crowd of celebrants in Hanoi, he read his "Declaration of Independence of the Democratic Republic of Vietnam" for the first time in public:

> All men are created equal. They are endowed by their Creator with certain inalienable rights, among them are Life, Liberty and the pursuit of Happiness.
>
> This immortal statement was made in the Declaration of Independence of the United States of America in 1776. In a broader sense, this means: All the peoples of the earth are equal from birth, and the peoples have a right to live, to be happy and free.

The United States did not agree to support Ho as requested, however; French colonialists returned, and combat soon raged across the country. America intervened as an ally of South Vietnam, fighting Ho's communist regime in a tragic and ultimately unsuccessful war that cost fifty-nine thousand lives during the 1960s and 1970s.

The Declaration's message hit home in a different way in 1963 when Dr. Martin Luther King spoke from the steps of the Lincoln Memorial during one of the signature moments of the civil rights movement, the "March on Washington for Jobs and Freedom." Referencing Lincoln, he harkened back to the Emancipation Proclamation one hundred years earlier—or, as King described it, "five score years ago." In a speech made famous by his signature phrase, "I have a dream," he challenged his country to live up, finally, to its founding ideals.

"In a sense we've come to our nation's capital to cash a check," King said. "When the architects of our republic wrote the magnificent words of the Constitution and the Declaration of Independence, they were signing a promissory note to which every American was to fall heir. This note was a promise that all men—yes, black men as well as white men—would be guaranteed the unalienable rights of life, liberty and the pursuit of happiness."

It was apparent by 1963 that the note had gone unfulfilled, but King was relentless, pushing on, undeterred. He still had a dream. "It is a dream deeply rooted in the American dream," he said. "I have a dream that one day this nation will rise up and live out the true meaning of its creed: We hold these truths to be self-evident, that all men are created equal."[36]

The Declaration, again.

CHAPTER 17

More Modern Perspectives

MILLIONS OF AMERICANS VISIT THE THOMAS JEFFERSON MEMORIAL IN Washington, DC, each year, marveling at a quote from the Declaration of Independence carved into one of its marble panels. Few are aware that it is historically inaccurate.

The words from the Declaration are not exact, and some of them were not even written by Jefferson.

How did this happen?

The Jefferson Memorial Committee was given the daunting task in 1941 of recapping the Declaration's spirit in just 325 letters. Space is often a challenge in memorial work, but it was especially acute here because the preamble's language is among the most famous—and familiar—in American history. Jefferson's great-grandson was one of three men assigned to carefully assess and pare down the wording.[1] They began by making a few tweaks and offered a first proposal that was reasonably close to the original:

> WE HOLD THESE TRUTHS TO BE SELF-EVIDENT THAT ALL MEN ARE CREATED EQUAL: THAT THEY ARE ENDOWED BY THEIR CREATOR WITH CERTAIN INALIENABLE RIGHTS: THAT AMONG THESE ARE LIFE, LIBERTY AND THE PURSUIT OF HAPPINESS; THAT TO SECURE THESE RIGHTS GOVERNMENTS ARE INSTI-TUTED AMONG MEN, DERIVING THEIR JUST POWERS FROM THE CONSENT OF THE GOVERNED. WHENEVER

ANY FORM OF GOVERNMENT BECOMES DESTRUCTIVE
OF THESE ENDS IT IS THE RIGHT OF THE PEOPLE TO
ALTER OR ABOLISH IT.[2]

Not bad, but not precise—and some of the edits were curious. Punctuation was changed; colons were inserted. "Unalienable" became "inalienable." A word was removed, creating a new sentence where there had been none, and some phrases were deleted altogether. Even with all that, the proposal was still too long—371 letters.[3]

Looking for support and guidance, the committee forwarded its work to President Franklin Delano Roosevelt on May 13, 1941. FDR was honored and delighted, responding two days later with his own detailed suggestions. "I think these inscriptions are excellent," he wrote, but "I do miss the last paragraph of the Declaration of Independence. It seems to me that it should appear somewhere. It could be condensed somewhat as follows:

> We . . . solemnly publish and declare that these United Colonies are, and of Right ought to be Free and Independent States. . . . And for the support of this Declaration, with a firm reliance on the protection of Divine Providence, we mutually pledge to each other our Lives, our Fortunes, and our Sacred honor.[4]

Other than the ellipses, his quotation is exact. But was Roosevelt aware that Jefferson had not written most of that section? The first sentence came from Richard Henry Lee's original resolution to Congress ("these United Colonies are, and of Right ought to be, Free and Independent States"), and much of the rest came from other congressional rewrites. It was strange, to say the least, because this was *Jefferson's* memorial.[5]

"Did no one have the nerve to tell the president?" historian Pauline Maier wondered. "Or were they unaware that much of the above quotation . . . was not of Jefferson's composition?"[6]

Complicating matters, Roosevelt increased the size to an unmanageable 515 letters, well over the limit. The committee told Roosevelt it would try to "fit this in" but reminded him of the space restrictions, "the number of letters to be used being only 325."[7]

Members reached for their pens and crossed out thirty-three words from their first proposal, trying to accommodate FDR. Among the casualties were two of Jefferson's core phrases—"deriving their just powers from the consent of the governed" and the "right of the people to alter or abolish" government (he would not have been pleased). They also edited Roosevelt's segment, cutting the word "United" before "Colonies" and dropping "to each other" from the last sentence. In a final oddity, the spelling of "honor" was changed to "honour."[8]

As inscribed on the Jefferson Memorial, which opened in 1943, the ode to the Declaration reads:

WE HOLD THESE TRUTHS TO BE SELF-EVIDENT: THAT ALL MEN ARE CREATED EQUAL, THAT THEY ARE ENDOWED BY THEIR CREATOR WITH CERTAIN INALIEN-ABLE RIGHTS, AMONG THESE ARE LIFE, LIBERTY AND THE PURSUIT OF HAPPINESS, THAT TO SECURE THESE RIGHTS GOVERNMENTS ARE INSTITUTED AMONG MEN. WE . . . SOLEMNLY PUBLISH AND DECLARE, THAT THESE COLONIES ARE AND OF RIGHT OUGHT TO BE FREE AND INDEPENDENT STATES . . . AND FOR THE SUP-PORT OF THIS DECLARATION, WITH A FIRM RELIANCE ON THE PROTECTION OF DIVINE PROVIDENCE, WE MUTUALLY PLEDGE OUR LIVES, OUR FORTUNES AND OUR SACRED HONOUR.[9]

The final passage was more than four hundred letters—still over the limit—but with Roosevelt's support and approval, they *did* manage to "fit it in."

That same year, 1943, on the two hundredth anniversary of Jefferson's birth, the Library of Congress commissioned the first true textual analysis of the country's founding document. Written and overseen by Jefferson scholar Julian P. Boyd, *The Declaration of Independence: The Evolution of the Text* sought to recount the history of the drafting process by presenting prints of all known drafts and copies in Jefferson's hand. "It is appropriate

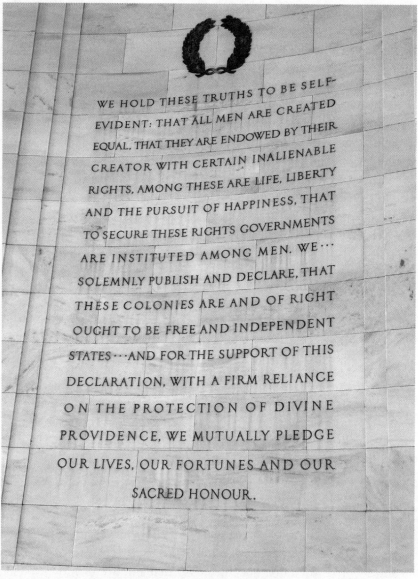

WE HOLD THESE TRUTHS TO BE SELF-EVIDENT: THAT ALL MEN ARE CREATED EQUAL, THAT THEY ARE ENDOWED BY THEIR CREATOR WITH CERTAIN INALIENABLE RIGHTS, AMONG THESE ARE LIFE, LIBERTY AND THE PURSUIT OF HAPPINESS, THAT TO SECURE THESE RIGHTS GOVERNMENTS ARE INSTITUTED AMONG MEN. WE··· SOLEMNLY PUBLISH AND DECLARE, THAT THESE COLONIES ARE AND OF RIGHT OUGHT TO BE FREE AND INDEPENDENT STATES···AND FOR THE SUPPORT OF THIS DECLARATION, WITH A FIRM RELIANCE ON THE PROTECTION OF DIVINE PROVIDENCE, WE MUTUALLY PLEDGE OUR LIVES, OUR FORTUNES AND OUR SACRED HONOUR.

Figure 17.1. This passage from the Declaration of Independence appears at the Thomas Jefferson Memorial in Washington, DC, although all of it was not written by Jefferson. *(Author photo)*

to all those who respect the precedents of freedom," the foreword said, "that the national library of the United States should publish in this year the various texts which illuminate the meaning of the Declaration of Independence." There was only one awkward factor: it assailed the British monarchy at a time when the United States and Great Britain were inseparable allies in a burgeoning world war against fascism.[10]

The congressional librarian, Archibald MacLeish, faced the delicate task of praising Jefferson's work in such a way that would not offend the British. Like Lincoln before him, he ignored the long segments that attacked King George III and focused on calls for freedom, equality, life, liberty, and the pursuit of happiness. It was decidedly deft footwork. "The Declaration of Independence is a positive and not a negative document," MacLeish wrote. "It is less a declaration of independence from Great Britain than a declaration of independence for the United States; less an act of revolution against the tyranny of a mediocre and stubborn king than an act of revolution for a society of free, and freedom-loving men."[11]

Whether Jefferson would have agreed with him (unlikely) was irrelevant. MacLeish offered a twentieth-century take that appeased folks on both sides of the Atlantic, and the book is still hailed today as "the preeminent textual presentation of the most fundamental document of the United States."[12]

* * *

The advent and reach of cinematography brought the independence story to life on new platforms in the twentieth and twenty-first centuries. At least two popular fictionalized productions had as much impact on the American public as anything printed in textbooks or historic narratives about the Declaration—the Broadway musical *1776* and the HBO miniseries *John Adams*.

Both were based on foundations of history, but shortcuts were taken out of necessity, scenes blended, facts rearranged, all in the name of entertainment. This is not a criticism, as neither pretended to be a documentary, but the power of stage and screen surely altered the views of modern-day Americans on how independence came about.

The play *1776* was a musical comedy conceived by a former high school history teacher, Sherman Edwards. No one who saw it will forget the early scene that had members of the Second Continental Congress telling a defiant John Adams: "Sit down, John! Sit down, John! For God's sake, John, sit down!" The play debuted at New York's 46th Street Theatre on March 16, 1969, to rave reviews and was performed 1,277 times over the next three years, on Broadway and across the country, almost always to packed houses. It won the Tony Award and the New York Drama Critics' Circle Award for best musical and became a cultural icon.[13]

Broadway's *Playbill* listed the following synopsis: "The founding fathers come alive in this classic American musical. John Adams, Benjamin Franklin, and Thomas Jefferson fight for independence against a deadlocked Continental Congress in a retelling filled with humor, romance, pathos and nail-biting tension."[14] But Edwards and playwright Peter Stone admitted that their numerous changes fell into five categories: "things altered, things surmised, things added, things deleted, and things rearranged." A review of opening night in the *New York Times* ignored the historical inaccuracies to praise its "style, humanity, wit, and passion," saying the authors "have really captured the Spirit of '76." Such acclaim continued when it was adapted to the big screen for a movie in 1972—perfect timing for the two hundredth anniversary of the Declaration in 1976.[15]

For many Americans, for many decades, *1776*, became the story of 1776.

Among other factual defects, however, Adams and Benjamin Franklin did not send Richard Henry Lee to Virginia to secure a motion on independence ("natural-LEE"); there was no "tally board" on the wall of Independence Hall, with "yea" and "nay" votes; Jefferson's wife, Martha, did not visit him in Philadelphia (she was ill at home in Virginia and could not travel); there is no record of a debate between Adams and Edward Rutledge of South Carolina over slavery; and the vote for independence, the editing of the Declaration, the approval of the Declaration, and the signing of the Declaration did not *all happen on the same day*.[16]

A much more fact-based account of the Declaration process is presented in episode 2 of the award-winning HBO miniseries *John Adams*, released in 2008. Although those consequential scenes were squeezed into less than an hour of screen time, producers had the benefit of having Adams's biographer, David McCullough, as a consultant. The tension of the July 1 debate between Adams and rival John Dickinson is palpable, and the twenty-five-seconds of silence after the vote for independence on July 2—as delegates pondered what they had wrought—is absolutely riveting television. But as with *1776*, there are leaps of faith and diversions from the record.

No one recorded what was said in real time, so much of the script is taken from letters delegates wrote that spring and summer—a reasonable alternative to fill the void. But there is no evidence that the historic triumvirate of Jefferson, Adams, and Franklin met together in person to review the draft of the Declaration (Franklin was laid up with gout). Edward Rutledge was portrayed as far too much of a villain by HBO, when, in fact, his proposals for delay on two occasions allowed the process to proceed. James Duane, who spoke for the opposition in the June–July debate scenes, had gone home to New York on May 31. Caesar Rodney returned to Philadelphia on his own for the dramatic final vote and was not, as the series showed, retrieved by Thomas McKean in Delaware. None of those miscues seem crucial on their own, but, as one critic noted, "fictionalized history can gain traction with alarming ease, spreading both factual errors and fundamental misconceptions; people tend to believe what they see on the screen."[17]

A sillier adaption of the Declaration story came in the movie *National Treasure*, starring Nicolas Cage and released in 2004. Cage played Benjamin Franklin Gates, son of Patrick Henry Gates and grandson of John Adams Gates. A secret passed down through the family held that there was a treasure map in invisible ink on the back of the Declaration.[18]

Ben Gates and his accomplices set off on a most improbable journey to sort this out; they *stole* the Declaration from the National Archives, took it to Independence Hall, outwitted a rival search crew, learned how to decipher the map, and, yes, located the long-lost ancient treasure. There were just enough hints of Declaration history to keep the theme going, including a shoutout to Timothy Matlack, the little-known congressional clerk who transcribed the original with iron gall ink. One of the clues Gates had to decode was the phrase, "Fifty-five in iron pen, Mr. Matlack can't offend." Fifty-five men had, indeed, signed the Declaration by January 1777 (only Thomas McKean signed later).[19]

The movie was a box-office hit, grossing more than $347 million, but it played to mixed critical views, including one that said, "National Treasure is no treasure, but it's a fun ride for those who can forgive its highly improbable plot." Nonetheless, there was at least a short-term spike in interest in the Declaration and an increase in visitation at the National Archives in the early 2000s.[20]

* * *

Then there was January 6, 2021.

One wonders what John Adams and Thomas Jefferson would have thought of images of election deniers storming the U.S. Capitol, carrying 1776 flags and "Don't Tread on Me" banners into the famed rotunda, where John Trumbull's painting, *The Declaration of Independence*, hangs in all its grandeur.

One wonders what Abraham Lincoln would have thought of Confederate flags breaching the Capitol's walls—a feat that Robert E. Lee and his powerful rebel army could not achieve during the American Civil War.

Many millions of law-abiding Americans were appalled by scenes of chaos that sent Congress members scurrying for safety, threatened the life of the vice president, injured Capitol police officers, caused multiple deaths, and, for the first time ever, interrupted the constitutionally mandated certification of votes. But a striking number of their fellow citizens saw it as legitimate protest, not an unlawful insurrection.

Especially since the early 1990s, disaffected Americans have rallied behind a radical statement Jefferson made in a private letter to Adams's son-in-law, William Stephens Smith, in 1787. "What country can preserve its liberties if their rulers are not warned from time to time that their people preserve the spirit of resistance," Jefferson wrote. "Let them take arms. . . . The tree of liberty must be refreshed from time to time with the blood of patriots and tyrants." (Jefferson, who was in France at the time, referenced the recent Shays' Rebellion in Massachusetts; what is rarely mentioned is that he said its motives were "founded in ignorance, not wickedness." He also wrote that "the remedy is to set them right as to facts, pardon and pacify them.")[21]

Taken out of context two hundred years later, Jefferson's words have been used by political extremists to justify wanton acts of criminal behavior. On April 19, 1995, Timothy McVeigh wore a T-shirt with Jefferson's quote when he attacked and blew up the Alfred P. Murrah Federal Building in Oklahoma City. The date was not chosen haphazardly—April 19 was the two-year anniversary of the FBI's deadly raid on the Branch Davidian complex in Waco, Texas, *and* the 220-year anniversary of Lexington and Concord. Meeting with an attorney shortly after his arrest, McVeigh explained his actions by reciting part of the Declaration's preamble: "When a long train of abuses and usurpations . . . evinces a design to reduce them under absolute despotism, it is their right, it is their duty, to throw off such government."[22]

Tenets of the revolution and the "Spirit of '76" also have been appropriated by both sides in America's modern culture wars. In August 2019, the *New York Times* published a provocative, multiplatform series reframing the roles of Black slavery and systemic racism as central to U.S. history, titled "The 1619 Project" (1619 being the year that enslaved Africans were first brought to Virginia). The work caused widespread introspection and was so impactful that it won a Pulitzer Prize for author Nikole Hannah-Jones, but even the *Times* would later concede that it had overreached in some areas, including the early assertion that 1619, not 1776, was the country's "true founding." The paper made a "clarification" in March 2020, writing, "we recognize that our original language could be read to suggest that protecting slavery was a primary motivation for *all of* the colonists [in the revolution]. The passage has been changed to make clear that this was a primary motivation for *some of* the colonists" (emphasis in original).[23]

The response was all too predictable. President Donald Trump created the President's Advisory 1776 Commission hoping to "better enable a rising generation to understand the history and principles of the founding of the United States in 1776." Announced in November 2020, one day before the presidential election, it promised to offer "a dispositive rebuttal of reckless 're-education' attempts that seek to reframe American history around the idea that the United States is not an exceptional country but an evil one." Some of this also was aimed at refuting critical race theory, an academic concept generating headlines and controversy. But former vice president Joe Biden defeated Trump in the election and dissolved the 1776 Commission by executive order on January 21, 2021, one day after his inauguration.[24]

By that time, the United States had been roiled by an unprecedented domestic attack on the U.S. Capitol building.

Trump disputed the election results even before Biden's victory was called on November 7. "If you count the legal votes, I easily win," Trump said in a November 5 speech. "If you count the illegal votes, they can try to steal the election from us."[25] The sitting president and his campaign were well aware that January 6, 2021, was the date set aside for Congress to certify the election, so it was no surprise that, as early as December 19, he was tweeting, "Big protest in D.C. on January 6th! Be there, will be wild!" That was followed on December 27 with "See you in Washington, DC, on January 6th. Don't miss it" and on January 1 with "The BIG Protest Rally in Washington, D.C. will take place at 11:00 A.M. on January 6th. Locational details to follow. StopTheSteal!"[26] His followers took it to heart.

Social media echo chambers lit up. Travel plans were made. Militias organized. A document allegedly given to the leader of one militia group called for protesters to occupy eight government buildings on January 6, including the Supreme Court and the Russell Senate Office Building (and, as an aside, to "at least egg [the] doorway" at CNN). It was titled, eerily, "1776 Returns."[27]

A leader of another militia group sent a note on January 3 that said, "1776 we are going to make history."[28]

They saw it as another American revolution—this time, against their own government.

It was noon on January 6 when Trump took the stage before a throbbing crowd of thousands at the Ellipse, just south of the White House. Earlier in the day he had made his final pitch to Vice President Mike Pence to overturn the election (Pence responded, correctly, that, even as president of the Senate, he had no legal power to do so). The only chance left was overt public protest. "They rigged an election . . . rigged it like they've never rigged an election before," Trump claimed. He and his followers had to "fight. We fight like hell, and if you don't fight like hell, you won't have a country anymore."

"We're going to walk down Pennsylvania Avenue . . . and we're going to the Capitol and we're going to . . . try and give them the kind of pride and boldness that they need to take back our country."[29]

Just as Trump finished his speech shortly after 1:00 p.m., members of militia groups broke through outer barriers at the Capitol complex. More protestors arrived from the Ellipse rally (yes, some via Pennsylvania Avenue), and Capitol police officers were soon outflanked and overwhelmed. By 2:30, advance elements of the mob smashed through windows and entered the building, swarming through its historic halls, chanting, "U-S-A!" and "hang Mike Pence." One man confronting officers was almost frothing at the mouth when he shouted, "1776, motherf—rs!"[30]

But it was not, as is often reported, the first time since the War of 1812 that the Capitol faced such a threat. There were similar fears on February 13, 1861, when Congress met to certify Lincoln's election just before the Civil War. One account published the next day carried "rumors of plots to take the city, blow up the public buildings, and prevent the inauguration of Lincoln." A mob of irate southerners gathered outside the Capitol, hoping to disrupt and overturn the electoral count.[31]

But the military was ready—in particular, the aging General Winfield Scott, who had served on active duty in some capacity since Jefferson was president. Scott posted armed soldiers around the building and made it clear how he would treat anyone who tried to intervene. Captured offenders would be "lashed to the muzzle of a twelve-pounder [cannon] and fired out the window of the Capitol." After that, Scott said, he would "manure the hills of Arlington with the fragments of his body."

Properly protected, Congress certified the election without interruption. Representative Charles Francis Adams, a grandson of John Adams, said that "the proceeding occupied two hours, but it was conducted in complete tranquility, which relieves us all of a great weight."[32]

There was no such tranquil scene on January 6, 2021. Authorities downplayed the readily apparent threat and failed to reinforce the out-manned Capitol Police force until it was almost too late. Protestors also found support in high places on the day of the attack. Representative Lauren Boebert of Colorado tweeted, "Today is 1776." Senator Josh Hawley of Missouri raised a fist of encouragement on his way into the building. Representative Marjorie Taylor Greene of Georgia called it "our 1776 moment."[33]

The intruders succeeded at first, bursting into the Capitol and forcing both houses of Congress into temporary recess. They paraded through the Senate chamber and the private office of the Speaker of the House, Nancy Pelosi, shuffling through documents and leaving taunting notes in their wake. But the arrival of additional police and the National Guard—and, finally, a message from Trump himself, calling them off—restored order after several hours. The election results were certified that night and announced by Pence, who did his job while avoiding the hangman's noose set up on the Capitol grounds.

When the dust had cleared, literally and figuratively, it was a remarkable, restorative moment for American democracy. After a fierce and unprecedented siege of the U.S. Capitol, the center of government held. Trump did not accept the result of the election, but he agreed to a transfer power on the designated date (in this case, January 20), as every president has done since George Washington passed the torch to Adams in 1797. He *did* become the first outgoing leader since Adams to snub his successor's inauguration, and yet he was back four years later to become his party's overwhelming choice as nominee, despite being convicted of a felony. It was a sign to many that the country was more divided in 2024 than at any time in its history, other than the Civil War.

* * *

But, being honest here, hasn't divisiveness been baked into the American experience from the start?

Isn't the resilience to endure and overcome it another key part of our national DNA?

The roots date back to 1776. A significant faction of the Second Continental Congress came into the year opposing independence. There was a contentious debate in May about the propriety of forming governments in each colony, and by mid-June, half the colonies still were not committed to breaking from England. On the night before the historic vote in July, four delegations had not yet come around.

Not even a successful revolution could tamp down the inherent strife. Individual feuds and regional squabbles remained long after the war was won. The Articles of Confederation failed miserably. Washington was criticized—often—as president. Alexander Hamilton undercut a member of his own party, Adams, and battled openly with Jefferson. Adams and Jefferson did not speak for more than a decade. The Declaration of Independence, the document that made them famous, was co-opted by rival parties for partisan purposes over the years, annoying both men. Our politics have been messy from the start.

Somehow, through it all, a country founded on revolution managed to adapt, survive, thrive, and become the world's dominant power by the twentieth century.

"You will never know how much it cost the present Generation to preserve your Freedom! I hope you will make good Use of it," Adams wrote with some exasperation in 1777.[34] How fitting. A purposeful rereading of the fraught political history of that era would do much to inform more cogent debate today.

ACKNOWLEDGMENTS

Any author delving into to America's independence era is deeply indebted to those who have conducted such exceptional scholarship over the past 250 years. This author and this work are no different.

The most recent, and impressive, deep dive into the Declaration of Independence came from Pauline Maier, with *American Scripture*, published in 1997. In particular, Maier was responsible for the focus on heretofore unknown "local" resolutions that supported and explained independence in 1776. She also was among the first to point out that, while Thomas Jefferson was the primary author of the Declaration, many others in the Second Continental Congress contributed to the final product.

My two favorite historians, David McCullough and Joseph Ellis, also provided helpful insight and road maps to research—McCullough with his Pulitzer Prize—winning *John Adams*, as well as *1776*, and Ellis with his marvelous *Revolutionary Summer*.

An unexpected gem was Emily Sneff, who, before earning her PhD from William & Mary University, was research manager of the Declaration Resources Project at Harvard. Her name appears often in the notes and bibliography because of her consistently remarkable work with Declaration resources and the Declaration in general. Dr. Sneff currently is consulting curator for exhibitions planned for the 250th anniversary of the Declaration in 2026 at the Museum of the American Revolution (Philadelphia) and other sites.

A phenomenal research outlet, available to anyone, for free—and online—is the Founders Online website, courtesy of the National Archives (www.founders.archives.gov). National archivists have digitized more than 184,000 searchable letters and other documents, fully anno-tated, from the Founding Fathers—Thomas Jefferson, John Adams, Benjamin Franklin, James Madison, Alexander Hamilton, and others. Thanks also to the Massachusetts Historical Society for its own digitized material, including the Adams Family Papers.

National Park Service rangers at Independence National Historical Park (Independence Hall) in Philadelphia are helpful to any visitor with questions.

I want to thank Gene Brissie, my editor at Globe Pequot / Lyons Press, for his interest, encouragement, and guidance. Thanks also to production editor Alden Perkins, copyeditor Nancy Syrett, typesetter Steven Williams, and proofreader Ariel Keith.

My literary agent, Uwe Stender, of Triada US Literary Agency in Sewickley, Pennsylvania, deserves special praise. Uwe helped me get my start as an author of history, and this, amazingly, is our fifth book. He is the best of the very best.

Finally, and most important, none of this happens without the love and support of my life partner and dearest friend, Colleen McMillan, probably as close to a reincarnation of Abigail Adams as one could imagine. (She tried to edit that last phrase out, but, hey, I'm the author. It's true.)

Appendix A

Jefferson's "original Rough draught" of the Declaration of Independence
A Declaration of the Representatives of the UNITED STATES OF AMERICA, in General Congress assembled.

When in the course of human events it becomes necessary for a people to advance from that subordination in which they have hitherto remained, & to assume among the powers of the earth the equal & independant station to which the laws of nature & of nature's god entitle them, a decent respect to the opinions of mankind requires that they should declare the causes which impel them to the change.

We hold these truths to be sacred & undeniable; that all men are created equal & independant, that from that equal creation they derive rights inherent & inalienable, among which are the preservation of life, & liberty, & the pursuit of happiness; that to secure these ends, governments are instituted among men, deriving their just powers from the consent of the governed; that whenever any form of government shall become destructive of these ends, it is the right of the people to alter or to abolish it, & to institute new government, laying it's foundation on such principles & organising it's powers in such form, as to them shall seem most likely to effect their safety & happiness. [P]rudence indeed will dictate that governments long established should not be changed for light & transient causes: and accordingly all experience hath shewn that mankind are more disposed to suffer while evils are sufferable, than to right themselves by abolishing the forms to which they are accustomed. [B]ut when a long train of abuses & usurpations, begun at a distinguished period, & pursuing invariably the same object, evinces a design to subject them to arbitrary power, it is their right, it is their duty, to throw off such government & to provide new guards for their future security. [S]uch has been the patient sufferance of these colonies; & such is now the necessity which constrains them to expunge their former systems of government. the history of his present majesty, is a history of unremitting injuries and usurpations, among which no one fact stands single or solitary to contradict the uniform tenor of the rest, all of which have in direct object the establishment of an absolute tyranny over these states. [T]o prove this, let facts be submitted to a candid world, for the truth of which we pledge a faith yet unsullied by falsehood.

- he has refused his assent to laws the most wholesome and necessary for the public good:

- he has forbidden his governors to pass laws of immediate & pressing importance, unless suspended in their operation till his assent should be obtained; and when so suspended, he has neglected utterly to attend to them.

- he has refused to pass other laws for the accomodation of large districts of people unless those people would relinquish the right of representation, a right inestimable to them, & formidable to tyrants alone:

- he has dissolved Representative houses repeatedly & continually, for opposing with manly firmness his invasions on the rights of the people:

- he has refused for a long space of time to cause others to be elected, whereby the legislative powers, incapable of annihilation, have returned to the people at large for their exercise, the state remaining in the mean time exposed to all the dangers of invasion from without, & convulsions within:

- he has endeavored to prevent the population of these states; for that purpose obstructing the laws for naturalization of foreigners; refusing to pass others to encourage their migrations hither; & raising the conditions of new appropriations of lands:

- he has suffered the administration of justice totally to cease in some of these colonies, refusing his assent to laws for establishing judiciary powers:
- he has made our judges dependant on his will alone, for the tenure of their offices, and amount of their salaries:
- he has erected a multitude of new offices by a self-assumed power, & sent hither swarms of officers to harrass our people & eat out their substance:
- he has kept among us in times of peace standing armies & ships of war:
- he has affected to render the military, independant of & superior to the civil power:
- he has combined with others to subject us to a jurisdiction foreign to our constitutions and unacknoleged by our laws; giving his assent to their pretended acts of legislation, for quartering large bodies of armed troops among us;
  - for protecting them by a mock-trial from punishment for any murders they should commit on the inhabitants of these states;
  - for cutting off our trade with all parts of the world;
  - for imposing taxes on us without our consent;
  - for depriving us of the benefits of trial by jury;
  - for transporting us beyond seas to be tried for pretended offences:
  - for taking away our charters, & altering fundamentally the forms of our governments;
  - for suspending our own legislatures & declaring themselves invested with power to legislate for us in all cases whatsoever:
- he has abdicated government here, withdrawing his governors, & declaring us out of his allegiance & protection:

- he has plundered our seas, ravaged our coasts, burnt our towns & destroyed the lives of our people:

- he is at this time transporting large armies of foreign mercenaries to compleat the works of death, desolation & tyranny, already begun with circumstances of cruelty & perfidy unworthy the head of a civilized nation:

- he has endeavored to bring on the inhabitants of our frontiers the merciless Indian savages, whose known rule of warfare is an undistinguished destruction of all ages, sexes, & conditions of existence:

- he has incited treasonable insurrections in our fellow-subjects, with the allurements of forfeiture & confiscation of our property:

- he has waged cruel war against human nature itself, violating it's most sacred rights of life & liberty in the persons of a distant people who never offended him, captivating & carrying them into slavery in another hemisphere, or to incur miserable death in their transportation thither. [T]his piratical warfare, the opprobrium of *infidel* powers, is the warfare of the CHRISTIAN king of Great Britain. determined to keep open a market where MEN should be bought & sold, he has prostituted his negative for suppressing every legislative attempt to prohibit or to restrain this execrable commerce: and that this assemblage of horrors might want no fact of distinguished die, he is now exciting those very people to rise in arms among us, and to purchase that liberty of which *he* has deprived them, by murdering the people upon whom *he* also obtruded them; thus paying off former crimes committed against the *liberties* of one people, with crimes which he urges them to commit against the *lives* of another.

[I]n every stage of these oppressions we have petitioned for redress in the most humble terms; our repeated petitions have been answered by repeated injury. [A] prince whose character is thus marked by every act which may define a tyrant, is unfit to be the ruler of a people who mean to be free. [F]uture ages will scarce believe that the hardiness of one man, adventured within the short compass of 12 years only, on so many acts of tyranny without a mask, over a people fostered & fixed in principles of liberty.

Nor have we been wanting in attentions to our British brethren. [W]e have warned them from time to time of attempts by their legislature to extend a jurisdiction over these our states. [W]e have reminded them of the circumstances of our emigration & settlement here, no one of which could warrant so strange a pretension: that these were effected at the expence of our own blood & treasure, unassisted by the wealth or the strength of Great Britain: that in constituting indeed our several forms of government, we had adopted one common king, thereby laying a foundation for perpetual league & amity with them: but that submission to their parliament was no part of our constitution, nor ever in idea, if history may be credited: and we appealed to their native justice & magnanimity, as well as to the ties of our common kindred to disavow these usurpations which were likely to interrupt our correspondence & connection. they too have been deaf to the voice of justice & of consanguinity, & when occasions have been given them, by the regular course of their laws, of removing from their councils the disturbers of our harmony, they have by their free election re-established them in power. [A]t this very time too they are permitting their chief magistrate to send over not only soldiers of our common blood, but Scotch & foreign mercenaries to invade & deluge us in blood. [T]hese facts have given the last stab to agonizing affection, and manly spirit bids us to renounce for ever these unfeeling brethren. we must endeavor to forget our former love for them, and to hold them as we hold the rest of mankind, enemies in war, in peace friends. [W]e might have been a free & a great people together; but a communication of grandeur & of freedom it seems is below their dignity. be it so, since they will have it: the road to glory & happiness is open to us too; we will climb it in a separate state, and acquiesce in the necessity which pronounces our everlasting Adieu!

We therefore the representatives of the United States of America in General Congress assembled do, in the name & by authority of the good people of these states, reject and renounce all allegiance & subjection to the kings of Great Britain & all others who may hereafter claim by, through, or under them; we utterly dissolve & break off all political connection which may have heretofore subsisted between us & the people or parliament of Great Britain; and finally we do assert and declare these colonies to be free and independant states, and that as free & independant states they shall hereafter have power to levy war, conclude peace, contract alliances, establish commerce, & to do all other acts and things which independant states may of right do. And for the support of this declaration we mutually pledge to each other our lives, our fortunes, & our sacred honour.

Source: National Archives
https://founders.archives.gov/documents/Jefferson/01-01-02-0176-0004

Appendix B

The final, approved version of the Declaration of Independence

In Congress, July 4, 1776
The unanimous Declaration of the thirteen united States of America

When in the Course of human events, it becomes necessary for one people to dissolve the political bands which have connected them with another, and to assume among the powers of the earth, the separate and equal station to which the Laws of Nature and of Nature's God entitle them, a decent respect to the opinions of mankind requires that they should declare the causes which impel them to the separation.

We hold these truths to be self-evident, that all men are created equal, that they are endowed by their Creator with certain unalienable Rights, that among these are Life, Liberty and the pursuit of Happiness.—That to secure these rights, Governments are instituted among Men, deriving their just powers from the consent of the governed,—That whenever any Form of Government becomes destructive of these ends, it is the Right of the People to alter or to abolish it, and to institute new Government, laying its foundation on such principles and organizing its powers in such form, as to them shall seem most likely to effect their Safety and Happiness. Prudence, indeed, will dictate that Governments long established should not be changed for light and transient causes; and accordingly all experience hath shewn, that mankind are more disposed to suffer, while evils are sufferable, than to right themselves by abolishing the forms to which they are accustomed. But when a long train of abuses and usurpations, pursuing invariably the same Object evinces a design to reduce them under absolute Despotism, it is their right, it is their duty, to throw off such Government, and to provide new Guards for their future security.—Such has been the patient sufferance of these Colonies; and such is now the necessity which constrains them to alter their former Systems of Government. The history of the present King of Great Britain is a history of repeated injuries and usurpations, all having in direct object the establishment of an absolute Tyranny over these States. To prove this, let Facts be submitted to a candid world.

- He has refused his Assent to Laws, the most wholesome and necessary for the public good.

- He has forbidden his Governors to pass Laws of immediate and pressing importance, unless suspended in their operation till his Assent should be obtained; and when so suspended, he has utterly neglected to attend to them.

- He has refused to pass other Laws for the accommodation of large districts of people, unless those people would relinquish the right of Representation in the Legislature, a right inestimable to them and formidable to tyrants only.

- He has called together legislative bodies at places unusual, uncomfortable, and distant from the depository of their public Records, for the sole purpose of fatiguing them into compliance with his measures.

- He has dissolved Representative Houses repeatedly, for opposing with manly firmness his invasions on the rights of the people.

- He has refused for a long time, after such dissolutions, to cause others to be elected; whereby the Legislative powers, incapable of Annihilation, have returned to the People at large for their exercise; the State remaining in the mean time exposed to all the dangers of invasion from without, and convulsions within.

- He has endeavoured to prevent the population of these States; for that purpose obstructing the Laws for Naturalization of Foreigners; refusing to pass others to encourage their migrations hither, and raising the conditions of new Appropriations of Lands.

- He has obstructed the Administration of Justice, by refusing his Assent to Laws for establishing Judiciary powers.

- He has made Judges dependent on his Will alone, for the tenure of their offices, and the amount and payment of their salaries.

- He has erected a multitude of New Offices, and sent hither swarms of Officers to harrass our people, and eat out their substance.

- He has kept among us, in times of peace, Standing Armies without the Consent of our legislatures.

- He has affected to render the Military independent of and superior to the Civil power.

- He has combined with others to subject us to a jurisdiction foreign to our constitution, and unacknowledged by our laws; giving his Assent to their Acts of pretended Legislation:

  - For Quartering large bodies of armed troops among us:
  - For protecting them, by a mock Trial, from punishment for any Murders which they should commit on the Inhabitants of these States:
  - For cutting off our Trade with all parts of the world:
  - For imposing Taxes on us without our Consent:
  - For depriving us in many cases, of the benefits of Trial by Jury:
  - For transporting us beyond Seas to be tried for pretended offences
  - For abolishing the free System of English Laws in a neighbouring Province, establishing therein an Arbitrary government, and enlarging its Boundaries so as to render it at once an example and fit instrument for introducing the same absolute rule into these Colonies:

- For taking away our Charters, abolishing our most valuable Laws, and altering fundamentally the Forms of our Governments:

- For suspending our own Legislatures, and declaring themselves invested with power to legislate for us in all cases whatsoever.

- He has abdicated Government here, by declaring us out of his Protection and waging War against us.

- He has plundered our seas, ravaged our Coasts, burnt our towns, and destroyed the lives of our people.

- He is at this time transporting large Armies of foreign Mercenaries to compleat the works of death, desolation and tyranny, already begun with circumstances of Cruelty & perfidy scarcely paralleled in the most barbarous ages, and totally unworthy the Head of a civilized nation.

- He has constrained our fellow Citizens taken Captive on the high Seas to bear Arms against their Country, to become the executioners of their friends and Brethren, or to fall themselves by their Hands.

- He has excited domestic insurrections amongst us, and has endeavoured to bring on the inhabitants of our frontiers, the merciless Indian Savages, whose known rule of warfare, is an undistinguished destruction of all ages, sexes and conditions.

In every stage of these Oppressions We have Petitioned for Redress in the most humble terms: Our repeated Petitions have been answered only by repeated injury. A Prince whose character is thus marked by every act which may define a Tyrant, is unfit to be the ruler of a free people.

Nor have We been wanting in attentions to our Brittish brethren. We have warned them from time to time of attempts by their legislature to extend an unwarrantable jurisdiction over us. We have reminded them of the circumstances of our emigration and settlement here. We have appealed to their native justice and magnanimity, and we have conjured them by the ties of our common kindred to disavow these usurpations, which, would inevitably interrupt our connections and correspondence. They too have been deaf to the voice of justice and of consanguinity. We must, therefore, acquiesce in the necessity, which denounces our Separation, and hold them, as we hold the rest of mankind, Enemies in War, in Peace Friends.

We, therefore, the Representatives of the united States of America, in General Congress, Assembled, appealing to the Supreme Judge of the world for the rectitude of our intentions, do, in the Name, and by Authority of the good People of these Colonies, solemnly publish and declare, That these United Colonies are, and of Right ought to be Free and Independent States; that they are Absolved from all Allegiance to the British Crown, and that all political connection between them and the State of Great Britain, is and ought to be totally dissolved; and that as Free and Independent States, they have full Power to levy War, conclude Peace, contract Alliances, establish Commerce, and to do all other Acts and Things which Independent States may of right do. And for the support of this Declaration, with a firm reliance on the protection of divine Providence, we mutually pledge to each other our Lives, our Fortunes and our sacred Honor.

Source: National Archives
https://www.archives.gov/founding-docs/declaration-transcript

Abbreviations for Notes

AP   The Adams Papers
CW   The Collected Works of Abraham Lincoln
DJA   Diary and Autobiography of John Adams
FO   Founders Online (National Archives)
JCC   Journals of the Continental Congress
LDC   Letters of Delegates to Congress
LOC   Library of Congress
LMCC   Letters of Members of the Continental Congress
MHS   Massachusetts Historical Society
NA   National Archives
NPS   National Park Service
PTJ   The Papers of Thomas Jefferson
WJA   The Works of John Adams

NOTES

INTRODUCTION

1. John Adams to Abigail Adams, April 26, 1777, Adams Family Papers, Massachusetts Historical Society (hereafter MHS), https://www.masshist.org/digitaladams/archive/doc?id=L17770426ja.

2. Representative Lauren Boebert (@Laurenboebert), "Today is 1776," Twitter, January 6, 2021, 8:30 a.m., https://x.com/laurenboebert/status/1346811381878845442?lang=en; Mark Hosenball, "Prosecutors Press Rhodes on Inflammatory Messages to Fellow Oath Keepers," *Yahoo News*, November 7, 2022, https://news.yahoo.com/prosecutors-press-rhodes-on-inflammatory-messages-to-fellow-oath-keepers-002717924.html; Marshall Cohen, "January 6 Was Opposite of 1776, Judge Tells Rioter Who Carried Revolutionary Flag into US Capitol," CNN, December 2, 2021, https://www.cnn.com/2021/12/02/politics/january-6-andrew-wrigley/index.html; "What Conspiracy Theorist Alex Jones Said in the Leadup to the Capitol Riot," PBS, January 12, 2021, https://www.pbs.org/wgbh/frontline/article/what-conspiracy-theorist-alex-jones-said-in-the-lead-up-to-the-capitol-riot/. In addition to Representative Boebert, Representative Marjorie Taylor Greene also tweeted a similar statement on April 23, 2022 (Representative Marjorie Taylor Greene [@RepMTG], "Today and everyday [*sic*] is 1776," Twitter, April 23, 2022, 9:05 a.m., https://x.com/RepMTG/status/1517852261963243521).

3. Natalie Wexler, "Why Kids Know Even Less about History Now—and Why It Matters," *Forbes*, April 24, 2020, https://www.forbes.com/sites/nataliewexler/2020/04/24/why-kids-know-even-less-about-history-now-and-why-it-matters/?sh=61e113d46a7a; Diana Ravitch, "Decline and Fall of Teaching History," *New York Times Magazine*, November 17, 1985; Eric Alterman, "The Decline of Historical Thinking," *New Yorker*, February 4, 2019, https://www.newyorker.com/news/news-desk/the-decline-of-historical-thinking.

4. "The Declaration of Independence: A Transcription," National Archives (hereafter NA), https://www.archives.gov/founding-docs/declaration-transcript.

5. Carter Braxton to Landon Carter, May 17, 1776, in *Letters of Delegates to Congress* (hereafter *LDC*), ed. Paul H. Smith (Washington, DC: Library of Congress [hereafter LOC], 1979), 4:19, 4:21–22n3. Congress voted on May 15 on a fiery preamble to a resolution calling for new state governments. Written by John Adams, it essentially called for a rejection of the king's authority and said, "all the powers of government [should

be] exerted under the authority of the people of the colonies." Although no official tally was recorded, Virginia delegate Carter Braxton said there was heated debate for two or three days and it passed "I think by 6 to 4." That would have meant that two colonies abstained, while Georgia's delegation was not yet present. The only other surviving account from that week was a diary entry by Philadelphia lawyer James Allen, who was not a delegate and not present. He said the vote was 7–4. A note in volume 4 of *LDC* said that if "Braxton's recollection is correct, the alignment of the colonies on the motion was probably: New Hampshire, Massachusetts, Rhode Island, Connecticut, Virginia and South Carolina; New York, New Jersey, Delaware and North Carolina opposed; and Pennsylvania and Maryland abstaining." As for a reflection of support for independence at that moment, Braxton was convinced that the language of Adams's preamble represented "a very important declaration & recommendation from Congress, which you will say falls little short of independence. . . . I find those out of doors on both sides of the question construe it in that manner." The original resolution, shorter and milder, had been agreed to on May 10, but a committee of three members, led by Adams, was assigned to write a preamble. See John Adams, "Preamble to Resolution on Independent Governments, 15 May 1776," Founders Online (hereafter FO), https://founders.archives .gov/documents/Adams/06-04-02-0001-0006. (This significant sequence of events will be examined in greater detail in chapter 7.)

6. Edward Rutledge to John Jay, June 8, 1776, in *Letters of Members of the Continental Congress* (hereafter *LMCC*), ed. Edmund C. Burnett (Washington, DC: Carnegie Institution of Washington, 1921; repr., London: Forgotten Books, 2018), 1:476.

7. Thomas Jefferson, "Notes of Proceedings in the Continental Congress, 7 June–1 August 1776," FO, 10, https://founders.archives.gov/documents/Jefferson/01-01-02-0160; *Journals of the Continental Congress* (hereafter *JCC*), ed. from the original records in the LOC (Washington, DC: Government Printing Office, 1906), 5:504–5. Official records do not provide details of the vote on July 1, saying only that it was "agreed to by the committee of the whole," with a final determination "postponed . . . till tomorrow." However, Jefferson wrote in his notes that nine colonies were in favor, with two opposed, one deadlocked, and one abstaining. "S. Carolina and Pennsylvania voted against it. Delaware having but two members present, they were divided." New York abstained because its provincial progress had not yet approved support. A one-day delay on the final vote was proposed by Edward Rutledge of South Carolina, and it was carried over to July 2.

8. "Continental Congress: Agreement of Secrecy," FO, November 9, 1775, https:// founders.archives.gov/documents/Jefferson/01-01-02-0132.

9. "Preface," in Burnett, *LMCC*, xxi; Abraham Clark to Elias Dayton, July 4, 1776, in Smith, *LDC*, 4:378; Caesar Rodney to Thomas Rodney, July 4, 1776, in Smith, *LDC*, 4:388. In addition, the private diary of delegate Robert Treat Paine had the following entry: "The Independence of the States Voted & declared" (Smith, *LDC*, 4:386). Several others had earlier written about independence being declared on July 1 and 2.

10. Adams wrote his autobiography between 1802 and 1807. Jefferson began his autobiography in 1821. They also addressed the independence process in private letters to other dignitaries in the 1820s—Adams to Timothy Pickering on August 22, 1822, and Jefferson to James Madison on August 30, 1823. Jefferson wrote that "in some of the

particulars, Mr. Adams's memory has led him into unquestionable error at the age of 88, and 47 years after the transactions of Independence [*sic*]." Jefferson himself was eighty at the time, but he claimed he had an advantage because he was working from contemporary notes. John Adams to Timothy Pickering, August 6, 1822, FO, https://founders.archives.gov/documents/Adams/99-02-02-7674; Thomas Jefferson to James Madison, August 30, 1823, FO, https://founders.archives.gov/documents/Jefferson/98-01-02-3728. The long-standing Adams-Jefferson debate from the 1800s is also addressed in detail in Pauline Maier, *American Scripture: Making the Declaration of Independence* (New York: Vintage, 1998), 99–101.

11. Pauline Maier interview excerpts: "Making the Declaration of Independence," YouTube, https://www.youtube.com/watch?v=ztAnlmmvAb0&t=40s.

12. *JCC*, 5:503–16; Gerard W. Gawalt, "Jefferson and the Declaration: Updated Work Studies Evolution of Historic Text," LOC, July 1999, https://www.loc.gov/loc/lcib/9907/jeffdec.html. There were eighty-six changes to Jefferson's original draft from mid-June, and almost forty of those were made during the full congressional sessions of July 2, 3, and 4.

13. According to the National Archives (NA) website: "Unlike other founding documents, the Declaration of Independence is not legally binding, but it is powerful" ("The Declaration of Independence," NA, https://www.archives.gov/founding-docs/declaration#:~:text=The%20Declaration%20of%20Independence%20states,binding%2C%20but%20it%20is%20powerful); also see Jeffrey Rosen and David Rubenstein, "The Declaration, the Constitution and the Bill of Rights," National Constitution Center, https://constitutioncenter.org/the-constitution/white-papers/the-declaration-the-constitution-and-the-bill-of-rights.

14. A good summation of the 1774–1775 time period can be found in Gordon S. Wood, *The American Revolution: A History* (New York: Modern Library, 2002), 48–54.

15. Smith, *LDC*, 3:63–64n1; "Delegate Discussions: *Common Sense*," Declaration Resources Project Blog, Harvard University, https://declaration.fas.harvard.edu/blog/dd-common-sense.

16. "John Dickinson's Notes for a Speech in Congress," July 1, 1776, in *JCC*, 5:351–56; and "John Dickinson Notes on Arguments Concerning Independence," July 1, 1776, in *JCC*, 5:357–58; Bernhard Kollenberg, "John Dickinson vs. John Adams, 1774–1776," *Proceedings of the American Philosophical Society* 107, no. 2 (April 15, 1963); "John Dickinson," U.S. Army Center of Military History, https://history.army.mil/books/revwar/ss/dickinson.htm.

17. "Declaring Independence: Drafting the Documents Timeline," Library of Congress Exhibitions, https://www.loc.gov/exhibits/declara/declara2.html.

CHAPTER 1

1. Diary of John Adams, October 27, 1775–October 13, 1776, "Residences of Delegates in Philadelphia," FO, https://founders.archives.gov/?q=1776&s=1511311112&r=46. Adams and the Massachusetts delegation stayed "at Mrs. Yards in 2d Street."

2. John Adams to Archibald Bulloch, July 1, 1776, in John Adams, *The Adams Papers* (hereafter *AP*), ed. Robert J. Taylor (Cambridge, MA: Belknap, 1979), 4:352.

3. John Adams to Abigail Adams, July 3, 1776, FO, https://founders.archives.gov /documents/Adams/04-02-02-0015. Although many believe the turning point in British-American relations came in 1763, shortly after the French and Indian War, Adams always thought it took place two years earlier. "I look back to the Year 1761," he wrote to Abigail, "and recollect the Argument concerning Writs of Assistance, in the Superior Court, which I have hitherto considered as the Commencement of the Controversy between Great Britain and America."

4. "By the King, a Proclamation, for Suppressing Rebellion and Sedition," August 11, 1775, Massachusetts Historical Society Collections, https://www.masshist.org/database /viewer.php?item_id=818&pid=2; Thomas Paine, *Common Sense and Other Writings*, ed. Gordon S. Wood (New York: Modern Library [Random House], 2003); first published January 1776.

5. "Daily Record, 1 July 1776–18 December 1799," LOC, Thomas Jefferson Papers, ser. 7, https://jefferson-weather-records.org/node/2. Jefferson recorded that it was 81.5 degrees at 9:00 a.m. on July 1, 1776, and 82 degrees at 7:00 p.m.

6. "Charter to Sir Walter Raleigh, 1584," Avalon Project, Yale Law School, https:// avalon.law.yale.edu/16th_century/raleigh.asp. Raleigh's name was spelled "Ralegh" in the original document.

7. Joseph J. Ellis, *Revolutionary Summer: The Birth of American Independence* (New York: Vintage, 2012), xxi.

8. *JCC*, 5:425. Other items in Lee's resolution called for developing foreign alliances and creating a plan of confederation. Both were important and necessary elements, but, at this time, independence had to come first.

9. Thomas Jefferson to the Editor of the *Journal de Paris*, August 29, 1787, FO, https: //founders.archives.gov/documents/Jefferson/01-12-02-0073; Pauline Maier, *American Scripture: Making the Declaration of Independence* (New York: Vintage, 1998), 41–42. Jefferson's letter to the Paris newspaper came eleven years after the fact, but it is believed to be much more reliable than his writings from the 1820s, when he was a very elderly man.

10. Thomas Jefferson, "Notes of Proceedings in the Continental Congress, 7 June–1 August 1776," FO, 7–8, https://founders.archives.gov/documents/Jefferson/01 -01-02-0160. The National Archives (NA) believes it is "highly probable" that Jefferson wrote these notes in the summer or early autumn of 1776—which would make them the most contemporary detailed account available of this crucial period in American history.

11. Maier, *American Scripture*, 103; Myron Magnet, *The Founders at Home: The Building of America, 1735–1817* (New York: Norton, 2014), 72. Lee and Wythe left for Virginia on June 13. For Jefferson's views on the importance of the state constitution, see Thomas Jefferson to Thomas Nelson, May 16, 1776, FO, https://founders.archives.gov/documents /Jefferson/01-01-02-0153. Jefferson had hoped to get the state assignment as well but was left in Philadelphia as a junior member of the delegation.

12. John Adams to Samuel Chase, July 1, 1776, in Adams, *AP*, 4:353.

13. "Editorial Note: The Declaration of Independence," FO, https://founders.archives .gov/documents/Jefferson/01-01-02-0176-0001.

14. Merrill Jensen, *The Founding of a Nation: A History of the American Revolution, 1763–1776* (Indianapolis, IN: Hackett, 2004), 241–42.

15. *JCC*, 2:140–57, 2:158–62; "Editorial Note: Declaration of the Causes and Necessity for Taking Up Arms," FO, https://founders.archives.gov/documents/Jefferson/01-01-02 -0113-0001; "John Dickinson's Notes for a Speech in Congress," July 1, 1776, in Smith, *LDC*, 4: 351–58. The eighteenth-century-style capitalization, which seems odd to the modern reader, is taken directly from notes of Dickinson's speech.

16. David McCullough, *John Adams* (New York: Simon & Schuster Paperbacks, 2001), 126–27; John Adams to William Cushing, June 9, 1776, in Smith, *LDC*, 4:178; John Adams to Samuel Chase, July 9, 1776, in Adams, *AP*, 4:372.

17. Jefferson, "Notes of Proceedings in the Continental Congress, 7 June–1 August 1776," FO, 10, https://founders.archives.gov/documents/Jefferson/01-01-02-0160; *JCC*, 5:505.

18. Caesar Rodney to Thomas Rodney, July 4, 1776, in Burnett, *LMCC*, 528; Thomas McKean to Caesar A. Rodney (nephew), September 22, 1813, in Burnett, *LMCC*, 534; *JCC*, 5:507; Maier, *American Scripture*, 45.

19. Jefferson, "Notes of Proceedings in the Continental Congress, 7 June–1 August 1776," FO, 10, https://founders.archives.gov/documents/Jefferson/01-01-02-0160.

20. Elbridge Gerry to James Warren, July 2, 1776, in Burnett, *LMCC*, 526; *Pennsylvania Evening Post* (vol. 2, no. 226), July 2, 1776, Seth Kellar Historic Documents and Legacy Collections, https://www.sethkaller.com/item/1000-The-First-Published -Announcement-of-Independence-(SOLD). This link includes an image of the historic newspaper page—it was the first time that independence had been announced in print.

21. John Adams to Abigail Adams, July 3, 1776 (first letter), in Smith, *LDC*, 4:374.

22. John Adams to Abigail Adams, July 3, 1776 (second letter), in Smith, *LDC*, 4:376.

23. *JCC*, 5:431, 491, 506–10; Gerard W. Gawalt, "Jefferson and the Declaration: Updated Work Studies Evolution of Historic Text," LOC, July 1999, https://www .loc.gov/loc/lcib/9907/jeffdec.html; Julian Boyd, *The Declaration of Independence: The Evolution of the Text*, rev. ed., ed. Gerard W. Gawalt (Washington, DC: LOC; Charlottesville, VA: Thomas Jefferson Memorial Foundation, 1999), 34–35; "The Declaration of Independence: A History," NA, https://www.archives.gov/founding-docs/declaration-history; Joseph J. Ellis, *American Creation* (New York: Vintage, 2005), 55.

24. "Dunlap Broadside," July 4, 1776, LOC, https://www.loc.gov/resource/gdcwdl.wdl _02716/.

25. *JCC*, 5:516 (also 5:516n1), 5:559–60, 5:590–91.

26. *JCC*, 5:626. The congressional journal reported on August 2 that "[t]he declaration of independence being engrossed and compared at the table was signed (by the members)"; "Declaration of Independence (1776)," NA, https://www.archives.gov/ milestone-documents/declaration-of-independence; "Declaring Independence: Drafting the Documents—Timeline," LOC, https://www.loc.gov/exhibits/declara/declara2.html; *JCC*, 7:48.

27. Adams uttered his legendary quote during his defensive of British soldiers in the Boston Massacre trial. "Adams' Argument for the Defense: 3–4 December 1770," FO, https://founders.archives.gov/documents/Adams/05-03-02-0001-0004-0016.

28. Thomas Jefferson to Benjamin Franklin (June 21, 1776), FO, https://founders .archives.gov/documents/Jefferson/01-01-02-0168; Thomas Jefferson to James Madison,

August 23, 1823, FO, https://founders.archives.gov/documents/Jefferson/98-01-02 -3728; Boyd, *The Declaration of Independence: The Evolution of the Text*, 28; Gawalt, "Jefferson and the Declaration," https://www.loc.gov/loc/lcib/9907/jeffdec.html. Jefferson's letter to Franklin in June 1776 is not dated, but he references a Friday, and scholars believe it was Friday, June 21. See Maier, *American Scripture*, 103.

29. Thomas Jefferson, *The Papers of Thomas Jefferson* (hereafter *PTJ*), ed. Julian P. Boyd (Princeton, NJ: Princeton University Press, 1950), 1:423–27; "Jefferson's 'original Rough draught' of the Declaration of Independence," LOC, https://www.loc.gov/exhibits/declara/ruffdrft.html.

30. "Declaration of Independence: A Transcription," July 4, 1776, NA, https://www.archives.gov/founding-docs/declaration-transcript.

31. Maier, *American Scripture*, 135. Dr. Maier writes that the sentiments Jefferson expressed in the preamble, which included the right to revolution, "were, in short, absolutely conventional among Americans of his time." The first sentence became increasingly important as time went on and is considered to be the most important element of the Declaration today. Also see "Pauline Maier: The Making of the Declaration of Independence," YouTube, https://www.youtube.com/watch?v=Ewyn5NkZfkY&t=1618s.

32. "Declaration of Independence: A Transcription," July 4, 1776, NA, https://www.archives.gov/founding-docs/declaration-transcript.

33. "What Is the Word Count of the Declaration of Independence," Declaration Resources Project, Harvard University, https://declaration.fas.harvard.edu/faq/what -word-count-declaration-independence#:~:text=If%20you%20include%20the%20title ,total%20word%20count%20is%201%2C458. There were 1,320 words in the final document. The section on charges against the king, including opening and closing sentences, has 749 words. There is an additional paragraph addressed to the British people.

34. "Jefferson's 'original Rough draught' of the Declaration of Independence," LOC, https://www.loc.gov/exhibits/declara/ruffdrft.html.

35. "The Enslaved Household of President Thomas Jefferson," White House Historical Association, https://www.whitehousehistory.org/slavery-in-the-thomas-jefferson-white -house#:~:text=Despite%20working%20tirelessly%20to%20establish,most%20of%20any %20U.S.%20president; "The Founding Fathers' View of Slavery," American Battlefield Trust, https://www.battlefields.org/learn/articles/founding-fathers-views-slavery.

36. Jefferson, "Notes of Proceedings in the Continental Congress, 7 June–1 August 1776," FO, 10, https://founders.archives.gov/documents/Jefferson/01-01-02-0160. Jefferson wrote that the clause "reprobating the enslaving of the inhabitants of Africa, was struck out in complaisance to South Carolina & Georgia, who had never attempted to restrain the importation of slaves, and who, on the contrary, still wished to continue it. [O]ur Northern brethren also I believe felt a little ender under those censures; for tho' their people have very few slaves themselves yet they had been pretty considerable carriers of them to others."

37. Samuel Johnson, "Taxation No Tyranny: An Answer to the Resolutions and Address of the American Congress," Samuel Johnson Sound Bite Page, https://www.samueljohnson.com/tnt.html.

38. Thomas Hutchinson, "Strictures upon the Declaration of the Congress at Philadelphia in a Letter to a Noble Lord, October 15, 1776," Teaching American History, https://teachingamericanhistory.org/document/strictures-upon-the-declaration-of-the-congress-at-philadelphia-in-a-letter-to-a-noble-lord-c/.

39. Comparison of Jefferson's original rough draft ("Jefferson's 'original Rough draught' of the Declaration of Independence," LOC, https://www.loc.gov/exhibits/declara/ruffdrft.html) with the final version of the Declaration of Independence ("Declaration of Independence: A Transcription," July 4, 1776, NA, https://www.archives.gov/founding-docs/declaration-transcript). Lee's resolution of June 7 is found at *JCC*, 5:425. The difference in language is subtle but important. Jefferson wrote that "we do assert and declare these colonies to be free and independent states." The Jefferson Memorial engraving is "that these colonies are and of right ought to be free and independent states." Congress wanted Lee's entire resolution to appear in the Declaration, to put an exclamation point on their achievement, and to tie it back to June 7—as opposed to the more generic sentence that Jefferson had crafted.

40. Emily Sneff, "July Highlight: George Rejected and Liberty Protected," Declaration Resources Project, Harvard University, July 4, 2016, 2–10, https://declaration.fas.harvard.edu/blog/july-proclamations. Sneff cites newspaper accounts from throughout the colonies.

41. "First Newspaper Printing of the Declaration of Independence," Museum of the American Revolution, https://www.amrevmuseum.org/collection/first-newspaper-printing-of-the-declaration-of-independence.

42. "Records of the Continental and Confederation Congresses and the Constitutional Convention," NA, https://www.archives.gov/research/guide-fed-records/groups/360.html#:~:text=Table%20of%20Contents&text=Note%3A%20Congress%20gave%20the%20Department,Continental%20and%20Confederation%20Congresses%2C%201789. Records of the Continental Congress were turned over to the Department of State in 1789 and transferred to the Library of Congress in 1903. They were published in a series of books in the early 1900s.

43. John Adams to Abigail Adams 2d [Adams's daughter], July 5, 1777, FO, https://founders.archives.gov/documents/Adams/04-02-02-0216. His daughter also was named Abigail, like her mother—but she went by "Nabby."

44. "Gettysburg Address—Delivered at Gettysburg, Pa., Nov. 19, 1863," LOC, https://www.loc.gov/resource/rbpe.24404500/?st=text.

45. "Independence Day," LOC, https://www.loc.gov/item/today-in-history/july-04/; "Federal Holidays," LOC, https://blogs.loc.gov/law/2012/12/federal-holidays/.

CHAPTER 2

1. "Charter to Sir Walter Raleigh, 1584," Avalon Project, Yale Law School, https://avalon.law.yale.edu/16th_century/raleigh.asp; "Europe Claims America: The Atlantic Joined," LOC, https://www.loc.gov/exhibits/1492/eurocla.html.

2. James Horn, *A Kingdom Strange: The Brief and Tragic History of the Lost Colony of Roanoke* (New York: Basic, 2010), 5–6; Karen Ordahl Kupperman, *Roanoke: The Abandoned Colony* (Lanham, MD: Rowman & Littlefield, 2007), 1, 9–11; "NPS Historical

Handbook: Fort Raleigh," National Park Service (hereafter NPS), https://www.nps.gov /parkhistory/online_books/hh/16/hh16b.htm. Gilbert's ships were battered by ferocious storms on the return trip to England, and the preternaturally calm Sir Humphrey was last seen alive on the deck of a small vessel, saying "we are as neere to heaven by sea as by land."

3. Comparison of Jefferson's original rough draft ("Jefferson's 'original Rough draught' of the Declaration of Independence," LOC, https://www.loc.gov/exhibits/declara/ruffdrft .html) with the final version of the Declaration of Independence ("Declaration of Independence: A Transcription," July 4, 1776, NA, https://www.archives.gov/founding-docs/ declaration-transcript). For Jefferson's opinions on English backing for early settlements, see "Refutation of the Argument That the Colonies were Established at the Expense of the British Nation," FO, https://founders.archives.gov/documents/Jefferson/01-01-02 -0147, and his "Summary View on the Rights of British America," Avalon Project, Yale Law School, https://avalon.law.yale.edu/18th_century/jeffsumm.asp; He also addressed it in his composition draft of the "Declaration of the Causes and Necessity for Taking Up Arms" (found in Jefferson, *PTJ*, 1:193) and in his "Notes on the State of Virginia," LOC, 106–7, https://tile.loc.gov/storage-services/service/gdc/lhbcb/04902/04902.pdf.

4. "Charter to Sir Walter Raleigh, 1584," Avalon Project, Yale Law School, https:// avalon.law.yale.edu/16th_century/raleigh.asp.

5. Richard Hakluyt, *The Principal Navigations, Voyages, Traffiques and Discoveries of the English Nation* (1904; repr., New York: Cambridge University Press, 2014), 8:i; also the "Thomas Jefferson Papers Timeline: 1776," LOC, https://www.loc.gov/collections/ thomas-jefferson-papers/articles-and-essays/the-thomas-jefferson-papers-timeline-1743 -to-1827/1774-to-1783/.

6. Arthur Barlowe, "The First Voyage to Roanoke, 1584: The First Voyage Made to the Coasts of America," Documenting the American South, https://docsouth.unc.edu/ nc/barlowe/barlowe.html.

7. Thomas Jefferson, "Refutation of the Argument That the Colonies Were Established at the Expense of the British Nation," FO, https://founders.archives.gov/documents/ Jefferson/01-01-02-0147.

8. "Letter from Ralph Lane," in Hakluyt, *Principal Navigations*, 317–20; "The First English Colony," NPS, https://www.nps.gov/fora/learn/education/the-first -english-colony.htm; "1585: The Military Colony," NPS, https://www.nps.gov/articles /1585voyage.htm.

9. Horn, *A Kingdom Strange*, 167, 189, 226–30; "The Fifth Voyage to Virginia," in Hakluyt, *Principal Navigations*, 416–17.

10. Jefferson, "Refutation of the Argument That the Colonies Were Established at the Expense of the British Nation," FO, https://founders.archives.gov/documents/Jefferson /01-01-02-0147.

11. Jefferson, "Notes on the State of Virginia," LOC, 115–16, https://tile.loc.gov/ storage-services/service/gdc/lhbcb/04902/04902.pdf.

12. "Colonial Charters, Grants and Related Documents," Avalon Project, Yale Law School, https://avalon.law.yale.edu/subject_menus/statech.asp#va; "The Colonial Period," U.S. Diplomatic Mission to Germany, https://usa.usembassy.de/etexts/history/ch2

.htm; "The English Establish a Foothold at Jamestown," LOC, https://www.loc.gov/classroom-materials/united-states-history-primary-source-timeline/colonial-settlement-1600-1763/english-at-jamestown-1606-1610/.

13. Alan Taylor, *American Colonies: The Settling of North America* (New York: Penguin, 2001), 136–37; Rebecca Beatrice Brooks, "The 13 Colonies in the Revolutionary War," *History of Massachusetts Blog*, December 12, 2017, https://historyofmassachusetts.org/13-colonies-revolutionary-war/; Tom Hand, "Royal, Self-governing and Proprietary Colonies: Advancing from British Rule toward American Independence," Constituting America, https://constitutingamerica.org/90day-aer-royal-self-governing-and-proprietary-colonies-advancing-from-british-rule-toward-american-independence-guest-essayist-tom-hand/.

14. Robert Middlekauff, *The Glorious Cause: The American Revolution, 1763–1789* (New York: Oxford University Press, 2005), 26–27.

15. Middlekauff, *The Glorious Cause*, 7–9, 55; "Jumonville Glen," NPS, https://www.nps.gov/articles/jumonville-glen.htm. "French and Indian War/Seven Years' War, 1754–1763," Office of the Historian, https://history.state.gov/milestones/1750-1775/french-indian-war. The war was called the Seven Years' War in the rest of the world. This link also includes a summation of the Treaty of Paris.

16. John Adams to William Tudor, Sr., March 29, 1817, FO, https://founders.archives.gov/documents/Adams/99-02-02-6735; Erick Trickey, "Why the Colonies' Most Galvanizing Patriot Never Became a Founding Father: James Otis, Jr. Used His Word to Whip Anti-British Sentiment into a Frenzy—So Why Isn't He Better Remembered Now?," *Smithsonian Magazine*, May 5, 2017, https://www.smithsonianmag.com/history/transformative-patriot-who-didnt-become-founding-father-180963166/.

17. James Otis, *Collected Political Writings of James Otis*, ed. Richard Samuelson (Indianapolis, IN: Liberty Fund, 2015), https://oll.libertyfund.org/title/collected-political-writings. The book includes Adams's notes on both of Otis's speeches.

18. John Adams to William Tudor, Sr., March 29, 1817, FO, https://founders.archives.gov/documents/Adams/99-02-02-6735.

19. "Proclamation of 1763: A Spotlight on a Primary Source of George III," Gilder Lehrman Institute of American History, https://www.gilderlehrman.org/history-resources/spotlight-primary-source/proclamation-1763-1763; Middlekauff, *The Glorious Cause*, 58–60.

20. "The Sugar Act," MHS, https://www.masshist.org/revolution/sugar.php; "The Stamp Act, 1765," Gilder Lehrman Institute of American History, https://www.gilderlehrman.org/history-resources/spotlight-primary-source/stamp-act-1765; "Britain Begins Taking the Colonies: The Sugar & Stamp Acts," Boston National Historical Park, NPS, https://www.nps.gov/articles/000/sugar-and-stamp-acts.htm#ftref3./.

21. "The Stamp Act, 1765," Gilder Lehrman Institute of American History, https://www.gilderlehrman.org/history-resources/spotlight-primary-source/stamp-act-1765; "Virginia Resolves on the Stamp Act (1765)," *Encyclopedia Virginia*, https://encyclopediavirginia.org/entries/virginia-resolves-on-the-stamp-act-1765/; "A Call for a Unified Response," MHS, https://www.masshist.org/database/viewer.php?item_id=293&pid=2; "Letter from Massachusetts Province," https://www.digitalhistory.uh.edu/disp

_textbook.cfm?smtID=3&psid=4116; "Resolutions of the Stamp Act Congress," Digital History, http://www.let.rug.nl/usa/essays/before-1800/the-stamp-act-and-the-sugar-act /resolutions-of-the-stamp-act-congress.php.

22. "Stamp Act Congress," Stamp Act, http://www.stamp-act-history.com/stamp-act/ stamp-act-congress/; "From the Providence Gazette Extraordinary; The following is said to be a copy of the Resolutions of the Congress held at New York, October 19, 1765," MHS, https://www.masshist.org/database/viewer.php?item_id=293&img_step=1&pid =2&mode=transcript#page1.

23. "Great Britain: Parliament—the Declaratory Act, March 18, 1766," Avalon Project, Yale Law School, https://avalon.law.yale.edu/18th_century/declaratory_act_1766.asp.

24. Stacy Schiff, *The Revolutionary: Samuel Adams* (New York: Little, Brown, 2022), 84–85, 122–23; "Samuel Adams, Boston's Radical Revolutionary," NPS, https://www.nps .gov/articles/000/samuel-adams-boston-revolutionary.htm; "Loyal Nine," Boston Tea Party Ships & Museum, https://www.bostonteapartyship.com/loyal-nine.

25. "Great Britain: Parliament—the Townshend Act, November 20, 1867," Avalon Project, Yale Law School, https://avalon.law.yale.edu/18th_century/townsend_act_1767 .asp; Schiff, *The Revolutionary: Samuel Adams*, 123; "British Reforms and Colonial Resis- tance, 1767–1772," LOC, https://www.loc.gov/classroom-materials/united-states-history -primary-source-timeline/american-revolution-1763-1783/british-reforms-1767-1772/. The Townshend Act was named for the chancellor of the exchequer, Charles Townshend.

26. "Massachusetts Circular Letter to the Colonial Legislatures, February 11, 1868," Avalon Project, Yale Law School, https://avalon.law.yale.edu/18th_century/mass_circ_let _1768.asp. James Otis was also one of the authors, along with Samuel Adams.

27. "Letters from a Farmer in Pennsylvania to the Inhabitants of the British Colonies," in *The American Revolution: Writings from the Pamphlet Debate 1764–1772 and 1773–1776*, ed. Gordon S. Wood (New York: Library of America, 2015), 432. There were twelve let- ters in all. The first was published in the *Pennsylvania Chronicle and Universal Advertiser*, December 3, 1767.

28. Merrill Jensen, *The Founding of a Nation: A History of the American Revolution 1763–1776* (Indianapolis, IN: Hackett, 2004), 252–57. Schiff, *The Revolutionary: Samuel Adams*, 134–35.

29. Schiff, *The Revolutionary: Samuel Adams*, 139–40; Jensen, *The Founding of a Nation*, 288–90.

30. Jensen, *The Founding of a Nation*, 296.

31. *Boston-Gazette and Country Journal*, December 5, 1768, 1, MHS, https://www .masshist.org/dorr/volume/2/sequence/341.

32. Samuel Adams, *The Writings of Samuel Adams*, ed. Harry Alonzo Cushing (New York: Putnam, 1904–1908), 1:201, 1:236, 1:254, 1:255, 1:282, 1:297, 1:316, 1:322, 1:336, 1:339; Schiff, *The Revolutionary: Samuel Adams*, 158–60.

33. Adams, *The Writings of Samuel Adams*, 1:264, 1:282; Samuel Adams to Dennys DeBerdt, November 16, 1769, cited in "Samuel Adams: Boston's Radical Revolutionary," NPS, 13, https://www.nps.gov/articles/000/samuel-adams-boston-revolutionary.htm.

34. Andrew Roberts, *The Last King of America: The Misunderstood Reign of George III* (New York: Viking, 2021), 204.

35. "The Remains of young Snider, the unfortunate Boy who was barbarously Murdered the 22nd of February last," *Boston-Gazette and Country Journal*, found at MHS, https://www.masshist.org/database/viewer.php?item_id=318&pid=2. The original protest was at the home of a Boston shop owner who was selling imported goods, Theophilus Lillie. Customs informer Ebenezer Richardson tried to break up the protest but was driven back to his own house, where he grabbed a gun and fired into the mob. The shots killed Seider (sometimes spelled Snider) and wounded a teenager. See "Christopher Seider: The First Casualty in the American Revolutionary Cause," New England Historical Society, https://newenglandhistoricalsociety.com/christopher-seider-the-first-casualty-in-the-american-revolutionary-cause/.

36. *Boston-Gazette and Country Journal*, March 5, 1770, MHS, https://www.masshist.org/dorr/browse-np/title/BGCJ/fYear/1770; "Samuel Adams: Boston's Radical Revolutionary," NPS, 13, https://www.nps.gov/articles/000/samuel-adams-boston-revolutionary.htm; Schiff, *The Revolutionary: Samuel Adams*, 178–79; "Christopher Seider: The First Casualty in the American Revolutionary Cause," New England Historical Society, https://newenglandhistoricalsociety.com/christopher-seider-the-first-casualty-in-the-american-revolutionary-cause/.

37. *Boston-Gazette and Country Journal*, March 12, 1770, MHS, https://www.masshist.org/database/viewer.php?item_id=316&img_step=1&pid=2&br=1&mode=transcript#page1; "Case of Capt. Thomas Preston of the 29th Regiment" (Preston's court testimony), MHS, https://www.masshist.org/database/viewer.php?item_id=462&mode=large&img_step=1&&pid=2; "The Boston Massacre," MHS, https://www.masshist.org/revolution/massacre.php; Schiff, *The Revolutionary: Samuel Adams*, 180–83; "Samuel Adams: Boston's Radical Revolutionary," NPS, 13, https://www.nps.gov/articles/000/samuel-adams-boston-revolutionary.htm.

38. *Boston-Gazette and Country Journal*, March 12, 1770, MHS, https://www.masshist.org/dorr/volume/3/sequence/101.

39. Schiff, *The Revolutionary: Samuel Adams*, 188–91; *Boston-Gazette and Country Journal*, March 12, 1770, MHS, https://www.masshist.org/database/viewer.php?item_id=316&img_step=1&pid=2&br=1&mode=transcript#page1; "The Bloody Massacre," MHS, https://www.masshist.org/database/2?ft=Boston%20Massacre&from=/features/massacre/visual&noalt=1&pid=34. Revere's work hit the market first and had the greatest impact. Henry Pelham's piece was titled "The Fruits of Arbitrary Power, or The Bloody Massacre."

40. "A Committee of the Town of Boston to Benjamin Franklin," July 13, 1770, in Adams, *The Writings of Samuel Adams*, 2:10.

41. Schiff, *The Revolutionary: Samuel Adams*, 196–200; "Samuel Adams: Boston's Radical Revolutionary," NPS, 13, https://www.nps.gov/articles/000/samuel-adams-boston-revolutionary.htm.

42. "[John] Adams' Argument for the Defense, 3–4 December, 1770," FO, https://founders.archives.gov/documents/Adams/05-03-02-0001-0004-0016; "Perspectives on the Boston Massacre: The Trials," MHS, https://www.masshist.org/features/massacre/trials.

43. Adams, *The Writings of Samuel Adams*, 2:77–162 (the ten pieces about the trial that Adams published as "Vindex" are included in this section, as well as some other unrelated

work); Schiff, *The Revolutionary: Samuel Adams*, 200, 203–4; "Samuel Adams: Boston's Radical Revolutionary," NPS, 14, https://www.nps.gov/articles/000/samuel-adams-boston-revolutionary.htm.

44. Richard Henry Lee to John Dickinson, July 25, 1768, found in Richard Henry Lee (grandson), *Memoir of the Life of Richard Henry Lee, and His Correspondence with the Most Distinguished Men in America and Europe* (n.p.: William Brown, 1825; repr., London: Forgotten Books, 2018), 1:65–66.

45. Schiff, *The Revolutionary: Samuel Adams*, 215.

46. Samuel Adams to James Warren, November, 4, 1772, MHS, https://www.masshist.org/database/viewer.php?item_id=438&img_step=1&pid=2&mode=transcript#page1.

47. Richard Henry Lee to Samuel Adams, February 4, 1773, and Samuel Adams to Richard Henry Lee, April 10, 1773, found in Lee, *Memoir of the Life of Richard Henry Lee*, 1:66–68; "Samuel Adams: Boston's Radical Revolutionary, NPS, 15, https://www.nps.gov/articles/000/samuel-adams-boston-revolutionary.htm.

48. "In the House of Burgesses in Virginia, March 1773" and "Extract of a letter from a Gentlemen of distinction in Virginia, to his Friend in this Town [Boston], dated March 14, 1773," MHS, https://www.masshist.org/database/viewer.php?item_id=442&img_step=1&pid=2&br=1&mode=transcript#page1; Thomas Cushing to Benjamin Franklin, April 20, 1773, FO, https://founders.archives.gov/documents/Franklin/01-20-02-0100; Benjamin Franklin to Thomas Cushing, July 7, 1773, FO, https://founders.archives.gov/documents/Franklin/01-20-02-0153.

49. "The Boston Tea Party," MHS, https://www.masshist.org/revolution/teaparty.php; Robert J. Allison, *The American Revolution: A Concise History* (New York: Oxford University Press, 2011), 16–17; "The Colonies Move toward Open Rebellion," LOC, https://www.loc.gov/classroom-materials/united-states-history-primary-source-timeline/american-revolution-1763-1783/colonies-rebellion-1773-1774/; "The Tea Act: The Catalyst of the Boston Tea Party," Boston Tea Party Ships & Museum, https://www.bostonteapartyship.com/the-tea-act#:~:text=The%20Tea%20Act%3A%20The%20Catalyst,sales%20in%20the%20American%20colonies; "The following was dispersed in Hand Bills among the worthy Citizens of Philadelphia," MHS, https://www.masshist.org/database/viewer.php?pid=2&old=1&mode=nav&ft=Coming%20of%20the%20American%20Revolution&item_id=450.

50. "The Boston Tea Party," MHS, https://www.masshist.org/revolution/teaparty.php; "Tradesmen's Protest against the Proceedings of the Merchants," MHS, https://www.masshist.org/database/viewer.php?item_id=398&img_step=1&pid=2&br=1&mode=transcript#page1.

51. *Boston-Gazette and Country Journal*, December 20, 1773, MHS, https://www.masshist.org/database/viewer.php?item_id=409&img_step=1&pid=2&br=1&mode=transcript#page1. Hutchinson, a Boston native and descendant of early New England settlers, had been promoted to governor by the Crown shortly after the Boston Massacre.

52. John Adams to James Warren, December 17, 1773, Papers of John Adams Digital Edition, vol. 2, MHS, https://www.masshist.org/publications/adams-papers/index.php/view/PJA02p1. The event was not labeled the "Boston Tea Party" until the 1800s.

53. Roberts, *The Last King of America*, 232.

Chapter 3

1. John Adams diary, December 17, 1773, FO, https://founders.archives.gov/documents/Adams/01-02-02-0003-0008.

2. Rick Atkinson, *The British Are Coming: The War for America, Lexington to Princeton, 1775–1777* (New York: Holt, 2019), 14; Andrew Roberts, *The Last King of America: The Misunderstood Reign of George III* (New York: Viking, 2021), 233.

3. "An Act to Block up Boston Harbour," MHS, https://www.masshist.org/database/viewer.php?item_id=675&img_step=1&pid=2&br=1&mode=dual#page1.

4. "The Coercive (Intolerable) Acts," MHS, https://www.masshist.org/revolution/coercive.php; "Great Britain: Parliament—the Massachusetts Government Act, May 20, 1774," Avalon Project, Yale University, https://avalon.law.yale.edu/18th_century/mass_gov_act.asp (all of the Coercive Acts are also available at this site); Atkinson, *The British Are Coming*, 14; Merrill Jensen, *The Founding of a Nation: A History of the American Revolution 1763–1776* (Indianapolis, IN: Hackett, 2004), 456–57; "The Coercive (Intolerable) Acts of 1774," George Washington's Mount Vernon, https://www.mountvernon.org/library/digitalhistory/digital-encyclopedia/article/the-coercive-intolerable-ydacts-of-1774/; "The Boston Tea Party—the Coercive Acts," History, https://www.history.com/topics/american-revolution/boston-tea-party. Some historians also include the Quebec Act, which, among other things, granted religious freedom to French Canadian Catholics under British rule—enraging the mostly Protestant colonists.

5. Jensen, *The Founding of a Nation*, 459, 465. Gage replaced Thomas Hutchinson, a loyalist New England native. Hutchison soon left for England and never returned to his homeland.

6. Jensen, *The Founding of a Nation*, 461, 463; "An American Describes the 'Patriotic Flame,' an excerpt from David Ramsay's *The History of the American Union*," America in Class, 2, https://americainclass.org/sources/makingrevolution/crisis/text7/coerciveactsresponse.pdf.

7. Samuel Adams to William Checkley, June 1, 1774, in Samuel Adams, *The Writings of Samuel Adams*, ed. Harry Alonzo Cushing (New York: Putnam, 1904–1908), 3:128.

8. Jack N. Rakove, *Revolutionaries: A New History of the Invention of America* (New York: First Mariner, 2011), 49; Jensen, *The Founding of a Nation*, 469.

9. "Proceedings of the Inhabitants of Philadelphia, June 18, 1774," Avalon Project, Yale Law School, https://avalon.law.yale.edu/18th_century/proc_in_pa_1774.asp. The Pennsylvania meeting was chaired by John Dickinson and included future congressmen Robert Morris and Charles Thomson.

10. Richard Henry Lee to Samuel Adams, June 23, 1774, in Richard H. Lee (grandson), *Memoir of the Life of Richard Henry Lee, and His Correspondence with the Most Distinguished Men in America and Europe* (n.p.: William Brown, 1825; repr., London: Forgotten Books, 2018), 1:97–99; Jensen, *The Founding of a Nation*, 475–77; Rakove, *Revolutionaries*, 48.

11. Samuel Adams to Richard Henry Lee, July 1774, in Lee, *Memoir of the Life of Richard Henry Lee*, 1:101. No specific date is given, but the letter was written in response to Lee's message of June 23.

12. Thomas Jefferson, *The Autobiography of Thomas Jefferson, 1743–1790*, ed. Paul Leicester Ford (1914; repr., Philadelphia: University of Pennsylvania Press, 2005), 13–14.

13. "Draft of Instructions to the Virginia Delegates in the Continental Congress (Text of 'A Summary View')," in Jefferson, *PTJ*, 1:121–35; Joseph Ellis, *Writing the Declaration of Independence* (New York: Vintage, 2015), e-book, 14–16.

14. "Draft Instructions of the Virginia Delegates in the Continental Congress," in Jefferson, *PTJ*, 1:121, 1:123, 1:125–26, 1:128, 1:130. This also may be found at "A Summary View of the Rights of British America," Avalon Project, Yale University, https://avalon .law.yale.edu/18th_century/jeffsumm.asp.

15. Jefferson, *PTJ*, 1:134–35.

16. Jefferson, *The Autobiography of Thomas Jefferson, 1743–1790*, 15; "Resolutions and Association of the Virginia Convention of 1774," in Jefferson, *PTJ*, 1:137–41.

17. "List of Delegates to Congress," in Smith, *LDC*, 1:xxxii.

18. John Adams, *The Works of John Adams* (hereafter *WJA*), vol. 2, *Diary, Notes of Debates, Autobiography* (repr., North Charleston, SC: Createspace, 2015), 173; "List of Delegates to Congress," in Smith, *LDC*, 1:xxviii. James Bowdoin was also appointed from Massachusetts but declined to attend. John Hancock did not become involved until the Second Continental Congress.

19. John Adams to Timothy Pickering, August 6, 1822, FO, https://founders.archives .gov/documents/Adams/99-02-02-7674; Adams, *WJA*, 2:174–75; Rakove, *Revolutionaries*, 51.

20. Adams, *WJA*, 2:176, 2:182; John Adams to Timothy Pickering, August 6, 1822, FO, https://founders.archives.gov/documents/Adams/99-02-02-7674. Among the men who met them at Frankford were Thomas Mifflin and Benjamin Rush.

21. Jack N. Rakove, *The Beginnings of National Politics: An Interpretive History of the Continental Congress* (Baltimore, MD: Johns Hopkins University Press, 1979), 43; "Continental Congress," History, https://www.history.com/topics/american-revolution/the -continental-congress; Adams, *WJA*, 2:182–85. The descriptions of other delegates from Adams's diary also are published in Smith, *LDC*, 1:3–9. His diary is available on numerous digital and printed platforms.

22. Stacy Schiff, *The Revolutionary: Samuel Adams* (New York: Little, Brown, 2022), 279. The secrecy agreement was referenced most specifically in a letter from Silas Dean to his wife on September 6: "Our proceedings for Various Reasons will be kept Secret. . . . (We) shall say Nothing until We break up, for though We may publish to the World the whole, it is improper to do so prematurely" (Smith, *LDC*, 1:29).

23. John Adams to William Tudor, September 29, 1774, FO, https://founders .archives.gov/documents/Adams/06-02-02-0052; David McCullough, *John Adams* (New York: Simon & Schuster Paperbacks, 2001), 79.

24. Joseph Galloway to William Franklin, September 3 and September 5, 1774, in Smith, *LDC*, 1:23–25, 27.

25. Smith, *LDC*, 1:xxiv, 1:xxvi–xxxii (for attendance), 1:13, 1:20, 1:30–31.

26. "James Duane's Notes of Debates," September 6, 1774, in Smith, *LDC*, 1:30.

27. John Adams' Diary, September 6, 1774, and Silas Deane to Elizabeth Deane, September 7, 1774, in Smith, *LDC*, 1:27, 1:29.

28. *JCC*, 1:26–28 (including *JCC*, 1:28n1).

29. Smith, *LDC*, 1:xxx. The dates of attendance by each delegate are listed at the start of this volume.

30. *JCC*, 1:31–40; Christian Di Spigna, *Founding Martyr: The Life and Death of Dr. Joseph Warren, the American Revolution's Lost Hero* (New York: Crown, 2018), 149–50; Jensen, *The Founding of a Nation*, 495.

31. *JCC*, 1:41, 1:43–50; Jensen, *The Founding of a Nation*, 498–99.

32. John Adams to Abigail Adams, October 9, 1774, in Smith, *LDC*, 1:164.

33. John Adams to Hezekiah Niles, February 13, 1818, FO, https://founders.archives .gov/documents/Adams/99-02-02-6854.

34. *JCC*, 1:42, 1:63–73; "The Bill of Rights: A List of Grievances, 14 October 1774," FO, https://founders.archives.gov/documents/Adams/06-02-02-0041-0005; Jensen, *The Founding of a Nation*, 504–6.

35. *JCC*, 1:62, 1:75–80, 1:81–89, 1:90–101, 1:105–13; "Continental Association, 20 October, 1774," FO, https://founders.archives.gov/documents/Jefferson/01-01-02 -0094; Rakove, *The Beginnings of National Politics*, 49–51.

36. "The Petition of the Grand American Continental Congress, to the King's Most Excellent Majesty," MHS, https://www.masshist.org/database/viewer.php?item_id=663 &pid=2; *JCC*, 1:115–23.

37. *JCC*, 1:102. It was recommended that "the same be held at the city of Philadelphia, and that all the Colonies, in North-America, chuse [*sic*] deputies, as soon as possible, to attend such Congress."

38. Jensen, *The Founding of a Nation*, 508; Rakove, *The Beginnings of National Politics*, 60–61.

39. John Dickinson to Arthur Lee, October 27, 1774, and Joseph Galloway to Thomas Nickleson, November 1, 1774, in Smith, *LDC*, 1:250–55. Galloway would not serve in Congress again and eventually fled to England.

40. Thomas Gage to Lord Dartmouth, November 15, 1774, Northern Illinois University Digital Library, https://digital.lib.niu.edu/islandora/object/niu-amarch%3A102747.

41. King George III to Lord North, November 18, 1774, in "George III's Official Correspondence July 1772–1783," Royal Collection Trust, https://www.rct.uk/collection /georgian-papers-programme/george-iiis-official-correspondence-july-1772-1783; Roberts, *The Last King of America*, 251. Gage wrote: "This province [Massachusetts] and the neighboring ones, particularly Connecticut, are preparing for war."

42. "The King's speech to both houses of Parliament, on the 30th of November, 1774," LOC, https://www.loc.gov/resource/rbpe.03704100/?st=text.

43. *JCC*, 1:123–24; Benjamin Franklin to Charles Thomson, February 5, 1775, FO, https://founders.archives.gov/documents/Franklin/01-21-02-0260 (and fn5); Roberts, *The Last King of America*, 255; Walter Isaacson, *Benjamin Franklin: An American Life* (New York: Simon & Schuster Paperbacks, 2003), 285. Congress originally titled its document "The Petition of the Grand American Continental Congress to the King's Most Excellent Majesty," but, according to a footnote with Franklin's February 5 letter at Founders Online, Dartmouth changed it to the far less compelling "Petition of sundry

Persons on Behalf of themselves and the Inhabitants of several of His Majesty's Colonies in America."

44. Abigail Adams to Mercy Otis Warren, February 3, 1775, FO, https://founders .archives.gov/documents/Adams/04-01-02-0122; "Abigail Adams Knows, February 2, 1775," Mass Moments, https://www.massmoments.org/moment-details/abigail-adams -knows.html.

CHAPTER 4

1. King George III to Lord Dartmouth, December 13, 1774, cited in Andrew Roberts, *The Last King of America: The Misunderstood Reign of George III* (New York: Viking, 2021), 254.

2. Lord Dartmouth to General Gage, January 27, 1775, cited in Rick Atkinson, *The British Are Coming: The War for America, Lexington to Princeton, 1775–1777* (New York: Holt, 2019), 51–52.

3. Merrill Jensen, *The Founding of a Nation: A History of the American Revolution 1763–1776* (Indianapolis, IN: Hackett, 2004), 584–585; Atkinson, *The British Are Coming*, 53–54. The duplicate copy of the order arrived first (two were sent to increase the odds that at least one would make it). But Gage waited for the original copy to reach him on April 16 before deciding to take action.

4. Order Given to Lt. Colonel Francis Smith from Thomas Gage, NPS, https:// www.nps.gov/common/uploads/teachers/lessonplans/primary%20source%203%20gage %20orders%20real.pdf.

5. Phillip S. Greenwalt and Robert Orrison, *A Single Blow: The Battles of Lexington and Concord and the Beginning of the American Revolution, April 19, 1775* (El Dorado Hills, CA: Savas Beatie, 2018), 28–33; Jensen, *The Founding of a Nation*, 585.

6. Stacy Schiff, *The Revolutionary: Samuel Adams* (New York: Little, Brown, 2022), 9, 18–22.

7. "April 19, 1775: Overview of Battle," NPS, https://www.nps.gov/mima/learn/ historyculture/april-19-1775.htm; Greenwalt and Orrison, *A Single Blow*, 41, 46–48.

8. John Parker testimony, *JCC*, 2:31.

9. John Robins testimony, *JCC*, 2:31.

10. "April 19, 1775: Overview of Battle," NPS, https://www.nps.gov/mima/learn/ historyculture/april-19-1775.htm; Atkinson, *The British Are Coming*, 63.

11. Greenwalt and Orrison, *A Single Blow*, 44–45; "April 19, 1775: Overview of Battle," NPS, https://www.nps.gov/mima/learn/historyculture/april-19-1775.htm.

12. Greenwalt and Orrison, *A Single Blow*, 71; "April 19, 1775: Overview of Battle," NPS, https://www.nps.gov/mima/learn/historyculture/april-19-1775.htm; "A Provincial Protest Becomes a World War," Erenow, https://erenow.net/modern/ paulreveresridedavidhackett/15.php.

13. Atkinson, *The British Are Coming*, 67–69; "April 19, 1775: Overview of Battle," NPS, https://www.nps.gov/mima/learn/historyculture/april-19-1775.htm.

14. "April 19, 1775: Overview of Battle," NPS, https://www.nps.gov/mima/learn/ historyculture/april-19-1775.htm.

15. Atkinson, *The British Are Coming*, 69.

16. John Dickinson to Arthur Lee, April 29, 1775, in Smith, *LDC*, 1:332.

17. Silas Deane to Elizabeth Deane, May 7, 1775, and Richard Caswell to William Caswell, May 11, 1775, in Smith, *LDC*, 1:335, 1:339–40; Pauline Maier, *American Scripture: Making the Declaration of Independence* (New York: Vintage, 1998), 5.

18. Silas Deane to Elizabeth Deane, May 12, 1775, in Smith, *LDC*, 1:346–47; Maier, *American Scripture*, 6.

19. *JCC*, 2:11–12.

20. David McCullough, *John Adams* (New York: Simon & Schuster Paperbacks, 2001), 87–88; "Pennsylvania State House (Independence Hall)," U.S. Department of State, https://history.state.gov/departmenthistory/buildings/section3#:~:text=The%20Second %20Continental%20Congress%20convened,Declaration%20of%20Independence %20was%20signed. The quote describing the State House Yard is from McCullough. The State Department document references a description of the building from the National Park Service.

21. *JCC*, 2:17–21.

22. "To the Honorable American Continental Congress," *JCC*, 2:24–25; Maier, *American Scripture*, 7–8.

23. Maier, *American Scripture*, 9–10; *JCC*, 2:49, 2:52, 2:55–56. Regarding the upstate New York actions, Congress was concerned about England making "a cruel invasion from the province of Quebec . . . for the purpose of destroying our lives and liberties." The troops taking Fort Ticonderoga were commanded by Benedict Arnold and Ethan Allen.

24. *JCC*, 2:53–54; John N. Rakove, *The Beginnings of National Politics: An Interpretive History of the Continental Congress* (Baltimore, MD: Johns Hopkins University Press, 1979), 71–72; Silas Deane's Diary, in Smith, *LDC*, 1:351. Calling a "committee of the whole" allowed Congress to hold informal discussions without official records being kept.

25. Silas Deane's Diary, in Smith, *LDC*, 1:352; Rakove, *The Beginnings of National Politics*, 72; *JCC*, 2:64–66. Dickinson's notes for his three speeches during this period are available in Smith, *LDC*, 2:371–90.

26. *JCC*, 2:58–59, 2:101–2.

27. Jensen, *The Founding of a Nation*, 609; *JCC*, 2:78.

28. *JCC*, 2:89–90.

29. *JCC*, 2:91 (including *JCC*, 2:91n1).

30. "John Adams Autobiography," Adams Family Papers: An Electronic Archive, June–August 1775, sheet 20 of 53, MHS, https://www.masshist.org/digitaladams/archive /doc?id=A1_20.

31. John Adams to James Lloyd, April 25, 1815, FO, https://founders.archives.gov/ documents/Adams/99-02-02-6460.

32. Jensen, *The Founding of a Nation*, 611; *JCC*, 2:91–92, including the full text of Washington's address to Congress on June 16, 1775. His commission was approved the next day and appears in *JCC*, 2:96.

33. Nathaniel Philbrick, *Bunker Hill: A City, a Siege, a Revolution* (New York: Penguin, 2013), 229–30; "Bunker Hill," American Battlefield Trust, https://www.battlefields.org/ learn/revolutionary-war/battles/bunker-hill; "The Battle of Bunker Hill," NPS, https:// www.nps.gov/articles/000/the-battle-of-bunker-hill.htm.

34. *JCC*, 2:103–5, 2:108–9; Jensen, *The Founding of a Nation*, 616–17.

35. *JCC*, 2:111–23.

36. *JCC*, 2:105, 2:108; "Editorial Note: Declaration of the Causes and Necessity for Taking Up Arms," FO, https://founders.archives.gov/documents/Jefferson/01-01-02-0113-0001; and https://founders.archives.gov/documents/Jefferson/01-01-02-0113-0005. The quote on Rutledge's draft is from another committee member, William Livingston. A copy of Rutledge's draft never has been found.

37. Maier, *American Scripture*, 19; *JCC*, 2:108, 2:127; "Editorial Note: Declaration of the Causes and Necessity for Taking Up Arms," FO, https://founders.archives.gov/documents/Jefferson/01-01-02-0113-0001; "Declaration of the Causes and Necessity for Taking Up Arms (26 June–6 July 1775)," FO, https://www.founders.archives.gov/ancestor/TSJN-01-01-02-0113. This last link includes several drafts of the declaration by Jefferson and Dickinson, as well as the final text approved by Congress.

38. Thomas Jefferson, *The Autobiography of Thomas Jefferson, 1743–1790*, ed. Paul Leicester Ford (1914; repr., Philadelphia: University of Pennsylvania Press, 2005), 18–19.

39. Maier, *American Scripture*, 20. Before Maier's work, which was published in early 1997, many historians accepted Jefferson's criticism, especially given Dickinson's reputation.

40. "Jefferson's Composition Draft, 26 June–6 July 1775," FO, https://www.founders.archives.gov/?q=Ancestor%3ATSJN-01-01-02-0113&s=1511311111&r=2.

41. "John Dickinson's Composition Draft, 26 June–6 July 1775," FO, https://www.founders.archives.gov/?q=Ancestor%3ATSJN-01-01-02-0113&s=1511311111&r=4; Maier, *American Scripture*, 20.

42. "The Declaration as Adopted by Congress (6 July 1775)," FO, https://www.founders.archives.gov/?q=Ancestor%3ATSJN-01-01-02-0113&s=1511311111&r=5; John Adams to Joseph Palmer, July 5, 1776, in Smith, *LDC*, 1:584.

43. *JCC*, 2:65.

44. "John Dickinson's Notes for a Speech in Congress" and "John Dickinson's Proposed Resolutions," May 23–25, 1775, in Smith, *LDC*, 1:371, 1:377, 1:380, 1:382–84.

45. Adams, *WJA*, 2:209–10.

46. *JCC*, 2:80, 2:127, 2:161 (Jay's draft of the petition is in *JCC*, 2:440–42); John Adams to James Warren, July 6, 1775, FO, https://founders.archives.gov/documents/Adams/06-03-02-0037.

47. Adams, *WJA*, 2:211.

48. John Adams to James Warren, July 24, 1775, FO, https://founders.archives.gov/documents/Adams/06-03-02-0052.

49. John Adams to James Warren, July 24, 1775, n.1–2, FO, https://founders.archives.gov/documents/Adams/06-03-02-0052; McCullough, *John Adams*, 95.

50. Adams, *WJA*, 2:215.

51. *JCC*, 2:162n2; Maier, *American Scripture*, 24.

Chapter 5

1. Andrew Roberts, *The Last King of America: The Misunderstood Reign of George III* (New York: Viking, 2021), 268. The second letter was written to Lord Sandwich.

2. Roberts, *The Last King of America*, 270.

3. *JCC*, 2:162n2; John Dickinson to Arthur Lee, July 1775, in Smith, *LDC*, 1:688. Editors of the congressional letters wrote that the date could not be read on the "mutilated" letter, but they believed it was written sometime shortly after the petition was signed on July 8.

4. "By the King, a Proclamation, For suppressing Rebellion and Sedition," MHS, https://www.masshist.org/database/viewer.php?item_id=818&pid=2; Pauline Maier, *American Scripture: Making the Declaration of Independence* (New York: Vintage, 1998), 24, 250.

5. *JCC*, 3:343n1; Richard Penn and Arthur Lee to the President of Congress, September 2, 1775, Northern Illinois University Digital Library, https://digital.lib.niu.edu/islandora/object/niu-amarch%3A95875.

6. *JCC*, 2:235, 2:239; Samuel Adams to Elizabeth Adams, July 30, 1775, in Smith, *LDC*, 1:683.

7. Jack N. Rakove, *The Beginnings of National Politics: An Interpretive History of the Continental Congress* (Baltimore, MD: Johns Hopkins University Press, 1979), 79.

8. Thomas Jefferson to John Randolph, August 25, 1775, in Smith, *LDC*, 1:707–8.

9. "Georgia's Credentials," *JCC*, 2:240–41.

10. *JCC*, 2:240, 2:245, 2:248–49, 2:253.

11. *JCC*, 3:298, 3:307, 3:319, 3:403–4; Merrill Jensen, *The Founding of a Nation: A History of the American Revolution 1763–1776* (Indianapolis, IN: Hackett, 2004), 639–40; Maier, *American Scripture*, 13. Similar advice to Virginia came in early December. Massachusetts had asked the same question in May 1775.

12. Rakove, *The Beginnings of National Politics*, 80; *JCC*, 3:343 (including the text of the letter, which appears on p. 343n1).

13. "John Dickinson's Proposed Instructions," November 9, 1775, in Smith, *LDC*, 2:319–20.

14. Rakove, *The Beginnings of National Politics*, 79–80.

15. David McCullough, *1776* (New York: Simon & Schuster Paperbacks, 2005), 3–4, 10.

16. "His Majesty's most gracious speech to both houses of Parliament," LOC, https://www.loc.gov/resource/rbpe.10803800/?st=text.

17. Roberts, *The Last King of America*, 270; Jensen, *The Founding of a Nation*, 615–16.

18. "His Majesty's most gracious speech to both houses of Parliament," LOC, https://www.loc.gov/resource/rbpe.10803800/?st=text.

19. McCullough, *1776*, 12–13, 18; Roberts, *The Last King of America*, 279. The two distinguished authors had slightly different tallies for the votes in both houses, but the margins were generally the same.

20. Joseph J. Ellis, *Revolutionary Summer: The Birth of American Independence* (New York: Vintage, 2012), 12.

21. Maier, *American Scripture*, 26.

22. "Lieutenant Henry Mowat to the People of Falmouth, October 16, 1775," *Naval Documents of the American Revolution*, 2:471, cited in Michael Cecere, "A Tale of Two Cities: The Destruction of Falmouth and the Defense of Hampton," *Journal of the American*

Revolution, https://allthingsliberty.com/2015/09/a-tale-of-two-cities-the-destruction-of
-falmouth-and-the-defense-of-hampton/#_ednref7.

23. Cecere, "A Tale of Two Cities," https://allthingsliberty.com/2015/09/a-tale-of
-two-cities-the-destruction-of-falmouth-and-the-defense-of-hampton/#_ednref7; *JCC,*
3:372.

24. "Lord Dunmore's Proclamation, 1775," Gilder Lehrman Institute of American
History, https://www.gilderlehrman.org/history-resources/spotlight-primary-source/lord
-dunmores-proclamation-1775; Jensen, *The Founding of a Nation,* 645; "Lord Dunmore," American Battlefield Trust, https://www.battlefields.org/learn/biographies/lord
-dunmore. Dunmore's regiment found some early success but was soundly defeated at
the Battle of Great Bridge in December 1775. Nonetheless, the proclamation inspired
thousands of slaves to seek freedom.

25. *JCC,* 3:319, 3:326–27.

26. John Adams to Richard Henry Lee, November 17, 1775, FO, https://founders
.archives.gov/documents/Adams/06-03-02-0163#:~:text=It%20is%20by%20ballancing
%20each,for%20an%20House%20of%20Commons; "Thoughts on Government, April
1776," FO, https://founders.archives.gov/?q=Ancestor%3AADMS-06-04-02-0026&s
=1511311111&r=4.

27. Thomas Jefferson to John Randolph, November 29, 1755, in Smith, *LDC,* 2:402–
3. It was in this letter that Jefferson informed Randolph of the death of Randolph's
brother, Peyton, the first president of the Continental Congress. Peyton Randolph died
shortly after suffering a stroke (called apoplexy at the time) on October 22.

28. *JCC,* 3:353, 3:392, 3:409–12; Roberts, *The Last King of America,* 285.

29. "A Collection of All the Statutes Now in Force; Relating to the Revenues and Officers of the Customs in Great Britain and the Plantations," 2:1459–60, HathiTrust, https:
//babel.hathitrust.org/cgi/pt?id=pst.000022133328&view=1up&seq=504.

30. Jensen, *The Founding of a Nation,* 649–50; Maier, *American Scripture,* 27–28; John
Hancock to Thomas Cushing, February 13, 1776, in Smith, *LDC,* 3:244.

Chapter 6

1. Richard Smith's Diary, January 8, 1776, in Smith, *LDC,* 3:60. Dunmore's men did,
indeed, attack Norfolk, but it was not understood until later that some of the damage was
caused by residents themselves.

2. Richard Smith's Diary, January 9, 1776, in Smith, *LDC,* 3:72; "John Dickinson's Proposed Resolutions on a Petition to the King," and "John Dickinson's Proposed Resolution
for Negotiating with Great Britain," January 9–24, 1776, in Smith, *LDC,* 3:63–64; Samuel Adams to John Adams, January 15, 1776, in Burnett, *LMCC,* 1:311. Pauline Maier,
American Scripture: Making the Declaration of Independence (New York: Vintage, 1998), 27.

3. *JCC,* 4:134–46 (and *JCC,* 4:146n1).

4. Thomas Paine, *Common Sense and Other Writings,* ed. Gordon S. Wood (New
York: Modern Library [Random House], 2003), 22, 26, 28–29, 31. Excellent background
and analysis of Paine and *Common Sense* can be found in Joseph J. Ellis, *Revolutionary
Summer: The Birth of American Independence* (New York: Vintage, 2012), 13–15; Maier,
American Scripture, 31–34; David McCullough, *John Adams* (New York: Simon &

Schuster Paperbacks, 2001), 96–97; and Jack N. Rakove, *Revolutionaries: A New History of the Invention of America* (New York: First Mariner, 2011), 94–95. All were helpful in understanding the impact of the pamphlet.

5. Rakove, *Revolutionaries*, 94; Ellis, *Revolutionary Summer*, 14; Richard Smith Diary, January 8, 1776, *LMCC*, 1:302–3.

6. Paine, *Common Sense*, 5, 9, 14–15.

7. Paine, *Common Sense*, 27.

8. Paine, *Common Sense*, 6, 30–31; Maier, *American Scripture*, 32.

9. John Adams to Abigail Adams, March 19, 1776, FO, https://founders.archives.gov/documents/Adams/04-01-02-0235.

10. Paine, *Common Sense*, 19, 48.

11. Samuel Ward to Henry Ward, February 19, 1776, in Smith, *LDC*, 3:285.

12. William Tudor to John Adams, February 29, 1776, FO, https://founders.archives.gov/documents/Adams/06-04-02-0013; John Adams to William Tudor, April 12, 1776, FO, https://founders.archives.gov/documents/Adams/06-04-02-0041; McCullough, *John Adams*, 97.

13. Paine, *Common Sense*, 42. This appeared near the end of his original text, but before an appendix that was added in later publications.

14. Maier, *American Scripture*, 30.

15. "Maryland Convention, January 1776," in *American Archives: A Documentary History of the English Colonies in North America*, 4th ser., ed. Peter Force (printed by Act of Congress, 1833; repr., London: Forgotten Books, 2019), 4:739.

16. Merrill Jensen, *The Founding of a Nation: A History of the American Revolution 1763–1776* (Indianapolis, IN: Hackett, 2004), 641–42.

17. "Instructions to the Representatives of Portsmouth, New-Hampshire," December 25, 1775, in Force, *American Archives*, 4th ser., 4:459.

18. Samuel Adams to John Adams, January 16, 1776, FO, https://founders.archives.gov/documents/Adams/06-03-02-0204#PJA03d254n1.

19. "John Jay's Essay on Congress and Independence," January 1776, in Smith, *LDC*, 3:175; "John Dickinson's Proposed Resolutions for Negotiating with Great Britain," January 1776, in Smith, *LDC*, 3:64.

20. James Duane to Robert Livingston, in Smith, *LDC*, 3:33–34; Rakove, *Revolutionaries*, 96.

21. Diary of John Adams, January 1776, FO, https://founders.archives.gov/documents/Adams/01-02-02-0006-0001; John Adams to George Washington, January 8, 1776, in Force, *American Archives*, 4th ser., 4:604.

22. Abigail Adams to John Adams, November 27, 1775, MHS, https://www.masshist.org/digitaladams/archive/doc?id=L17751127aa&rec=sheet&archive=&hi=&numRecs=&query=&queryid=&start=&tag=&num=10&bc=. The Adams letter to R. H. Lee on November 15 is covered and attributed in chapter 5.

23. Danielle Allen, interview by Liz Covart, *Ben Franklin's World* (podcast), episode 141, July 4, 2017, https://benfranklinsworld.com/episode-141-declaration-draft/. Also see "Danielle Allen: John Adams and the Declaration," Houghton Library, Harvard

University, https://houghton75.org/2017/06/02/danielle-allen-john-adams-and-our
-declaration/.

24. "A Proclamation by the General Court, 19 January 1776," FO, https://founders
.archives.gov/documents/Adams/06-03-02-0195-0005.

25. "A Proclamation by the General Court, 19 January 1776," FO, https://founders
.archives.gov/documents/Adams/06-03-02-0195-0005; comparisons with "Declaration
of Independence: A Transcription," July 4, 1776, NA, https://www.archives.gov/founding
-docs/declaration-transcript.

26. "A Proclamation by the General Court, 19 January 1776," note 1, FO, https://
founders.archives.gov/documents/Adams/06-03-02-0195-0005.

27. Thomas Jefferson to Henry Lee, May 8, 1825, FO, https://founders.archives.gov/
documents/Jefferson/98-01-02-5212.

28. Allen, interview by Liz Covart, *Ben Franklin's World* (podcast), https://
benfranklinsworld.com/episode-141-declaration-draft/.

29. John Adams, *Diary and Autobiography of John Adams* (hereafter *DJA*), ed. L. H. Butterfield (Cambridge, MA: Belknap, 1961), 2:231–33, including n1; McCullough, *John
Adams*, 89. It has frustrated historians that this February 1776 memorandum by Adams
was not dated. Editors of his diary say that it was likely written between February 10 and
February 15 and "certainly before February 23." The author believes it was closer to February 15 because of the time it would have taken to consult with Samuel Adams and R.
H. Lee, after just returning to Congress on February 9.

30. *JCC*, 4:173–75; Richard Smith Diary, in Burnett, *LMCC*, 1:366; "A Collection of
All the Statutes Now in Force; Relating to the Revenues and Officers of the Customs
in Great Britain and the Plantations" (Prohibitory Act), 2:1459–74, HathiTrust, https://
babel.hathitrust.org/cgi/pt?id=pst.000022133328&view=1up&seq=503.

31. John Adams to Horatio Gates, March 23, 1776, in Smith, *LDC*, 3:429–31; Richard Henry Lee to Landon Carter, April 1, 1776, in Smith, *LDC*, 3:470; Robert Morris
to Robert Herries, February 15, 1776, in Smith, *LDC*, 3:258; Maier, *American Scripture*,
27–28; Jensen, *The Founding of a Nation*, 655.

32. "The Committee of Secret Correspondence: Instructions to Silas Deane, 2 March
1776," FO, https://founders.archives.gov/documents/Franklin/01-22-02-0222#BNFN
-01-22-02-0222-fn-0006-ptr. The committee's purpose, when it was formed on November 29, 1775, was to communicate with "our friends . . . in other parts of the world." Committee members were Benjamin Franklin, Benjamin Harrison, John Dickinson, Robert
Morris, and John Jay, although the instructions were likely written by Franklin. Also
see *JCC*, 3:92 for the committee's creation, and "Secret Committee of Correspondence,"
U.S. Department of State, https://2001-2009.state.gov/r/pa/ho/time/ar/91718.htm.

33. *JCC*, 4:215–20.

34. *JCC*, 4:215–16; Gene Procknow, "Franklin's Failed Diplomatic Mission," *Journal of
the American Revolution*, January 27, 2015, https://allthingsliberty.com/2015/01/franklins
-failed-diplomatic-mission/#_edn5. Benjamin Franklin to Josiah Quincy, April 15, 1776,
FO, https://founders.archives.gov/documents/Franklin/01-22-02-0240.

35. David McCullough, *1776* (New York: Simon & Schuster Paperbacks, 2005),
24–25, 39.

36. McCullough, *1776*, 82–90; "Dragging Cannon from Fort Ticonderoga to Boston," Gilder Lehrman Institute of American History, https://www.gilderlehrman.org/history -resources/spotlight-primary-source/dragging-cannon-fort-ticonderoga-boston-1775#: ~:text=Knox%20and%20his%20men%20moved,largest%20guns%20on%20Dorchester %20Heights. This item includes a letter from Knox to Washington on December 17, 1775.

37. Abigail Adams to John Adams, March 16–18, 1775, MHS, https://www.masshist .org/digitaladams/archive/doc?id=L17760316aa; McCullough, *1776*, 93–94. Howe's quote appears in the Abigail Adams letter. She said she heard the quote attributed to him.

38. McCullough, *1776*, 104–5; "This Day in History: American Forces Occupy Dorchester Heights," History, https://www.history.com/this-day-in-history/american -forces-occupy-dorchester-heights; "Dorchester Heights," NPS, https://www.nps.gov/ bost/learn/historyculture/dohe.htm.

39. Timothy Newell, "A Journal Kept during the Time Boston Was Shut Up in 1775–6," MHS, 275–76, https://archive.org/details/s4collections01massuoft/page/n301 /mode/2up?view=theater.

40. Joseph Ward to John Adams, March 23, 1776, Adams, *AP*, 4:60.

41. *JCC*, 4:229–33; "In Congress March 23, 1776," MHS, https://www.masshist.org /database/viewer.php?item_id=961&pid=2; "Privateers in the American Revolution," NPS, https://www.nps.gov/articles/privateers-in-the-american-revolution.htm.

42. *JCC*, 4:247–48.

43. John Hancock to George Washington, April 2, 1776, Papers of John Adams, MHS, https://www.masshist.org/publications/adams-papers/index.php/view/ADMS-06-04-02 -0001-0005.

CHAPTER 7

1. Richard Smith's Diary, March 26, 1776, in Smith, *LDC*, 3:448; "Thoughts on Government, ante March 27–April 1776," in Adams, *AP*, 4:65; Lindley S. Butler, "Provincial Congresses," *NCpedia*, https://www.ncpedia.org/provincial-congresses#:~:text =In%20the%20process%2C%20these%20Provincial,constitution%20that%20established %20the%20state. The British fought a battle at Mill's Creek Bridge and attempted to take Cape Fear.

2. "Thoughts on Government," in Adams, *AP*, 4:65, 78–79; John Adams to Abigail Adams, March 19, 1776, FO, https://founders.archives.gov/documents/Adams/04-01 -02-0235.

3. "Thoughts on Government," in Adams, *AP*, 4:65–68; John Adams to James Warren, April 20, 1776, FO, https://founders.archives.gov/documents/Adams/06-04-02-0048.

4. David McCullough, *John Adams* (New York: Simon & Schuster Paperbacks, 2001), 103; John Adams to John Penn, ante March 27, 1776, "Thoughts on Government," in Adams, *AP*, 4:79.

5. "Thoughts on Government," in Adams, *AP*, 4:86–93; Joseph J. Ellis, *American Creation* (New York: Vintage, 2005), 46–48; McCullough, *John Adams*, 102–3; Joseph J. Ellis, *Revolutionary Summer: The Birth of American Independence* (New York: Vintage, 2012), 19–20.

6. "Thoughts on Government," Adams, *AP*, 4:85, 92–93. An image of the published cover is in Adams, *AP*, 85.

7. Adams, *AP*, 70; "The Halifax Resolves," *NCpedia*, https://www.ncpedia.org/history /usrevolution/halifax-resolves; John Penn to John Adams, April 17, 1776, FO, https:// founders.archives.gov/documents/Adams/06-04-02-0046. This was a slow process. North Carolina did not settle on a constitution until December 1776.

8. "Carter Braxton: An Address to the Convention of the Colony and Ancient Dominion of Virginia, on the Subject of Government in General," University of Chicago, https: //press-pubs.uchicago.edu/founders/documents/v1ch18s10.html and University of Wisconsin, https://wisc.pb.unizin.org/ps601/chapter/carter-braxton-an-address/.

9. Carter Braxton to Landon Carter, April 14, 1776, in Smith, *LDC*, 3:522.

10. "Act of Renunciation, 1776," Rhode Island State Archives, https://docs.sos .ri.gov/documents/civicsandeducation/teacherresources/Act-of-Renunciation.pdf; "Rhode Island Declares Independence," Triverton Historical Society, http://www .tivertonhistorical.org/tiverton-stories/rhode-island-declares-independence/; Merrill Jensen, *The Founding of a Nation: A History of the American Revolution 1763–1776* (Indianapolis, IN: Hackett, 2004), 679.

11. "Fifth Revolutionary Convention," Library of Virginia, https://edu.lva.virginia.gov /oc/stc/entries/fifth-virginia-revolutionary-convention-called-for-independence-may-15 -1776; Jensen, *The Founding of a Nation*, 680.

12. Richard Henry Lee to Samuel Purviance, Jr., May 6, 1776, in Smith, *LDC*, 3:632.

13. Pauline Maier, *American Scripture: Making the Declaration of Independence* (New York: Vintage, 1998), 47–50, 59–61. Maier recognized the importance of these local declarations and was the first historian to write about them in detail. The wording of the Massachusetts resolution of May 10, 1776, may be found at https://archives.lib.state .ma.us/bitstream/handle/2452/280938/ocm39986874-1926-SB-0389.pdf?sequence=1 &isAllowed=y. Local resolutions also were drawn up throughout Virginia and Maryland.

14. *JCC*, 4:330, 4:342; William Hogeland, *Declaration: The Nine Tumultuous Weeks When America Became Independent, May 1–July 4, 1776* (New York: Simon & Schuster Paperbacks, 2010), 46–48.

15. Jensen, *The Founding of a Nation*, 683–84; Hogeland, *Declaration*, 78–81, 88–89; "Forester Letter IV," *Pennsylvania Journal*, May 8, 1776, Thomas Paine National Historical Association, https://www.thomaspaine.org/works/essays/american-revolution/the -forester-s-letters.html.

16. *JCC*, 4:357–58.

17. *JCC*, 4:357–58; McCullough, *John Adams*, 108–9.

18. Carter Braxton to Landon Carter, May 17, 1776, in Smith, *LDC*, 4:19.

19. "Notes of Debates in the Continental Congress, May 13–15, 1776," FO, from the diary of John Adams, https://founders.archives.gov/documents/Adams/01-02-02-0006 -0007-0001.

20. "Notes of Debates in the Continental Congress, May 13–15, 1776," FO, https:// founders.archives.gov/documents/Adams/01-02-02-0006-0007-0001. There also is an effective recounting of the debate in Hogeland, *Declaration*, 95–100.

21. *JCC*, 4:347–58; Carter Braxton to Landon Carter, May 17, 1776, in Burnett, *LMCC*, 1:453–54; "Notes of Debates in the Continental Congress, May 13–15, 1776," FO, n4, https://founders.archives.gov/documents/Adams/01-02-02-0006-0007 -0001. For the Maryland instructions, see chapter 6.

22. John Adams to James Warren, May 15, 1776, in Adams, *AP*, 4:186.

23. John Adams to Abigail Adams, May 17, 1776, in Smith, *LDC*, 4:17–18.

24. Robert R. Livingston to John Jay, May 17, 1776, in Smith, *LDC*, 4:28–29; Carter Braxton to Landon Carter, May 17, 1776, in Burnett, *LMCC*, 1:453–54; James Duane to John Jay, May 18, 1776, in Smith, *LDC*, 4:34–35.

25. Caesar Rodney to Thomas Rodney, May 17, 1776, and Oliver Wolcott to Samuel Lyman, May 16, 1776, in Smith, *LDC*, 4:16–17, 4:30; Stephen Hopkins to Nicolas Cooke, May 15, 1776, in Smith, *LDC*, 3:681.

26. John Adams to James Warren, May 20, 1776, in Adams, *AP*, 4:195–96.

27. "List of Delegates to Congress," in Smith, *LDC*, 4:xxii (this section includes the dates served by each delegate); *JCC*, 4:352; Jon Meacham, *Thomas Jefferson: The Art of Power* (New York: Random House Trade Paperbacks, 2012), 94–95, 97–99; Thomas Jefferson to Thomas Nelson, May 16, 1776, in Smith, *LDC*, 4:12–13.

28. "Fifth Revolutionary Convention," Library of Virginia, https://edu.lva.virginia.gov /oc/stc/entries/fifth-virginia-revolutionary-convention-called-for-independence-may-15 -1776; Jensen, *The Founding of a Nation*, 681.

29. Preamble and Resolution of the Virginia Convention, May 15, 1776, Avalon Project, Yale Law School, https://avalon.law.yale.edu/18th_century/const02.asp; "James Madison," *Encyclopedia Virginia*, https://encyclopediavirginia.org/entries/madison-james -1751-1836/.

30. John Adams to Richard Lee, June 4, 1776, in Smith, *LDC*, 4:135–36n2. The recipient of the letter was Richard Lee, a delegate to the Virginia Convention—not to be confused with Richard Henry Lee, who was serving in Congress in Philadelphia.

31. Gene Procknow, "Franklin's Failed Diplomatic Mission," *Journal of the American Revolution*, January 27, 2015, https://allthingsliberty.com/2015/01/franklins-failed -diplomatic-mission/; Walter Isaacson, *Benjamin Franklin: An American Life* (New York: Simon & Schuster Paperbacks, 2003), 307.

32. Commissioners in Canada to John Hancock, May 6, 1776, in Smith, *LDC*, 3:628– 29; Benjamin Franklin to the Commissioners in Canada, May 27, 1776, in Smith, *LDC*, 4:85; Procknow, "Franklin's Failed Diplomatic Mission," https://allthingsliberty.com /2015/01/franklins-failed-diplomatic-mission/; Andrew Roberts, *The Last King of America: The Misunderstood Reign of George III* (New York: Viking, 2021), 291; Maier, *American Scripture*, 40. The final American defeat in Canada came on June 8 at Trois-Rivières.

33. John Hancock to the Massachusetts Assembly, May 16, 1776, in Smith, *LDC*, 4:7; Maier, *American Scripture*, 39.

34. *JCC*, 4:369–70; Caesar Rodney to Thomas Rodney, May 22, 1776, in Smith, *LDC*, 4:61–62. The soldier's adventure it also recounted in Josiah Bartlett to John Langdon, May 21, 1776, in Smith, *LDC*, 4:55 and 4:55n2. The committee included John Adams, Jefferson, and Lee.

35. Jack N. Rakove, *The Beginnings of National Politics: An Interpretive History of the Continental Congress* (Baltimore, MD: Johns Hopkins University Press, 1979), 98; Roberts, *The Last King of America*, 291–92.

36. John Hancock to George Washington, May 16, 1776, in Smith, *LDC*, 4:8–9; "Expense Account of [Washington's] Journey to and from Philadelphia, May 21–June 12, 1776," FO, https://founders.archives.gov/documents/Washington/03-04-02-0298 (see notes).

37. *JCC*, 4:383–84, 4:387–88, 4:391, 4:398–402; "Expense Account of [Washington's] Journey to and from Philadelphia, May 21–June 12, 1776," FO, https://founders.archives.gov/documents/Washington/03-04-02-0298 (see notes).

38. *JCC*, 4:402. The other committee members were George Wythe and Edward Rutledge.

39. George Washington to John Augustine Washington, May 31–June 4, 1776, FO, https://founders.archives.gov/documents/Washington/03-04-02-0333 (and n2 for Martha Washington's smallpox inoculation).

40. Jensen, *The Founding of a Nation*, 685–86; Hogeland, *Declaration*, 126–30, 143–45; also see "The Pennsylvania Assembly: Instructions to Its Delegates to Congress, June 14, 1776, FO, https://founders.archives.gov/documents/Franklin/01-22-02-0280.

41. John Hancock to George Washington, June 3, 1776, and John Hancock to Certain Colonies, June 4, 1776, in Smith, *LDC*, 4:132, 4:136–37. Although Hancock and Washington were both in Philadelphia on June 3, Hancock wrote a letter because he was bed-ridden with gout. He told Washington that he had "fully accomplished that View of Congress in requesting your Attendance in this City." The colonies who received the June 4 letter were New Hampshire, Massachusetts, New York, New Jersey, Delaware and Maryland (Smith, *LDC*, 4:137, notes). He was concerned about the impact on northern colonies following the defeat in Canada.

CHAPTER 8

1. John Adams to Patrick Henry, June 3, 1776, in Smith, *LDC*, 4:122.

2. *JCC*, 4:409–16 and *JCC*, 5:417–24; Robert Morris to Silas Deane, June 5, 1776, in Smith, *LDC*, 4:146–47; Pauline Maier, *American Scripture: Making the Declaration of Independence* (New York: Vintage, 1998), 42; Merrill Jensen, *The Founding of a Nation: A History of the American Revolution 1763–1776* (Indianapolis, IN: Hackett, 2004), 682.

3. *JCC*, 5:420–24.

4. Samuel Adams to James Warren, June 6, 1776, in Smith, *LDC*, 4:151.

5. *JCC*, 5:424–25.

6. William Hogeland, *Declaration: The Nine Tumultuous Weeks When America Became Independent, May 1–July 4, 1776* (New York: Simon & Schuster Paperbacks, 2010), 131; David McCullough, *John Adams* (New York: Simon & Schuster Paperbacks, 2001), 118. Lee lost four fingers of his left hand when his gun barrel exploded.

7. *JCC*, 5:425; "Lee Resolution (1776)," NA, https://www.archives.gov/milestone-documents/lee-resolution#atranscript.

8. "Great Britain: Parliament—the Declaratory Act, March 18, 1766," Avalon Project, Yale Law School, https://avalon.law.yale.edu/18th_century/declaratory_act_1766.asp.

9. *JCC*, 5:426; "Thomas Jefferson's Notes of Proceedings in the Continental Congress, June 7–August 1, 1776," in Jefferson, *PTJ*, 1:309. Jefferson's notes also are found at Thomas Jefferson, "Notes of Proceedings in the Continental Congress, June 7–August 1, 1776," FO, https://founders.archives.gov/documents/Jefferson/01-01-02-0160.

10. "Thomas Jefferson's Notes of Proceedings," in Jefferson, *PTJ*, 1:299, 1:308–9. The editors of his papers believed it is "highly probable [that] Jefferson wrote the 'Notes' in the late summer or early autumn of 1776," when his memory would have been relatively fresh. He may have compiled them while referencing shorter notes jotted during the congressional debates in June and July. Complicating matters for historians, however, both Jefferson and John Adams also wrote about this period in the 1820s, almost fifty years after the fact, when memories certainly *had* faded.

11. Jefferson, *PTJ*, 1:309. There are also detailed descriptions of the June 8–10 debates, based on the notes from Jefferson and John Dickinson, in Jensen, *The Founding of a Nation*, 688–90, and Maier, *American Scripture*, 42–43. It should be noted that James Duane, who had been a prominent moderate voice to this point, and is portrayed as playing a major role in the HBO series *John Adams*, returned to New York on May 31 and did not attend Congress during June or July.

12. "John Dickinson's Notes for a Speech in Congress," in Smith, *LDC*, 4:165–67.

13. "Thomas Jefferson's Notes of Proceedings," in Jefferson, *PTJ*, 1:309–11.

14. "John Dickinson's Notes for a Speech in Congress," in Smith, *LDC*, 4:167.

15. "Thomas Jefferson's Notes of Proceedings," in Jefferson, *PTJ*, 1:311–13.

16. Edward Rutledge to John Jay, June 8, 1776, in Smith, *LDC*, 4:174–175; John Dickinson to Thomas Willing, June 8, 1776, in Smith, *LDC*, 4:169; New York Delegates to the New York Convention, June 8, 1776, in Smith, *LDC*, 4:171.

17. John Adams to William Cushing, June 9, 1776, in Smith, *LDC*, 4:177–79. The other letters written by Adams that day were to James Warren and Samuel Cooper. Keep in mind that none of the recipients would have been aware that Lee's motion on independence had been presented on June 7.

18. *JCC*, 5:427–28; Jensen, *The Founding of a Nation*, 689–90; "Thomas Jefferson's Notes of Proceedings," in Jefferson, *PTJ*, 1:312. Jefferson didn't specifically credit Adams with this quote, but Adams was the most combative of the radical speakers, and the words fit perfectly with his thinking at the time. Adams and Dickinson were the lead orators for their respective sides.

19. Edward Rutledge to John Jay, June 8, 1776, in Smith, *LDC*, 4:174–75; *JCC*, 5:428–29. The vote is recorded in "Maryland Delegates to the Maryland Committee of Safety, June 11, 1776," in Burnett, *LMCC*, 1:485–86. Also see Jensen, *The Founding of a Nation*, 690–91.

20. John Hancock to George Washington, June 10, 1776, in Smith, *LDC*, 4:183.

21. Elbridge Gerry to James Warren, June 11, 1776, in Smith, *LDC*, 4:187.

22. *JCC*, 5:429–31; Robert G. Parkinson, *The Common Cause: Creating Race and Nation in the American Revolution* (Chapel Hill: University of North Carolina Press, 2016), 242.

23. *JCC*, 5:431; John Adams to Timothy Pickering, August 6, 1822, FO, https://founders.archives.gov/documents/Adams/99-02-02-7674. Writing years later, Adams

said, "I think [Jefferson] had one more vote than any other, and that placed him at the head of the Committee. I had the next highest number, and that placed me second."

24. Maier, *American Scripture*, 48; "John Adams Autobiography, May 25–June 12, 1776," MHS, https://www.masshist.org/digitaladams/archive/doc?id=A1_37&bc=%2Fdigitaladams%2Farchive%2Fbrowse%2Fautobio1.php; Thomas Jefferson to Thomas Nelson, May 16, 1776, FO, https://founders.archives.gov/documents/Jefferson/01-01-02-0153#:~:text=16.,1776.&text=I%20arrived%20here%20last%20Tuesday,the%20naval%20engagement%20in%20Delaware; Richard H. Lee (grandson), *Memoir of the Life of Richard Henry Lee, and His Correspondence with the Most Distinguished Men in America and Europe* (n.p.: William Brown, 1825; repr., London: Forgotten Books, 2018), 1:173.

25. George Mason to Richard Henry Lee, May 18, 1776, Constitutional Sources Project (ConSource), https://www.consource.org/document/george-mason-to-richard-henry-lee-1776-5-18/; Richard Henry Lee to Landon Carter, June 2, 1776, in Smith, *LDC*, 4:117–18.

26. *JCC*, 5:431, 5:433.

27. *JCC*, 5:434–35, 5:438.

28. *JCC*, 5:439.

29. Peter Force, ed., *American Archives: A Documentary History of the English Colonies in North America*, 4th ser. (printed by Act of Congress, 1833), 6:867–68, 6:902, https://ia600202.us.archive.org/26/items/americanarchivea46forc/americanarchivea46forc.pdf; Maier, *American Scripture*, 63. Maier offers an overall account of the change in colonial instructions in Maier, *American Scripture*, 63–67.

30. Force, *American Archives*, 4th ser., 6:1029–30, https://ia600202.us.archive.org/26/items/americanarchivea46forc/americanarchivea46forc.pdf; Jensen, *The Founding of a Nation*, 692; "Delaware in the American Revolution," https://www.americanrevolutioninstitute.org/wp-content/uploads/2018/09/Delaware-in-the-American-Revolution-2002.pdf.

31. Maier, *American Scripture*, 64; Force, *American Archives*, 4th ser., 6:1627–28, https://ia600202.us.archive.org/26/items/americanarchivea46forc/americanarchivea46forc.pdf; Jonathan Dickinson Sergeant to John Adams, June 15, 1776, in Smith, *LDC*, 4:224.

32. "The Pennsylvania Assembly: Instructions to Its Delegates in Congress, June 14, 1776," FO, https://founders.archives.gov/documents/Franklin/01-22-02-0280; Hogeland, *Declaration*, 152–53; John Adams to William Tudor, June 24, 1776, in Smith, *LDC*, 4:306; Jensen, *The Founding of a Nation*, 686–87.

33. Carl G. Karsch, "Pennsylvania: From Colony to State," Carpenters' Hall, https://www.carpentershall.org/pennsylvania-from-colony-to-state; Force, *American Archives*, 4th ser., 6:963, https://ia600202.us.archive.org/26/items/americanarchivea46forc/americanarchivea46forc.pdf; Maier, *American Scripture*, 64–66.

34. John Adams to Benjamin Kent, June 22, 1776, in Smith, *LDC*, 4:290.

35. Maier, *American Scripture*, 97.

36. Thomas Jefferson to Benjamin Franklin, June 21, 1776, in Smith, *LDC*, 4:286; Benjamin Franklin to George Washington, June 21, 1776, in Smith, *LDC*, 4:280–81; Benjamin Franklin to Benjamin Rush, June 26, 1776, in Smith, *LDC*, 4:325.

37. Patrick Spero, interview by Liz Covart, *Ben Franklin's World* (podcast), episode 141, July 4, 2017, https://benfranklinsworld.com/episode-141-declaration-draft/.

38. Many historians credit Franklin for "self-evident," but there is no conclusive evidence from any of the participants, or in the congressional records, to support it. This will be discussed in greater detail in chapter 9.

39. "Thomas Jefferson's Notes of Proceedings," in Jefferson, *PTJ*, 1:313; Thomas Jefferson to James Madison, August 30, 1823, FO, https://founders.archives.gov/documents/Jefferson/98-01-02-3728.

40. Adams, *DJA*, 3:336.

41. Adams, *DJA*, 2:391–92; Maier, *American Scripture*, 97–101. I draw on much of Maier's deep and detailed research for this period.

42. Joseph J. Ellis, *Revolutionary Summer: The Birth of American Independence* (New York: Vintage, 2012), 71.

Chapter 9

1. Much of this is taken from "Thomas Jefferson and Robert Hemings in Philadelphia," NPS, https://www.nps.gov/articles/independence-jeffersonphiladelphia.htm, and Doris Devine Fanelli, "Furnishings Plan for the Graff House, Philadelphia, PA," NPS, https://irma.nps.gov/DataStore/DownloadFile/603989. Brief descriptive accounts are also found in Jon Meacham, *Thomas Jefferson: The Art of Power* (New York: Random House Trade Paperbacks, 2012), 103, and David McCullough, *John Adams* (New York: Simon & Schuster Paperbacks, 2001), 120. The house was owned at the time by Jacob Graff, a tailor and bricklayer, and Jefferson had two rooms on the second floor, a parlor and a bed chamber. His enslaved servant, Bob Hemings, was the older brother of Sally Hemings, another enslaved person from Monticello with whom Jefferson fathered several children. During his time at the Graff house, Bob likely slept in the "garret," or attic.

2. Thomas Jefferson to John Randolph, August 25, 1775, FO, https://founders.archives.gov/documents/Jefferson/01-01-02-0121#:~:text=They%20have%20taken%20it%20into,as%20it%20exists%20in%20truth.

3. Adams, *DJA*, 3:336.

4. Thomas Jefferson to James Madison, August 30, 1823, FO, https://founders.archives.gov/documents/Jefferson/98-01-02-3728.

5. *JCC*, 5:446–58; Julian P. Boyd, *The Declaration of Independence: The Evolution of the Text*, rev. ed., ed. Gerard W. Gawalt (Washington, DC: LOC; Charlottesville, VA: Thomas Jefferson Memorial Foundation, 1999), 26–28; Pauline Maier, *American Scripture: Making the Declaration of Independence* (New York: Vintage, 1998), 101–3;

6. Jefferson, *PTJ*, 1:329–65 (for all three of Jefferson's drafts); McCullough, *John Adams*, 121. The Virginia Convention eventually adopted its own constitution, but Jefferson's drafts are valuable because they lay out his thoughts on government during this period. It is clear that he was impacted by Adams's earlier work.

7. Thomas Jefferson to Henry Lee, May 8, 1825, FO, https://founders.archives.gov/documents/Jefferson/98-01-02-5212.

8. *JCC*, 5:491–92 (which also includes the eventual edits). An image of the handwritten "John Adams copy," without those edits, may be found in Boyd, *The Declaration of Independence*, 60.

9. "Jefferson's 'Original Rough Draught' of the Declaration of Independence," FO, https://founders.archives.gov/documents/Jefferson/01-01-02-0176-0004.

10. John Locke, *Second Treatise on Government*, Project Gutenberg e-book, chap. 2, sec. 6, https://www.gutenberg.org/files/7370/7370-h/7370-h.htm#CHAPTER_II.

11. McCullough, *John Adams*, 121; "A Proclamation by the General Court, January 18, 1776," FO, https://founders.archives.gov/documents/Adams/06-03-02-0195-0005.

12. *Pennsylvania Gazette*, June 12, 1776, image of the front page found at https://images.wydaily.com/wp-content/uploads/2014/07/Pennsylvania-Gazette-June-12-1776.jpg.

13. *Pennsylvania Gazette*, June 12, 1776.

14. Maier, *American Scripture*, 104.

15. Peter Onuf, interview by Liz Covart, *Ben Franklin's World* (podcast), episode 141, July 4, 2017, https://benfranklinsworld.com/episode-141-declaration-draft/. Onuf is the Thomas Jefferson Foundation Professor Emeritus in the Corcoran Department of History at the University of Virginia.

16. "Jefferson's Rough Draft of the Declaration of Independence," image of the handwritten copy, in Boyd, *The Declaration of Independence*, 67–71. Changes attributed to Franklin and Adams are noted in the margins.

17. Walter Isaacson, *Benjamin Franklin: An American Life* (New York: Simon & Schuster Paperbacks, 2003), 312; "Jefferson's Rough Draft of the Declaration of Independence," image of the handwritten copy, in Boyd, *The Declaration of Independence*, 67–71.

18. It is possible to compare the early Adams copy with the draft Jefferson presented to Congress in Boyd, *The Declaration of Independence*, 60–63, 67–71. This also is addressed by Carl Lotus Becker in *The Declaration of Independence: A Study in the History of Political Ideas* (New York: Harcourt, Brace, 1922; repr., 2017), 80–81. Becker believed that the draft was submitted to Franklin twice.

19. "Jefferson's 'Original Rough Draught' of the Declaration of Independence," FO, https://founders.archives.gov/documents/Jefferson/01-01-02-0176-0004.

20. Pauline Maier, "Who Really Wrote the Declaration," in *Declaring Independence: The Origin and Influence of America's Founding Document*, ed. Christian Y. Dupont and Peter S. Onuf (Charlottesville: University of Virginia Library, 2008), 2. Maier also addresses this topic in *American Scripture*, 126. Chapter 3 (part 2, 105–23) of that book features a very detailed look at the charges against the king.

21. Robert G. Parkinson, "Twenty-Eight Reasons for Independence," in *Declaring Independence: The Origin and Influence of America's Founding Document*, ed. Christian Y. Dupont and Peter S. Onuf (Charlottesville: University of Virginia Library, 2008), 11.

22. Parkinson, "Twenty-Eight Reasons for Independence," 12; Maier, *American Scripture*, 107.

23. Comparisons of "Jefferson's 'Original Rough Draught' of the Declaration of Independence," FO, https://founders.archives.gov/documents/Jefferson/01-01-02-0176

-0004 and "Declaration of Independence: A Transcription," July 4, 1776, NA, https://www.archives.gov/founding-docs/declaration-transcript.

24. "Jefferson's 'Original Rough Draught' of the Declaration of Independence," FO, https://founders.archives.gov/documents/Jefferson/01-01-02-0176-0004; Jefferson, *PTJ*, 1:338; Parkinson, "Twenty-Eight Reasons for Independence," 12, 14.

25. "Jefferson's 'Original Rough Draught' of the Declaration of Independence," FO, https://founders.archives.gov/documents/Jefferson/01-01-02-0176-0004.

26. "Jefferson's 'Original Rough Draught' of the Declaration of Independence," FO, https://founders.archives.gov/documents/Jefferson/01-01-02-0176-0004; "Slavery FAQs—Property," Thomas Jefferson, Monticello, https://www.monticello.org/slavery/slavery-faqs/property/#:~:text=How%20many%20people%20did%20Thomas,people%20were%20enslaved%20at%20Monticello.

27. "Jefferson's 'Original Rough Draught' of the Declaration of Independence," FO, https://founders.archives.gov/documents/Jefferson/01-01-02-0176-0004.

28. "Jefferson's 'Original Rough Draught' of the Declaration of Independence," FO, https://founders.archives.gov/documents/Jefferson/01-01-02-0176-0004; Maier, *American Scripture*, 142.

29. Thomas Jefferson to Benjamin Franklin, June 21, 1776, FO, https://founders.archives.gov/documents/Franklin/01-22-02-0284. The note was undated, other than to say it was a "Friday morn," but scholars have concluded that it was written on Friday, June 21. It is highly unlikely that Jefferson could have written the document and already shown it to the committee for review by the morning of Friday, June 14, and the final edited draft was presented to Congress on Friday, June 28.

30. Benjamin Franklin to George Washington, June 21, 1776, in Smith, *LDC*, 4:280–81; Benjamin Franklin to Benjamin Rush, June 26, 1776, in Smith, *LDC*, 4:325.

31. Jefferson, *PTJ*, 1:414, 1:420–32; Boyd, *The Declaration of Independence*, 35, 55; Gerard W. Gawalt, "Jefferson and the Declaration: Updated Work Studies Evolution of the Historic Text," LOC, July 1999, https://www.loc.gov/loc/lcib/9907/jeffdec.html.

32. Thomas Jefferson to James Madison, August 30, 1823, FO, https://founders.archives.gov/documents/Jefferson/98-01-02-3728.

33. This is from a comparison of the Adams draft and Jefferson's "Original Rough Draught," as well as versions included side-by-side in the June 28, 1776, entry of the *Journals of the Continental Congress* (*JCC*, 5:491–92). Confusion still exists over when the change to "Creator" was made, but Jefferson copied versions of the draft that were submitted Congress and sent them to various colleagues after July 4. One of these was sent to Richard Henry Lee and includes the phrase "endowed by their Creator." It is reproduced in Boyd, *The Declaration of Independence*, 73–74. Jefferson said it was a copy of the draft as "originally framed." It was sent to Lee to on July 8, 1776.

34. Boyd, *The Declaration of Independence*, 33–34.

35. John Adams to Samuel Chase, June 24, 1776, in Smith, *LDC*, 4:303–4; Merrill Jensen, *The Founding of a Nation: A History of the American Revolution 1763–1776* (Indianapolis, IN: Hackett, 2004), 695.

36. Peter Force, ed., *American Archives: A Documentary History of the English Colonies in North America*, 4th ser. (printed by Act of Congress, 1833), 6:1485, https://archive.org/details/americanarchivea46forc/page/801/mode/2up.

37. John Adams to Samuel Chase, June 24, 1776, in Smith, *LDC*, 4:304.

38. Force, *American Archives*, 4th ser., 6:1491, https://archive.org/details/americanarchivea46forc/page/805/mode/2up; Samuel Chase to John Adams, June 28, 1776, FO, https://founders.archives.gov/documents/Adams/06-04-02-0140.

39. *JCC*, 5:491; Thomas Jefferson, *The Autobiography of Thomas Jefferson, 1743–1790* (1914; repr., Philadelphia: University of Pennsylvania Press, 2005), 28.

40. John Adams to Timothy Pickering, August 6, 1822, FO, https://founders.archives.gov/documents/Adams/99-02-02-7674; John Adams diary [In Congress, May–July 1776], FO, https://founders.archives.gov/documents/Adams/01-03-02-0016-0029.

41. Edward Rutledge to John Jay, June 29, 1776, in Smith, *LDC*, 4:337–38.

CHAPTER 10

1. George Washington to John Hancock, June 28, 1776, FO, https://founders.archives.gov/documents/Washington/03-05-02-0089 (see note 13 for the report that Washington's rolls included 10,368 men, but only 7,389 were "present and fit for duty"); George Washington to William Livingston, June 28, 1776, FO, https://founders.archives.gov/?q=%20Author%3A%22Washington%2C%20George%22&s=1111311111&r=9832; Joseph J. Ellis, *Revolutionary Summer: The Birth of American Independence* (New York: Vintage, 2012), 78–79, 93; David McCullough, *1776* (New York: Simon & Schuster Paperbacks, 2005), 133–35, 147; Ron Chernow, *Washington: A Life* (New York: Penguin, 2010), 235–36.

2. George Washington to John Hancock, June 29, 1776, FO, https://founders.archives.gov/?q=%20Author%3A%22Washington%2C%20George%22&s=1111311111&r=9837.

3. Joseph Hewes to James Iredell, June 28, 1776, and John Penn to Samuel Johnston, June 28, 1776, in Smith, *LDC*, 4:331–33. For an examination of the change in Joseph Hewes's thinking in late spring and early summer 1776, see Allan J. McCurry, "Joseph Hewes and Independence: A Suggestion," *North Carolina Historical Review* 40, no. 4 (October 1963), https://www.jstor.org/stable/23517596?read-now=1&seq=8#page_scan_tab_contents.

4. John Adams to Archibald Bulloch, July 1, 1776, and Josiah Bartlett to John Langdon, July 1, 1776, in Smith, *LDC*, 4:345–46, 350–51.

5. *JCC*, 5:503–4.

6. John Adams's Diary, August 29–September 5, 1774, in Smith, *LDC*, 1:5; Autobiography of John Adams, July 1, 1776, FO, https://founders.archives.gov/documents/Adams/01-03-02-0016-0142.

7. John Dickinson's Notes for a Speech in Congress, July 1, 1776, in Smith, *LDC*, 4:351–56.

8. John Adams to Samuel Chase, July 1, 1776, in Smith, *LDC*, 4:347; Autobiography of John Adams, July 1, 1776, FO, https://founders.archives.gov/documents/Adams/01-03-02-0016-0142.

9. Autobiography of John Adams, July 1, 1776, FO, https://founders.archives.gov/
documents/Adams/01-03-02-0016-0142; John Adams to William Cushing, June 9,
1776, in Smith, *LDC*, 4:178.

10. "Editorial Note: The Declaration of Independence," FO, https://founders.archives
.gov/documents/Jefferson/01-01-02-0176-0001; David McCullough, *John Adams* (New
York: Simon & Schuster Paperbacks, 2001), 128; Pauline Maier, *American Scripture: Making the Declaration of Independence* (New York: Vintage, 1998), 44–45.

11. "Thomas Jefferson's Notes of Proceedings in the Continental Congress," in Jefferson, *PTJ*, 1:314.

12. Thomas McKean to Alexander James Dallas, September 26, 1796, in Burnett,
LMCC, 1:533–34; Merrill Jensen, *The Founding of a Nation: A History of the American
Revolution 1763–1776* (Indianapolis, IN: Hackett, 2004), 700.

13. Edward Rutledge to John Jay, June 8, 1776, in Smith, *LDC*, 4:174–75.

14. Thomas McKean to Alexander James Dallas, September 26, 1796, in Burnett,
LMCC, 1:533–34; Jensen, *The Founding of a Nation*, 700.

15. "Thomas Jefferson's Notes of Proceedings," in Jefferson, *PTJ*, 1:314.

16. *JCC*, 5:506–7.

17. Thomas McKean to Alexander James Dallas, September 26, 1796, in Burnett,
LMCC, 1:533–34.

18. Thomas McKean to Caesar A. Rodney (nephew), September 22, 1813, in Burnett,
LMCC, 1:534; John Adams's Diary, in Smith, *LDC*, 1:8–9.

19. "Thomas Jefferson's Notes of Proceedings," in Jefferson, *PTJ*, 1:314; Thomas McKean to Alexander James Dallas, September 26, 1796, in Burnett, *LMCC*, 1:533–34. Delaware's vote for independence was 2–1. Pennsylvania's was 3–2 (with Franklin, Morton, and Wilson in support). South Carolina's exact tally was never recorded.

20. McCullough, *John Adams*, 129.

21. *JCC*, 5:507.

22. *Pennsylvania Evening Post* (vol. 2, no. 226), July 2, 1776, Seth Kellar Historic
Documents and Legacy Collections, https://www.sethkaller.com/item/1000-The-First
-Published-Announcement-of-Independence-(SOLD); McCullough, *John Adams*, 130;
Elbridge Gerry to James Warren, July 2, 1776, in Burnett, *LMCC*, 1:526; *Pennsylvania
Gazette*, July 3, 1776, 2 cited in Charles Warren, "Fourth of July Myths," *William & Mary
Quarterly* 2, no. 3 (July 1945): 240n5; Maier, *American Scripture*, 161, 274n14.

23. John Adams to Abigail Adams, July 3, 1776 (first letter), in Smith, *LDC*, 4:374.

24. John Adams to Abigail Adams, July 3, 1776 (second letter), in Smith, *LDC*, 4:376.

25. George Washington to John Hancock, July 3, 1776, FO, https://founders.archives
.gov/documents/Washington/03-05-02-0127,

26. *JCC*, 5:508–9.

27. "General Orders, July 2, 1776," FO, https://founders.archives.gov/documents/
Washington/03-05-02-0117#:~:text=The%20fate%20of%20unborn%20Millions,Honor
%2C%20all%20call%20upon%20us.

28. Chernow, *Washington: A Life*, 235–36; George Washington to John Hancock, July 3,
1776, FO, https://founders.archives.gov/documents/Washington/03-05-02-0127.

29. *JCC*, 5:508–9.

30. Thomas Jefferson to James Madison, August 30, 1823, FO, https://founders
.archives.gov/documents/Jefferson/98-01-02-3728; Richard Henry Lee to Thomas Jefferson, July 21, 1776, FO, https://founders.archives.gov/documents/Jefferson/01-01-02
-0190#:~:text=I%20thank%20you%20much%20for,should%20be%20so%20unhappily
%20applied; Joseph J. Ellis, *American Creation* (New York: Vintage, 2005), 55; Thomas
Jefferson to Thomas Nelson, May 16, 1776, FO, https://founders.archives.gov/documents
/Jefferson/01-01-02-0153.

31. In addition to comparing copies of Jefferson's "Original Rough Draught" with the
final version, readers can find very detailed studies of the editing process in Maier, *Ameri-
can Scripture*, chap. 3 (especially 143–53 for the congressional changes) and Julian P. Boyd,
The Declaration of Independence: The Evolution of the Text, rev. ed., ed. Gerard W. Gawalt
(Washington, DC: LOC; Charlottesville, VA: Thomas Jefferson Memorial Foundation,
1999), 32–36. Other good resources on the writing and editing of the document are Carl
Lotus Becker, *The Declaration of Independence: A Study in the History of Political Ideas* (New
York: Harcourt, Brace, 1922; repr., 2017); and John Hampden Hazelton, *The Declaration
of Independence: Its History* (Cambridge, MA: University Press, 1906).

32. Maier, *American Scripture*, 145.

33. Comparisons of "Jefferson's 'Original Rough Draught' of the Declaration of
Independence," FO, https://founders.archives.gov/documents/Jefferson/01-01-02-0176
-0004 with "Declaration of Independence: A Transcription," July 4, 1776, NA, https://
www.archives.gov/founding-docs/declaration-transcript.

34. "Declaration of Independence: A Transcription," July 4, 1776, NA, https://www
.archives.gov/founding-docs/declaration-transcript.

35. Thomas Jefferson, *The Autobiography of Thomas Jefferson, 1743–1790* (1914; repr.,
Philadelphia: University of Pennsylvania Press, 2005), 33.

36. John Adams to Timothy Pickering, August 6, 1822, FO, https://founders.archives
.gov/documents/Adams/99-02-02-7674. Adams once called slavery "a foul contagion of
the human character."

37. Comparisons of "Jefferson's 'Original Rough Draught' of the Declaration of
Independence," FO, https://founders.archives.gov/documents/Jefferson/01-01-02-0176
-0004 with "Declaration of Independence: A Transcription," July 4, 1776, NA, https:
//www.archives.gov/founding-docs/declaration-transcript; Maier, *American Scripture*,
147–48.

38. Jefferson, *The Autobiography of Thomas Jefferson*, 33.

39. "Thomas Jefferson's Anecdotes of Benjamin Franklin," December 4, 1818, FO,
https://founders.archives.gov/documents/Jefferson/03-13-02-0407; Maier, *American
Scripture*, 149–50.

40. Ellis, *American Creation*, 55.

41. *JCC*, 5:510.

42. Abraham Clark to Elias Dayton and Caesar Rodney to Thomas Rodney, July 4,
1776, in Smith, *LDC*, 4:378, 4:388. Among those writing letters about the debates on
July 1 and 2 about the votes and independence were John Adams (2), Josiah Bartlett (2),
Thomas Jefferson, Francis Lightfoot Lee, Elbridge Gerry, and the New York delegation
(to its convention), in Smith, *LDC*, 4:342–72. Adams also wrote two letters on July 3.

43. Jefferson, *PTJ*, 1:315; *JCC*, 5:516–18; Emily Sneff, "December Highlight: Dunlap," Declaration Resources Project, Harvard University, December 4, 2017, https://declaration.fas.harvard.edu/blog/december-dunlap. Additional detail is found in notes to a letter in Smith, *LDC*, 4:379–82, titled "Committee of Congress to the Lancaster Associators." These notes estimate that a vote on the Declaration was "probably taken sometime before 11:00 A.M." They added that "it seems clear that when the delegates convened [on July 4] at approximately 9:00 A.M., very little work remained to be done on the Declaration, that it was completed in less than two hours without much additional controversy, and that Congress then proceeded to several other pressing matters, which consumed the greater part of their time this memorable day."

Chapter 11

1. Emily Sneff, "December Highlight: Dunlap," Declaration Resources Project, Harvard University, December 4, 2017, https://declaration.fas.harvard.edu/blog/december-dunlap; "John Dunlap," *Dictionary of American Biography*, ed. Dumas Malone (Oxford: Oxford University Press, 1935), 5:514–15, https://archive.org/details/in.ernet.dli.2015.163970/page/n523/mode/2up.

2. "Dunlap Broadside," LOC, https://www.loc.gov/resource/gdcwdl.wdl_02716/; Megan Huang, "Dunlap's Declaration of Independence," NA, https://prologue.blogs.archives.gov/2018/07/03/dunlaps-declaration-of-independence/; David McCullough, *John Adams* (New York: Simon & Schuster Paperbacks, 2001), 137; Wilfred J. Ritz, "From the Here of Jefferson's Handwritten Rough Draft of the Declaration of Independence to the There of the Printed Dunlap Broadside," *Pennsylvania Magazine of History and Biography* 116, no. 4 (October 1992): 499–512. The argument for Jefferson writing the updated copy for Dunlap is based on unusual markings that appeared in a very early version of Dunlap's work. These may have been markings that Jefferson himself had made to remind him of the need to pause when reading the Declaration out loud. Then again, Jefferson was very upset after his colleagues made their changes, and Congress was in session for much of the rest of the day.

3. "Dunlap Broadside," LOC, https://www.loc.gov/resource/gdcwdl.wdl_02716/.

4. "Declaration of Independence: A Transcription," July 4, 1776, NA, https://www.archives.gov/founding-docs/declaration-transcript; *JCC*, 5:516.

5. John Hancock to the New Jersey Convention, July 5, 1776, in Smith, *LDC*, 4:392. In the New Jersey letter, Hancock also advised the convention to relocate British prisoners to Pennsylvania.

6. Abraham Clark to William Livingston, July 5, 1776, and Elbridge Gerry to James Warren, July 5, 1776, in Smith, *LDC*, 4:391–92.

7. John Hancock to George Washington, July 6, 1776, in Smith, *LDC*, 4:397.

8. Jared Keller, "How the Declaration of Independence Went Viral," *Pacific Standard*, June 28, 2016, https://psmag.com/news/how-the-declaration-of-independence-went-viral; Daniel Crown, "The German-Language Newspaper That Got the Scoop on American Independence," *Atlas Obscura*, July 3, 2019, https://www.atlasobscura.com/articles/german-language-newspaper-declaration-independence-day-signing.

9. *Pennsylvania Evening Post*, July 6, 1776, found in the New York Public Library Digital Collections, https://digitalcollections.nypl.org/items/951d8421-1918-ef56-e040-e00a1806382f.

10. Jay Hinesley, Independence National Historic Park, interview by Liz Covart, *Ben Franklin's World*, (podcast), episode 245, July 2, 2019, https://benfranklinsworld.com/episode-245-celebrating-the-fourth/; Roland M. Baumann, "The Pennsylvania Revolution," US History, https://www.ushistory.org/pennsylvania/birth2.html; Carl G. Karsch, "Pennsylvania: From Colony to State," Carpenters' Hall, https://www.carpentershall.org/pennsylvania-from-colony-to-state.

11. *Dunlap's Maryland Gazette*, July 16, 1776, cited in Emily Sneff, "July Highlight: George Rejected and Liberty Protected," Declaration Resources Project, Harvard University, July 4, 2016, https://declaration.fas.harvard.edu/blog/july-proclamations; *Pennsylvania Gazette*, July 10, 1776; John Adams to Samuel Chase, July 9, 1776, in Smith, *LDC*, 4:414; John Hampden Hazelton, *The Declaration of Independence: Its History* (Cambridge, MA: University Press, 1906), 242; Hinesley, interview by Liz Covart, *Ben Franklin's World* (podcast), https://benfranklinsworld.com/episode-245-celebrating-the-fourth/.

12. Ritz, "From the Here of Jefferson's Handwritten Rough Draft of the Declaration of Independence to the There of the Printed Dunlap Broadside," https://journals.psu.edu/pmhb/article/view/44820/44541; Chris Coelho, "The First Reading of the Declaration of Independence, July 4, 1776," *Journal of the American Revolution*, July 1, 2021, https://allthingsliberty.com/2021/07/the-first-public-reading-of-the-declaration-of-independence-july-4-1776/; *Autobiography of Charles Biddle*, 86, LOC, https://www.loc.gov/resource/gdcmassbookdig.autobiographyofc00bidd/?sp=104&st=image&r=-0.299,0.22,1.706,0.825,0; Pauline Maier, *American Scripture: Making the Declaration of Independence* (New York: Vintage, 1998), 156, 273–74n5.

13. *Pennsylvania Evening Post*, July 11, 1776; *Dunlap and Claypoole's American Daily Advertiser*, July 15, 1776 (both reports of July 8 events), cited in Sneff, "July Highlight: George Rejected and Liberty Protected," https://declaration.fas.harvard.edu/blog/july-proclamations.

14. Thomas Jefferson to Richard Henry Lee, July 8, 1776, FO, https://founders.archives.gov/documents/Jefferson/01-01-02-0179; Richard Henry Lee to Thomas Jefferson, FO, July 21, 1776, https://founders.archives.gov/documents/Jefferson/01-01-02-0190#:~:text=I%20thank%20you%20much%20for,should%20be%20so%20unhappily%20applied; Thomas Jefferson to James Madison, August 30, 1823, FO, https://founders.archives.gov/documents/Jefferson/98-01-02-3728.

15. The Committee of Secret Correspondence to Silas Deane, July 8, 1776, FO, https://founders.archives.gov/documents/Franklin/01-22-02-0298; Maier, *American Scripture*, 130.

16. Maier, *American Scripture*, 130.

17. New York Delegates to the New York Provincial Congress, July 2, 1776, in Smith, *LDC*, 4:371–72n1.

18. Walter Stahr, *John Jay* (London and New York: Hambledon, 2005), 61–63; "Reading of the Declaration of Independence, White Plains, July 11, 1776," Westchester

County Historical Society, *LOC*, https://www.loc.gov/resource/rbpe.10901900/?st=text. The Declaration was read in public two days after the July 9 vote.

19. *JCC*, 5:560. The resolution written by Jay also called for the Declaration to be published and distributed, while authorizing New York's congressional delegates to "adopt all such measures as they may seem conducive to the happiness and welfare of the United States of America."

20. "Celebrating the 9th of July, New York's True Independence Day," *New York Times*, June 30, 1996, https://www.nytimes.com/1996/06/30/nyregion/celebrating-the-9th-of -july-new-york-s-true-independence-day.html.

21. John Aslop to the New York Provincial Congress, July 16, 1776, in Smith, *LDC*, 4:466–68n1.

22. General Orders, July 9, 1776, FO, https://founders.archives.gov/documents/ Washington/03-05-02-0176.

23. General Orders, July 9, 1776, FO, https://founders.archives.gov/documents/ Washington/03-05-02-0176; Hazelton, *The Declaration of Independence: Its History*, 252–53; *Dunlap and Claypoole's American Daily Advertiser*, July 15, 1776, 3, cited in Sneff, "July Highlight: George Rejected and Liberty Protected," https://declaration.fas.harvard .edu/blog/july-proclamations; Joseph J. Ellis, *Revolutionary Summer: The Birth of American Independence* (New York: Vintage, 2012), 86.

24. *JCC*, 5:425, 433.

25. John Adams to Abigail Adams, July 11, 1776, in Smith, *LDC*, 4:434–35n2. John Adams did not leave Congress until October 13, 1776. Edward Rutledge to John Jay, June 29, 1776, in Smith, *LDC*, 4:337–39.

26. "Josiah Bartlett's and John Dickinson's Draft Articles of Confederation, June– July 1776," in Smith, *LDC*, 4:233–55, and especially p. 251n1; Josiah Bartlett to John Langdon, June 17, 1776, and Bartlett to Nathaniel Folsom, July 1, 1776, in Smith, *LDC*, 4:255–57, 4:348–50; Edward Rutledge to John Jay, June 29, 1776, in Smith, *LDC*, 4:337– 38; "John Dickinson's Notes for a Speech in Congress," July 1, 1776, in Smith, *LDC*, 4:355; "Articles of Confederation," NA, https://www.archives.gov/milestone-documents /articles-of-confederation. Though Bartlett's manuscript is identified as "his" draft, it is believed to be a clean copy of one of Dickinson's drafts (Smith, *LDC*, 4:252). Dickinson also had at his disposal a plan of confederation that Benjamin Franklin had unsuccessfully proposed to Congress in 1775.

27. Josiah Bartlett to John Langdon, June 17, 1776, in Smith, *LDC*, 4:255–57; Edward Rutledge to John Jay, June 29, 1776, in Smith, *LDC*, 4:337–38; "John Dickinson's Notes for a Speech in Congress," July 1, 1776, in Smith, *LDC*, 4:355.

28. Jefferson, *PTJ*, 1:320, 323; "Articles of Confederation," NA, https://www.archives .gov/milestone-documents/articles-of-confederation. Issues of debate included the sectional split between northern and southern colonies over slavery, the extent of western boundaries, and the power of the central government.

29. *JCC*, 5:425; Adams, *DJA*, 2:231–32, 2:236; Adams, *DJA*, vol. 3, "June–August 1776," MHS, https://www.masshist.org/publications/adams-papers/index.php/view/ DJA03d299.

30. *JCC*, 5:433; Adams, *DJA*, vol. 4, "Editorial Note," MHS, https://www.masshist.org /publications/adams-papers/index.php/view/ADMS-06-04-02-0116-0001.

31. *JCC*, 5:575–89, 5:768, 5:813.

32. Ellis, *Revolutionary Summer*, 93–94, 101. Some estimates had the British/Hessian force at more than forty thousand.

33. Lord Howe to George Washington, July 13, 1776, FO, https://founders.archives .gov/documents/Washington/03-05-02-0212.

34. "The Howe Brothers," Museum of the American Revolution, Philadelphia, PA (in-person visit by author); Ellis, *Revolutionary Summer*, 95.

35. Lord Howe to George Washington, July 13, 1776, FO, https://founders.archives .gov/documents/Washington/03-05-02-0212; George Washington to John Hancock, July 14, 1776, FO, https://founders.archives.gov/documents/Washington/03-05-02-0218 #:~:text=My%20last%20of%20friday%20evening,upper%20end%20of%20the%20Island; Henry Knox to William Knox, July 15, 1776, Gilder Lehrman Institute of American History, https://www.gilderlehrman.org/collection/glc0243700378; David McCullough, *1776* (New York: Simon & Schuster Paperbacks, 2005), 144.

36. George Washington to John Hancock, July 14, 1776, FO, https: //founders.archives.gov/documents/Washington/03-05-02-0218#:~:text =My%20last%20of%20friday%20evening,upper%20end%20of%20the%20Island; Ellis, *Revolutionary Summer*, 96.

37. "Memorandum of an Interview with Lieutenant Colonel James Patterson, July 20, 1776," FO, https://founders.archives.gov/documents/Washington/03-05-02-0295. The memo was written by Washington's aide, Joseph Reed.

38. McCullough, *1776*, 146. The quote was from Henry Knox in a July 22 letter to his wife.

39. Benjamin Franklin to Lord Howe, July 20, 1776, FO, https://founders.archives.gov /documents/Franklin/01-22-02-0307#BNFN-01-22-02-0307-fn-0006.

40. Benjamin Franklin to Lord Howe, July 20, 1776, FO, https://founders.archives.gov /documents/Franklin/01-22-02-0307#BNFN-01-22-02-0307-fn-0006.

41. Danielle Allen, *Our Declaration: A Reading of the Declaration of Independence in Defense of Equality* (New York: Liveright, 2014), 75–77; Chris Coelho, "Timothy Matlack: Scribe of the Declaration of Independence," *Journal of the American Revolution*, August 24, 2021, https://allthingsliberty.com/2021/08/timothy-matlack-scribe-of-the -declaration-of-independence/; Mary Lynn Ritzenthaler and Catherine Nicholas, "The Declaration of Independence and the Hand of Time," *Prologue Magazine* 48, no. 3 (Fall 2016), https://www.archives.gov/publications/prologue/2016/fall/declaration. Ritzenthaler was chief of conservation and Nicholson deputy chief of conservation at the National Archives (NA).

42. Comparisons of the two documents are available in many online and published images.

43. John Adams to Samuel Chase, July 9, 1776, in Smith, *LDC*, 4: 414–15; "Proposal for the Great Seal of the United States (before August 14, 1776)," FO, https://founders .archives.gov/documents/Franklin/01-22-02-0330 (the seal was not approved until

1782); *JCC*, 5:590–91, 626. Members did not start to sign until August 2, which will be examined in detail in chapter 12.

CHAPTER 12

1. "Newspaper Editions of the DECLARATION OF INDEPENDENCE: Published in July and August 1776 in the 13 United States of America," Declaration Resources Project, Harvard University, https://declaration.fas.harvard.edu/files/declaration/files/map_for_website_-_printable.jpg?m=1468950586.

2. *New Hampshire Gazette*, July 20, 1776. Many contemporary local accounts are compiled in Emily Sneff, "July Highlight: George Rejected and Liberty Protected," Declaration Resources Project, Harvard University, July 4, 2016, https://declaration.fas.harvard.edu/blog/july-proclamations.

3. "Boston," *Dunlap and Claypoole's American Daily Advertiser*, August 5, 1776, 2, cited in Sneff, "July Highlight: George Rejected and Liberty Protected," https://declaration.fas.harvard.edu/blog/july-proclamations.

4. Abigail Adams to John Adams, July 21, 1776, MHS, https://www.masshist.org/digitaladams/archive/doc?id=L17760721aa.

5. Charles B. Desbler, "How the Declaration Was Received in the Old Thirteen," *Harper's New Monthly Magazine* 75, July 1892, 173–174. Desbler was quoting from the *Massachusetts Spy* on July 24, 1776. He found twenty-seven accounts of contemporary celebrations in July and early August 1776—probably the most valuable single source of Americans' immediate reaction to the Declaration.

6. *New-York Journal*, August 8, cited in Sneff, "July Highlight: George Rejected and Liberty Protected," https://declaration.fas.harvard.edu/blog/july-proclamations; Pauline Maier, *American Scripture: Making the Declaration of Independence* (New York: Vintage, 1998), 158.

7. "Declaration Database: 1776 Periodicals," Declaration Resources Project, Harvard University, 4–9, https://declaration.fas.harvard.edu/sites/projects.iq.harvard.edu/files/declaration/files/declaration_database_august_2018_2023_update.pdf; John Hampden Hazelton, *The Declaration of Independence: Its History* (Cambridge, MA: University Press, 1906), 27; *Pennsylvania Journal*, September 18, 1776.

8. Hazelton, *The Declaration of Independence: Its History*, 279–81; Desbler, "How the Declaration Was Received in the Old Thirteen," 186–87.

9. Emily Sneff, "Unsullied by Falsehood: The Signing," Declaration Resources Project, Harvard University, https://declaration.fas.harvard.edu/blog/signing.

10. *JCC*, 5:590–91, 626.

11. David McCullough, *John Adams* (New York: Simon & Schuster Paperbacks, 2001), 137.

12. Herbert Friedenwald, *The Declaration of Independence: An Interpretation and an Analysis* (New York: Macmillan, 1904), 137, 149.

13. Samuel Chase to John Adams, July 5, 1776, FO, https://founders.archives.gov/documents/Adams/06-04-02-0148; John Adams to Samuel Chase, July 9, 1776, FO, https://founders.archives.gov/documents/Adams/06-04-02-0155; Elbridge Gerry to

Samuel and John Adams, July 21, 1776, MHS, https://www.masshist.org/publications/adams-papers/index.php/view/ADMS-06-04-02-0174.

14. Thomas Jefferson, "Notes of Proceedings in the Continental Congress, 7 June–1 August 1776," FO, https://founders.archives.gov/documents/Jefferson/01-01-02-0160; Friedenwald, *The Declaration of Independence*, 142–50; Sneff, "Unsullied by Falsehood: The Signing," https://declaration.fas.harvard.edu/blog/signing. In later years, John Adams also tried to claim that the Declaration was signed on July 4, probably part of the "golden haze" that developed around that date.

15. Friedenwald, *The Declaration of Independence*, 146.

16. Friedenwald, *The Declaration of Independence*, 141–42.

17. Sneff, "Unsullied by Falsehood: The Signing," https://declaration.fas.harvard.edu/blog/signing.

18. Robert Morris to Joseph Reed, July 21, 1776, in Smith, *LDC*, 4:510.

19. Sneff, "Unsullied by Falsehood: The Signing," https://declaration.fas.harvard.edu/blog/signing; Friedenwald, *The Declaration of Independence*, 142–50. The modern-day research done by Sneff and her colleagues was remarkable.

20. Michael Hancock, "John Hancock and His Signature," NA, September 12, 2019, https://prologue.blogs.archives.gov/2019/09/12/john-hancock-and-his-signature/ (the blog item was also posted by Jessie Kratz); Sneff, "Unsullied by Falsehood: The Signing," https://declaration.fas.harvard.edu/blog/signing; Ben Blatt, "Was John Hancock's Signature Too Big?," *Slate*, August 5, 2014, https://www.slate.com/articles/news_and_politics/history/2014/08/john_hancock_s_declaration_of_independence_signature_was_it_too_big.html.

21. Sneff, "Unsullied by Falsehood: The Signing," https://declaration.fas.harvard.edu/blog/signing.

22. Sneff, "Unsullied by Falsehood: The Signing," https://declaration.fas.harvard.edu/blog/signing; *JCC*, 7:48.

23. Benjamin Rush to John Adams, July 20, 1776, FO, https://founders.archives.gov/documents/Adams/99-02-02-5659.

24. Howard H. Peckham, "Independence: The View from Britain," *Proceedings of the American Antiquarian Society* 8, pt. 2 (October 1875): 389–90, https://www.americanantiquarian.org/proceedings/44498108.pdf; "First Foreign Printing of the Declaration of Independence," RR Auction, https://www.rrauction.com/auctions/lot-detail/343389905923011-first-foreign-printing-of-the-declaration-of-independence; Emily Sneff, "September Highlight: Extravagant and Inadmissible Claim of Independency," Declaration Resources Project, Harvard University, https://declaration.fas.harvard.edu/blog/september-kings-speech.

25. Peckham, "Independence: The View from Britain," 389–90, https://www.americanantiquarian.org/proceedings/44498108.pdf; "The First Printing of the Declaration of Independence in Britain," Sotheby's, https://www.sothebys.com/en/buy/auction/2021/constitutions-and-related-documents-from-the-collection-of-dorothy-tapper-goldman-part-1/declaration-of-independence-the-first-printing-of.

26. *Scots Magazine*, August 1776, cited in "British Reactions to America's Declaration of Independence," British Newspaper Archive, July 4, 2017, https://blog

.britishnewspaperarchive.co.uk/2017/07/04/british-reaction-to-americas-declaration
-of-independence/#:~:text=For%20the%20most%20part%2C%20the,rebels%20and
%20supported%20their%20independence.

27. *Kentish Gazette*, August 24 and 31, 1776, cited in "British Reactions to America's Declaration of Independence," British Newspaper Archive, July 4, 2017, https://blog
.britishnewspaperarchive.co.uk/2017/07/04/british-reaction-to-americas-declaration
-of-independence/#:~:text=For%20the%20most%20part%2C%20the,rebels%20and
%20supported%20their%20independence.

28. Peckham, "Independence: The View from Britain," 391, https://www
.americanantiquarian.org/proceedings/44498108.pdf; *Kentish Gazette*, February 21, 1776, cited in "British Reactions to America's Declaration of Independence," British Newspaper Archive, July 4, 2017, https://blog.britishnewspaperarchive.co.uk/2017/07/04/
british-reaction-to-americas-declaration-of-independence/#:~:text=For%20the%20most
%20part%2C%20the,rebels%20and%20supported%20their%20independence.

29. Sneff, "September Highlight: Extravagant and Inadmissible Claim of Independency," https://declaration.fas.harvard.edu/blog/september-kings-speech.

30. Maier, *American Scripture*, 106. Lind was not successful in his dream of serving in Parliament.

31. John Lind, "An Answer to the Declaration of the American Congress," HathiTrust, https://babel.hathitrust.org/cgi/pt?id=aeu.ark:/13960/t2f76xt2z&seq=8; "An Answer to the Declaration of the American Congress," American Battlefield Trust, https://www
.battlefields.org/learn/primary-sources/answer-declaration-american-congress.

32. Thomas Hutchinson, "Strictures upon the Declaration of the Congress at Philadelphia in a Letter to a Noble Lord," October 15, 1776, Teaching American History, https://
teachingamericanhistory.org/document/strictures-upon-the-declaration-of-the-congress
-at-philadelphia-in-a-letter-to-a-noble-lord-c/.

33. George Washington to Jesse Root, August 7, 1776, FO, https://founders.archives
.gov/documents/Washington/03-05-02-0459.

34. Ron Chernow, *Washington: A Life* (New York: Penguin, 2010), 144–45.

35. Joseph J. Ellis, *Revolutionary Summer: The Birth of American Independence* (New York: Vintage, 2012), 135; David McCullough, *1776* (New York: Simon & Schuster Paperbacks, 2005), 156–57.

36. General Orders, August 23, 1776, FO, https://founders.archives.gov/documents/
Washington/03-06-02-0100#:~:text=The%20officers%20of%20the%20militia,on%20his
%20bundle%2C%20and%20keep.

37. "Brooklyn Battle Facts and Summary," American Battlefield Trust, https://www
.battlefields.org/learn/revolutionary-war/battles/brooklyn; McCullough, *1776*, 168–77; Ellis, *Revolutionary Summer*, 140–42; Chernow, *Washington: A Life*, 146–48. The American defenses were designed by Nathaniel Greene, Washington's top subordinate, but Greene fell ill with a "raging fever" before the battle. He was replaced briefly by John Sullivan and then, after a few days, by Israel Putnam.

38. Ellis, *Revolutionary Summer*, 143–45; A. J. Langguth, *Patriots: The Men Who Started The American Revolution* (New York: Simon & Schuster, 1988), 377, 383–84.

39. Chernow, *Washington: A Life*, 249–51; McCullough, *1776*, 186–91; Ellis, *Revolutionary Summer*, 146–51.

40. General Orders, August 31, 1776, FO, https://founders.archives.gov/documents/Washington/03-06-02-0143.

41. James Grant to Edward Harvey, September 2, 1776, cited in McCullough, *1776*, 179.

CHAPTER 13

1. Thomas Jefferson to John Page, August 20, 1776, FO, https://founders.archives.gov/documents/Jefferson/01-01-02-0207; John Adams to Abigail Adams, August 30, 1776, FO, https://founders.archives.gov/documents/Adams/04-02-02-0073.

2. George Washington to John Hancock, August 31, 1776, FO, https://founders.archives.gov/documents/Washington/03-06-02-0144. Sullivan was among those supporting John Adams in his opposition to the Olive Branch Petition in summer 1775.

3. For Howe's message to the Americans as well as communication between Sullivan and Howe, see *JCC*, 5:730–31.

4. John Adams to James Warren, September 4, 1776, in Smith, *LDC*, 5:102–3n3 for Rush's comments; "John Witherspoon's Speech in Congress," September 5, 1776, in Smith, *LDC*, 5:108–13n4.

5. "John Witherspoon's Speech in Congress," September 5, 1776, in Smith, *LDC*, 5:112; *JCC*, 5:737.

6. *JCC*, 5:738; John Adams to Abigail Adams, September 6, 1776, FO, https://founders.archives.gov/documents/Adams/04-02-02-0078; Benjamin Franklin to Lord Howe, September 8, 1776, in Smith, *LDC*, 5:123; Adams, *DJA*, 3:418.

7. Adams, *DJA*, 3:419; David McCullough, *John Adams* (New York: Simon & Schuster Paperbacks, 2001), 155–56.

8. "Henry Strachey's Notes on Lord Howe's Meeting with a Committee of Congress," September 11, 1776, in Smith, *LDC*, 5:158, 5:160; Adams, *DJA*, 3:420, 3:422; Joseph J. Ellis, *Revolutionary Summer: The Birth of American Independence* (New York: Vintage, 2012), 158–60.

9. Adams, *DJA*, 3:421, 3:423. Adams wrote in his autobiography that "I was informed in England, afterwards, that a Number were excepted by name from Pardon, by the privy Council, and that John Adams was one of them, and that this List of Exceptions was given to both Howes, with their commission."

10. McCullough, *John Adams*, 158.

11. Council of War, September 12, 1776, FO, https://founders.archives.gov/documents/Washington/03-06-02-0230; George Washington to John Hancock, September 14, 1776, FO, https://founders.archives.gov/documents/Washington/03-06-02-0247.

12. Ellis, *Revolutionary Summer*, 179–81. The British attack began with four thousand troops, although a second wave of nine thousand, led by William Howe himself, arrived soon afterward.

13. "Declaration of Lord Howe and Sir William Howe," September 19, 1776, Northern Illinois Digital Library, https://digital.lib.niu.edu/islandora/object/niu-amarch%3A96725.

14. Ellis, *Revolutionary Summer*, 182.

15. George Washington to John Hancock, September 25, 1776, FO, https://founders .archives.gov/documents/Washington/03-06-02-0305#:~:text=To%20bring%20men %20to%20a,mixture%20of%20Troops%20as%20have.

16. *JCC*, 5:762–63, 5:787–807; Adams, *DJA*, 3:433–34; McCullough, *John Adams*, 159–60.

17. Ellis, *Revolutionary Summer*, 192.

18. *JCC*, 5:82; "Resolution of Congress: Appointing Franklin, Deane, and Jefferson as Commissioners to France, September 26, 1776," Jefferson, *PTJ*, 1:521–22; Thomas Jefferson to John Hancock, September 30, 1776, Jefferson, *PTJ*, 1:524; McCullough, *John Adams*, 162.

19. Rick Atkinson, *The British Are Coming: The War for America, Lexington to Princeton, 1775–1777* (New York: Holt, 2019), 418, 439. The Americans left a very small force to hold Fort Washington in Manhattan for "as long as possible."

20. Emily Sneff, "September Highlight: Extravagant and Inadmissible Claim of Independency," Declaration Resources Project, Harvard University, https://declaration.fas .harvard.edu/blog/september-kings-speech.

21. Ron Chernow, *Washington: A Life* (New York: Penguin, 2010), 264.

22. David McCullough, *1776* (New York: Simon & Schuster Paperbacks, 2005), 247, 258; "Acquackonock Bridge Signs," Revolutionary War New Jersey, https://www .revolutionarywarnewjersey.com/new_jersey_revolutionary_war_sites/towns/passaic_nj _revolutionary_war_sites.htm.

23. McCullough, *1776*, 258; George Washington to John Hancock, December 1, 1776, FO, https://founders.archives.gov/documents/Washington/03-07-02-0176; George Washington to Richard Humpton, December 1, 1776, FO, https://founders.archives.gov /documents/Washington/03-07-02-0179.

24. Atkinson, *The British Are Coming*, 493–95.

25. George Washington to John Hancock, December 9, 1776, FO, https://founders .archives.gov/documents/Washington/03-07-02-0222#:~:text=I%20did%20myself %20the%20honor,Stores%20except%20a%20few%20Boards; McCullough, *1776*, 255; "The Period of the Continental Congress, September 1774–October 1781," U.S. Department of State, https://history.state.gov/departmenthistory/buildings/section1.

26. McCullough, *1776*, 258, 264–65, 267.

27. Atkinson, *The British Are Coming*, 486–88; Chernow, *Washington: A Life*, 271; "How Thomas Paine's Other Pamphlet Saved the Revolution," National Constitution Center, December 19, 2023, https://constitutioncenter.org/blog/how-thomas-paines-other -pamphlet-saved-the-revolution.

28. "The American Crisis (No. 1) by the Author of *Common Sense*," LOC, https://www .loc.gov/resource/rbpe.03902300/?st=text; Travis Shaw, "Summer Soldiers and Sunshine Patriots," American Battlefield Trust, https://www.battlefields.org/learn/articles/summer -soldiers-and-sunshine-patriots-american-crisis.

29. Jeff Conner, "The American Crisis before Crossing Delaware," *Journal of the American Revolution*, February 25, 2015, https://allthingsliberty.com/2015/02/american-crisis -before-crossing-the-delaware/; Atkinson, *The British Are Coming*, 519.

30. George Washington to John Hancock, September 8, 1776, *FO*, https://founders .archives.gov/documents/Washington/03-06-02-0203; George Washington to Jonathan Trumbull, December 14, 1776, FO, https://founders.archives.gov/documents /Washington/03-07-02-0272; Joseph Reed to George Washington, December 22, 1776, FO, https://founders.archives.gov/documents/Washington/03-07-02-0324; McCullough, *1776*, 271–72.

31. "Trenton Battle Facts and Summary," American Battlefield Trust, https://www .battlefields.org/learn/revolutionary-war/battles/trenton; McCullough, *1776*, 280–82; Chernow, *Washington: A Life*, 272–76.

32. Chernow, *Washington: A Life*, 278–83.

33. Continental Congress Executive Committee to George Washington, January 7, 1777, FO, https://founders.archives.gov/?q=%20Recipient%3A%22Washington%2C %20George%22&s=1111311121&r=2888 (this letter was signed by Robert Morris, George Walton, and George Clymer); Continental Congress Executive Committee to George Washington, December 28, 1776, FO, https://founders.archives.gov/?q= %20Recipient%3A%22Washington%2C%20George%22&s=1111311121&r=2859; John Hancock to George Washington, January 1, 1777, FO, https://founders.archives.gov/?q= %20Recipient%3A%22Washington%2C%20George%22&s=1111311121&r=2875.

34. *JCC*, 7:48.

35. Emily Sneff, "March Highlight: Mary Katherine Goddard," Declaration Resources Project, Harvard University, March 4, 2016, https://declaration.fas.harvard.edu/blog/ march-goddard.

36. Circular Letter from John Hancock to the State Legislatures, January 31, 1777, Documenting the American South, https://docsouth.unc.edu/csr/index.html/document /csr11-0249. This item references Hancock's letter, with the Goddard broadside, to the "Convention of the State of North Carolina."

37. "Broadside of the Declaration of Independence," New York Public Library, https: //www.nypl.org/events/exhibitions/galleries/beginnings/item/3570; "Mary Katharine Goddard Takes a Stance," NPS, https://www.nps.gov/articles/independence-goddard .htm; Erick Trickey, "Mary Katharine Goddard: The Woman Whose Name Appears on the Declaration of Independence," *Smithsonian Magazine*, November 14, 2018, https: //www.smithsonianmag.com/history/mary-katharine-goddard-woman-whose-name -appears-declaration-independence-180970816/; "Which Version Is This, and Why Does It Matter?," Declaration Resources Project, Harvard University, https://declaration .fas.harvard.edu/resources/which-version-and-why. The Harvard item reports that the Matlack parchment "was entrusted to (congressional secretary Charles) Thomson, was rolled up with other documents, and traveled with the Continental Congress as they moved locations over the course of the Revolutionary War."

CHAPTER 14
1. Pauline Maier, *American Scripture: Making the Declaration of Independence* (New York: Vintage, 1998), 160.

2. Alex Shashkevich, "It Took over a Decade for the Declaration of Independence to Matter in American Life, Stanford Historian Says," *Stanford News*, July 2, 2019, https://news.stanford.edu/stories/2019/07/americans-forgot-declaration-independence.

3. John Adams to Abigail Adams 2d. [Adams's daughter], July 5, 1777, FO, https://founders.archives.gov/documents/Adams/04-02-02-0216.

4. John Adams to Abigail Adams 2d. [Adams's daughter], July 5, 1777, FO, https://founders.archives.gov/documents/Adams/04-02-02-0216; Charles Warren, "Fourth of July Myths," *William and Mary Quarterly* 2, no. 3 (July 1945): 254–56; Thomas Burke to Richard Caswell, July 5, 1777, Documenting the American South, https://docsouth.unc.edu/csr/index.php/document/csr11-0395.

5. Diana Karter Appelbaum, *The Glorious Fourth: An American Holiday, an American History* (New York: Facts on File, 1989), 17–18.

6. "Brandywine Battle Facts and Summary," American Battlefield Trust, https://www.battlefields.org/learn/revolutionary-war/battles/brandywine; *JCC*, 8:751–52; "The Period of the Continental Congress, September 1774–October 1781," U.S. Department of State, https://history.state.gov/departmenthistory/buildings/section1.

7. Samuel Mostyn, "Loyalists and the British Evacuation of Philadelphia, 1778," Gilder Lehrman Institute of American History, https://www.gilderlehrman.org/history-resources/spotlight-primary-source/loyalists-and-british-evacuation-philadelphia-1778; "British Abandon Philadelphia, 1778," History, https://www.history.com/this-day-in-history/british-abandon-philadelphia.

8. *JCC*, 11:641. The three members chosen were John Hancock, William Duer, and John Matthews.

9. Warren, "Fourth of July Myths," 256–57; General Orders, July 3, 1778, https://founders.archives.gov/documents/Washington/03-16-02-0014.

10. Warren, "Fourth of July Myths," 257–58; *Acts and Resolves of Massachusetts, 1780–81*, 691, Secretary of the Commonwealth, https://archive.org/details/actsresolvespass178081mass/page/690/mode/2up.

11. Shashkevich, "It Took over a Decade for the Declaration of Independence to Matter in American Life," https://news.stanford.edu/stories/2019/07/americans-forgot-declaration-independence.

12. "Battle of Yorktown in the American Revolution," American Battlefield Trust, https://www.battlefields.org/learn/revolutionary-war/battles/yorktown. North's first replacement was Charles Watson-Wentworth, who died fourteen weeks later. Lord Shelburne was the next choice.

13. "Treaty of Paris 1783," U.S. Department of State, https://2001-2009.state.gov/r/pa/ho/time/ar/14313.htm; "The Treaty of Paris," American Battlefield Trust, https://www.battlefields.org/learn/articles/treaty-paris.

14. Walter Stahr, *John Jay* (London and New York: Hambledon, 2005), 146, 158, 162; John P. Kaminski, "Preserving the Alliance: The Artful Diplomacy of Benjamin Franklin," Center for the Study of the American Constitution, University of Wisconsin–Madison, https://csac.history.wisc.edu/wp-content/uploads/sites/281/2018/03/Kaminski-benjaminFranklin.pdf; David McCullough, *John Adams* (New York: Simon & Schuster Paperbacks, 2001), 273–75.

15. John Jay to John Adams, September 1, 1782, FO, https://founders.archives.gov/documents/Adams/06-13-02-0173; John Jay to John Adams, September 28, 1782, *The Papers of John Jay*, Columbia University, https://dlc.library.columbia.edu/jay/ldpd:48404. The Americans were supposed to negotiate on a treaty with England and France at the same time, but Jay and Franklin determined that the best course was to negotiate directly with the British. McCullough, *John Adams*, 275–76.

16. Stahr, *John Jay*, 167–72; McCullough, *John Adams*, 279, 283; "The Treaty of Paris," American Battlefield Trust, https://www.battlefields.org/learn/articles/treaty-paris.

17. "Preliminary Articles of Peace," November 30, 1782, FO, https://founders.archives.gov/documents/Franklin/01-38-02-0286.

18. The American Peace Commissioners to Robert R. Livingston, December 14, 1782, FO, https://founders.archives.gov/documents/Adams/06-14-02-0076; John Adams to Robert R. Livingston, December 14, 1782, notes 3, 4, FO, https://founders.archives.gov/documents/Adams/06-14-02-0075.

19. "The Definitive Treaty of Peace between the United States and Great Britain," September 3, 1783, FO, https://founders.archives.gov/documents/Franklin/01-40-02-0356; McCullough, *John Adams*, 285.

20. "Signing of the Treaty of Paris," National Portrait Gallery, https://npg.si.edu/object/npg_1957.0856; "The Treaty of Paris," American Battlefield Trust, https://www.battlefields.org/learn/articles/treaty-paris.

21. "The Definitive Treaty of Peace between the United States and Great Britain," September 3, 1783, FO, https://founders.archives.gov/documents/Franklin/01-40-02-0356.

22. The treaty was ratified by Congress on January 14, 1784.

23. John Hancock to the New Jersey Convention, July 5, 1776, in Smith, *LDC*, 4:392.

24. "Articles of Confederation," NA, https://www.archives.gov/milestone-documents/articles-of-confederation#transcript.

25. Richard R. Beeman, "The Constitutional Convention of 1787: A Revolution in Government," National Constitution Center, https://constitutioncenter.org/the-constitution/white-papers/the-constitutional-convention-of-1787-a-revolution-in-government; "Constitution of the United States—a History," NA, https://www.archives.gov/founding-docs/more-perfect-union.

26. *JCC*, 31:678–80. Dickinson's letter was dated September 1786—one year and three days before a new, world-changing constitution was approved by Congress.

27. *JCC*, 31:71–74.

28. Beeman, "The Constitutional Convention of 1787," https://constitutioncenter.org/the-constitution/white-papers/the-constitutional-convention-of-1787-a-revolution-in-government; Richard Beeman, *Plain, Honest Men: The Making of the American Constitution* (New York: Random House, 2009), 52–54.

29. "Constitution of the United States—a History," NA, https://www.archives.gov/founding-docs/more-perfect-union.

30. "Constitution of the United States—a History," NA, https://www.archives.gov/founding-docs/more-perfect-union; "The Records of the Federal Convention of 1787, Vol. 1," LOC, xi, 2–3, https://www.loc.gov/resource/llscdam.llfr001/?st=pdf&pdfPage=29.

31. "The Records of the Federal Convention of 1787, Vol. 1," LOC, 2–4, https://www
.loc.gov/resource/llscdam.llfr001/?st=pdf&pdfPage=30; "Constitution of the United
States—a History," NA, https://www.archives.gov/founding-docs/more-perfect-union.
The quote attributed to Washington is from Madison's notes of May 25.

32. Beeman, "The Constitutional Convention of 1787," https://constitutioncenter.org
/the-constitution/white-papers/the-constitutional-convention-of-1787-a-revolution-in
-government; "Constitution of the United States—a History," NA, https://www.archives
.gov/founding-docs/more-perfect-union. The quote attributed to Washington is from
Madison's notes of May 25.

33. "The Records of the Federal Convention of 1787, Vol. 1," LOC, 29–31, https://
www.loc.gov/resource/llscdam.llfr001/?st=pdf&pdfPage=58.

34. Beeman, "The Constitutional Convention of 1787," https://constitutioncenter.org
/the-constitution/white-papers/the-constitutional-convention-of-1787-a-revolution-in
-government; "The Records of the Federal Convention of 1787, Vol. 2," July 16, 1787,
Online Library of Liberty, https://oll.libertyfund.org/titles/farrand-the-records-of-the
-federal-convention-of-1787-vol-2.

35. Beeman, *Plain, Honest Men*, xxiv.

36. Beeman, *Plain, Honest Men*, 345–46; "Constitution of the United States—a History," NA, https://www.archives.gov/founding-docs/more-perfect-union.

37. "The Constitution of the United States: A Transcription," NA, https://www
.archives.gov/founding-docs/constitution-transcript.

38. Beeman, *Plain, Honest Men*, 346. Beeman quotes a letter that Madison wrote to
historian Jared Sparks in 1831.

39. "Top Myths about the Constitution on Constitution Day," National Constitution
Center, September 17, 2023, https://constitutioncenter.org/blog/top-10-myths-about
-the-constitution-on-constitution-day#:~:text=Only%20six%20Founders%20signed
%20both,James%20Wilson%2C%20and%20Roger%20Sherman; "Constitution of the
United States—a History," NA, https://www.archives.gov/founding-docs/more-perfect
-union; "The Bill of Rights: A Transcription," NA, https://www.archives.gov/founding
-docs/bill-of-rights-transcript. The only delegates in attendance on September 17 who
did not sign were George Mason, Edmund Randolph, and Elbridge Gerry.

40. Walter Isaacson, *Benjamin Franklin: An American Life* (New York: Simon & Schuster Paperbacks, 2003), 457–58. Franklin was one of only six men to sign both the Declaration of Independence and the Constitution. The others were George Clymer, Robert
Morris, George Read, Roger Sherman, and James Wilson.

41. Shashkevich, "It Took over a Decade for the Declaration of Independence to
Matter in American Life," https://news.stanford.edu/stories/2019/07/americans-forgot
-declaration-independence. The scholar was Jonathan Gienapp of Stanford University.

42. Ezra Stiles, "The United States Elevated to Glory and Honor," May 8, 1783, Digital
Commons at the University of Nebraska–Lincoln, 46, https://digitalcommons.unl.edu/
cgi/viewcontent.cgi?article=1041&context=etas.

43. Thomas Jefferson to the Editor of the *Journal de Paris*, August 29, 1787 (unpublished), FO, https://founders.archives.gov/documents/Jefferson/01-12-02-0073; Maier,
American Scripture, 169.

44. "A Fourth of July Tribute to Jefferson," July 4, 1789, in *The Papers of Thomas Jefferson Digital Edition*, ed. James P. McClure and J. Jefferson Looney, University of Virginia, https://rotunda.upress.virginia.edu/founders/default.xqy?keys=TSJN-print-01-15-02-0229&mode=deref; Maier, *American Scripture*, 169.

45. Shira Lurie, interview by Liz Covart, *Ben Franklin's World* (podcast), episode 245, July 2, 2019, https://benfranklinsworld.com/episode-245-celebrating-the-fourth/.

46. Maier, *American Scripture*, 170–71; Warren, "Fourth of July Myths," 261; Philip F. Detweiler, "The Changing Reputation of the Declaration of Independence: The First Fifty Years," *William and Mary Quarterly* 19, no. 4 (October 1962): 565.

47. Warren, "Fourth of July Myths," 264–65.

48. Warren, "Fourth of July Myths," 267, quoting from the *Independent Chronicle*, July 26, 1802.

49. Warren, "Fourth of July Myths," 270, quoting from the *Columbian Centinel*, June 21, 1804.

50. Maier, *American Scripture*, 171; "Presidential Elections of 1816 and 1820: A Resource Guide," LOC, https://www.loc.gov/rr/program/bib/elections/election1816.html. In 1816, Monroe received 183 electoral votes to King's 34—Monroe therefore had 84 percent of the vote to King's 16 (68 points). Monroe's 1820 reelection was unopposed, although one delegate cast a vote for John Quincy Adams, making the official tally 231–1.

CHAPTER 15

1. Lester J. Cappon, ed., *The Adams-Jefferson Letters: The Complete Correspondence between Thomas Jefferson & Abigail & John Adams* (Chapel Hill: University of North Carolina Press, 1959), 244, 264, 290; David McCullough, *John Adams* (New York: Simon & Schuster Paperbacks, 2001), 569.

2. "The Electoral Count for the Presidential Elections of 1789," Washington Papers, University of Virginia, https://washingtonpapers.org/resources/articles/the-electoral-count-for-the-presidential-election-of-1789/.

3. McCullough, *John Adams*, 415; Jon Meacham, *Thomas Jefferson: The Art of Power* (New York: Random House Trade Paperbacks, 2012), 232.

4. Meacham, *Thomas Jefferson*, 249–50, 252, 259–60, 262, 264; Gordon S. Wood, *Friends Divided: John Adams and Thomas Jefferson* (New York: Penguin, 2018), 270.

5. "Neutrality Proclamation," April 22, 1793, FO, https://founders.archives.gov/documents/Washington/05-12-02-0371; Wood, *Friends Divided*, 270; Thomas Jefferson to George Washington, July 31, 1793, FO, https://founders.archives.gov/documents/Jefferson/01-26-02-0533; Thomas Jefferson to George Washington, December 31, 1793, LOC, https://www.loc.gov/resource/mtj1.019_1253_1253/?st=text.

6. John Adams to Abigail Adams, January 6, 1794, MHS, https://www.masshist.org/digitaladams/archive/doc?id=L17940106ja&rec=sheet&archive=all&hi=1&numRecs=1364&query=I+always+consider+the+settlement+of+America+with+reverence+and+wonder%2C+as+the+opening+of+a+grand+scene+and+design+in+Providence+for+the+illumination+of+the+slavish+part+of+mankind+all+over+the+earth.&queryid=&start=40&tag=text&num=10&bc=.

7. McCullough, *John Adams*, 423; Meacham, *Thomas Jefferson*, 299.

8. John Adams to Abigail Adams, January 7, 1796, MHS, https://www.masshist.org/digitaladams/archive/doc?id=L17960107ja&bc=%2Fdigitaladams%2Farchive%2Fbrowse%2Fletters_JA.php.

9. McCullough, *John Adams*, 471; C. James Taylor, "John Adams: Campaigns and Elections," Miller Center, University of Virginia, https://millercenter.org/president/adams/campaigns-and-elections.

10. John Adams to Abigail Adams, January 3, 1797, MHS, https://www.masshist.org/digitaladams/archive/doc?id=L17970103ja&bc=%2Fdigitaladams%2Farchive%2Fbrowse%2Fletters_1796_1801.php; Meacham, *Thomas Jefferson*, 301; Joseph J. Ellis, *First Family: Abigail and John Adams* (New York: Vintage, 2011), 176.

11. Thomas Jefferson to John Adams, December 28, 1796, in Cappon, *The Adams-Jefferson Letters*, 262–63.

12. Thomas Jefferson to James Madison, January 1, 1797, FO, https://founders.archives.gov/?q=%20Author%3A%22Jefferson%2C%20Thomas%22%20Recipient%3A%22Madison%2C%20James%22&s=1111311113&r=313.

13. Meacham, *Thomas Jefferson*, 304; Ellis, *First Family*, 176.

14. McCullough, *John Adams*, 473–75; Wood, *Friends Divided*, 290–94.

15. Taylor, "John Adams: Campaigns and Elections," Miller Center, University of Virginia, https://millercenter.org/president/adams/campaigns-and-elections; Meacham, *Thomas Jefferson*, 312–13; Ellis, *First Family*, 188–91.

16. McCullough, *John Adams*, 543–45; Peter Onuf, "Thomas Jefferson: Campaigns and Elections," Miller Center, University of Virginia, https://millercenter.org/president/jefferson/campaigns-and-elections.

17. "Tally of Votes for the 1800 Presidential Election," NA, https://www.archives.gov/legislative/features/1800-election/1800-election.html. One elector from Rhode Island cast a vote for John Jay instead of Pinckney. In 1804, the Twelfth Amendment to the Constitution solved one of the unanticipated issues, calling for separate votes for the president and vice president.

18. McCullough. *John Adams*, 560, 565; Wood, *Friends Divided*, 323.

19. "Presidential Historians Survey 2021," C-Span, https://www.c-span.org/presidentsurvey2021/?page=overall (Jefferson ranked seventh out of forty-four, just behind Harry Truman and just ahead of John F. Kennedy); "Election Listing," American Presidency Project, https://www.c-span.org/presidentsurvey2021/?page=overall; "Exhibit: Louisiana Purchase—National Archives," NA, https://www.archives.gov/exhibits/american_originals/loupurch.html#:~:text=The%20lands%20acquired%20stretched%20from,largest%20nations%20in%20the%20world.

20. Thomas Jefferson to John Adams, March 8, 1801, FO, https://founders.archives.gov/?q=%20Author%3A%22Jefferson%2C%20Thomas%22&s=1111311113&r=8619; John Adams to Thomas Jefferson, March 24, 1801, in Cappon, *The Adams-Jefferson Letters*, 264.

21. Cappon, *The Adams-Jefferson Letters*, 284–85; Benjamin Rush to Thomas Jefferson, January 2, 1811, FO, https://founders.archives.gov/?q=%20Recipient%3A%22Jefferson%2C%20Thomas%22&s=1111311123&r=20329.

22. Thomas Jefferson to Benjamin Rush, December 5, 1811, LOC, https://www.loc.gov/item/mtjbib020752/; Wood, *Friends Divided*, 360.

23. Benjamin Rush to John Adams, December 16, 1811, FO, https://founders.archives.gov/?q=%20Recipient%3A%22Adams%2C%20John%22&s=1111311113&r=7408.

24. John Adams to Thomas Jefferson, January 1, 1811, and Thomas Jefferson to John Adams, January 21, 1811, in Cappon, *The Adams-Jefferson Letters*, 290–92.

25. "Contents," in Cappon, *The Adams-Jefferson Letters*, xvi–xxii.

26. John Adams to Thomas Jefferson, May 1, 1812, FO, https://founders.archives.gov/documents/Jefferson/03-05-02-0001; John Adams to Thomas Jefferson, FO, https://founders.archives.gov/documents/Jefferson/03-06-02-0247.

27. Benjamin Rush to John Adams, February 17, 1812, cited in McCullough, *John Adams*, 604.

28. "Declaration of Independence," Architect of the Capitol, https://www.aoc.gov/explore-capitol-campus/art/declaration-independence; Olivia B. Waxman, "This Painting Is How You Probably Imagine the Original Fourth of July: Here's What's Wrong with It," *Time*, July 3, 2018, https://time.com/5323460/declaration-of-independence-john-trumbull/.

29. Wood, *Friends Divided*, 399.

30. Pauline Maier, *American Scripture: Making the Declaration of Independence* (New York: Vintage, 1998), 175; "Declaration of Independence," Architect of the Capitol, https://www.aoc.gov/explore-capitol-campus/art/declaration-independence and https://www.aoc.gov/sites/default/files/painting_key_declaration-of-independence_aoc.png (this last link identifies everyone in the painting).

31. McCullough, *John Adams*, 627.

32. John Quincy Adams to John Adams, December 14, 1818, FO, https://founders.archives.gov/?q=%20Recipient%3A%22Adams%2C%20John%22&s=1111311113&r=8172.

33. Catherine Nicholson, "The Stone Engraving: Icon of the Declaration," *Prologue Magazine* 35, no. 3, https://www.archives.gov/publications/prologue/2003/fall/stone-engraving.html.

34. "The Declaration of Independence—Stone Facsimile," Independence National Historical Park, NPS, https://www.nps.gov/articles/stone.htm.

35. "The Declaration of Independence—Stone Facsimile," Independence National Historical Park, NPS, https://www.nps.gov/articles/stone.htm. The White House holds one of only thirty-one copies of the original Stone engraving known to exist today.

36. Timothy Pickering to John Adams, August 2, 1822, FO, https://founders.archives.gov/?q=%20Recipient%3A%22Adams%2C%20John%22&s=1111311113&r=8645; Maier, *American Scripture*, 171–72.

37. John Adams to Timothy Pickering, August 6, 1822, FO, https://founders.archives.gov/documents/Adams/99-02-02-7674.

38. "Col. Pickering's observations introductory to reading the Declaration of Independence, at Salem, July 4, 1823," Internet Archive, https://archive.org/details/colpickeringsobs00pick/page/n3/mode/2up.

39. Thomas Jefferson to James Madison, August 30, 1823, FO, https://founders.archives.gov/documents/Jefferson/98-01-02-3728.

40. Thomas Jefferson to Henry Lee, May 8, 1825, FO, https://founders.archives.gov/documents/Jefferson/98-01-02-5212.

41. Thomas Jefferson to James Madison, August 30, 1823, FO, https://founders.archives.gov/documents/Jefferson/98-01-02-3728.

42. Thomas Jefferson to John Adams, March 25, 1826, and John Adams to Thomas Jefferson, April 17, 1826, in Cappon, *The Adams-Jefferson Letters*, 613–14.

43. Thomas Jefferson to Roger C. Weightman, June 24, 1826, in "Declaring Independence: Drafting the Documents," LOC, https://www.loc.gov/exhibits/declara/rcwltr.html.

44. Meacham, *Thomas Jefferson*, 490, 493–94.

45. McCullough, *John Adams*, 645–46.

46. McCullough, *John Adams*, 647; Wood, *Friends Divided*, 1.

47. Caleb Cushing eulogy, July 15, 1826, in *A Selection of Eulogies Pronounced in the Several States in Honor of Those Illustrious Patriots and Statesmen, John Adams and Thomas Jefferson*, various authors (Hartford, CT: Robinson and Norton & Russell, 1826), 23–24.

CHAPTER 16

1. "Prince Hall: Petition to the Massachusetts Legislature (1777)," National Constitution Center, https://constitutioncenter.org/media/files/12.3_Primary_Source__Prince_Hall%2C_Petition_to_the_Massachusetts_Legislature_%281777%29_.pdf.

2. "First Women's Rights Convention," NPS, https://www.nps.gov/wori/learn/historyculture/the-first-womens-rights-convention.htm.

3. Abigail Adams to John Adams, March 31, 1776, FO, https://founders.archives.gov/documents/Adams/04-01-02-0241.

4. "Declaration of Sentiments," NPS, https://www.nps.gov/wori/learn/historyculture/declaration-of-sentiments.htm.

5. "Signers of the Declaration of Sentiments," NPS, https://www.nps.gov/wori/learn/historyculture/signers-of-the-declaration-of-sentiments.htm; "The Rights of Women," *North Star*, July 28, 1848, LOC, https://www.loc.gov/exhibitions/women-fight-for-the-vote/about-this-exhibition/seneca-falls-and-building-a-movement-1776-1890/seneca-falls-and-the-start-of-annual-conventions/frederick-douglass-speaks-in-support/.

6. "The Declaration of Sentiments," Women's Rights National Historical Park, NPS, https://www.nps.gov/articles/declaration-of-sentiments.htm#:~:text=Elizabeth%20Cady%20Stanton%20wrote%20the,gender%20inequality%20in%20the%20U.S.

7. David W. Blight, *Frederick Douglass: Prophet of Freedom* (New York: Simon & Schuster, 2018), 227, 229–36. July 4 also fell on a Sunday, but Blight wrote that moving events to July 5 had "long been a practice among New York State African American communities."

8. "What to the Slave Is the 4th of July?," in *Great Speeches by Frederick Douglass*, ed. James Daley (Mineola, NY: Dover, 2013), 26–30, 36; Olivia B. Waxman, "'What to the Slave Is the Fourth of July?': The History of Frederick Douglass' Searing Independence Day Oration," *Time*, July 3, 2019, https://time.com/5614930/frederick-douglass-fourth-of-july/; Blight, *Frederick Douglass*, 230–33.

9. "What to the Slave Is the 4th of July?," in Daley, *Great Speeches by Frederick Douglass*, 46.

10. Blight, *Frederick Douglass*, 236.

11. "The Slaveholders' Rebellion: An Address Delivered in Himrod's, New York on July 4, 1862," Frederick Douglass Papers Project, https://frederickdouglasspapersproject.com /s/digitaledition/item/10537. Hillel Italie, "Frederick Douglass' July 4 Speeches Trace American History," Associated Press, July 1, 2018, https://apnews.com/article/393ae428 732c4cc8905f3e3af01128d7.

12. "Address at Independence Hall," February 22, 1861, NPS, https://www.nps.gov/ liho/learn/historyculture/independence-hall.htm.

13. Jon Meacham, *And There Was Light: Abraham Lincoln and the American Struggle* (New York: Random House, 2022), 30–31 (also see William Grisham, *History of the United States* (Philadelphia, PA: Warner, 1821), 271, Google Books, https://books.google .com/books/about/History_of_the_United_States.html?id=Ud8RAAAAIAAJ. Meacham wrote that Grisham's book was "possibly the first time Lincoln had ever encountered the document."

14. Lyceum Address," January 27, 1838, https://www.abrahamlincolnonline.org/ lincoln/speeches/lyceum.htmc; "Temperance Address," February 22, 1842, Abraham Lincoln Online, https://www.abrahamlincolnonline.org/lincoln/speeches/temperance .htm#:~:text=Turn%20now%2C%20to%20the%20temperance,orphans%20starving%2C %20no%20widows%20weeping; David Herbert Donald, *Lincoln* (New York: Simon & Schuster, 1995), 80–82.

15. Meacham, *And There Was Light*, 115–16; Katie Uva, "Parson Weems," Mount Vernon, https://www.mountvernon.org/library/digitalhistory/digital-encyclopedia/article/ parson-weems/; Mason L. Weems, *The Life of Washington* (Cambridge, MA: Harvard University Press, 1962), 80, Google Books, https://books.google.com/books/about/The _Life_of_Washington.html?id=GJsVo9RvEs4C. Meacham wrote that "Weems got all the details wrong, but the young Lincoln, reading about the heroic events, could not have known that. It probably would not have mattered if he had. The tale was all."

16. Abraham Lincoln to Henry L. Pierce and Others, April 6, 1859, Abraham Lincoln Online, https://www.abrahamlincolnonline.org/lincoln/speeches/pierce.htm; Meacham, *And There Was Light*, 116–17.

17. "Lincoln's Autobiography, December 20, 1859," Abraham Lincoln Online, https: //www.abrahamlincolnonline.org/lincoln/speeches/autobiog.htm; Joseph R. Fornieri, "Speech on the Repeal of the Missouri Compromise at Peoria," Teaching American History, https://teachingamericanhistory.org/resource/the-lincoln-exhibit/speech-on-the -repeal-of-the-missouri-compromise-at-peoria/.

18. Fornieri, "Speech on the Repeal of the Missouri Compromise at Peoria," https:// teachingamericanhistory.org/resource/the-lincoln-exhibit/speech-on-the-repeal-of-the -missouri-compromise-at-peoria/.

19. "Lincoln's Peoria Speech, October 16, 1854," NPS, https://www.nps.gov/liho/learn /historyculture/peoriaspeech.htm.

20. "Speech of Senator Douglas," July 9, 1858, Northern Illinois University Digital Library, https://digital.lib.niu.edu/islandora/object/niu-lincoln:36302.

21. "Lincoln Speech at Chicago, Illinois," July 10, 1858, Teaching American History, https://teachingamericanhistory.org/document/speech-at-chicago-illinois/.

22. "Speech Delivered at Springfield, Ill, by Senator S. A. Douglas," July 17, 1858, Northern Illinois University Digital Library, https://digital.lib.niu.edu/islandora/object/niu-lincoln%3A35822; "(Lincoln) Speech at Springfield," July 17, 1858, Mr. Lincoln and Freedom, https://www.mrlincolnandfreedom.org/pre-civil-war/house-divided-speech/speech-springfield-july-17-1858/#:~:text=Under%20the%20operation%20of%20that,half%20slave%20and%20half%20free.

23. Abraham Lincoln to Henry L. Pierce and Others, April 6, 1859, Abraham Lincoln Online, https://www.abrahamlincolnonline.org/lincoln/speeches/pierce.htm. Jefferson's birthday was April 13.

24. "Republican Party Platform of 1860," American Presidency Project, https://www.presidency.ucsb.edu/documents/republican-party-platform-1860.

25. "1860 Election," American Presidency Project, https://www.presidency.ucsb.edu/statistics/elections/1860. Lincoln received 1.1 percent Virginia. He got no popular votes in Alabama, Arkansas, Florida, Georgia, Louisiana, Mississippi, North Carolina, Tennessee, or Texas. South Carolina's electors were chosen by the state legislature.

26. "War Declared: States Secede from the Union," NPS, https://www.nps.gov/kemo/learn/historyculture/wardeclared.htm.

27. "Address at Independence Hall," NPS, https://www.nps.gov/liho/learn/historyculture/independence-hall.htm; "Old Abe Raises Stars and Stripes," *Philadelphia North American and United States Gazette*, February 23, 1861, found at LOC, https://www.loc.gov/exhibits/lincoln/interactives/journey-of-the-president-elect/feb_22/article_1_504j_highlight_1.html; Donald, *Lincoln*, 277; "Presidential Visit to Independence Hall—Abraham Lincoln, February 22, 1881," Constitutional Walking Tour, posted February 15, 2021, https://www.theconstitutional.com/blog/2021/02/14/presidential-visit-independence-hall-abraham-lincoln-february-22-1861.

28. "First Inaugural Address of Abraham Lincoln," March 4, 1861, Avalon Project, Yale Law School, https://avalon.law.yale.edu/19th_century/lincoln1.asp.

29. Response to a Serenade," July 7, 1862, in Abraham Lincoln, *The Collected Works of Abraham Lincoln* (hereafter *CW*), ed. Roy P. Basler (New Brunswick, NJ: Rutgers University Press, 1953), 6:319–20.

30. "Final Text: Address Delivered at the Dedication of the Cemetery at Gettysburg," in Lincoln, *CW*, 7:22–23.

31. Meacham, *And There Was Light*, 312.

32. Garry Wills, *Lincoln at Gettysburg: The Words That Remade America* (New York: Simon & Schuster, 1992), 120.

33. Scott Douglas Gerber, ed., *The Declaration of Independence: Origins and Impact* (Washington, DC: CW Press, 2002), 183, 208–10. Among the essays referenced are David Thelen's "Reception of the Declaration of Independence" and Bonnie L. Ford's "Women, Equality, and the Declaration of Independence."

34. "Churchill on the Fourth of July," Churchill Project, https://winstonchurchill.hillsdale.edu/churchill-on-july-4th/.

35. "Independence Hall and the Declaration of Common Aims of 1918," NPS, https://www.nps.gov/articles/000/declaration-of-common-aims.htm.

36. "Read Dr. Martin Luther King's 'I Have a Dream' Speech in Its Entirety," NPR, https://www.npr.org/2010/01/18/122701268/i-have-a-dream-speech-in-its-entirety; "March on Washington for Jobs and Freedom," NPS, https://www.nps.gov/articles/march-on-washington.htm#:~:text=It%20was%20the%20largest%20gathering,from%20all%20over%20the%20country.

Chapter 17

1. Frank Whitson Fetter, "The Revision of the Declaration of Independence in 1941," *William and Mary Quarterly* 31, no. 1 (January 1974): 133–34. The three-man committee was Stuart G. Gibboney, president of the Thomas Jefferson Memorial Association; Senator Elbert D. Thomas (D-Utah), a former professor of political science; and Brigadier General Jefferson Randolph Kean, one of Jefferson's great-grandsons.

2. Fetter, "The Revision of the Declaration of Independence in 1941," 134–35.

3. Pauline Maier, *American Scripture: Making the Declaration of Independence* (New York: Vintage, 1998), 210.

4. Franklin D. Roosevelt to Stuart G. Gibboney, May 15, 1941, cited in Fetter, "The Revision of the Declaration of Independence in 1941," 135.

5. Maier, *American Scripture*, 211.

6. Maier, *American Scripture*, 211.

7. Fetter, "The Revision of the Declaration of Independence in 1941," 135.

8. Fetter, "The Revision of the Declaration of Independence in 1941," 136–37; also see Nicholas D. Kristof, "Literary Liberties: Jefferson Memorial Quotes Declaration Imperfectly," *Washington Post*, July 4, 1982, https://www.washingtonpost.com/archive/politics/1982/07/04/literary-liberties/d8516924-1eca-44c7-a181-c3891bf79350/. Kristof also wrote about it in the edition of the *New York Times*: Nicholas Kristof, "For July 4, Fix the Jefferson Memorial!," *New York Times*, July 4, 2009, https://archive.nytimes.com/kristof.blogs.nytimes.com/2009/07/04/for-july-4-fix-the-jefferson-memorial/.

9. Author visit to Jefferson Memorial, January 2024.

10. Julian P. Boyd, *The Declaration of Independence: The Evolution of the Text*, rev. ed., ed. Gerard W. Gawalt (Washington, DC: LOC; Charlottesville, VA: Thomas Jefferson Memorial Foundation, 1999), 9, 13–14. Maier, *American Scripture*, 212–13.

11. Archibald McLeish, "Foreword," in Boyd, *The Declaration of Independence*, 13–14.

12. Gerard W. Gawalt, "Preface," in Boyd, *The Declaration of Independence*, 9.

13. Steve Yates, "About the Playwright: *1776*," Utah Shakespeare Festival, https://www.bard.org/study-guides/about-the-playwright-1776/; "*1776*: Full Synopsis," Music Theatre International, https://www.mtishows.com/print/node/925.

14. "*1776*," Playbill, https://playbill.com/production/1776-46th-street-theatre-vault-0000003101.

15. Emily Sneff, "Presenting the Facts: 1776," Declaration Resources Project, Harvard University, March 28, 2017, https://declaration.fas.harvard.edu/blog/facts-1776; "*1776*: Full Synopsis," Music Theatre International, https://www.mtishows.com/print/node/925.

16. Author viewing of *1776*; Sneff, "Presenting the Facts: 1776," https://declaration.fas .harvard.edu/blog/facts-1776.

17. "List of Delegates to Congress," in Smith, *LDC*, 4:xix (the record has Duane attending from April 21, 1775 to May 31, 1776); Jeremy Stern, "What's Wrong with HBO's Dramatization of John Adams's Story," History News Network, https: //www.historynewsnetwork.org/article/whats-wrong-with-hbos-dramatization-of-john -adamss; author viewing of *John Adams*, HBO, episode 2.

18. Sneff, "Presenting the Facts: National Treasure," Declaration Resources Project, Harvard University, December 19, 2016, https://declaration.fas.harvard.edu/blog/facts -nationaltreasure.

19. Sneff, "Presenting the Facts: National Treasure," https://declaration.fas.harvard.edu /blog/facts-nationaltreasure; "National Treasure—Mr. Matlack," YouTube, https://www .youtube.com/watch?v=h4ey-CsLTBw.

20. "National Treasure," Rotten Tomatoes review, https://www.rottentomatoes.com/m /national_treasure; Zack Sharf, "Nicolas Cage Can't Say 'Steal the Declaration of Inde-pendence,' without Laughing: How Do You Sell Something 'So Profoundly Ridiculous'?," *Variety*, November 22, 2023, https://variety.com/2023/film/news/nicolas-cage-national -treasure-profoundly-ridiculous-1235805396/.

21. Thomas Jefferson to William Stephens Smith, November 13, 1787, FO, https: //founders.archives.gov/documents/Jefferson/01-12-02-0348. Smith was married to John Adams's daughter, Nabby, and was serving on Adams's diplomatic staff in London. For Smith's background, see "William Stephens Smith," Biographical Directory of the United States Congress, https://bioguide.congress.gov/search/bio/S000638.

22. Nolan Clay, "Jury View Slogan-Bearing Shirt, McVeigh's Other Clothes," *Okla-homan*, May 16, 1997, https://www.oklahoman.com/story/news/1997/05/16/jury-views -slogan-bearing-shirt-mcveighs-other-clothes/62314279007/; Jeffrey Toobin, *Home-grown: Timothy McVeigh and the Rise of Right-Wing Extremism* (New York: Simon & Schuster, 2023), 4.

23. Lovi Gyarke, "How the 1619 Project Came Together," *New York Times*, August 18, 2019, https://www.nytimes.com/2019/08/18/reader-center/1619-project-slavery -jamestown.html; Jake Silverstein, "The 1619 Project and the Long Battle over U.S. His-tory," *New York Times Magazine*, November 9, 2021, https://www.nytimes.com/2021/11 /09/magazine/1619-project-us-history.html; Carlos Lozada, "The 1619 Project Started as History. Now It's Also a Political Program," *Washington Post*, November 19, 2021, https://www.washingtonpost.com/outlook/2021/11/19/1619-project-book-history/; Jake Silverstein, "An Update to the 1619 Project," *New York Times*, March 11, 2020, https://www.nytimes.com/2020/03/11/magazine/an-update-to-the-1619-project.html.

24. "Establishing the President's Advisory 1776 Commission," White House news release, November 2, 2020, https://www.federalregister.gov/documents/2020/11/05 /2020-24793/establishing-the-presidents-advisory-1776-commission; "1776 Commis-sion Takes Historic and Scholarly Step in Restoring Understanding of the Greatness of the American Founding," Trump White House Archives, https://trumpwhitehouse .archives.gov/briefings-statements/1776-commission-takes-historic-scholarly-step -restore-understanding-greatness-american-founding/; Caroline Kelly, "Biden Rescinds

1776 Commission with Executive Order," CNN, January 21, 2021, https://www.cnn
.com/2021/01/20/politics/biden-rescind-1776-commission-executive-order/index.html.

25. Jonathan Martin and Alexander Burns, "Biden Wins Presidency, Ending
Four Tumultuous Years under Trump," *New York Times*, November 7, 2020, https://
www.nytimes.com/2020/11/07/us/politics/biden-election.html; "Remarks by President
Trump on the Election," NA, November 5, 2020, https://trumpwhitehouse.archives.gov/
briefings-statements/remarks-president-trump-election/.

26. Dan Barry and Sheera Frenkel, "'Be There. Will Be Wild!': Trump All but Circled
the Date," *New York Times*, January 6, 2021, https://www.nytimes.com/2021/01/06/us/
politics/capitol-mob-trump-supporters.html.

27. Alan Feuer, "Document in Jan. 6 Case Shows Plan to Storm Government Buildings," *New York Times*, March 14, 2022, https://www.nytimes.com/2022/03/14/us/
politics/enrique-tarrio-jan-6-document.html; Kyle Cheney, "Jan. 6 Committee Interview
Sheds Light on Origins of Proud Boys '1776 Returns' Document," *Politico*, December
27, 2022, https://www.politico.com/news/2022/12/27/jan-6-committee-interview-sheds
-light-on-origins-of-proud-boys-1776-returns-document-00075637; "1776 Returns,"
https://s3.documentcloud.org/documents/22060772/1776returns.pdf.

28. Michael Kunzelman, "Trial: Trump Tweet about 'Wild' Protest Energized Extremists," Associated Press, October 14, 2022, https://apnews.com/article/capitol-siege
-florida-donald-trump-conspiracy-congress-040a763522081e592af10fae682fda70.

29. "Read: Former President Donald Trump's January 6 Speech," CNN, February
8, 2021, https://www.cnn.com/2021/02/08/politics/trump-january-6-speech-transcript/
index.html; Maggie Haberman, "Trump Told Crowd 'You Will Never Take Back Our
Country with Weakness,'" *New York Times*, January 15, 2022, https://www.nytimes.com
/2021/01/06/us/politics/trump-speech-capitol.html.

30. "How a Pro-Trump Mob Besieged the Capitol," *Washington Post*, January 7, 2021,
https://www.cnn.com/interactive/2021/01/politics/us-capitol-siege/ (eight journalists
contributed to this story); Toobin, *Homegrown*, 2.

31. "Affairs of the Nation: Highly Important News from Washington; The Electoral
Vote Counted," February 14, 1861, *New York Times*, https://timesmachine.nytimes.com
/timesmachine/1861/02/14/78651365.pdf?pdf_redirect=true&ip=0; Ted Widmer, "The
Capitol Takeover That Wasn't," *New York Times*, January 8, 2021, https://www.nytimes
.com/2021/01/08/opinion/capitol-protest-1861-lincoln.html.

32. Erik Larson, *The Demon of Unrest* (New York: Crown, 2024), 240–41.

33. Representative Lauren Boebert (@Laurenboebert), "Today is 1776," Twitter,
January 6, 2021, 8:30 a.m., https://x.com/laurenboebert/status/13468113818788454
42?lang=en; "Sen. Hawley Criticized for Saluting Capitol Rioters with Fist Pump,"
KTVI St. Louis, January 27, 2021, https://www.abc27.com/news/sen-hawley-criticized
-for-saluting-capitol-protesters-with-fist-pump/; "Marjorie Taylor Greene Testifies at
Jan. 6 Candidacy hearing: 'Our 1776 Moment' Comment about 'Courage to Object.'"
AL.com, https://www.al.com/news/2022/04/marjorie-taylor-greene-testifies-at-jan-6
-candidacy-hearing-our-1776-moment-about-the-courage-to-object.html.

34. John Adams to Abigail Adams, April 26, 1777, Adams Family Papers, MHS, https:
//www.masshist.org/digitaladams/archive/doc?id=L17770426ja.

Selected Bibliography

Primary Sources
Books

Adams, John. *The Adams Papers*. Vols. 3–4. Edited by Robert J. Taylor. Cambridge, MA: Belknap, 1979.

———. *Diary and Autobiography of John Adams*. Vols. 1–4. Edited by L. H. Butterfield. Cambridge, MA: Belknap, 1961.

———. *The Works of John Adams*. Vols. 1–3. Reprint, North Charleston, SC: Createspace, 2015.

Adams, Samuel. *The Writings of Samuel Adams*. 4 vols. Edited by Harry Alonzo Cushing. New York: Putnam, 1904–1908.

Burnett, Edmund C., ed. *Letters of Members of the Continental Congress*. Washington, DC: Carnegie Institution of Washington, 1921. Reprint, London: Forgotten Books, 2018.

Cappon, Lester J., ed. *The Adams-Jefferson Letters: The Complete Correspondence between Thomas Jefferson & Abigail & John Adams*. Chapel Hill: University of North Carolina Press, 1959.

Daley, James, ed. *Great Speeches by Frederick Douglass*. Mineola, NY: Dover, 2013.

Dickinson, John. *Letters from a Farmer in Pennsylvania to the Inhabitants of the British Colonies*. 1768. Reprint, Middletown DE: Amazon Made-on-Demand, 2022.

Force, Peter, ed. *American Archives: A Documentary History of the English Colonies in North America*. 4th ser. Vol. 4. Printed by Act of Congress, 1833. Reprint, London: Forgotten Books, 2019.

Hakluyt, Richard. *The Principal Navigations, Voyages, Traffiques and Discoveries of the English Nation*. Vol. 8. 1904; written in the 16th century. Reprint, New York: Cambridge University Press, 2014.

Jefferson, Thomas. *The Autobiography of Thomas Jefferson, 1743–1790*. Edited by Paul Leicester Ford. 1914. Reprint, Philadelphia: University of Pennsylvania Press, 2005.

———. *The Papers of Thomas Jefferson, 1760–1776*. Vol. 1. Edited by Julian A. Boyd. Princeton, NJ: Princeton University Press, 1950.

Journals of the Continental Congress, 1774–1789. 34 vols. Edited from the original records in the Library of Congress. Washington, DC: Government Printing Office, 1906.

Lincoln, Abraham. *The Collected Works of Abraham Lincoln*. Vols. 6–7. Edited by Roy P. Basler. New Brunswick, NJ: Rutgers University Press, 1953.

Paine, Thomas. *Common Sense and Other Writings*. Edited by Gordon S. Wood. New York: Modern Library (Random House), 2003.

Smith, Paul H., ed. *Letters of Delegates to Congress, 1774–1789*. 26 vols. Washington, DC: Library of Congress, 1979.

Wood, Gordon S., ed. *The American Revolution: Writings from the Pamphlet Debate, 1764–1772 and 1773–1776*. New York: Library of America, 2015.

Digital Sources

Abraham Lincoln Online. https://www.abrahamlincolnonline.org/index.html.

The Avalon Project. "Documents in Law, History and Diplomacy." Yale Law School. https://avalon.law.yale.edu/.

Columbia University. *The Papers of John Jay*. https://dlc.library.columbia.edu/jay/.

The Constitutional Sources Project (ConSource). https://www.consource.org.

Documenting the American South. https://docsouth.unc.edu.

Force, Peter, ed. *American Archives: A Documentary History of the English Colonies in North America*. 4th ser. Vol. 6. Printed by Act of Congress, 1833. https://ia600202.us .archive.org/26/items/americanarchivea46forc/americanarchivea46forc.pdf; https: //archive.org/details/americanarchivea46forc/page/801/mode/2up.

Founders Online (National Archives). "Correspondence and Other Writings of Seven Major Shapers of the United States." https://founders.archives.gov/.

Gilder Lehrman Institute of American History. https://www.gilderlehrman.org/history -resources.

Liberty Fund Network. "Collected Political Writings." https://oll.libertyfund.org/people.

Library of Congress. www.loc.gov.

Library of Virginia. https://edu.lva.virginia.gov.

Massachusetts Historical Society. Adams Family Papers: An Electronic Archive. https:// www.masshist.org/digitaladams/archive/.

———. Collections. https://www.masshist.org/collections.

———. Digital Collections. https://www.masshist.org/digital-collections.

———. Thomas Jefferson Papers: An Electronic Archive. https://www.masshist.org/ thomasjeffersonpapers/.

National Archives. "The Declaration of Independence: A Transcription." July 4, 1776. https://www.archives.gov/founding-docs/declaration-transcript.

———. "Records of the Continental and Confederation Congresses and the Con- stitutional Convention." https://www.archives.gov/research/guide-fed-records /groups/360.html#:~:text=Table%20of%20Contents&text=Note%3A %20Congress%20gave%20the%20Department,Continental%20and%20 Confederation%20Congresses%2C%201789.

———. "The U.S. Constitution: A Transcription." https://www.archives.gov/founding -docs/constitution-transcript.

National Constitution Center. https://constitutioncenter.org/.

National Park Service. www.nps.gov.

———. "Declaration of Sentiments." https://www.nps.gov/wori/learn/historyculture/declaration-of-sentiments.htm.

New York Public Library. "Broadside of the Declaration of Independence." https://www.nypl.org/events/exhibitions/galleries/beginnings/item/3570.

Northern Illinois University Digital Library. https://digital.lib.niu.edu.

Pennsylvania Evening Post (vol. 2, no. 226), July 2, 1776. Seth Kellar Historic Documents and Legacy Collections. https://www.sethkaller.com/item/1000-The-First-Published-Announcement-of-Independence-(SOLD).

Essays and Periodicals

Hutchinson, Thomas. "Strictures upon the Declaration of the Congress at Philadelphia in a Letter to a Noble Lord, October 15, 1776." Teaching American History. https://teachingamericanhistory.org/document/strictures-upon-the-declaration-of-the-congress-at-philadelphia-in-a-letter-to-a-noble-lord-c/

Johnson, Samuel. "Taxation No Tyranny: An Answer to the Resolution of the American Congress. Samuel Johnson Sound Bite Page. https://www.samueljohnson.com/tnt.html.

Locke, John. *Second Treatise on Government*. Project Gutenberg e-book. https://www.gutenberg.org/files/7370/7370-h/7370-h.htm#CHAPTER_II

Newell, Timothy. "A Journal Kept during the Time Boston Was Shut Up in 1775–6." Massachusetts Historical Society. https://archive.org/details/s4collections01massuoft/page/n301/mode/2up?view=theater.

Paine, Thomas. "The American Crisis (No. 1)." Library of Congress. https://www.loc.gov/resource/rbpe.03902300/?st=text.

Stiles, Ezra. "The United States Elevated to Glory and Honor." May 8, 1783, 46. Digital Commons at the University of Nebraska–Lincoln. https://digitalcommons.unl.edu/cgi/viewcontent.cgi?article=1041&context=etas.

Secondary Sources
Books

Allen, Danielle. *Our Declaration: A Reading of the Declaration of Independence in Defense of Equality.* New York: Liveright, 2014.

Allison, Robert J. *The American Revolution: A Concise History.* New York: Oxford University Press, 2011.

Anderson, Fred. *Crucible of War: The Seven Years' War and the Fate of the Empire in British North America, 1754–1766.* New York: Vintage, 2001.

Appelbaum, Diana Karter. *The Glorious Fourth: An American Holiday, an American History.* New York: Facts on File, 1989.

Atkinson, Rick. *The British Are Coming: The War for America, Lexington to Princeton, 1775–1777.* New York: Holt, 2019.

Beck, Derek W. *Igniting the American Revolution 1773–1775.* Naperville, IL: Sourcebooks, 2015.

Becker, Carl Lotus. *The Declaration of Independence: A Study in the History of Political Ideas*. New York: Harcourt, Brace, 1922. Reprint, 2017.

Beeman, Richard. *Plain, Honest Men: The Making of the American Constitution*. New York: Random House, 2009.

Blight, David W. *Frederick Douglass: Prophet of Freedom*. New York: Simon & Schuster, 2018.

Boyd, Julian P. *The Declaration of Independence: The Evolution of the Text*. Rev. ed. Edited by Gerard W. Gawalt. Washington, DC: Library of Congress; Charlottesville, VA: Thomas Jefferson Memorial Foundation, 1999.

Bryant, Rick. *The Forever War: America's Unending Conflict with Itself*. London: Bloomsburg Continuum, 2024.

Chernow, Ron. *Washington: A Life*. New York: Penguin, 2010.

Dangerfield, George. *Chancellor Robert R. Livingston of New York, 1746–1813*. New York: Harcourt, Brace, 1960.

Di Spigna, Christian. *Founding Martyr: The Life and Death of Dr. Joseph Warren, the American Revolution's Lost Hero*. New York: Crown, 2018.

Donald, David Herbert. *Lincoln*. New York: Simon & Schuster, 1995.

Dupont, Christian Y., and Peter S. Onuf, eds. *Declaring Independence: The Origin and Influence of America's Founding Document*. Charlottesville: University of Virginia, 2008.

Ellis, Joseph J. *American Creation*. New York: Vintage, 2005.

———. *First Family: Abigail and John Adams*. New York: Vintage, 2011.

———. *Revolutionary Summer: The Birth of American Independence*. New York: Vintage, 2012.

———. *Writing the Declaration of Independence*. New York: Vintage, 2015. E-book.

Ferling, John. *Adams and Jefferson: The Tumultuous Election of 1800*. New York: Oxford University Press, 2004.

Friedenwald, Herbert. *The Declaration of Independence: An Interpretation and an Analysis*. New York: Macmillan, 1904.

Gerber, Scott Douglas, ed. *The Declaration of Independence: Origins and Impact*. Washington, DC: CW Press, 2002.

Greenwalt, Phillip S., and Robert Orrison. *A Single Blow: The Battles of Lexington and Concord and the Beginning of the American Revolution, April 19, 1775*. El Dorado Hills, CA: Savas Beatie, 2018.

Hazelton, John Hampden. *The Declaration of Independence: Its History*. Cambridge, MA: University Press, 1906.

Hogeland, William. *Declaration: The Nine Tumultuous Weeks When America Became Independent, May 1–July 4, 1776*. New York: Simon & Schuster Paperbacks, 2010.

Horn, James. *A Kingdom Strange: The Brief and Tragic History of the Lost Colony of Roanoke*. New York: Basic, 2010.

Isaacson, Walter. *Benjamin Franklin: An American Life*. New York: Simon & Schuster Paperbacks, 2003.

Jensen, Merrill. *The Founding of a Nation: A History of the American Revolution 1763–1776*. Indianapolis, IN: Hackett, 2004.

Kaplan, Fred. *His Masterly Pen: A Biography of Jefferson the Writer.* New York: Harper-Collins, 2022.

Kupperman, Karen Ordahl. *Roanoke: The Abandoned Colony.* Lanham, MD: Rowman & Littlefield, 2007.

Langguth, A. J. *Patriots: The Men Who Started the American Revolution.* New York: Simon & Schuster, 1988.

Larson, Erik. *The Demon of Unrest.* New York: Crown, 2024.

Lee, Richard H. (grandson). *Memoir of the Life of Richard Henry Lee, and His Correspondence with the Most Distinguished Men in America and Europe.* Vols. 1–2. N.p.: William Brown, 1825. Reprint, London: Forgotten Books, 2018.

Magnet, Myron. *The Founders at Home: The Building of America, 1735–1817.* New York: Norton, 2014.

Maier, Pauline. *American Scripture: Making the Declaration of Independence.* New York: Vintage, 1998.

———. *From Resistance to Revolution: Colonial Radicals and the Development of American Opposition to Britain, 1765–1776.* New York: Norton, 1872.

McCullough, David. *John Adams.* New York: Simon & Schuster Paperbacks, 2001.

———. *1776.* New York: Simon & Schuster Paperbacks, 2005.

Meacham, Jon. *And There Was Light: Abraham Lincoln and the American Struggle.* New York: Random House, 2022.

———. *Thomas Jefferson: The Art of Power.* New York: Random House Trade Paperbacks, 2012.

Middlekauff, Robert. *The Glorious Cause: The American Revolution, 1763–1789.* New York: Oxford University Press, 2005.

Middleton, Richard, and Anne Lombard. *Colonial America: A History to 1763.* Malden, MA: Wiley-Blackwell, 2011.

Parkinson, Robert G. *Common Cause: Creating Race and Nation in the American Revolution.* Chapel Hill: University of North Carolina Press, 2016.

Philbrick, Nathaniel. *Bunker Hill: A City, a Siege, a Revolution.* New York: Penguin, 2013.

Rakove, Jack N. *The Beginnings of National Politics: An Interpretive History of the Continental Congress.* Baltimore, MD: Johns Hopkins University Press, 1979.

———. *Revolutionaries: A New History of the Invention of America.* New York: First Mariner, 2011.

Roberts, Andrew. *The Last King of America: The Misunderstood Reign of George III.* New York: Viking, 2021.

Ramsay, David. *The History of the American Revolution.* 1789. Reprint, Bedford, MA: Applewood, 2009.

Schiff, Stacy. *The Revolutionary: Samuel Adams.* New York: Little, Brown, 2022.

Stahr, Walter. *John Jay.* London and New York: Hambledon, 2005.

Taylor, Alan. *American Colonies: The Settling of North America.* New York: Penguin, 2001.

Toobin, Jeffrey. *Homegrown: Timothy McVeigh and the Rise of Right-Wing Extremism.* New York: Simon & Schuster, 2023.

Various Authors. *A Selection of Eulogies Pronounced in the Several States, in Honor of Those Illustrious Patriots and Statesmen, John Adams and Thomas Jefferson.* Hartford, CT: Robinson and Norton & Russell, 1826.

Will, Garry. *Lincoln at Gettysburg: The Words That Remade America.* New York: Simon & Schuster, 1992.

Wills, Garry. *Inventing America: Jefferson's Declaration of Independence.* New York: Vintage, 1978.

Wright, Louis B. *The Thirteen Colonies.* Rockville, MD: American Heritage, 2016.

Wood, Gordon S. *The American Revolution: A History.* New York: Modern Library, 2002.

———. *Friends Divided: John Adams and Thomas Jefferson.* New York: Penguin, 2018.

Digital Sources

American Battlefield Trust. "Brooklyn Battle Facts and Summary." https://www.battlefields.org/learn/revolutionary-war/battles/brooklyn.

———. "Trenton Battle Facts and Summary." https://www.battlefields.org/learn/revolutionary-war/battles/trenton.

American Presidency Project. "Election Listing." C-Span. https://www.c-span.org/presidentsurvey2021/?page=overall.

British Newspaper Archive. "British Reactions to America's Declaration of Independence." July 4, 2017. https://blog.britishnewspaperarchive.co.uk/2017/07/04/british-reaction-to-americas-declaration-of-independence/#:~:text=For%20the%20most%20part%2C%20the,rebels%20and%20supported%20their%20independence.

Covart, Liz. *Ben Franklin's World.* Podcast, episode 141, July 4, 2017. https://benfranklinsworld.com/episode-141-declaration-draft/.

C-Span. "Presidential Historians Survey 2021." https://www.c-span.org/presidentsurvey2021/?page=overall

Declaration Resources Project. Harvard University. https://declaration.fas.harvard.edu/.

Journal of the American Revolution. https://allthingsliberty.com/.

Library of Congress Exhibitions. "Declaring Independence: Drafting the Documents Timeline." https://www.loc.gov/exhibits/declara/declara4.html.

National Park Service. "April 19, 1775: Overview of Battle." https://www.nps.gov/mima/learn/historyculture/april-19-1775.htm.

National Portrait Gallery. "Signing of the Treaty of Paris." https://npg.si.edu/object/npg_1957.0856.

RR Auction. "First Foreign Printing of the Declaration of Independence." https://www.rrauction.com/auctions/lot-detail/343389905923011-first-foreign-printing-of-the-declaration-of-independence.

Sotheby's. "The First Printing of the Declaration of Independence in Britain." https://www.sothebys.com/en/buy/auction/2021/constitutions-and-related-documents-from-the-collection-of-dorothy-tapper-goldman-part-1/declaration-of-independence-the-first-printing-of.

Thomas Jefferson, Monticello. www.monticello.org.

Triverton Historical Society. http://www.trivertonhistorical.org.

U.S. Department of State. "Pennsylvania State House (Independence Hall)." https://history.state.gov/departmenthistory/buildings/section3#:~: text=The%20Second%20Continental%20Congress%20convened ,Declaration%20of%20Independence%20was%20signed.

———. "The Period of the Continental Congress, September 1774–October 1781." https://history.state.gov/departmenthistory/buildings/section1.

———. "Treaty of Paris 1783." https://2001-2009.state.gov/r/pa/ho/time/ar/14313.htm.

Washington Papers. "The Electoral Count for the Presidential Elections of 1789." University of Virginia. https://washingtonpapers.org/resources/articles/the-electoral -count-for-the-presidential-election-of-1789/.

Essays and Periodicals

American Battlefield Trust. "The Founding Fathers' View of Slavery." https://www .battlefields.org/learn/articles/founding-fathers-views-slavery.

Architect of the Capitol. "Declaration of Independence." https://www.aoc.gov/explore -capitol-campus/art/declaration-independence.

Baumann, Roland M. "The Pennsylvania Revolution." US History. https://www.ushistory .org/pennsylvania/birth2.html.

Beeman, Richard R. "The Constitutional Convention of 1787: A Revolution in Government." National Constitution Center. https://constitutioncenter.org/the -constitution/white-papers/the-constitutional-convention-of-1787-a-revolution -in-government.

Blatt, Ben. "Was John Hancock's Signature Too Big?" *Slate*, August 5, 2014. https: //www.slate.com/articles/news_and_politics/history/2014/08/john_hancock_s _declaration_of_independence_signature_was_it_too_big.html.

Butler, Lindley S. "Provincial Congresses." *NC*pedia. https://www.ncpedia.org/ provincial-congresses#:~:text=In%20the%20process%2C%20these%20Provincial ,constitution%20that%20established%20the%20state.

Coelho, Chris. "The First Reading of the Declaration of Independence, July 4, 1776." *Journal of the American Revolution*, July 1, 2021. https://allthingsliberty.com/2021 /07/the-first-public-reading-of-the-declaration-of-independence-july-4-1776/.

———. "Timothy Matlack: Scribe of the Declaration of Independence." *Journal of the American Revolution*, August 24, 2021. https://allthingsliberty.com/2021/08/ timothy-matlack-scribe-of-the-declaration-of-independence/.

Conner, Jeff. "The American Crisis before Crossing the Delaware." *Journal of the American Revolution*, February 25, 2015. https://allthingsliberty.com/2015/02/american -crisis-before-crossing-the-delaware/.

Crown, Daniel. "The German-Language Newspaper That Got the Scoop on American Independence." *Atlas* Obscura, July 3, 2019. https://www.atlasobscura.com/articles /german-language-newspaper-declaration-independence-day-signing.

Declaration Resources Project. "Declaration Database: 1776 Periodicals." Harvard University. https://declaration.fas.harvard.edu/sites/projects.iq.harvard.edu/files/ declaration/files/declaration_database_august_2018_2023_update.pdf.

———. "Which Version Is This, and Why Does It Matter?" Harvard University. https:// declaration.fas.harvard.edu/resources/which-version-and-why.

De Peyster, Frederic. "A Biographical Sketch of Robert R. Livingston: Read Before the N.Y. Historical Society, October 3, 1876." London: Forgotten Books, 2012.

Desbler, Charles B. "How the Declaration Was Received in the Old Thirteen." *Harper's New Monthly Magazine* 75 (July 1892): 186–87.

Detweiler, Philip F. "The Changing Reputation of the Declaration of Independence: The First Fifty Years." *William and Mary Quarterly* 19, no. 4 (October 1962).

Fetter, Frank Whitson. "The Revision of the Declaration of Independence in 1941." *William and Mary Quarterly* 31, no. 1 (January 1974).

Fornieri, Joseph R. "Speech on the Repeal of the Missouri Compromise at Peoria." Teaching American History. https://teachingamericanhistory.org/resource/the -lincoln-exhibit/speech-on-the-repeal-of-the-missouri-compromise-at-peoria/.

Gawalt, Gerard W. "Jefferson and the Declaration: Updated Work Studies Evolution of Historic Text." Library of Congress, July 1999. https://www.loc.gov/loc/lcib/9907 /jeffdec.html.

Hancock, Michael. "John Hancock and His Signature." National Archives, September 12, 2019. Posted by Jessie Kratz. https://prologue.blogs.archives.gov/2019/09/12/john -hancock-and-his-signature/.

Huang, Megan. "Dunlap's Declaration of Independence." National Archives. https:// prologue.blogs.archives.gov/2018/07/03/dunlaps-declaration-of-independence/.

Italie, Hillel. "Frederick Douglass' July 4 Speeches Trace American History." Associated Press, July 1, 2018. https://apnews.com/article/393ae428732c4cc8905f3e3af011 28d7.

Kaminski, John P. "Preserving the Alliance: The Artful Diplomacy of Benjamin Franklin." Center for the Study of the American Constitution, University of Wisconsin–Madison. https://csac.history.wisc.edu/wp-content/uploads/sites/281/2018/03 /Kaminski-benjaminFranklin.pdf.

Karsch, Carl G. "Pennsylvania: From Colony to State." Carpenters' Hall. https://www .carpentershall.org/pennsylvania-from-colony-to-state.

Keller, Jared. "How the Declaration of Independence Went Viral." *Pacific Standard*, June 28, 2016. https://psmag.com/news/how-the-declaration-of-independence-went -viral.

Kollenberg, Bernhard. "John Dickinson vs. John Adams, 1774–1776." *Proceedings of the American Philosophical Society* 107, no. 2 (April 15, 1963).

Lind, John. "An Answer to the Declaration of the American Congress." HathiTrust. https://babel.hathitrust.org/cgi/pt?id=aeu.ark:/13960/t2f76xt2z&seq=8.

Maier, Pauline. "Who Really Wrote the Declaration." In *Declaring Independence: The Origin and Influence of America's Founding Document*, edited by Christian Y. Dupont and Peter S. Onuf. Charlottesville: University of Virginia Library, 2008.

Mass Moments. "Abigail Adams Knows." https://www.massmoments.org/moment -details/abigail-adams-knows.html.

McCurry, Allan J. "Joseph Hewes and Independence: A Suggestion." *North Carolina Historical Review* 40, no. 4 (October 1963). https://www.jstor.org/stable/23517596 ?read-now=1&seq=8#page_scan_tab_contents.

Mostyn, Samuel. "Loyalists and the British Evacuation of Philadelphia, 1778." Gilder Lehrman Institute of American History. https://www.gilderlehrman.org/history -resources/spotlight-primary-source/loyalists-and-british-evacuation-philadelphia -1778.

National Constitution Center. "Top Myths about the Constitution on Constitution Day." September 17, 2023, https://constitutioncenter .org/blog/top-10-myths-about-the-constitution-on-constitution -day#:~:text=Only%20six%20Founders%20signed%20both ,James%20Wilson%2C%20and%20Roger%20Sherman.

National Park Service. "The Declaration of Independence—Stone Facsimile." Independence National Historical Park. https://www.nps.gov/articles/stone.htm.

Nicholson, Catherine. "The Stone Engraving: Icon of the Declaration." *Prologue Magazine* 35, no. 3. https://www.archives.gov/publications/prologue/2003/fall/stone -engraving.html.

Onuf, Peter. "Thomas Jefferson: Campaigns and Elections." Miller Center, University of Virginia. https://millercenter.org/president/jefferson/campaigns-and-elections.

Parkinson, Robert G. "Twenty-Seven Reasons for Independence." In *Declaring Independence: The Origin and Influence of America's Founding Document*, edited by Christian Y. Dupont and Peter S. Onuf. Charlottesville: University of Virginia, 2008.

Peckham, Howard H. "Independence: The View from Britain." *Proceedings of the American Antiquarian Society* 8, pt. 2 (October 1875). https://www.americanantiquarian.org/ proceedings/44498108.pdf.

Procknow, Gene. "Franklin's Failed Diplomatic Mission." *Journal of the American Revolution*, January 27, 2015. https://allthingsliberty.com/2015/01/franklins-failed -diplomatic-mission/#_edn5.

Ritz, Wilfred J. "From the Here of Jefferson's Handwritten Rough Draft of the Declaration of Independence to the There of the Printed Dunlap Broadside." *Pennsylvania Magazine of History and Biography* 116, no. 4 (October 1992).

Ritzenthaler, Mary Lynn, and Catherine Nicholas. "The Declaration of Independence and the Hand of Time." *Prologue Magazine* 48, no. 3 (Fall 2016). https://www .archives.gov/publications/prologue/2016/fall/declaration.

Rosen, Jeffery, and David Rubenstein. "The Declaration, the Constitution and the Bill of Rights." National Constitution Center. https://constitutioncenter.org/ the-constitution/white-papers/the-declaration-the-constitution-and-the-bill-of -rights.

Sharf, Zach. "Nicolas Cage Can't Say 'Steal the Declaration of Independence,' without Laughing: How Do You Sell Something 'So Profoundly Ridiculous'?" *Variety*, November 22, 2023. https://variety.com/2023/film/news/nicolas-cage-national -treasure-profoundly-ridiculous-1235805396/.

Shashkevich, Alex. "It Took over a Decade for the Declaration of Independence to Matter in American Life, Stanford Historian Says." *Stanford News*, July 2, 2019. https://news.stanford.edu/stories/2019/07/americans-forgot-declaration-independence.

Shaw, Travis. "Summer Soldiers and Sunshine Patriots." American Battlefield Trust. https://www.battlefields.org/learn/articles/summer-soldiers-and-sunshine-patriots-american-crisis.

Sneff, Emily. "December Highlight: Dunlap." Declaration Resources Project, Harvard University, December 4, 2017. https://declaration.fas.harvard.edu/blog/december-dunlap.

———. "July Highlight: George Rejected and Liberty Protected." Declaration Resources Project, Harvard University, July 4, 2016. https://declaration.fas.harvard.edu/blog/july-proclamations.

———. "March Highlight: Mary Katherine Goddard." Declaration Resources Project, Harvard University, March 4, 2016. https://declaration.fas.harvard.edu/blog/march-goddard.

———. "Presenting the Facts: National Treasure." Declaration Resources Project, Harvard University, December 19, 2016. https://declaration.fas.harvard.edu/blog/facts-nationaltreasure.

———. "Presenting the Facts: 1776." Declaration Resources Project, Harvard University, March 28, 2017. https://declaration.fas.harvard.edu/blog/facts-1776.

———. "September Highlight: Extravagant and Inadmissible Claim of Independency." Declaration Resources Project, Harvard University, September 4, 2016. https://declaration.fas.harvard.edu/blog/september-kings-speech.

———. "Unsullied by Falsehood: The Signing." Declaration Resources Project, Harvard University, July 27, 2016. https://declaration.fas.harvard.edu/blog/signing.

Stern, Jeremy. "What's Wrong with HBO's Dramatization of John Adams's Story." History News Network. https://www.historynewsnetwork.org/article/whats-wrong-with-hbos-dramatization-of-john-adamss.

Taylor, C. James. "John Adams: Campaigns and Elections." Miller Center, University of Virginia. https://millercenter.org/president/adams/campaigns-and-elections.

Trickey, Erick. "Mary Katharine Goddard: The Woman Whose Name Appears on the Declaration of Independence." *Smithsonian Magazine*, November 14, 2018. https://www.smithsonianmag.com/history/mary-katharine-goddard-woman-whose-name-appears-declaration-independence-180970816/.

Uva, Katie. "Parson Weems." Mount Vernon. https://www.mountvernon.org/library/digitalhistory/digital-encyclopedia/article/parson-weems/.

Warren, Charles. "Fourth of July Myths." *William and Mary Quarterly* 2, no. 3 (July 1945).

Waxman, Olivia B. "This Painting Is How You Probably Imagine the Original Fourth of July: Here's What's Wrong with It." *Time*, July 3, 2018. https://time.com/5323460/declaration-of-independence-john-trumbull/.

———. "'What to the Slave Is the Fourth of July?': The History of Frederick Douglass' Searing Independence Day Oration." *Time*, July 3, 2019. https://time.com/5614930/frederick-douglass-fourth-of-july/.

Yates, Steve. "About the Playwright: *1776*." Utah Shakespeare Festival. https://www.bard
.org/study-guides/about-the-playwright-1776/.

Newspapers, Periodicals, and News Services
Associated Press
Boston-Gazette and Country News
Dunlap and Claypoole's American Daily Advertiser
Dunlap's Maryland Gazette
Kentish Gazette
Massachusetts Spy
New Hampshire Gazette
New York Journal
New York Times
North Star
Pennsylvania Evening Post
Pennsylvania Gazette
Scots Magazine
Time
Washington Post

INDEX

Act for the Impartial Administration of Justice, 42

Adams, Charles Francis, 281

Adams, John, 106–7; Adams-Lee proposal preamble by, 109–10; autobiography of, 302n10; Board of War and Ordnance assignment of, 130; Boston Massacre and, 35–36, 305n27; on Boston Tea Party, 38, 41; Bulloch correspondence with, 7; closing arguments of, 8, 10, 12; on *Common Sense*, 89, 91, 103; on consent, 140; Cushing, W., correspondence with, 126; death of, 20, 251; debate correspondence of, 334n42; on Declaration of Independence, 134–35; Declaration of Independence case by, 155–56; on Declaration of Independence timing, 132; on "Declaration of the Causes and Necessity of Taking Up Arms," 70; delegate descriptions, 314n21; diary timeline of, 322n29; on Dickinson, 47, 154–55; Dickinson and, relationship between, 71–73; on Duane, 47; Ellis on, 105; on facts, 36; Federalists on, 235; on First Continental Congress, 47–48, 51–52; on freedom, 1; on King George III, 109–10; Hooper correspondence with, 103–5; independence motion seconded by, 121; on independence proposal, 127; on independent statehood, 13–14; January 1776 activities of, 93–94; Jefferson compared with, 8; Jefferson on memory of, 302n10; Jefferson's feud with, 237–44; Jefferson's pre-inaugural correspondence with, 239–40; July 4th and, 19–20, 161, 221–22, 340n14; Lee, R. H., correspondence with, 104, 119; on Lee, R. H., 47; legislature plan of, 105; "Letter from a Gentleman to His Friend," 105–7; on Lynch, 47; Madison on, 240; McCullough on, 10; "Memorandum of Measures to be Pursued in Congress," 96; as monarchist, 241; on New York City, 46; on Olive Branch Petition, 70; on Otis, 28; on Paine, T., 89, 91, 103; peace delegations and, 225–26; Penn, J., correspondence with, 103–5; phrase experimentations of, 10, 12; "Plan of Treaties," 180; portrait of, *11*; "Preamble to Resolution on Independent Governments," 301n5; presidential achievements of, 240–41; presidential appointment of, 239; private letters of, 302n10; "Proclamation of the General Court," 94–96; on Prohibitory Act, 97; on Randolph, P., 47; reliability of, 327n11; on revolutionary foundations, 96; on Rodney, 47; Rush on, 242; on separation of powers, 84, 95; on slavery, 334n36; on Thomson, 47; *Thoughts on Government*,

Applicable to the Present State of the American Colonies, 84, 94, 104–7; on three-branch government model, 84; treason and, 342n9; on treaty of commerce, 180; on turning point with England, 304n3; on Washington, 93; Washington nominated to lead Continental Army by, 66–67; Wythe correspondence with, 104
Adams, John Quincy, 246
Adams, Nabby, 307n43
Adams, Samuel: on Adams-Lee proposal, 111; background work of, 47; in *Boston-Gazette and Country Journal*, 32; Boston Massacre and, 35; Boston Port Act and, 42–43; on committee of correspondence, 36–37; Hutchinson meeting with, 35; Lee, R. H., relationship with, 37; propaganda of, 32; pseudonyms of, 32–33, 311n43; responding to King George III, 87–88; Schiff on, 32, 47; Seider funeral procession organized by, 33–34; at Stamp Act Congress, 29; on Townshend Revenue Acts, 31; "Vindex" pseudonym of, 32–33
Adams-Lee proposal, 108, 114; Adams, J., preamble to, 109–10; Adams, S., on, 111; Braxton on, 111; debate over, 110–13; Dickinson, John on, 109–10; Duane on, 110; Hopkins on, 112; McKean on, 110–11; Rodney on, 112; vote on, 111; Wilson on, 111; Wolcott on, 112
Alien and Sedition Acts, 240–41
Allen, Danielle: on Declaration of Independence, 96; on "Proclamation of the General Court," 94–96
Allen, Ethan, 317n23
Allen, James, 301n5
"The American Crisis" (Paine, T.), 215
American Gazette, 187
American Philosophical Society Library, 133

American Seal, 193; approval of, 338n43
Answer to the Declaration of the American Congress (Lind), 199
Antietam, Battle of, 257, 263
antiseparation, 93
"Arguments in Congress in Favour of a Reconciliation & sending over persons to lay the Colonies at the Feet of his Majesty and pray(ing) for Peace" (Dickinson), 70–71
Arnold, Benedict: Canada invasion by, 98; Fort Ticonderoga taken by, 317n23; wounding of, 86
Articles of Confederation and Perpetual Union, 178; approval of, 179; debate over, 179, 337n28; Dickinson draft, 179; flaws in, 227–28; narratives of, 179; ratification of, 179; revision committee, 229; slavery debate and, 337n28; submission of, 179
Aslop, John, 177
Assembly Room, Pennsylvania State House (Independence Hall), 64, *159*, 230; Lincoln at, 262–63

Barrett, James, 61
Bartlett, Josiah: debate correspondence of, 334n42; on Declaration of Independence, 154
Bell, Robert, 88
Bernard, Francis, 31–32
Biddle, Charles, 174
Biden, Joe, 280
Bill of Rights, U.S. Constitution, 231
"The Bloody Massacre perpetuated in King Street, Boston" (Revere), 35
Boebert, Lauren, 282
Boston-Gazette and Country Journal: Adams, S., in, 32; on Boston Tea Party, 38; on Seider, 33
Boston Massacre, 7; Adams, J., and, 35–36, 305n27; Adams, S., and, 35; conflicting accounts of, 34; engravings of, 35; Franklin, B., and, 35; Hancock

and, 35; Hutchinson and, 34; mob at, 34; Preston and, 34–36; Revere and, 35
Boston Port Act, 41; Adams, S., and, 42–43; East India Company and, 42
Boston Tea Party, 7; Adams, J., and, 38, 41; *Boston-Gazette and Country Journal* on, 38; King George III and, 39; naming of, 312n52; reactions to, 38–39, 41
Bowdoin, James, 314n18
Boyd, Julian P., 147, 273, 275; on Declaration of Independence, 148
Brandywine Creek, Battle of, 222
Braxton, Carter: on Adams-Lee proposal, 111; on alignment of colonies, 301n5; on "Preamble to Resolution on Independent Governments," 301n5; on *Thoughts on Government, Applicable to the Present State of the American Colonies*, 106–7
Brunswick (Duke), 115
Bulloch, Archibald, 7
Bunker Hill, Battle of, 67; casualties, 68, 76
Burr, Aaron, 241

Cape Fear, 323n1
capitalization, eighteenth-century-style, 305n15
Capitol, U.S., riots at, 1, 279–82; reactions to, 278
Carroll, Charles: Canada mission of, 98–99; signing and, 195
Chase, Samuel: Canada mission of, 98–99; holdout colonies and, 150; on signing, 193
Clark, Abraham, 170
Clarke, Jonas, 58–59
Clinton, Henry, 201–2
Clymer, George, 195
Coercive Acts, 7, 41, 144–45, 313n4; addressing, 43; Jefferson on, 44; Ramsay on, 42. *See also Specific* Acts
Coles, Edward, 242–43
colonial charters, 27

commerce, treaty of, 180
"Committee of Congress to the Lancaster Associators," 335n43
Committee of Detail, 231
Committee of Five, 130; Lee, R. H., omitted from, 129; Livingston in, 129; members of, 128–29
Committee of Prisoners, 128
Committee of Safety, 172
Committee of Secret Correspondence: Deane representing, 97–98; Declaration of Independence sent to France by, 175; Franklin, B., instructions for, 322n32; members of, 322n32; purpose of, 322n32
Committee of Style and Substance, 231
Committee of the Whole, 108, 123, 127; reasons for forming, 317n24
Common Sense (Paine, T.): Adams, J., on, 89, 91, 103; appendix to, 321n13; impact of, 320n4; publication of, 4, 7–8, 88–89, *90*; as rally cry, 88; sales of, 91
Confederacy: defeat of, 263, 265; Fort Sumter attacked by, 263; surrender of, 265
Connecticut Compromise, 231
consent of the governed, 4, 95, 140, 227, 254; in Declaration of Independence, 271–72
Constitution, U.S.: Committee of Detail, 231; Committee of Style and Substance, 231; Declaration of Independence against, 232–36; final draft of, 231–32; Morris, G., and, 231–32; preamble, 231–32; preparation of, 231; Twelfth Amendment, 349n17
Constitutional Convention, 229, 231–32; first official act of, 230
Continental Army: enlistment form, 66; first appearance of term, 66; Washington accepting leadership of, 67; Washington drafting regulations

for, 66; Washington nominated to lead, 66–67

Continental Congress: records of, 307n42. *See also* First Continental Congress; *Journals of the Continental Congress*; Second Continental Congress

"Convention of the Representatives of the State of New York" (Jay), 176; Aslop on, 177; authorizations in, 337n19

"Convention of the State of North Carolina" (Hancock), 344n36

Coolidge's Inn, 46

Cornwallis, Charles, 201–2; in New Brunswick, 213–14; surrender of, 224

correspondence, committee of: Adams, S., on, 36–37; Jefferson appointed to, 37; Lee, R. H, on, 37; Virginia establishing, 37–38

Crisis, 197–98

Croatoan tribe, 26

Cushing, Caleb, 251

Cushing, Thomas, 37–38

Cushing, William, 126

Dartmouth, 38

Dartmouth (Lord), 75

Dawes, William, 58–59

Deane, Silas: on Agreement of Secrecy, 314n22; Committee of Secret Correspondence and, 97–98; cover for, 98; on First Continental Congress, 46, 63; France trip of, 97–99; on Gage, 49

Declaration of Common Aims, 268

Declaration of Independence, U.S.: Adams, J., arguing case for, 155–56; Adams, J., on, 134–35; Adams, J., on timing of, 132; Allen, D., on, 96; *American Gazette* publishing, 187; approval of, 3; authenticated copy of, 196, 219; authorship questions, 233; Bartlett on, 154; Boyd on, 148; changes made during congressional sessions to, 303n12; Clark introduction letter to, 170; Constitution against,

232–36; "Creator" change in, 331n33; *Crisis on*, 197–98; Declaration of Rights and, 141; declaratory conclusion of, 146–47; Dickinson's notes in *Journals of the Continental Congress*, 155; distributing to public, 170, 187; Douglass on, 255–57; draft committee, 14; Dunlap broadsides, 169, *171*, 217, 335n2; *Dunlap's and Claypool's American Daily Advertiser* announcing, 173; Easton ceremony, 174; editing of, 14, 18–19, 139–40, 142–43, 163–67, 303n12, 331n33; Ellis on, 135, 166; fairly engrossed on parchment, 183–84; festive events around, 19; final meeting before vote on, 151; final section of, 146; final version of, 293–97; first formal public reading, 173–74; first publishing of, 14; formal vote on, 2; Franklin, B., and, 133–34, 147–48; Franklin, B., informing France of, 175; Friedenwald on, 191; Gawalt on, 148; *Gentleman's Magazine* on, 197; King George III and, 198, 212; Gerry introduction letter to, 170–71; Gienapp on, 224; Goddard broadside, *218*, 219–20; Goddard printing, 219–20; Hall and, 253; Hancock introduction letter to, 170, 172; Hewes on, 154; holdouts on, 154; Howe, W., on, 196; Hutchinson on, 199–200; influence of, 267–69; introduction edits, 139; Isaacson on, 142; Jay's formal resolution on, 176–77, 337n19; Jefferson comparing versions of, 174–75; Jefferson Memorial language differences with, 307n39; Jefferson's "original Rough draught" of, 14, 134–35, 137–52, 287–92; *Kentish* Gazette on, 197; language differences between versions, 307n39; legality of, 303n13; Library of Congress textual analysis of, 273, 275; Lincoln on, 258, 260–63, 266; Lind on, 199; list of charges in, 143–45,

189; *London Chronicle* publishing, 196; MacLeish and, 275; Maier on, 133, 221, 306n31; as marketing, 4; Matlack and, 184–85, 191, *192*; Morris, R., informing France of, 175; narratives of, 133, 142, 174, 340n14; Nixon reading, 173; Onuf on, 141; original title of, 183–84; Parkinson on, 143; passing of, 158–59; pause notes, 335n2; Penn, J., on, 153–54; *Pennsylvania Evening Post* on, 160, 173; *Pennsylvania Gazette* on, 160; *Pennsylvanischer* Staatsbote announcing, 172–73; preamble edits, 139–40, 142–43; preliminary vote on, 2; presentation of, 151; printing of, 167, 169, *171*, 217, 219–20, 335n2; "Proclamation of the General Court" and, 95; public readings of, 173–74, 177, 187–90, *188*; resources for, 334n31; revival of, 232–36; Rodney on, 167; *Scots Magazine* on, 197; self-evident wording in, 141–42, 149, 329n38; sent to France by Committee of Secret Correspondence, 175; signing of, 5, 14–15, 169–70, 183, 185, 191–96, *192*, 220, 245, 340n14; slavery and, 145, 164–65; *South-Carolina and American General Advertiser* publishing, 187; *St. James's Chronicle* publishing, 196–97; State House Yard reading of, 14; Stone copying, 246–47; thematic organization of, 143–47; timeline, 132, 305n26; time to complete, 137–38; tone of, 139; tour of, 344n37; as treason, 198; updated title of, 219; *Virginia Gazette* publishing, 190; Washington reading, 177; word count of, 306n33

The Declaration of Independence (Boyd), 273, 275

Declaration of Independence (Trumball), 244, *247*; Adams, J. Q., on, 246; idea for, 245; public display of, 245–46

Declaration of Rights (Mason), 138; Declaration of Independence and,

141; introduction to, 141; Stamp Act Congress passing, 29–30

Declaration of Sentiments (Stanton), 253–54

"Declaration of the Causes and Necessity of Taking Up Arms" (Dickinson), 10; Adams, J., on, 70; committee for, 69; draft of, 69–72; grievances in, 70; Jefferson draft of, 69–70, 138; Maier on, 69; purpose of, 70; racial insecurities and, 71; voting on, 72

Declaratory Act, 144–45; Lee, R. H., and, 30, 121; wording of, 30

Definitive Treaty of Paris, 28–29, *228*; Article 1st, 227; ratification of, 346n22; signing, 226–27

Delaware independent vote, 333n19

Department of State records, 307n42

Dickinson, John, 9; Adams, J., and, relationship between, 71–73; Adams, J., on, 47, 154–55; on Adams-Lee proposal, 109–10; "Arguments in Congress in Favour of a Reconciliation & sending over persons to lay the Colonies at the Feet of his Majesty and pray(ing) for Peace," 70–71; Articles of Confederation and Perpetual Union draft, 179; background of, 10; closing arguments of, 10; confederation plan of, 337n26; counters from, 79; credit for independence, 233; Declaration of Independence notes in *Journals of the Continental Congress*, 155; "Declaration of the Causes and Necessity of Taking Up Arms," 10, 69–72, 138; example of, 4–5; on First Continental Congress, 54; on governmental defects, 228–29; independence opposed by, 93, 124–26, 154–55, 157; legacy of, 69; "Letters from a Farmer in Pennsylvania to the Inhabitants of the British Colonies," 31; loyalty to King George III, 71; "Olive Branch Petition," 4, 7, 10, 70,

73, 76–77, 79, 342n2; pacific system and, 71–72; portrait of, *156*; on preparing for war, 65; racial insecurities and, 71; reputation of, 318n39; signing and, 194; at Stamp Act Congress, 29; Townshend Revenue Act and, 31; Wilson backed by, 87

Dorchester Heights: cannons at, 99–100; Howe, W., attacking, 100; Newell on, 100

Douglas, Stephen A., 259

Douglass, Frederick, 253; on Declaration of Independence, 255–57; on July 4th, 255–56; portrait of, *257*; on slavery, 255–58; "What to the Slave Is the 4th of July?," 255–56

"Draft of Instructions to the Virginia Delegates in the Continental Congress" (Jefferson), 44

Drake, Francis, 25

Drummond (Lord), 93

Duane, James, 46; Adams, J., on, 47; on Adams-Lee proposal, 110; on Henry, 48–49; opposition to independence of, 93; role in *John Adams*, 327n10

Dunlap, John, 167, *171*; background of, 169

Dunlap broadsides, 169, *171*, 217; Jefferson updating writing for, 335n2; markings on, 335n2. *See also* Declaration of Independence

Dunlap's and Claypool's American Daily Advertiser, 173

Dunlap's Maryland Gazette, 173

Dunmore (Lord): attacking Norfolk, 87, 320n1; defeat of, 320n24; Jensen on, 83; on slavery, 7, 82–83, 320n24

East India Company: Boston Port Act and, 42; monopoly of, 38

Edwards, Sherman, 276

Ellis, Joseph, 8; on Adams, J., 105; on Declaration of Independence, 135, 166

Elm Brook Hill, 62

Emancipation Proclamation, 257, 263

equality: gender, 253–54; Locke on, 140; Wilson on, 140. *See also* Declaration of Independence; slavery

"Establishment of an Army indispensably necessary" (Hancock), 64

Eve, Oswald, 120

Falmouth, Massachusetts: burning of, 82–83; Mowat warning to, 82–83; report on, 83

Federalists, 232–33; on Adams, J., 235; July 4th and, 234; Republicans competing with, 234–35

Fifth Revolutionary Convention, 113–14

First Continental Congress, 56; Adams, J., notes on, 47–48, 51–52; appointments to, 45; boycotts of, 52–53; at Carpenters' Hall, *50*, 54; committees of, 49; Deane on, 46, 63; delegates of, 47; Dickinson on, 54; documents approved by, 52–53; first stop of, 45–46, 63; focus of, 4; Gage on, 55; Galloway on, 48, 54; King George III and, 53, 55; Hancock appointed president of, 66; instructions to delegations, 64; Jefferson joining, 66; militia security for, 63; at Pennsylvania State House, 64–66; procedural issues of, 48; Randolph, P., elected president of, 48; reports of, 46; second meeting, 63–66; secrecy of, 47; template of, 54; Thomson elected secretary of, 48

First Maryland Regiment, 202

Folsom, Nathan, 47

Ford, Bonnie L., 353n24

Fort Lee, 212

Fort Sumter, Confederacy attacking, 263

Fort Ticonderoga: Allen, E., taking, 317n23; Arnold taking, 317n23; militia seizing, 65

Fort Washington, 212; holding force, 343n19

Founders Online, 95

Fourth Provincial Congress, 103

Franklin, Benjamin: Boston Massacre and, 35; Canada mission of, 98–99; on Canada support, 114–15; Committee of Secret Correspondence instructions from, 322n32; Declaration of Independence and, 133–34, 147–48; on editing, 166; Howe, W., correspondence with, 182–83; informing France of Declaration of Independence, 175; Paine, T., recommended by, 88; sickness of, 133; Spero on, 133
Franklin, William, 131
French and Indian War, 8, 27–28
Friedenwald, Herbert: on Declaration of Independence,193, 191; on treason, 191
"The Fruits of Arbitrary Power" (Pelham), 311n39

Gage, Thomas: Boston attack of, 49; Deane on, 49; disruptions from, 43; on First Continental Congress, 55; Howe, W., replacing, 80, 82; Hutchinson replaced by, 313n5; installed as royal governor of Massachusetts, 42; ordered to stop rebellion, 57–58; Smith, F., instructions from, 58; on war preparations, 315n40
Galloway, Joseph: on First Continental Congress, 48, 54; joint plan of, 51; leaving for England, 315n39
Gates, Horatio, 116
Gawalt, Gerard W., 148
gender equality, 253–54
"General Orders" (Washington), 162, 201, 203
Gentleman's Magazine, 197
George III (King): accusations from, 76; Adams, J., on, 109–10; Adams, S., responding to, 87–88; Boston Tea Party and, 39; Lord Dartmouth correspondence with, 75; Declaration of Independence and, 198, 212; Dickinson's loyalty to, 71; First

Continental Congress and, 53, 55; foreign troop treaties of, 115; Jefferson's indictment of, 16, 44–45, 85; July 1, 1775 letter from, 75; military buildup approved by, 76, 80–81; mock funerals for, 190–91; Paine, T., on, 88–89; Parliament speech January 9, 1770, 33; portrait of, 81; rejection of City of London peace, 116; slavery and, 16, 145; suppressing Rebellion and Sedition proclamation of, 76; Westminster Palace speech by, 79–80; Wilson responding to, 87–88
Georgia charter, 27
Germain, George, 196
Gerry, Elbridge: debate correspondence of, 334n42; Declaration of Independence letter, 170–71; on independent statehood, 13; secrecy agreement violated by, 127–28; signing and, 193–95; Warren, James, correspondence with, 127–28
Gettysburg, Battle of, 263, 265
Gettysburg Address, 266–67; July 4th and, 20
Gibboney, Stuart G., 354n1
Gienapp, Jonathan, 224
Gilbert, Humphrey, 23; storms hitting, 307n2
The Glorious Cause (Middlekauf), 27
Goddard, Mary Katharine, 218; Declaration of Independence printed by, 219–20
Goddard broadside, 218, 219–20. See also Declaration of Independence
Graff, Jacob, 329n1
Grant, James, 203–4
Grant, Ulysses S., 265
Great Bridge, Battle of, 320n24
Greene, Marjorie Taylor, 282
Greene, Nathanial, 215; defense designed by, 341n37; illness of, 341n37; Putnam replacing, 341n37; Sullivan replacing, 341n37

Grisham, William, 258, 352n13

Hakluyt, Richard, 24
Hall, Prince, 253
Hamilton, Alexander, 237
Hanau (Count), 115
Hancock, John, 14–15; appointed
    president of First Continental
    Congress, 66; Boston Massacre and,
    35; on Canadian defeat, 326n41;
    "Convention of the State of North
    Carolina," 344n36; Declaration of
    Independence introduction letter,
    170, 172; "Establishment of an Army
    indispensably necessary," 64; on for-
    eign reinforcements, 115; Hutchinson
    meeting with, 35; on independence
    proposal, 127; on prisoner relocations,
    335n5; on Prohibitory Act, 86; signing
    and, 195
Hannah-Jones, Nikole, 279
Harrison, Benjamin, 129
Hartley, David, 226
Hawley, Josh, 282
Hemings, Bob, 137, 329n1
Hemings, Sally, 329n1
Henry, Patrick, 107; Duane on, 48–49;
    Stamp Act and, 29
hereditary succession, 89
Hesse Cassel (Landgrave), 115
Hewes, Joseph, 154
Hillsborough (Lord), 31
History of the United States (Grisham),
    258, 352n13
Ho Chi Minh, 268
Hogeland debate, 324n20
Hooper, William: Adams, J., corre-
    spondence with, 103–5; at Fourth
    Provincial Congress, 103
Hopkins, Stephen, 112
Howe, Richard, 153; arrival in Long
    Island Sound, 180–81; peace commis-
    sioner appointment of, 181

Howe, William, 153; attacking
    Dorchester Heights, 100; on
    Declaration of Independence, 196;
    Franklin, B., correspondence with,
    182–83; Gage replaced by, 80, 82; New
    York attack by, 201–2, 342n12; peace
    commissioner appointment of, 181;
    Philadelphia taken by, 223; proposal
    of, 205–9; Putnam on, 202; retreat of,
    100; Washington rejecting, 181–82;
    winter camp of, 214
Hume, David, 142
Humphreys, Charles, 157
Hutchinson, Thomas: Adams, S., meeting
    with, 35; Boston Massacre and, 34; on
    Declaration of Independence, 199–
    200; Gage replacing, 313n5; Hancock
    meeting with, 35; leaving for England,
    313n5; Preston imprisoned by, 34;
    promotion of, 312n51; on slavery, 18;
    Sons of Liberty and, 38

independent statehood: Adams, J., on,
    13–14; arguing against, 9; arguing for,
    9; Gerry on, 13; Jefferson on, 9; Lee,
    R. H., introducing, 9; Pennsylvania
    Evening Post on, 13, 18–19; Second
    Continental Congress passing, 13;
    voting for, 12–13
Intolerable Acts, 7, 41, 144–45, 313n4;
    addressing, 43; Jefferson on, 44;
    Ramsay on, 42. See also Specific Acts

Isaacson, Walter, 142
Jamestown, 8, 26–27
Jay, John, 46, 237; on boycotts, 52–53;
    "Convention of the Representatives
    of the State of New York," 176–77,
    337n19; Declaration of Independence
    formal resolution by, 176–77, 337n19;
    opposition to independence of, 93;
    peace delegations and, 225–27;
    Rutledge, E., correspondence with, 152

Jefferson, Thomas: Adams, J., compared with, 8; Adams, J., feud with, 237–44; on alignment of colonies, 302n7; autobiography of, 302n10; on backing for early settlements, 308n3; children with Hemings, S., 329n1; on Coercive Acts, 44; committee of correspondence appointment of, 37; credit for independence, 233–34; death of, 20, 251; debate correspondence of, 334n42; Declaration of Independence "original Rough draught" of, 14, 134–35, 137–52, 287–92; Declaration of Independence versions compared by, 174–75; "Declaration of the Causes and Necessity of Taking Up Arms" draft by, 69–70, 138; "Draft of Instructions to the Virginia Delegates in the Continental Congress," 44; Dunlap broadsides writing updates, 335n2; George III (King) indicted by, 16, 44–45, 85; goals of, 95–96; gravestone of, 252; on independence delays, 124–25; independence role of, 138–39; on independent statehood, 9; joining First Continental Congress, 66; July 4th and, 20; legacy of, 69; Lincoln on, 259, 262; literary skill of, 44; on memory of Adams, J., 302n10; National Archives on, 304n10; "Notes on the State of Virginia," 308n3; portrait of, 17; preamble of, 15–16; pre-inaugural correspondence with Adams, J., 239–40; presidential achievements of, 242; presidential appointment of, 234–35, 241; primary task of, 16; private letters of, 302n10; on Raleigh, 23, 25–26; Randolph, J., correspondence with, 77–78, 84–85; reactions to editing, 164–66; "Refutation of the Argument that the Colonies Were Established at the Expense of the British Nation," 26, 308n3; reliability of, 304n9, 327n11; resignation of, 238; on resistance,

278–79; return of, 113; Rush on, 242; second paragraph of, 15; signing claim of, 193–94; on slavery, 16, 306n36; Smith, W., correspondence with, 278–79; "Summary View of the Rights of British America," 44–45, 69, 138, 308n3; writing reputation of, 69
Jefferson Memorial, 274; Declaration of Independence language differences with, 307n39; inaccuracy of, 271–73; Roosevelt and, 272–73
Jefferson Memorial Committee, 271
Jensen, Merrill, 83
John Adams (HBO miniseries), 275, 276; Duane role in, 327n10; McCullough consulting on, 277
Johnson, Samuel, 18
Johnson, Thomas, 66–67
Journals of the Continental Congress: Agreement of Secrecy and, 3; Dickinson's notes on Declaration of Independence in, 155
July 9, 1776: New York's Independence Day exhibition, 177
July 4th celebration, 3; Adams, J., and, 19–20, 161, 221–22, 340n14; Congress establishment of, 20–21; Douglass on, 255–56; Federalists and, 234; first, 20, 221–22; Gettysburg Address and, 20; Jefferson and, 20; Lincoln and, 20; McKean on, 223–24; Monroe and, 20; official recognition of, 223–24; Pennsylvania Evening Post on, 222; Pennsylvania Packet on, 223; Republicans and, 234

Kansas-Nebraska Act, 259
Kean, Jefferson Randolph, 354n1
Kentish Gazette, 197
Kerber, Linda, 254
King, Martin Luther, Jr., 268–69
King Street. See Boston Massacre
Knox, Henry, 99, 237

Ladies' Anti-Slavery Society, 255–56
Laurens, Henry, 225; peace delegations and, 226
Lee, Arthur, 76
Lee, Charles, 214
Lee, Francis Lightfoot, 334n42
Lee, Richard Henry, 5; Adams, J., correspondence with, 104, 119; Adams, J., on, 47; Adams, S., relationship with, 37; background of, 121; called back to Virginia, 9–10, 304n11; on committee of correspondence, 37; Committee of Five omitting, 129; Declaratory Act and, 30, 121; on foreign mercenaries, 107; Harrison conflict with, 129; independence resolution of, 18, 121, 123, *123*, 125; independent statehood introduced by, 9; Mason's correspondence with, 129; portrait of, *122*; on Prohibitory Act, 97; signing and, 194–95
Lee, Robert E., 263, 265
legalized piracy, 86
"Letter from a Gentleman to His Friend" (Adams, J.), 105–7
"Letters from a Farmer in Pennsylvania to the Inhabitants of the British Colonies" (Dickinson), 31
Lewis and Clark Expedition, 242
Lexington, Battle of, 59; Paine, T., on, 89; return engagement, 62
liberal youth education, 105
Library of Congress: Declaration of Independence textual analysis, 273, 275; records, 307n42
The Life of Washington (Weems), 258–59, 352n15
Lillie, Theophilus, 311n35
Lincoln, Abraham, 257; at Assembly Room, Pennsylvania State House (Independence Hall), 262–63; death of, 267; on Declaration of Independence, 258, 260–63, 266; influences on, 258–59; on Jefferson, 259,

262; July 4th and, 20; "Perpetuation of Our Political Institutions," 258; on popular sovereignty, 260–61; presidential appointment of, *264*; on slavery, 259–61; threats to, 281; votes for, 353n24; Wills on, 267
Lincoln at Gettysburg (Wills), 267
Lind, John: *Answer to the Declaration of the American Congress*, 199; on Declaration of Independence, 199; political failures of, 341n30
Livingston, Robert R., 9, 93; in Committee of Five, 129; independence opposed by, 124; signing and, 194
Locke, John, 235; on equality, 140
London Chronicle, 196
Lost Colony, 25–26
Louisiana Purchase, 242
Lurie, Shira, 234
Lynch, Thomas, 47

MacLeish, Archibald, 275
Madison, James, 242; on Adams, J., 240
Maier, Pauline, 3; on Declaration of Independence, 133, 221, 306n31; on "Declaration of the Causes and Necessity of Taking Up Arms," 69; historical revisions by, 318n39; on local resolutions, 324n13; on revolution, 306n31
Marshall, John, 241
Maryland convention, 92
Maryland Journal, 219
Mason, George: "Declaration of Rights," 29–30, 138, 141; Lee, R. H., correspondence with, 129
Massachusetts Government Act, 42
Massachusetts Spy, 339n5
Matlack, Timothy, 169, 246; calligraphy style of, 184; Declaration of Independence and, 184–85, 191, *192*
McConkey's Ferry, 216–17
McCullough, David, 191; on Adams, J., 10; consulting on *John Adams*, 277

McKean, Thomas: on Adams-Lee proposal, 110–11; on July 4th, 223–24; signing and, 193–96
M'Clintock, Mary Ann, 254
McVeigh, Timothy, 279
"Memorandum of Measures to be Pursued in Congress" (Adams, J.), 96
Menotomy, 62
Meriam's Corner, 62
Middlekauff, Robert, 27
Mifflin, Thomas, 116
militia law, 105
Miller, Heinrich, 172–73
Mill's Creek Bridge, 323n1
Milton, John, 106
minute men, 60–62
Missouri Compromise, 259
Monroe, James, 242; death of, 20; electoral votes of, 348n50; July 4th and, 20; presidential appointment of, 235
Montgomery, Richard: Canada invasion by, 98; death of, 86, 98
Morris, Gouverneur, 231–32
Morris, Lewis, 194–95
Morris, Robert, 217; backpedaling of, 119–20; independence opposed by, 157; informing France of Declaration of Independence, 175; Prohibitory Act received by, 97; signing and, 194; voluntary absence of, 12
Mowat, Henry, 82–83

National Archives (NA), 338n41; on Jefferson, 304n10
National Treasure (movie), 277–78
New Brunswick, 213–14
Newell, Timothy, 100
Nicholas, Catherine, 338n41
Nixon, John, 173
Norfolk, 87, 320n1
North Carolina Constitution, 324n7
"Notes on the State of Virginia" (Jefferson), 308n3

Oklahoma City Bombing, 279
Olive Branch Petition (Dickinson), 4, 7, 10; Adams, J., on, 70; Lee, A., delivering, 76; Penn delivering, 73, 76; rejection of, 76–77, 79; Sullivan and, 342n2
Onuf, Peter, 141
Oswald, Richard, 225–26
Otis, James, Jr., 28

pacific system, 71–72
Paine, Robert Treat, 302n9
Paine, Thomas, 4, 7–8; Adams, J., on, 89, 91, 103; "The American Crisis," 215; background of, 88; on Battle of Lexington, 89; enlistment of, 215–16; failures of, 88; "Forester" pseudonym of, 109; Franklin recommending, 88; on King George III, 88–89; on governmental systems, 89; on hereditary succession, 89; intended audience of, 89–91; on overthrowing Pennsylvania, 109; in Pennsylvania Journal, 109; Tudor on, 91; Ward, S., on, 91; writing style of, 88
Parker, John, 59; statue of, 60
Parker's Revenge, 62
Parkhurst, Noah, 62
Parkinson, Robert, 143
Patterson, James, 182
peace delegation: Adams, J., and, 225–26; France and, 346n15; Hartley and, 226; Jay and, 225–27; Laurens and, 226; main issues, 226; Oswald and, 225–26
Peale, Charles Willson, 160
Pelham, Henry, 311n39
Pelosi, Nancy, 282
Penn, John: on Declaration of Independence, 153–54; at Fourth Provincial Congress, 103
Penn, Richard, 73, 76
Pennsylvania Evening Post: on Declaration of Independence, 160; Declaration of Independence full copy printed by,

173; on independent statehood, 13, 18–19; on July 4th, 222
Pennsylvania Gazette, 160
Pennsylvania independent vote, 333n19
Pennsylvania Journal, 109
Pennsylvania Packet, 223
Pennsylvanischer Staatsbote, 172–73
Percy, Hugh Early, 62
"Perpetuation of Our Political Institutions" (Lincoln), 258
"Petition of sundry Persons on Behalf of themselves and the Inhabitants of several of His Majesty's Colonies in America," 315n43
"The Petition of the Grand American Continental Congress to the King's Most Excellent Majesty," 53; title change of, 315n43
Pickering, Thomas, 249
Pickett's Charge, 263, 265
Pinckney, Charles, 241
Pinckney, Thomas, 239
Pitcairn, John, 59
"Plan of Treaties" (Adams, J.), 180
popular sovereignty, 260–61
"Preamble to Resolution on Independent Governments" (Adams, J.), 301n5
Preliminary Articles of Peace, 226
Prescott, Samuel, 60–61
President's Advisory 1776 Commission, 279–80
Preston, Thomas: acquittal of, 36; Boston Massacre and, 34–36; Hutchinson imprisoning, 34; trial of, 35–36
Price, Richard, 198
Princeton, Battle of, 217
The Principal Navigations, Voyages, Traffiques and Discoveries of the English Nation (Hakluyt), 24
Proclamation of Neutrality, 238
"Proclamation of the General Court" (Adams, J.): Allen, D., on, 94–96; Declaration of Independence and, 95

Prohibitory Act, 144–45; Adams, J., on, 97; Hancock on, 86; Lee, R. H., on, 97; Morris, R., receiving, 97; proposal of, 85–86; reactions to, 97–98, 101; Smith, R., on, 97
Provincial Conference, 132
Putnam, Israel: Greene, N., replaced by, 341n37; on Howe, W., 202

Quartering Act, 42
Quebec Acts, 313n4
Quebec City, Battle of, 86, 98

Rakove, Jack, 77
Raleigh, Walter: charter granted to, 8, 23; first explorer group of, 24–25; funding, 23, 24; Jefferson on, 23, 25–26
Ramsay, David, 42
Randolph, Edmond, 230
Randolph, John, 77–78, 84–85
Randolph, Peyton, 45; Adams, J., on, 47; called back to Virginia, 65–66; death of, 320n27; elected president of First Continental Congress, 48
Read, George, 195
"Reception of the Declaration of Independence" (Thelen), 353n24
Reed, Joseph, 216
"Refutation of the Argument that the Colonies Were Established at the Expense of the British Nation" (Jefferson), 26, 308n3
Republicans, 232–36; Federalists competing with, 234–35; July 4th and, 234
Revere, Paul: "The Bloody Massacre perpetuated in King Street, Boston," 35; Boston Massacre and, 35; capture of, 59; Suffolk Resolves and, 49; Warren, Joseph, sending, 58–59
revolution: Adams, J., on foundations of, 96; Maier on, 306n31
Revolutionary War, first shot of, 59
Rhode Island independence, 107
Richardson, Ebenezer, 311n35

Ritzenthaler, Mary Lynn, 338n41
Roanoke Island, North Carolina, 25
Rodney, Caesar, 12; Adams, J., on, 47;
    on Adams-Lee proposal, 112; arrival
    for independence vote, 159; on
    Declaration of Independence, 167; at
    Stamp Act Congress, 29
Rogers, John, 195
Roosevelt, Franklin Delano, 272–73
Ross, George, 195
Royal Ethiopian Regiment, 83
Rush, Benjamin: on feud between
    Jefferson and Adams, J., 242; signing
    and, 195–96
Rutledge, Edward, 9, 47; delay called
    by, 12, 302n7; independence delayed
    by, 127, 130–31, 158; independence
    opposed by, 124–27; Jay's correspon-
    dence with, 152
Rutledge, John, 47; on defining goals, 65;
    at Stamp Act Congress, 29

Sandwich (Lord), 318n1
Schiff, Stacy, 32, 47
Scots Magazine, 197
Scott, Winfield, 281
search warrants, 7; Otis on, 28
Second Continental Congress: colonies
    urged to create government by, 78–79,
    84; focus of, 4; illegal proclamations
    committee, 85; independent state-
    hood passed by, 13; official stance of,
    85; Rakove on, 77; recess, 77; second
    session of, 78
Second Treatise on Government
    (Locke), 140
Secrecy, Agreement of, 2; Board of
    War and Ordnance, 130; Deane on,
    314n22; First Continental Congress
    and, 47; Gerry breaking, 127–28;
    Journals of the Continental Congress
    and, 3; violations of, 3, 127–28
Seider, Christopher: Adams, S., orga-
    nizing funeral procession for, 33–34;

Boston-Gazette and Country Journal on,
    33; original protest killing, 311n35;
    tributes to, 33–34
separation of powers, 84, 95
1776 (musical), 275; awards for, 276;
    synopsis of, 276
Seven Years' War. See French and
    Indian War
Shelburne (Lord), 225, 345n12
Sherman, Roger, 46
Six Nations Indian confederacy, 128
"The 1619 Project," 279
slavery: Adams, J., on, 334n36; Articles
    of Confederation and debates over,
    337n28; attacks on, 16, 18; contra-
    dictions around, 18; Declaration of
    Independence and, 145, 164–65;
    Douglass on, 255–58; Dunmore on, 7,
    82–83, 320n24; King George III and,
    16, 145; Hall on, 253; Hutchinson on,
    18; Jefferson on, 16, 306n36; Johnson,
    S., on, 18; Lincoln on, 259–61. See also
    Emancipation Proclamation
Smith, Francis, 58
Smith, James, 195
Smith, Richard, 97
Smith, William Stephens: background
    of, 355n21; Jefferson's correspondence
    with, 278–79
Sneff, Emily, 307n40
Sons of Liberty, 38
South-Carolina and American General
    Advertiser, 187
Sparks, Jared, 347n38
Spero, Patrick, 133
St. James's Chronicle, 196–97
Stamp Act, 7; Henry and, 29; repeal of,
    30; taxation without representation
    and, 29
Stamp Act Congress: Adams, S., at, 29;
    attendees at, 29; Declaration of Rights
    passed by, 29–30; Dickinson at, 29;
    resolutions of, 30; Rodney at, 29;
    Rutledge, J., at, 29

Stanton, Elizabeth Cady, 253–54
State House Yard reading, 14
Stone, William J.: Declaration of
    Independence copy by, 246–47; owner-
    ship of engravings by, 350n35
Strachey, Henry, 208
*Strictures upon the Declaration of the
    Congress at Philadelphia in a Letter to a
    Noble Lord* (Hutchinson), 199–200
Suffolk Resolves: approval of, 51; passing
    of, 54; Revere and, 49; Warren, Joseph,
    and, 49
Sugar Act, 7, 29
Sullivan, John, 71; capture of, 203, 205;
    Greene, N., replaced by, 341n37;
    message from, 205–6; Olive Brance
    Petition and, 342n2
"Summary View of the Rights of British
    America" (Jefferson), 44–45, 69, 138,
    308n3

taxation without representation, 29
Taylor, George, 195
Tea Act, 38
Thelen, David, 353n24
Thomas, Elbert D., 354n1
Thomas Jefferson Papers, 147
Thomson, Charles, 14–15, 169; Adams,
    J., on, 47; elected secretary of First
    Continental Congress, 48; signing
    and, 194
Thornton, Matthew, 194, 195
*Thoughts on Government, Applicable to the
    Present State of the American Colonies*
    (Adams, J.), 84; anonymity of, 105–6;
    Braxton on, 106–7; foundational pil-
    lars of, 104–5; as foundation for state
    constitutions, 94; publication of, 104;
    reactions to, 106–7
three-branch government model, 84
Townshend, Charles, 310n25
Townshend Revenue Acts, 310n25;
    Adams, S., on, 31; Dickinson and, 31;
    passing of, 30; repeal of, 36

treason: Adams, J., and, 342n9;
    Declaration of Independence as, 198;
    Friedenwald on, 191
Trois-Rivières, Battle of, 325n32
Trumball, John, 244–46, *247*
Trump, Donald, 279, 282; disputing
    election, 280–81
Tudor, William, 91
Twelfth Amendment, U.S. Constitution,
    349n17

United States (U.S.). *See specific topics*

Vindex pseudonym, 32–33; trial pieces by,
    311n43
Virginia Company, 26–27
Virginia Convention, 329n6
Virginia Dynasty, 242
Virginia Gazette, 190
Virginia Plan, 230–31

Waco Massacre, 279
Walker, Charles, 120
War and Ordnance, Board of, 130
Ward, Artemis, 67
Ward, Samuel, 91
War of 1812, 3, 235
Warren, James, 72; Gerry's correspon-
    dence with, 127–28
Warren, Joseph: Dawes sent as courier
    by, 58–59; Revere sent as courier by,
    58–59; Suffolk Resolves and, 49
Washington, George: Adams, J., advice
    for, 93; Adams, J., nomination
    for Army leadership by, 66–67;
    Brandywine Creek defeat, 222;
    Continental Army acceptance of, 67;
    Continental Army regulations drafted
    by, 66; crossing Delaware, 216–17;
    Declaration of Independence read by,
    177; farewell address of, 238; "General
    Orders," 162, 201, 203; Howe, W.,
    rejection by, 181–82; myths surround-
    ing, 258–59; New York City defense

plan, 209–12; New York return trip of, 117–18; nominated to lead Continental Army, 66–67; Patterson meeting with, 182; Philadelphia visit of, 116–17; presidential nomination of, 230, 237; Proclamation of Neutrality issued by, 238; reinforcements requested by, 153, 161–62; retreat of, 202–3, 213; success of, 217; Trenton attack of, 216–17; war strategy of, 116–17

Watson-Wentworth, Charles, 345n12

Weems, Mason L., 258–59, 352n15

West, Benjamin, 226–27

"What to the Slave Is the 4th of July?" (Douglass), 255–56

White, John, 25–26

White Plains, 212

Williams, William, 195

Willing, Thomas, 157

Wills, Garry, 267

Wilson, James, 9; on Adams-Lee proposal, 111; Dickinson backing, 87; on equality, 140; independence opposed by, 124; responding to King George III, 87–88

Wolcott, Oliver: on Adams-Lee proposal, 112; signing and, 194–95

"Women, Equality, and the Declaration of Independence" (Ford), 353n24

Women's Rights Convention, 253–54

Wythe, George: Adams, J., letter to, 104; called back to Virginia, 9–10, 304n11; on independence resolution, 125; signing and, 194–95